2004
Merry
Christmas
Dear Bill
Think you'll
like these!
Love Lil'
Jeanne

The D. L. Moody Collection

THE HIGHLIGHTS OF HIS WRITINGS, SERMONS, ANECDOTES, AND LIFE STORY

Edited and Compiled by

JAMES S. BELL, JR.

MOODY PRESS
CHICAGO

ISBN: 0-8024-1715-9

Printed in the United States of America

To Lyle W. Dorsett of Wheaton College,
my friend and mentor,
and the author of
A Passion for Souls: The Life of D. L. Moody

If God calls a man to a work, He will be with him in that work, and he will succeed no matter what the obstacles may be.

D. L. Moody

CONTENTS

Section 4: Daily Devotions

Section 5: Sermons

INTRODUCTION

D. L. Moody never set out to become an author. He was primarily an evangelist, and preaching was his way of dialoguing with sinners. Yet he knew that preaching had its limitations, and he wanted to get the gospel message into the hands of those who couldn't attend his meetings or buy expensive books. He thus—perhaps inadvertently—became a publisher, and because he needed a clear gospel message for the masses, he became an author.

Reading Moody is like sitting in a pew and hearing him preach. Everything of substance that he believed, lived, and taught is found in his sermons. Indeed, most of the book excerpts in sections 2, 4, and 5 of this work are adapted from Moody's sermons. The cadence and directness of the evangelist's speech will be easy to hear as you read these passages.

Numerous biographies and reminiscences have been published recounting Moody's amazingly fruitful ministry. His sermons have been packaged as anecdotes, thoughts, quotes, and devotionals. So why still another volume of his messages?

The obvious reason is that much of the content herein is currently out of print. Some volumes, whether in print or out of print, do not give you enough of Moody's thought on one topic, while others take an entire book to cover one theme. I strive to find a middle ground—numerous topics of about a chapter each.

More importantly, no publication exists that serves as a general introduction to the great evangelist's life and work. For this reason, I have combined a mixture of biographical material with the highlights of his compiled preaching found in books of sermons, anthologies, anecdotes, etc. The result is more than just a "sampler"; this is a compendium that is really a new genre—a combined life/work.

I have compartmentalized the material into five categories: biography, Moody classics, anthologies, daily devotions, and sermons. To understand Moody the evangelist and the man, I begin with a short yet complete biography by A. P. Fitt (only slightly abridged). Fitt was a keen observer and helper of Moody—the first assistant treasurer of Moody's Bible institute as well as superintendent and editor of the Bible Institute Colportage Association (BICA, the forerunner of Moody Press). As Moody's son-in-law, Fitt also brought a personal family perspective to the biography. I also include *Why God Used D. L. Moody,* Reuben A. Torrey's insightful analysis of the spiritual power and character of D. L. Moody. Torrey, an educator trained at Yale, was the first president (then called superintendent) of Moody Bible Institute. Section 2 features excerpts from nineteen books, beginning with *The Way to God,* Moody's second book for BICA. They represent the diversity of Moody's topics and illustrations and clearly reveal his passion for the lost. Sections 3–5 are writings featured in anthologies in which Moody was one contributor, daily devotional books, and some of Moody's best sermons. Only minor style changes have been made.

This volume should aid the novice who needs an introduction to Moody the man before delving into a representation of his most significant contributions. The reader familiar with some of Moody's writings will add a single volume "reference" work to his shelf that will fill in the gaps and provide a comprehensive overview of the highlights of the person and the scope of his ministry. In collecting this material, I intended its purpose to go far beyond the reference shelf; rather, I want it to get into the heart and life of the reader. Therefore, I have included spiritual self-evaluation exercises to help you put into practice the teaching and preaching of the great evangelist. Moody challenged both the believer and unbeliever by what he said. Rather than mere head knowledge, he expected life change. Here is a way to measure it.

It is my humble desire that a reader would scan this volume from cover to cover, and if it were the only volume he or she ever read regarding D. L. Moody, the reader would feel satisfied that he or she adequately understood both the man and his essential message. If this occurs, I will be eternally grateful, for God has certainly used His servant mightily, and the sum total of his life and work speaks far more eloquently than my collected work.

James S. Bell, Jr.
1997

SECTION 1
BIOGRAPHY

1

THE SHORTER LIFE OF D. L. MOODY
by A. P. Fitt

Early Life at Northfield

Some day you will read in the papers that D. L. Moody, of East Northfield, is dead. Don't you believe a word of it! At that moment I shall be more alive than I am now. I shall have gone up higher, that is all, gone out of this old clay tenement into a house that is immortal, a body that death cannot touch, that sin cannot taint, a body like unto His own glorious body. I was born of the flesh in 1837. I was born of the Spirit in 1856. That which is born of the flesh may die. That which is born of the Spirit will live forever."

Those are the words of D. L. Moody—his autobiography compressed into a few sentences. Between his birth in the flesh on February 5, 1837, and his departure to be with Christ on December 22, 1899, there were crowded more, and more varied, experiences than fall to the general lot of men; and he firmly believed to the last that the opening portals of heaven would only admit him to larger and truer service for his God and Savior in unseen worlds.

By the grace of God, he was what he was; but his life was largely influenced, under God, by his mother. Betsy Hilton was born February 5, 1805. She came of old Puritan stock that had settled in Northfield, Massachusetts, as early as 1673. She married Edwin Moody on January 3, 1828. He was a mason by trade.

They had a comfortable home in Northfield, with an acre or two of land. Seven children were born to them, of whom Dwight Lyman Ryther was the sixth.

On May 28, 1841, young Dwight was at school. A neighbor put his head in at the window, and asked if any of Ed Moody's children were there, saying that their father had just died suddenly. That morning he had gone about his work as usual; but a pain in his side sent him home to rest. About one o'clock in the afternoon he staggered to the bed, and was found dead a few minutes later, kneeling beside it as if in prayer.

The death of his father was the earliest thing that Dwight could remember. He could recall nothing about the funeral, but the shock of the sudden death made a lasting impression on him.

The widow was left in trying circumstances, which, however, only served to develop her sterling and heroic character. Her eldest child was only thirteen years old. Twins were born a month after her husband's death. He died a bankrupt, and she had no one on whom she could lean heavily for support.

When the neighbors would come in and tell her to bind out her children, she would say:

"Not as long as I have these two hands."

"Well," they would say, "you know one woman cannot bring up seven boys. They will turn up in jail, or with a rope around their necks."

She toiled on, and none of her children went to jail, and none has had a rope around his neck.

"If everyone had a mother like that mother," said Mr. Moody on the occasion of her funeral, "if the world was mothered by that kind of mother, there would be no need for jails."

The creditors swept away nearly everything, even the kindling. Once when there came on a snowstorm, she had to make the children stay in bed next morning until school-time, for want of wood to make a fire.

She was always bright and cheerful in the presence of her children, but that first year after her husband died she wept herself to sleep every night. Her sorrows drove her to God, and she claimed His promises for the fatherless and the widow.

In spite of all its privations, home was the sweetest place on earth to the Moody children, and as long as that mother remained on earth, occupying that same home, but with all the comforts she desired, Dwight and her other children were drawn thither by the strong bands of love.

Dwight's early life differed little, in the main, from that of the ordinary New England boy. He continued to go to school in the winter, and learned the three R's and a little algebra. In the summer he "hired out." The first thing he did to earn money was to turn some neighbor's cows out to pasture on a mountain near by, receiving a cent a day as wages.

Many anecdotes are told that prove that he was full of fun and loved practical jokes—a characteristic that he retained undiminished to the end. They indicate also those qualities of leadership which were so marked a feature of his later career.

At the closing exercises one school term, the boys gave recitations and dialogues. Dwight chose Mark Antony's oration over Caesar's body as his piece. He brought a box with him to serve as a coffin, and put it on the table. The audience, which included the local ministers, school committee, teachers, parents, and friends of the children, was moved to tears as he proceeded. Presently he lifted the cover of the box to take a last look at Caesar, and out jumped a tom-cat!

"Scat!" shouted Dwight; and great was the uproar and laughter.

Some of the boys brought a pail to the cider mill one afternoon, but not wishing to be seen carrying the cider home by daylight, they left it on one side until they should return later. Dwight had watched them, and when they were gone he got the pail and brought it home. One of his brothers thought he would add to the joke, so when supper-time came he filled a glass with vinegar and set it at his own place at the table. Dwight fell into the trap. Supposing that his brother had helped himself to the cider, he reached over and proceeded to drink to the toast:

"Here's to the health of George Washington!"

But he enjoyed the joke himself.

On one occasion he wrote a notice summoning a temperance meeting in the schoolhouse on a given date, and signed a certain deacon's name in disguised handwriting. There was a crowded attendance, but no speaker appeared. In that school district there were two parties. One party said that boys could not possibly be controlled without the cane, and they kept a schoolmaster who acted on their plan; the other party said they should be controlled by love. The struggle went on, and at last, on one election day, the first party was put out and the other ruled in their stead. The boys said to each other that they were going to have a grand time that winter. There would be no more corporal punishment; they were going to be ruled by love.

The new teacher was a lady, and she opened the school with prayer. The boys hadn't seen that done before, and they were impressed, especially when she prayed that she might have grace and strength to rule with love. School went on for several weeks, and they saw no rattan.

Dwight, always the ringleader, was one of the first to break the rules. The teacher asked him to stay behind. He thought the cane was coming out again, and was in a fighting mood. She took him alone, sat down, and began to talk to him kindly. That was worse than the cane; he did not like it. She said:

"I have made up my mind that if I cannot control the school by love, I will give it up. I will have no punishment. If you love me, try to keep the rules."

Love conquered him, and he became a firm ally of that teacher.

When he was about eight years old, an incident happened that he ever afterward spoke of with gratitude. One of his elder brothers went to the town of Greenfield, twelve miles away, to work in a store for his board and attend school. He was so lonely that he found a place for Dwight. The incident can be best related in Mr. Moody's own words:

"One cold day in November my brother came home, and said he had a place for me. I said I wouldn't go but after it was talked over, they decided I should. That night was a long one.

"The next morning we started. We went up on the hill and had a last sight of the old house. We sat down there and cried. I thought that would be the last time I should ever see that old home. I cried all the way down to Greenfield. There, my brother introduced me to an old man who was so old that he could not milk his cows and do the chores, so I was to do his errands, milk his cows, and go to school. I looked at the old man, and saw he was cross. I took a good look at his wife, and thought she was crosser than the old man. I stayed there an hour, and it seemed like a week. I went around then to my brother, and said:

"'I am going home.'

"'What for?'

"'I am homesick.'

"'Oh, well, you will get over it in a few days.'

"'I never will. I don't want to.'

"He said: 'You will get lost if you start for home now; it is getting dark.'

"I was frightened then, and I said: 'I will go at day-break tomorrow morning.'

"He took me to a shop window where they had some jackknives and other things, and tried to divert my mind. What did I care for those old jackknives? I wanted to get back home to my mother and brothers; it seemed as if my heart was breaking.

"All at once my brother said: 'Dwight, here comes a man that will give you a cent.'

"'How do you know he will?' I asked.

"'Oh, he gives every new boy that comes to town a cent.'

"I brushed away the tears, for I wouldn't have that man see my crying, and I got right into the middle of the sidewalk, where he couldn't help but see me, and kept my eyes right on him. I remember how that old man looked as he came tottering down the sidewalk. Oh, such a bright, cheerful, sunny face he had! When he came opposite to where I was, he stopped, took my hat off, put his hand on my head, and said to my brother:

"'This is a new boy in town, isn't he?'

"'Yes, sir, he is; just came today.'

"I watched to see if he would put his hand into his pocket. I was thinking of that cent. But he began to talk to me so kindly that I forgot all about it. He told me that God had an only Son, and He sent Him down here, and wicked men killed Him; and he said He died for me.

"He talked only five minutes, but he took me captive. After he had given me this little talk, he put his hand into his pocket and took out a brand-new old-fashioned cent, a copper that looked just like gold. He gave me that. I thought it was gold, and didn't I hold it tight! I never felt so rich before or since. I don't know what became of that cent. I have always regretted that I didn't keep it; but I can feel the pressure of that old man's hand on my head today. Fifty years have rolled away, and I can hear those kind words ringing yet. I never shall forget that act."

At the age of sixteen, when he was still considered a small boy, he was taken one night to a lyceum meeting, where the townspeople had a debate. Toward the close of the meeting, when feeling was running high, he stood up, and in a few pointed impromptu sentences proved the weaker side in the debate to be right, and changed the current of the whole meeting.

He was immediately appointed leader of the next lyceum meeting, by acclamation, and went home feeling proud.

He selected as subject for the coming meeting the wrongs to which the Indians were subjected. He wrote out a speech of ten or fifteen minutes' duration, and for days his mother heard him tramping back and forth in his bedroom as he memorized this speech. When at last he appeared on the platform he recited the first few sentences, but memory failed him in his excitement, and he closed abruptly with the remark:

"The Indians went to the North Pole, and got froze up as stiff as steelyards."

Not long ago, he comforted a student of Mount Hermon School, of whom much had been expected, but who broke down during his final oration, by saying:

"Never mind! I broke down the first time I tried. You will get through next time."

Naturally, the reader will inquire if Dwight showed any special aptitude in a religious direction during these early years. The answer must be no.

His mother was a religious woman—that quiet, home religion that characterizes New England. She was then a Unitarian of the Channing school, differing very little in her beliefs from orthodox Congregationalists, and apparently having a vital faith in the widow's God. Northfield is not far from the scene of Jonathan Edwards' revival labors, but the wave of his influence did not reach the Moodys.

About the only books in the home were a Bible and a book of devotions. Every morning Mrs. Moody read to her children from these. On Sunday all the children were sent to the Unitarian church, over a mile away, and they stayed through Sabbath-school. It was never a debatable question whether they should go or not. The boys used to go barefoot, carrying their shoes and stockings in their hands, and only putting them on when they came in sight of the church.

Mr. Everett, pastor of the Unitarian church, was very kind to the widow Moody in the days of her trial. At one time Dwight boarded with him and did his chores. But attendance at the Sunday services was irksome. Dwight could not understand the sermons. In fact, Sunday was a day the boys disliked, and at sundown—they began to observe Sabbath at sundown on Saturday in those days —they would run out and throw up their caps, and let off their jubilant spirits.

The only water baptism D. L. Moody received was at the hands of this Unitarian minister, but it was in the name of Father, Son, and Holy Ghost.

His mother tried to induce him to pray, but he said he had tried it, and it didn't work. Once, however, when he was about six years old, a rail fence fell over on him. He could not extricate himself, and his cries for help were in vain, as he was too far away from any house. But he happened to think, "Maybe God will help me." So he prayed in his extremity, and believed that God answered his cry, as he was presently able to lift away the rails.

One lesson the mother taught the boys was, that their word, once given, like the laws of the Medea, altered not. No excuse would ever be accepted for failure to perform a promise. The question she always asked was, "Did you say you would?" not, "Can you?" Once, when Dwight went to his brother George and sought release from an agreement to work for a neighbor for his board during the winter while he was also attending school, the case was carried to their mother. Dwight's cause of complaint was that for nineteen consecutive meals his only food had been milk and corn-meal, varied occasionally by the addition of some old crusts that were too hard for the family. When his mother found that he had enough to eat, such as it was, Dwight was sent back to keep his agreement.

Nothing that is recalled of his boyhood gives any reason to expect the large things that followed in Mr. Moody's life. But his love of harmless fun, his keen appreciation of a joke, even upon himself, his sensitive compassionate nature, and his leadership of boy comrades, were features which remained with him throughout the years that followed.

BUSINESS AND CONVERSION IN BOSTON

As Dwight grew older he became ambitious for a change. The confines in which he found himself were too narrow. He began to appreciate the value of education, and tried to make the most of his schooling opportunities.

One day in the spring of 1854, when he was up in the woods cutting and hauling logs, he said to his brother Edwin, who was with him:

"I'm tired of this. I'm not going to stay 'round here any longer; I'm going off to get some other work."

He had two uncles in the boot and shoe business in Boston, of whom he sought work, but with little encouragement. Finally, he left Northfield and went to Clinton, Massachusetts, where another brother was employed. He got a job in a stationery and book store, addressing wrappers for the first paper issued in that town; but he wasn't satisfied. Soon he went to Boston, where he had a homesick and trying time seeking work and finding none. At last he approached his uncles again, and was probably in such a condition that they were able to make their own terms with him. They agreed to take him into their store if he would promise to board at a place selected by them, to attend the Mount Vernon Church and Sabbath-school, and not to drink or gamble.

Dwight accepted the terms, and became the store boy, to do odds and ends. His ambition now was to make one hundred thousand dollars, and be a successful merchant. He spent his spare moments learning the prices of goods, and quietly familiarizing himself with the details of the business.

Although he was little acquainted with city ways and city manners, it soon became evident that he made up for deficiencies in polish and externals by a natural wit and brightness that lifted him out of his lowly position and brought him to the front as a salesman.

Letters that he wrote home at this time show that his boyish heart turned constantly toward Northfield. A postscript to a letter written to his mother on August 22, 1854, is characteristic of his correspondence. "Ho, George," he wrote, addressing his elder brother, "tell me what kind of a crop of corn this year, and potatoes also."

Nor did business so engross his attention as to crowd out the old tendency and liking for practical jokes. Before he had been in the store long, he settled on a tall cobbler, to plague him. One day he slit the leather seat of this cobbler's box, and placed a basin of water underneath. When the cobbler sat down, of course he got wet. This was repeated three times before the cobbler kicked the box over to see what was the matter. Immediately he grabbed a knife and started for young Moody, who was waiting on customers in the front part of the store. Moody was taking it all in, and rushed out into the street when he saw the cobbler coming.

One evening when he was aching for fun, a young man about his own age came along the sidewalk just as he was leaving the store. Moody stepped to his side and walked along with him, looking into his eyes all the time. The young man hurried; so did Moody. Finally the other commenced to run, and Moody kept up with him until the young man was thoroughly scared.

He had his share in all the legitimate excitement of the city. The abolition cause appealed strongly to him, and he attended stirring meetings in Faneuil Hall. He took part in the attack on the old court house to free the slave Anthony Burns. He used to tell how they took great planks to stave in the door, but when the soldiers fired and the crowd smelt powder, they backed away.

His first definite spiritual experience came to him during his stay in Boston—his conversion.

Attendance at church and Sabbath-school was obligatory, under agreement with his uncle. But it was merely formal at first. There was many an Elias, Abinadab, or Shammah on whom the anointing of the Spirit would more likely come than on this David.

Mount Vernon Church was organized as a revival church, particularly to retain in Boston the fiery eloquence, holy zeal, and glowing fervor of Dr. Edward N. Kirk—just such a church as Mr. Moody's own church in Chicago later became. But the earnest, cultured addresses of Dr. Kirk did not reach young Moody. It is said that he chose a seat in one of the obscurest pews in the gallery, and that, wearied with the hard work of the week, he used to sleep most of the time during the Sunday services.

In the Sabbath-school he was placed in a class taught by Edward Kimball. The teacher handed him a Bible, and told him the lesson was in John. Moody took the book, and hunted all through the Old Testament for John. The other young men (among whom were some Harvard students) detected his ignorance, and nudged each other. The teacher saw his embarrassment, and found the place for him. "I put my thumb in the place and held on," said Mr. Moody afterward; "I said then that if ever I got out of that scrape, I would not be caught there again." An incident that exhibits not merely his ignorance of the Bible, but also his dogged purpose to learn from his mistakes.

He gave close, respectful attention to his teacher from the first, and his demeanor in class was always earnest, quiet, and attentive. He seldom said anything. Once, when Mr. Kimball was teaching about Moses, trying to show that he was a man of self-control, wise and statesmanlike, who would have been at the head of affairs in any age or nation, Moody asked, with hesitancy:

"Mr. Kimball, don't you think Moses was *smart?*"

This word from his limited New England country vocabulary truly expressed Mr. Kimball's idea, and proved that he was anxious to grasp his teacher's meaning.

Before long, Mr. Kimball determined to speak to his new scholar about his spiritual condition. He went to Hilton's shoe store one day, and found Moody in the back part of the store wrapping up shoes in paper and putting them on the shelves. Mr. Kimball told him of Christ's love and sacrifice. Evidently the young man was ripe for the gospel message, although he had hardly felt that he had a soul till then. The light of heaven flashed upon him, and never afterward grew dim.

How tenderly Mr. Moody used to refer to that transaction between himself and his Savior! Preaching in Tremont Temple, early in 1898, he said: "I can almost throw a stone from Tremont Temple to the spot where I found God over forty years ago. I wish I could do something to lead some young men to that same God. I wish I could make people understand what He has been to me. He has been a million times better to me than I have been to Him."

At other times he used to say: "The morning I was converted I went outdoors and fell in love with everything. I never loved the bright sun shining over the earth so much before. And when I heard the birds singing their sweet songs, I fell in love with the birds. Everything was different."

The natural zeal and energy of the man at once sought to find expression in service for the new Master whose cause he had entered. One of the first things he did was to go before the church committee with a view to joining the church. He was then only eighteen years old. He had been in Mr. Kimball's class only a few months. The committee was composed of earnest, sympathetic men (among them Mr. Kimball), who made the examination very carefully and gently, knowing young Moody's limited knowledge and hesitation. The questions had to be shaped so that the answers would be simply "yes" or "no." At length one of the deacons asked:

"Mr. Moody, what has Jesus Christ done for you, and for us all, that specially entitles Him to our love and obedience?"

The question embarrassed him. It was too long and too wordy for him to answer promptly, but he said:

"I think He has done a good deal for all of us, but I don't think of anything He has done in particular as I know of."

Nothing, therefore, was elicited at this examination that could be considered satisfactory evidence of conversion. Under the circumstances the committee deferred recommending him for admission to the church, but three of their number were appointed to take care of his case, and to seek to open up to him the way of God more perfectly. When he came before the committee again, no more doctrinal questions were asked of him than previously; but his earnest desire to be among God's people, and the feeling that he would get more good in the church than from being either refused or delayed admission, and the conviction that he would do no harm in the church anyway, although he was still unable to give any intelligent information as to his religious experience—these reasons led to his being recommended for membership in May, 1856.

Mr. Moody never complained of the action of the committee in this case. On the contrary, he thought they had done the wise and proper thing. He was very solicitous in later years about persons being admitted to membership in our churches without having really been "born again," and directed his efforts to bring men and women face to face with this question, to see not only if they had become partakers of the divine nature, but also that with Paul they should be able to say, "I *know* whom I have believed, and *am persuaded* that he is able to keep that which I have committed unto him."

Stories are current—whether true or not it is impossible to verify in every case, although in some instances they are known to be false—of one and another trying to rebuke young Moody for speaking at prayer-meetings, and seeking to repress his zeal. It can easily be credited that he was whole-hearted and active in religion just as he was in other things. But Mr. Kimball, whose loving interest in his Sabbath-school pupil never abated, says that while Moody attended the Friday evening church prayer-meetings quite regularly, he has no recollection of hearing him speak except a few times, when he was invited by the leader of the meeting to take part. "I can truly say (and in saying it I magnify the infinite grace of God as bestowed upon Mr. Moody)," wrote Mr. Kimball, "that I have seen few persons whose minds were spiritually darker when he came into my Sabbath-school class, or one who seemed more unlikely ever to become a Christian of clear, decided views of gospel truth, still less to fill any sphere of extended public usefulness." Dr. Kirk and the church officers lived to thank God for Mr. Moody's marvelous development in grace and in the knowledge and service of our Lord and Savior Jesus Christ.

EARLY CHICAGO CAREER

"Chicago, September 20, 1856—I reached this far-famed city of the West one week ago, in the night . . . I went into a prayer-meeting last night, and as soon as I made myself known I had friends enough. After meeting they came to me, and seemed to be as glad to see me as if I were their earthly brother. God is the same here as He was in Boston, and in Him I can find peace . . . I wish you could have seen a couple of ladies that came on with me. I was introduced to them at the depot at Boston. They were so good Christians. They stayed here until Friday night, and then went South, and I felt as if Christ was the only friend I had in Chicago. But since then I have found some nice people . . ."

These extracts are from the first letter D. L. Moody wrote to his mother after reaching Chicago.

His ambition had been stirred by the opening up of the great West. Boston proved too conservative for him. He was not comfortable in his surroundings, and privately decided to strike out where there was more room for a young man with push and enthusiasm to succeed in business. His home folks were opposed to his going to the then far-away city of Chicago, but he wrote his mother that if God would bring him there, he would devote his whole life to God's service. While he undoubtedly did not mean this to imply giving up business, as his ambition was still to become a successful merchant, it shows how ready he was to follow God's leading, and make his whole life tell for Christ.

After reaching Chicago, he secured employment in Wiswall's boot and shoe store. Though personal appearances were still against him, his ability as a salesman soon asserted itself. He became popular with the rougher class of customers, and used to take especial delight in handling difficult people.

After a time, when Wiswall added a jobbing department to his business, Moody found himself still more in his element. It gave him a chance to push out in his own interests, to exercise his tireless energies outside the routine of the store. He used to visit the depots, and inspect the hotel registers for incoming visitors. When the store closed at night, he would accost passers-by and try to sell them rubbers or other seasonable goods. He was all the time on the lookout for customers.

On December 16, 1856, he wrote his brother Samuel at Northfield as follows:

"I suppose you would like to know how I am doing. Well, I am doing first-rate. Shall be on there in the summer, if not before. I came very near going last week. A man offered to pay my fare if I would go with him to buy some goods, but Mr. Wiswall was so driven for help that he could not spare me. I should like to come back to the Bay State once more. Things don't look out here much as they do in Boston. A good many of the stores are kept open on the Sabbath-day. It is a great holiday out here."

The same day he wrote his mother:

"I have made thirty dollars a week ever since I came out here

. . . Don't let Uncle Samuel get hold of it, but as it has turned out, I have done the very best thing in coming out here. My expenses are a good deal, but I can make more money here than in Boston. I will send you a bill of fare on the house where I board, and then you can judge whether I shall starve or not."

One joke that Mr. Moody used to tell about himself with great enjoyment occurred at this period.

It was during President Lincoln's first presidential campaign, and Mr. Moody was traveling through Southern Illinois. The train had stopped at a small village. A farmer was sauntering up and down the platform, and as he came opposite Mr. Moody's window the latter asked him if he knew that Lincoln was on the train. The man showed great interest, and said:

"No! Is he?"

"I don't think he is," answered Mr. Moody. "I only asked you if you knew that he was."

The farmer said nothing, but continued his walk on the platform. As he came opposite the window again he remarked that their town had had some excitement.

"What's the matter?" Mr. Moody asked.

"The authorities wouldn't let some folks bury a woman," replied the farmer.

"Why not?"

"She wasn't dead," was the laconic reply.

The first Sunday he was in Chicago he attended the morning Sabbath-school in the First Baptist Church. His future wife sat there among the pupils, a girl in her teens. He brought with him a letter to the Plymouth Congregational Church, with which he immediately identified himself. Here he undertook his earliest form of Christian activity. He realized that there were many young men in this growing Western city, away from home and friends as he was, and who felt diffidence about attending churches where the pews were all engaged. He therefore rented four pews in Plymouth church, and invited young men to attend and sit in his pew, a form of ministry that he prosecuted with unusual success.

At this time he also joined the Young Men's Mission Band of the First Methodist Episcopal Church, whose purpose was to visit hotels and boarding houses on Sunday mornings, distributing tracts and inviting people to the church services. Sunday afternoons he devoted to a little mission Sabbath-school on the corner of Chicago Avenue and Wells Street. He offered to take a class. The

superintendent said he had twelve teachers already and only sixteen scholars, but if he could work up a class of his own, he would
be welcome. Next Sunday Moody appeared with eighteen ragged
and dirty "hoodlums," gathered off the streets, but each none the
less needing to be saved. Turning these children over to some of the
other teachers, Moody sought out more scholars, until he filled the
school to overflowing. He had no idea that he could teach himself,
but devoted to God his one talent of being able to "drum up" re-
cruits, both young men and children, for the services of the house
of God.

While Mr. J. B. Stillson, of Rochester, New York, was at this
time engaged in the erection of the old Chicago custom-house, he
used to distribute tracts and hold meetings along the river. One day
he met Moody, who struck him as "a young man of earnest purpose,
plain habits, and not very much education." The two became co-
workers in scattering religious reading among sailors, in saloons
and boarding houses, and in hundreds of poor families living in
that portion of the city known as "the Sands," on the north side of
the city, extending from the jail to the lake.

Letters written home at this period prove that he was rapidly
ripening in Christian experience, however little he knew of correct
doctrine. Writing to his brother George, on March 17, 1857, he said:

"I can make more money here in a week than I could in Boston
in a month. But that is not all. I have enjoyed more religion here
than ever in my life. Oh, George, I hope you will hold on to the
promises in the Bible. I find the better I live the more enjoyment I
have, and the more I think of God and His love the less I think of
this world's troubles. George, don't let anything keep you from the
full enjoyment of God's love. I think we have things sometimes
come upon us to try our faith, and God likes to see us cling on. As
the Psalmist says in one place, God likes to chastise them whom He
loves. So let us pray for each other, for I think it becomes Christians
to pray for each other. I have brought you before God in my prayers,
and I hope you have done the same for me."

A year later (May 21, 1858) he wrote his mother as follows:

"I have a good situation, and I mean to work my cards to make
it better. I have been very successful so far, and if nothing happens
I will do well. Luther (his brother) thought it was very foolish in my
leaving Wiswall's, but I have got me a situation that is worth five of
that. If I have my health, and my God is with me, I shall succeed
better here in Chicago than I ever thought. Mother, I hope you will

not forget to pray for your son here in the West, surrounded by temptations on all sides. I never worked in a place since my conversion that there were so many wild young men as here. I hope you will plead with God that I may live a consistent Christian life before them, that they may not lead me astray. I am in hopes to live so before them that I may succeed in winning their souls to Christ. Pray for me, dear mother."

In the fall of 1858, Mr. Moody started a Sabbath-school of his own in a vacant saloon, his helpers being Mr. Stillson and a Mr. Carter, who led the singing. Larger quarters were immediately needed, and when the mayor of the city understood the plan for trying to save the children in that submerged portion of the city, he gladly gave the use of the North Market Hall for Sabbath-school work.

This was a large hall over a market, owned by the city, and rented nearly every Saturday night for balls, when liquor and refreshments and cigars were freely used. It was commodious and convenient to that tough quarter in which Mr. Moody delighted to work.

Seeking out some of the street [urchins] who did not like the Wells Street mission school and had therefore dropped out, Mr. Moody invited them to *assist* him in his new venture. The boys were pleased to become partners, and willingly entered upon the work. One of those boys subsequently became postmaster of Chicago and commander-in-chief of the Grand Army of the Republic.

In preparing the hall for balls, the chairs, class banners, and other furniture used by Mr. Moody were thrown into a miscellaneous heap at one end of the hall. He and his "partners" used, therefore, to get around at 6 A.M. Sunday mornings to sweep out the hall, remove the beer-barrels, cigar-stumps, and other debris of the ball, and rearrange their furniture and banners for the 3 P.M. service. Sweeping the floors was in his eyes as true a service for God as superintending the school.

The Sabbath-school meetings were not creatures of routine. Mr. Moody's genius was taxed to keep control. The boys indulged in all sorts of cat-calls, whistling, etc., while there was no semblance of classes.

One Sunday Mr. John V. Farwell came by invitation to visit the school.

About half of the boys rushed forward to shine his shoes as he came in. Presently Mr. Moody invited him to make a speech, at the

close of which he was elected superintendent of the school by acclamation, to his utter surprise.

Said Mr. Moody to one man: "I want you to teach these lambs."
"*Lambs? Wolves,* you mean!" replied the other.

Mr. Moody or some helper would read a passage of Scripture,
sing a hymn, tell an anecdote—anything to fill up the time. By degrees the school increased to fifteen hundred, and as new teachers
enlisted, order was achieved out of chaos. It was before the day of
International Lessons, however, and scholars and teachers simply
had their common text-book, the New Testament. Denominational
lines were not recognized.

Mr. Moody's devices for running the school were eminently
successful.

He issued stock certificates of the "North Market Sabbath-
school Association; capital, ten thousand dollars; forty thousand
shares at twenty-five cents each." These certified the purchase of
shares "for the erection of a new building." "For dividends apply at
the school each Sabbath at 3 P.M."

His plan for disposing of unfit teachers was automatic. Scholars were allowed, by permission of the superintendent, to transfer
from one class to another. The inevitable result was that teachers
who failed to interest their scholars were speedily left without classes.

When he bought an Indian pony in order to save time in making calls, he used to let the boys ride the pony while he was indoors.
Three or four would ride at a time.

He used to make much of picnics, entering into the sports with
as great a zest as the youngest. He was then a very fast runner. At
one picnic he picked up a barrel partly filled with apples, and holding it so that the apples would spill out, ran ahead, followed by the
boys. One of the latter ran in front of him, and lay down on the
ground, so that Mr. Moody, who was watching the apples, fell over
him, barrel and all.

Thirteen street [urchins] were promised a new suit each at
Christmas if they would attend regularly every Sunday until that
time. Their nicknames were: Red Eye, Smikes, Madden the Butcher, Jackey Candles, Giberick, Billy Blucannon, Darby the Cobbler,
Butcher Lilroy, Greenhorn, Indian, Black Stovepipe, Old Man, Rag-
breeches Cadet. All but one fulfilled the conditions. Mr. Moody had
them photographed "before" and "after," the pictures (which are
still in existence) being known by the titles, "Will it pay?" and "It

does pay!" This uniformed group became known as "Moody's body-guard."

Thirteen years later a friend called at a railway ticket office. The agent asked him to step inside, and said:

"You do not seem to know me?"

"No, I have not that pleasure."

"You know 'Moody's bodyguard?'"

"Yes; I have a picture of them in my home."

"Well," said the agent, "when you go home, take a square look at the ugliest of the lot, and you will see your humble servant, now a church member and heir to Mr. Moody in that work."

Volumes might be written relating incidents connected with the gathering of his scholars and the general conduct of the school.

One of his first principles was that the worse the boy was, the more reason against ejecting him. Hence, expulsion was never thought of.

One young bully of fifteen years was especially noisy and troublesome, and all the usual means failed to tame him. At last Mr. Moody said to Mr. Farwell:

"If that boy disturbs his class today, and you see me go for him and take him into the anteroom, you ask the school to rise and sing a very loud hymn until I return."

The program was executed as arranged. Mr. Moody seized the boy, hurried him into the anteroom before he realized what was happening, and locked the door. He gave the boy a terrible thrashing, and presently returned, with face flushed, but wearing an expression of victory.

Said he, "I believe that boy is saved."

The boy was converted soon afterward, and years later acknowledged that he was still enjoying the benefits of that gospel exercise.

The neighboring Roman Catholic children were a source of great trial to Mr. Moody, disturbing his meetings and breaking windows in the hall. When all other resources had failed to stop this vandalism, he went to see Bishop Duggan. He called at the bishop's residence, and was told the bishop was not in.

"Then I'll wait for him," said he.

By and by the two came together, and he stated his complaint, and requested the bishop to exercise control over his parishioners. The bishop met him kindly, but said a man of his zeal ought to be inside the true church. Mr. Moody said he wanted to be right, but that if he became a Roman Catholic, he would have to give up his noon prayer-meeting.

"No, you won't," said the bishop.

"But I couldn't pray with Protestants?"

"Yes, you could."

"Then," said Mr. Moody, "if a Roman Catholic can pray with a Protestant, won't you kneel down right here and pray that God may open our eyes to the truth?"

They kneeled and prayed together, and as a result of that interview, Mr. Moody had no more organized persecution from his Roman Catholic neighbors.

When Abraham Lincoln was president-elect he spent a Sunday in Chicago, and visited the school on Mr. Farwell's invitation, on condition that he should not be asked to make a speech. When the boys learned who he was, their enthusiasm burst all restraints. As Lincoln rose to leave, Mr. Moody announced the conditions of his visit, but added:

"If Mr. Lincoln finds it in his heart to say a few words for our encouragement, of course we will listen attentively."

Thus taken, Mr. Lincoln made a helpful address, based upon his own early experiences, earnestly admonishing the boys to be attentive to their teachers and put in practice what they learned, and by so doing some day, perhaps, any one of them might become President of the United States.

An older brother of one pupil was in the South, and on hearing of Mr. Moody's influence over his family, he wrote home that he would "whip Moody within an inch of his life" on his return. When he got back he was taken down with typhoid fever, and Mr. Moody helped to nurse him. The man was so touched that his wrath disappeared, he became converted, and remained a firm friend of the work.

One day a forgetful or careless scholar took his seat with his cap on. One of "Moody's bodyguards" discovered him, planted a stunning blow between his eyes, and sent him sprawling to the floor, with the remark:

"I'll teach you not to enter Moody's Sunday-school with your hat on."

On one of his recruiting excursions, Mr. Moody reached a house where there were not only children, but also a jug of whiskey, which the father had laid in for his Sunday carouse. Mr. Moody got the whiskey and emptied it into the street. Next week when he returned, bent on a similar errand, the man was awaiting him. As he confessed to demolishing the whiskey-jug, the man took off his coat to fight him. But Mr. Moody said:

"I emptied the jug for the good of yourself and your family. If I am to be thrashed for it, let me pray for you all before you do it." Falling on his knees, he prayed earnestly for the father, mother, and children, as he had learned to pray under such circumstances; and when he rose from his knees the father's anger had cooled down, and he was permitted to have the children for his school.

Writing to a brother at Northfield from La Crosse, Wisconsin, on July 18, 1859, he said:

"How are you getting along with your Sabbath-school, and who is superintendent of it now? And how large a school have you got? Tell me all about it. If I were in your place, I would not have it stopped every winter, but keep it a-going. I shall expect to have a good time next Sunday when I get home, for I have been away some time now, and the children are so glad to see me when I return. I think I have got the best school there is in the West; anyway, it is the largest school this side of New York. I wish you could see it."

As here intimated, Mr. Moody loved his school, and his scholars loved him. Many of them were as brands plucked from the burning, and were knitted to him by the common love of God which had been shed abroad in their hearts. One scholar moved to another part of the city. The little fellow kept up his attendance, although it meant a long, tiresome walk each way. Someone asked him why he went so far, and said that there were plenty of other schools just as good nearer his home.

"They may be as good for others, but not for me," was the boy's reply.

"Why not?"

"Because they love a fellow over there," he replied.

"If only we could make the world believe that we love them," said Mr. Moody, "there would be fewer empty churches and a smaller proportion of our populations who never darken a church door. Let *love* replace *duty* in our church relations, and the world will soon be evangelized."

HOW HE CAME TO GIVE UP BUSINESS

In 1860 Mr. Moody was led to give up business and devote all his time to Christian work.

In addition to the Sabbath-school held on Sunday afternoons

in the North Market Hall, he used to hold Sunday evening services for the boys in a smaller room connected with the hall. From the beginning he taught the importance of confessing Christ as one's Savior, of giving testimony as to Christian experience, and also of engaging in active work. Later on these evening meetings multiplied as parents became interested. During the week Mr. Moody spent much time daily in visiting in the homes of the scholars.

As a result of the revival of 1857–58, the Y.M.C.A. was organized in Chicago. A daily noon prayer-meeting, similar to the Fulton Street prayer-meeting in New York, was held. Mr. Moody used to attend this meeting. At first there was not much general interest in it, but being aroused to action by the example of an old Scotchman who was the only attendant one day, when he went through the program of hymn, prayer, and Scripture-reading all alone, Mr. Moody and others began to work up the attendance, and very soon the meeting was flourishing.

Meanwhile, he prosecuted his boot and shoe business with unabated zeal and unfailing success. Events succeeded each other that had important bearings on his future. After two years with Mr. Wiswall, he had found employment as a commercial traveler for Mr. C. N. Henderson, a gentleman who was interested in the North Market Hall work. This position gave him greater liberty for mission work, as his time was now his own; he worked on commission, and could get away without encroaching upon his employer's rights to his time.

A letter he wrote home under date January 2, 1859, shows his feelings toward Mr. Henderson:

"On my return from the country last week I found my hopes all vanished. The one whom I had looked to for advice and counsel, and had proved to be more than a friend to me, was dead. . . . That man was my employer, Mr. Henderson. I shall miss him very much. He was the truest friend I have met since I left home. He seemed to take as much interest in my welfare as he would in the welfare of his own son."

The confidence in which Mr. Moody was held was shown when a year later Mrs. Henderson insisted that he settle up their business. A young man of only twenty-three years, he shrunk from the responsibility of handling an estate that was so large; but "I feel greatly honored," he wrote his mother, "for they had a great many friends who are good business men. I never have been put in so responsible a position in my life, and my prayer is that I may do myself credit. I am in hopes that you will not forget to pray for me, for I am nothing without the same God that has been with me since I started out in life. Do not say anything about this, will you?"

Results proved that Mrs. Henderson's confidence was not misplaced.

He next found employment with the firm of Buel, Hill & Granger, devoting a large share of every day to visitation and other work connected with his Sabbath-school, while meetings multiplied still more at night. Before a year elapsed, he cut loose altogether from business.

The story may be told in his own words:

"I had never lost sight of Jesus Christ since the first night I met Him in the store at Boston, but for years I really believed that I could not work for God. No one had ever asked me to do anything.

"When I went to Chicago, I hired four pews in a church, and used to go out on the street and pick up young men and fill these pews. I never spoke to those young men about their souls; that was the work of the elders, I thought. After working for some time like that, I started a mission Sabbath-school. I thought numbers were everything, and so I worked for numbers. When the attendance ran below one thousand, it troubled me; and when it ran to twelve or fifteen hundred, I was elated. Still none were converted; there was no harvest.

"Then God opened my eyes.

"There was a class of young ladies in the school who were without exception the most frivolous set of girls I ever met. One Sunday the teacher was ill, and I took that class. They laughed in my face, and I felt like opening the door and telling them all to get out and never come back.

"That week the teacher of the class came into the store where I worked. He was pale, and looked very ill.

"'What is the trouble?' I asked.

"'I have had another hemorrhage of my lungs. The doctor says I cannot live on Lake Michigan, so I am going to New York State. I suppose I am going home to die.'

"He seemed greatly troubled, and when I asked the reason, he replied:

"'Well, I have never led any of my class to Christ. I really believe I have done the girls more harm than good.'

"I had never heard any one talk like that before, and it set me thinking.

"After awhile I said: 'Suppose you go and tell them how you feel. I will go with you in a carriage, if you want to go.'

"He consented, and we started out together. It was one of the best journeys I ever had on earth. We went to the house of one of the girls, called for her, and the teacher talked to her about her soul. There was no laughing then! Tears stood in her eyes before long. After he had explained the way of life, he suggested that we have prayer. He asked me to pray. True, I had never done such a thing in my life as to pray God to convert a young lady there and then. But we prayed, and God answered our prayer.

"We went to other houses. He would go upstairs, and be all out of breath, and he would tell the girls what he had come for. It wasn't long before they broke down and sought salvation.

"When his strength gave out, I took him back to his lodgings. The next day we went out again. At the end of ten days he came to the store with his face literally shining.

"'Mr. Moody,' he said, 'the last one of my class has yielded herself to Christ.'

"I tell you we had a time of rejoicing.

"He had to leave the next night, so I called his class together that night for a prayer-meeting, and there God kindled a fire in my soul that has never gone out. The height of my ambition had been to be a successful merchant, and if I had known that meeting was going to take that ambition out of me, I might not have gone. But how many times I have thanked God since for that meeting!

"The dying teacher sat in the midst of his class, and talked with them, and read the fourteenth chapter of John. We tried to sing 'Blest Be the Tie that Binds,' after which we knelt down to pray. I was just rising from my knees when one of the class began to pray for her dying teacher. Another prayed, and another, and before we rose the whole class had prayed. As I went out I said to myself:

"'O God, let me die rather than lose the blessing I have received tonight!'

"The next evening I went to the depot to say good bye to that teacher. Just before the train started, one of the class came, and before long, without any prearrangement, they were all there. What a meeting that was! We tried to sing, but we broke down. The last we saw of that dying teacher he was standing on the platform of the rear car, his finger pointing upward, telling us to meet him in heaven.

"I didn't know what this was going to cost me. I was disqualified for business; it had become distasteful to me. I had got a taste of another world, and cared no more for making money. For some days after, the greatest struggle of my life took place. Should I give up business and give myself wholly to Christian work, or should I not? God helped me to decide aright, and I have never regretted my choice. Oh, the luxury of leading some one out of the darkness of this world into the glorious light and liberty of the gospel!"

The last eight months he spent in business, he made five thousand dollars—quite a large sum in those days. The first year in Christian work he did not receive more than three hundred dollars. But he never wavered. He believed Christ would provide him means as long as He had use for him. It meant living on crackers and cheese, sleeping on benches and settees in the Y.M.C.A. hall, and other "hardships," but through all his privations, he remained steadfast to the commission he knew he had received from on high.

When his purpose became known, he was dubbed "Crazy Moody." Later, when his efforts proved successful, and he became one of the leading religious factors of the city and of the Northwest, he became "Brother Moody." Later still, when his reputation extended over two continents, his title became "Mr. Moody," and plain "Mr. Moody" or "D. L. Moody" he remained until his coronation.

He was now free to prosecute with greater activity the many labors entailed by his Sabbath-school and his new love, the Y.M.C.A. Under his leadership the latter became, like the former, a live popular institution whose influence was soon felt throughout the whole city.

He never received a regular salary from any source after leaving business.

MISSIONARY LABORS IN CHICAGO

Most of the children who attended the North Market Hall were gathered from homes where there was no Christian influence or training. Mr. Moody felt (as he expressed it) that he had the children an hour a week and the devil had them the rest of the time. That led him to start the Sunday night meetings, and as interest increased, he was forced, and not unwillingly, to open up every night. Presently it was necessary to find larger quarters than the small anteroom occupied Sunday nights, and he hired a corner store that had been used as a saloon, fitted it up conveniently, and held meetings every night for prayer and exhortation.

The tide kept coming in, and as converts increased it became a serious question what to do with them. Mr. Moody tried to get them to join existing churches, but the poorer classes felt strange and out of place in the beautiful edifices. Besides, they had an affection for the place where they had first been blessed, and the rough and ready methods of Mr. Moody suited them better than the more deliberate proceedings of the ordinary church service. Most of the converts had no religious antecedents, and hence had no preference for one denomination rather than another. The tie that bound them to the mission could not exist toward any church.

It was inevitable, therefore, that some permanent organization should be founded, and Mr. Moody undertook the task of providing a building suitable for their needs. The outcome was the Illinois Street Church.

This building was adapted for Sabbath-school as well as church purposes. It held fifteen hundred people in the main hall, and also had several class-rooms.

It was dedicated early in 1864, and became one of the most thriving and active churches in the city. Mr. Moody was a deacon, and deacons and members alike were kept hard at work. In addition to ordinary meetings, there were also special meetings for men, young men, and boys; for mothers and girls; Bible, gospel, praise, prayer, and testimony meetings; without mentioning special cases, such as watch-night and thanksgiving services. Besides all these, cottage meetings were held at the homes of the members, and open-air meetings. The church building was almost in constant use, and Mr. Moody was the life and moving spirit of all. It was the scene of continuous revival activity and zeal.

"It is believed that if Pandemonium were accessible," wrote a visitor to Chicago, who attended this church, "Mr. Moody would have a mission started there within a week."

It became his custom to preach here at the Sunday morning service, and conduct the Sabbath-school (numbering a thousand scholars and upward) in the afternoon. In the evening he repeated his morning address at Farwell Hall, with an inquiry meeting following, while some visiting minister or friend conducted the meeting at the church.

Mr. Moody never let a man pass by without getting him to preach, if he was able. This happy faculty of enlisting others brought him into close personal touch with most of the leading Christian workers who came to Chicago, among whom may be mentioned Dr. Punshon and John Darby, of England.

All these years, he was in growing demand as a speaker at

Sabbath-school and Y.M.C.A. conventions. He and his fellow-laborers used to take these by storm and sweep away all rules, with the result that as often as not the convention work would be swallowed up in a revival.

"I have been to prayer meetings every night but two for eight months," he wrote his mother as early as June 5, 1861. "The Lord is blessing my labors, and I think you would say, 'God bless you, go forward.' . . . I was away all last week to Sabbath-school conventions. Have got to go again this week, and all of next week, so you see I am driven more than I ever was in my life. I have crowded houses wherever I go. Last week the house was full, and the sidewalk outside, so they had to open another church, and I had to speak in two houses. The Lord blessed me very much, and the work commenced in good earnest, so they have sent for me again. Oh, mother, if you could be out here you never would be sorry I gave up my business, for if I had not I suppose I should have lost everything I was worth, for all but one or two merchants in the boot and shoe trade have failed. . . ."

Many anecdotes might be related to illustrate his direct method of approach on religious questions. . . .

At one town Mr. Moody visited, he asked to be taken to the home of the worst man in the place. They sent him to the home of an infidel carpenter, whose wife, however, was a Christian. By and by he went into the man's shop, and asked him:

"Do you know that Jesus of Nazareth was a carpenter?"

"No," was the surly answer; "I don't know, and don't care."

But Mr. Moody interested him, and before leaving town told the carpenter's wife that her husband would be converted. Said he:

"I'll be passing through here in two days on the train. Won't you signal me if he has come into the light?"

When the time came, he had the joy of seeing the woman standing on the porch of her house, which stood near the track, excitedly waving a large white tablecloth.

An overzealous critic, who was not an overactive worker, took Mr. Moody to task for his defects in speech, in the early days.

"You oughtn't to speak in public," he said; "you make so many mistakes in grammar."

"I know I make mistakes," was the reply, "and I lack a great many things; but I'm doing the best I can with what I've got. But look here, friend, you've got grammar enough; what are you doing with it for Jesus?"

On one occasion Mr. Moody was one of several speakers at a

convention. A minister who followed him took occasion in his speech
to criticize him, saying that his address was made up of newspaper
clippings, etc. When he sat down, Mr. Moody stepped to the front
again, and said he recognized his want of learning and his inability
to make a fine address; he thanked the minister for pointing out his
shortcomings, and asked him to lead in prayer that God would help
him to do better.

It is reported that he once heard someone say:

"The world has yet to see what God can do *with*, and *for*, and
through, and *in* a man who is fully and wholly consecrated to Him."

The statement took hold of him. He thought to himself: "He
did not say a great man, or a learned man, or a rich man, or an eloquent man, or a clever man; simply a man. Well, I am a man. It lies
with the man himself whether he will or will not make that full and
entire consecration. I will try my utmost to be that man."

That spirit was evidently animating him. Letters written at this
period of his life exhibited his inner purposes.

"Tell all my friends," he wrote home on February 12, 1861,
"there is nothing like the religion of Jesus Christ. I am in hopes the
family altar is kept up at home . . ."

"I hope you will do all you can personally for your Savior," he
wrote to his brother Sam, February 13, 1865. "Talk for Him. Pray to
Him. Labor for Him, and do all things for Him, and the good Lord
will never leave you. Read often the fourteenth chapter of John."

The wideness of his charity was illustrated by his conduct toward a man who used to attend the noon prayer-meetings and
open-air meetings in order to make disturbance. Even Mr. Moody
could not suppress him. While he stood at the door shaking hands
with people at the close of the prayer-meeting one day, this man
came along. After a moment's hesitation, Mr. Moody stretched out
his hand, and said:

"I suppose if Jesus Christ could eat the Last Supper with Judas
Iscariot, I ought to shake hands with you."

HOW MR. MOODY PREPARED HIS SERMONS

For years, he never expected to do more in the way of preaching than to give five or ten minute addresses to his Sabbath-school
children. By and by he procured a copy of the "Topical Text Book"
as a help in Bible study, and began to prepare an address on "The
Bible." This was the subject of his first attempt at a Bible reading.

His method was simple, and suited to the needs of the case. He would call upon some one in the audience to read a certain text. This would give him time to collect his thoughts, and he would then say a few words or relate an anecdote to light up the text. When he found himself running dry, he would call for another text to be read, and on this he would offer a few comments in a similar fashion.

When his audiences became larger, so that he had to read the texts himself, he had to make better preparation beforehand, as there was less opportunity for impromptu comment. Before long he received an invitation from Dr. Goodwin, pastor of the First Congregational Church, Chicago, to repeat one of these Bible readings in his church.

"I rubbed my eyes," he said, "to see who I was!"

He had never anticipated that he would get that far in public ministry. The Bible reading he gave at Dr. Goodwin's church was on the Holy Spirit—a neglected subject, which, largely owing to Mr. Moody's efforts, now occupies a very prominent place in the study and thought of Bible students throughout the world.

He next received an invitation to give a Bible reading in the Third Presbyterian Church, and by degrees his reputation spread throughout the city and beyond.

He never really changed his method of making sermons, which was as follows:

Having decided to prepare an address on any topic or text (he preferred to use subjects mostly), his first step was to take a large envelope, and on the outside write the title or reference: "Heaven"— "Psalm 23"—"Backsliders"—"Let the wicked forsake"—"How to deal with inquirers."

Into such envelopes he crowded extracts copied from sermons and commentaries, cuttings from newspapers, original thoughts and suggestions, anecdotes and illustrations from his own experience—scraps of all kinds that had any bearing on the subject under consideration. Hundreds of these envelopes are in his study, many of them fat and showing signs of frequent use, but many representing sermons in embryo.

Whenever Mr. Moody wished to preach on a certain subject, he ran through the envelope of thoughts and clippings, and selected such points and anecdotes as he wished to use on that occasion. Weaving these into an outline, and taking sheets of note-paper, he wrote out catchwords, and fastened the sheets into his Bible by means of elastic bands.

[For example, in one sermon on repentance,] he began by considering objections. First: "I do not feel enough for my sins."

This objection he proposed to meet by quoting Ezekiel 33:11; so he cut that verse out of a large-print Bible and pasted it onto this sheet, in order to avoid the necessity of turning up the reference.

At some later period he added, "Has not struck me," to remind him of another frequent excuse that he met with in dealing with the unsaved.

Second objection: "How much and long should I feel sorry for my sins?"

This he met with 2 Corinthians 7:9, 10. Also with the command of Isaiah 55:7: "Let the wicked forsake his way, and the unrighteous man his thoughts; and let him return unto the Lord."

"I have repented far more since I came to Christ than before," he next wrote down, reminding himself of a line of thought that he was fond of pressing home—namely, that repentance and the new birth are only the beginnings of an experience during which the Christian may constantly need to repent of sin, and rely on the Savior's help. This method of making sermons he found to possess many advantages.

It gives full opportunity for impromptu inspiration, as the preacher is not bound hard and fast to a written manuscript. Many of Mr. Moody's best and most often quoted sayings were unpremeditated. He always insisted that what the church needs is "men who can think on their feet."

It avoids monotony and formality in the frequent repetition of a sermon. "People say I repeat my sermons," said Mr. Moody. "Of course I do; I am glad to do so. Some ministers are afraid if they repeat their sermons, they will lose their reputation. Give up your reputation, and you will get along all right! If you have a sermon that has been blessed of God, don't be afraid to use it again and again." He must have repeated some of his sermons hundreds, if not thousands, of times, and they always sounded fresh to one who had heard them again and again. The secret undoubtedly lays in part in the nature of his subject, as no one could listen to an actor or lecturer repeatedly deliver the same selection without losing interest—the same being the reason why the Bible remains a fountain of perennial interest. Part was due to his freshness of delivery; but credit must also be given to his method of sermon-making, which permitted a variation of outline that meant continual freshness in the substance of his address, and in the order in which his points and anecdotes were marshaled.

There are three books which he advised every Christian to pro-cure: (1) a good substantial copy of the Bible, with large clear print; (2) a Cruden's Concordance; and (3) a topical text-book.

We have already seen how he turned to the last named when preparing for Bible readings. He always kept one at hand in his study, and also a concordance. He was a Christian five years before he heard of the latter. A skeptic in Boston got hold of him shortly af-ter his conversion, and young Moody tried to defend the Bible and Christianity. The skeptic made a misquotation. Moody said it wasn't in the Bible, and hunted for days and days to prove the skeptic wrong. He came later to realize that if he had had a concordance, he could have found the passage in question in a few moments.

His Bibles are among the most precious treasures that he left behind. He had a large number—upward of a score—in constant use. In his study are to be seen several that have been almost worn out; leaves loose and ragged-edged, but invaluable because of the notes and suggestions written on the margins and blank spaces.

He had a dozen "interleaved" Bibles—that is, Bibles in which every other page was left blank for inscribing notes and comments upon the Scriptures facing the pages. He found that notebooks and clippings accumulated quickly, and were likely to be laid aside and never referred to again. He therefore adopted these interleaved Bibles, where notes were always at hand. From these he used to give out "nuggets" at his meetings, and when friends borrowed a Bible in order to copy off the notes, they were expected to write in some nuggets before returning it.

"Don't be afraid to borrow or lend Bibles," he used to say. "Some time ago a man wanted to take my Bible home to get a few things out of it; and when it came back I found this note in it:

"*Jesus only:*
The light of heaven is the face of Jesus
The joy of heaven is the presence of Jesus
The melody of heaven is the name of Jesus
The harmony of heaven is the praise of Jesus
The theme of heaven is the work of Jesus
The employment of heaven is the service of Jesus
The duration of heaven is the eternity of Jesus
The fullness of heaven is Jesus Himself."

He used to say it would be worth going a thousand miles to get a good thought. With what keenness he listened to other preachers for good thoughts and illustrations, and how his face lit up with a smile as he took out the notebook he kept in his hip-pocket for nuggets! He urged this habit of making notes of all the good things one read and heard, believing that it would make the Bible more deeply interesting day by day.

He was an untiring Bible student. He usually arose about daybreak in summer, in order to have two or three hours alone with his Bible and his God, while his mind was fresh, and before the activities of the day divided his attention. The walls of his library are occupied from floor to ceiling with bookshelves.

Among the volumes he prized most is a large pulpit Bible that contains the following inscription:

"Mr. D. L. Moody, from Mrs. C. H. Spurgeon, in tender memory of the beloved one gone home to God. This Bible has been used by my precious husband, and is now given with unfeigned pleasure to the one in whose hands its blessed service will be continued and extended.

"S. Spurgeon.

"Westwood, London, November 20, 1892."

This is the original Bible in which C. H. Spurgeon kept track of his sermons as they were printed. By means of red ink entries in the margin, he knew at once in what volume or magazine any sermon might be found. It was not the Bible Mr. Spurgeon used daily, but Mrs. Spurgeon transcribed the inscription from that one and pasted it on the fly-leaf of the copy she gave Mr. Moody. It reads as follows:

"C. H. Spurgeon. 1856.

The lamp of my study.

The light is as bright as ever. 1861.

O that mine eyes were more opened! 1864.

Being worn to pieces, rebound 1870. The lantern mended and the light as joyous to mine eyes as ever."

Since Mr. Spurgeon's Bible came into Mr. Moody's possession (and at the same time a complete set of his sermons), he was in the habit of turning to it first to see if Mr. Spurgeon had preached on any text he was studying.

THE CIVIL WAR PERIOD

The outbreak of the Civil War opened up another avenue of Christian activity to Mr. Moody.

He had been an abolitionist since his Boston days, and took keen interest in the progress of current events. The day Lincoln's calls for soldiers was issued, he was at a Sabbath-school convention at Sycamore, Illinois. Turning to a friend, K. A. Burnell, he said:

"We'll have to go, but we're here now. Let us do what we can to win a multitude of souls to Christ today."

Lincoln's visit to the North Market Hall had awakened intense feelings of patriotism in the scholars, and seventy-five of them responded to his call. Naturally, Mr. Moody's heart followed them into service. A camp was formed near the southern limits of Chicago, Camp Douglas, whither ten thousand rebel prisoners were later sent on parole. An army and navy committee was immediately organized at the Y.M.C.A. With this the Northwestern Branch of the United States Christian Commission was affiliated, after the parent organization was founded, November 16, 1861. Mr. Moody did not care to engage himself to the Christian Commission, as he feared it would curtail his liberty and embarrass him in his wider work, in which he was having many conversions; nor would he accept urgent invitations to become a chaplain for similar reasons.

In a letter to his mother dated November 19, 1861, he wrote:

"I think you would like to attend our meetings in the North Market Hall. They are very large and interesting. Some nights fifteen or twenty rise for prayers . . . I am now at work among the soldiers a good deal. I had a good time in Kentucky. The boys wanted to have me become their chaplain, but my friends would not let me go, so I shall remain in the city . . . I would like to see you all, and talk with you about my Savior, who seems so near to me. Oh, what would life be without Christ! I sometimes get to looking down on this dark world of sin, but when I look to Jesus it makes me look up."

One of his brothers (Warren) enlisted, and this fact also turned his heart toward the army camps. Writing to his mother on September 13, 1862, he asked to be kept exactly informed as to Warren's movements, so that he could send him books. "I am holding meetings at the camp every night with the soldiers. A good many of them are turning from the error of their ways. Tell George and Ed (two brothers at Northfield) not to let that prayer-meeting go down. Pray on. They have great reason to pray now. God seems to be waiting to have this nation call on Him. I do hope these meetings will be kept up, and that the friends of Jesus will not grow weary, and Mother, I wish you would talk to Warren about his soul. Tell him that you will pray for him daily, and God will answer your prayers. Tell him not to play cards, for it leads to gambling, and gambling leads to hell."

By gospel services, prayer-meetings, song services (religious and patriotic), distribution of Bibles, books and tracts, and by personal visitations, he tried to win the soldiers to Christ. He organized the professed Christians into "Bands of Brothers," who were to carry "the Banner of Christ" with them, and be loyal to each other and to the cause they professed. The Seventy-second Illinois Regiment was first called the "Y.M.C.A. Regiment," the idea being to have a regiment of Ironsides, every man in the ranks a Christian. He reveled in the abundant opportunities the gathering of the troops gave him for Christian activity.

Nine times he went to the front, sometimes as a member of the Christian Commission to preach and minister to the soldiers, sometimes at the request of the Sanitary Commission or the Chicago Citizens' Committee to take supplies to the wounded after battle. He was on the ground ministering to the wounded after the battles of Fort Donelson, Pittsburgh Landing, Shiloh, and Murfreesboro, with the army at Cleveland and Chattanooga, and among the first to enter Richmond.

He was a great favorite with the soldiers, and highly respected for his self-sacrificing labors. Each evening, while at the front, the boys would gather round a blazing camp-fire and listen to his earnest appeals. It was his habit to drop into the tents and talk earnestly to the soldiers, remonstrating with those who indulged in profanity. Knowing many of the soldiers in several of the regiments, he was personally solicitous for their welfare, and prayed God to give them victory over sin, Satan, and the rebels. His voice might often be heard rising in prayer from the tents of the ungodly. While serving with the command of General O. O. Howard, who was in thorough sympathy with his efforts, his ministry was especially fruitful.

In many ways these war experiences served to prepare him for his larger work. It brought him prominently before the whole country. The Chicago noon prayer-meetings became a rallying-ground, where Mr. Moody and his fellow-workers met and reported on their frequent excursions to the front. People from all over the Northwest sent in requests for prayer at these meetings, on behalf of husbands, brothers, sons. Mr. Moody learned, in dealing with the dying, how dangerous it is to delay in the matter of eternal salvation, and hence his faculty of prompt personal dealing with the unsaved was developed. He learned precious truths as to the comforts of the gospel, the readiness of God to hear and answer prayer, and the value of His promises. His own faith increased. Besides, he gathered a fund of anecdotes and incidents which proved effective in after years in lighting up his sermons.

FARWELL HALL ACTIVITIES

One of the turning points in the history of the Y.M.C.A. in Chicago, and indeed throughout the world, occurred that day when three young men—L. M. Beam, B. F. Jacobs, and D. L. Moody—met and signed a covenant to pray and work for a building for the Association, which at that time held meetings in rented quarters that offered only limited facilities for its work.

The board of managers of the Y.M.C.A. thought, planned, and prayed for a building of their own; they did everything but act. Finally it was proposed that Mr. Moody, who had recently been successful in erecting the Illinois Street Church, should be elected president, and John V. Farwell, vice-president. But Mr. Moody was considered too radical to head the ticket, so the names were reversed. While the election was proceeding, he was out getting pledges, and before night a building was assured that should contain a hall with seating capacity of three thousand, as well as rooms for smaller meetings, and offices. It was claimed to be the first Y.M.C.A. building in existence.

Cyrus McCormick, who had full confidence in Mr. Moody, subscribed ten thousand dollars, the largest money gift that had been entrusted to him up to that time.

The dedication of this building to the service of Almighty God on September 26, 1867, was a notable event in religious annals. George H. Stuart, president of the United States Christian Commission, traveled eight hundred miles to be present. The hall was filled to its utmost capacity, many visitors gathering from other towns and states. The interdenominational character of the Y.M.C.A. was proved by the presence of ministers of all denominations—and this at a time when its work was only beginning, and jealous eyes were watching, lest it should prove to be a rival of the churches.

Mr. Moody's speech that night recounted the goodness of God in leading them from small beginnings to their present position of influence. He advocated aggressive attack upon the strongholds of sin, saying they had been on the defensive too long. He prophesied that the work was only in its infancy.

It was intended to name the hall after Mr. Moody, in honor of his strenuous and successful efforts on its behalf; but when the

proper moment came he took the platform and made a short, pas-
sionate appeal that the audience name it "Farwell Hall," in honor of
the man who was chairman of the Building Committee and a liberal helper. The proposal was carried with acclamation.

He raised money at one time and another for the erection of
scores of churches, missions, and Association buildings in Great
Britain and America, but he disclaimed all honor for his share in
the work, and always suppressed attempts to use his name.

The following January the building was burned, entailing
great loss, as it was only partially insured. Mr. Moody took matters
in hand so promptly, however, that the noon prayer-meeting was
held without break, in other quarters, and it was said he had sub-
scriptions for a new building before the fire was out. The following
year the second Farwell Hall was completed and dedicated, superi-
or in many respects to the first. This second building followed its
predecessor in the great fire of 1871, when the original covenant,
referred to above, was also burned.

For two years, Mr. Moody was president of the Y.M.C.A.

FIRST VISIT TO ENGLAND AND THE CONTINENT, IN 1867

In 1867, the doctor suggested a sea voyage for Mrs. Moody,
who had a harassing cough. As Mr. Moody had an earnest desire to
hear and meet Spurgeon and Mueller, it was therefore decided that
they make a journey to England. They started on February 22 of
that year.

At this time Mr. Moody was unknown in England, except to
such friends as had visited America. Among these was Fountain J.
Hartley, secretary of the London Sabbath-school Union, who invited him to speak at an anniversary meeting in Exeter Hall. It is
customary in England for a speaker on such an occasion to be connected with a formal resolution, as its mover or seconder, in order
to give him a right to the floor. Mr. Moody was therefore assigned
to move a vote of thanks to the chairman of the evening, who in this
instance was the well-known Earl of Shaftesbury.

Toward the close of the meeting the chairman yielded his place
to the vice-chairman, in order that such a resolution could be offered. The vice-chairman announced that they were glad to
welcome their "American cousin, the Reverend Mr. Moody, of
Chicago," who would now "move a vote of thanks to the noble Earl"
who had presided on this occasion.

This program was quite out of Mr. Moody's way of doing

things. With refreshing frankness and an utter disregard of conventionalities and mere compliments, he burst upon the audience with the bold announcement:

"The chairman has made two mistakes. To begin with, I'm not the 'reverend' Mr. Moody at all. I'm plain D. L. Moody, a Sabbath-school worker. And then I'm not your 'American cousin.' By the grace of God I'm your brother, who is interested, with you, in our Father's work for His children.

"And now about this vote of thanks to 'the noble Earl' for being our chairman this evening. I don't see why we should thank him, any more than he should thank us. When at one time they offered to thank our Mr. Lincoln for presiding over a meeting in Illinois, he stopped it. He said he'd tried to do his duty, and they'd tried to do theirs. He thought it was an even thing all around."

That opening fairly took the breath away from the audience. Its novelty was delightful, and he carried his English hearers from that time on.

He soon found his way to the Y.M.C.A. in Aldersgate Street, and his experiences of gospel work in Chicago were told with a freshness and vigor that captivated all who heard him. The unique and original way in which he pursued his declamatory efforts among the rough and lawless children of Chicago were described with thrilling interest.

He had an interview with Mr. Spurgeon, but failed to induce him to make a trip to America. He also went to Bristol. "Bristol," he wrote to his mother, "is where George Mueller's great orphan schools are. He has 1,150 children in his house, but never asks a man for a cent of money to support them. He calls on God, and God sends the money to him. It is wonderful to see what God can do with a man of prayer."

Before sailing from New York, a friend had advised him strongly not to miss meeting missionary veteran Dr. Duff, and also to see Dr. Guthrie's work at Edinburgh. Thither, therefore, he went; and while he failed in his special purpose, he had the opportunity of speaking one night in the Free Assembly Hall, and met several prominent religious leaders.

He also visited Dublin, Ireland, and met Harry Moorehouse, "the boy preacher," who introduced himself, and said he would like to come to Chicago and preach. This incident had an important sequel, which may be told in Mr. Moody's own words, as follows:

"I looked at him. He was a beardless boy; didn't look as if he was more than seventeen; and I said to myself: 'He can't preach.' He wanted me to let him know what boat I was going on, as he would like to return with me. I thought he could not preach, and did not let him know. But I had not been in Chicago a great many weeks before I got a letter which said he had arrived in this country, and that he would come to Chicago and preach for me if I wanted him. I sat down and wrote a very cold letter: 'If you come west, call on me.' I thought that would be the last I should hear of him, but soon I got another letter, saying that he was still in this country, and would come on if I wanted him. I wrote again, telling him if he happened to come west to drop in on me. In the course of a few days I got a letter stating that next Thursday he would be in Chicago. What to do with him I did not know. I had made up my mind he couldn't preach. I was going to be out of town Thursday and Friday, and I told some of the officers of the church:

"'There is a man coming here Thursday and Friday who wants to preach. I don't know whether he can or not. You had better let him try, and I will be back Saturday.'

"They said there was a good deal of interest in the church, and they did not think they should have him preach then; he was a stranger, and he might do more harm than good.

"'Well,' I said, 'you had better try him. Let him preach two nights'; and they finally let him preach.

"When I got back Saturday morning, I was anxious to know how he got on. The first thing I said to my wife when I got in the house was:

"'How is that young Irishman coming along?' (I had met him in Dublin, and took him to be an Irishman, but he happened to be an Englishman.) 'How do the people like him?'

"'They like him very much.'

"'Did you hear him?'

"'Yes.'

"'Did you like him?'

"'Yes, very much. He has preached two sermons from John 3:16, "For God so loved the world, that he gave his only begotten Son, that whosoever believeth in him should not perish, but have everlasting life"; and I think you will like him, although he preaches a little different from what you do.'

"'How is that?'

"'Well, he tells sinners God loves them.'

"'Well,' said I, 'he is wrong.'

"She said: 'I think you will agree with him when you hear him, because he backs up everything he says with the Word of God. You think if a man doesn't preach as you do, he is wrong.'

"I went down that night to church, and I noticed every one brought his Bible.

"'My friends,' began Moorehouse, 'if you will turn to the third chapter of John and the sixteenth verse, you will find my text.'

"He preached a most extraordinary sermon from that verse. He did not divide the text into 'secondly' and 'thirdly' and 'fourthly' —he just took it as a whole, and then went through the Bible, from Genesis to Revelation, to prove that in all ages God loved the world; that He sent prophets and patriarchs and holy men to warn them, and last of all sent His Son. After they murdered Him, He sent the Holy Ghost.

"I never knew up to that time that God loved us so much. This heart of mine began to thaw out, and I could not keep back the tears. It was like news from a far country. I just drank it in.

"The next night there was a great crowd, for the people like to hear that God loves them, and he said: 'My friends, if you will turn in your Bible to the third chapter of John and the sixteenth verse, you will find my text.' He preached another extraordinary sermon from that wonderful verse, and he went on proving God's love again, from Genesis to Revelation. He could turn to almost any part of the Bible, and prove it. I thought that sermon was better than the other one, he struck a higher chord than ever, and it was sweet to my soul to hear it.

"The next night—it is pretty hard to get out a crowd in Chicago on Monday night, but they came. Women left their washing, or if they washed, they came, and brought their Bibles; and he said again: 'My friends, if you will turn to the sixteenth verse of the third chapter of John, you will find my text'; and again he followed it out to prove that God loves us. He just beat it down into our hearts, and I have never doubted it since.

"I used to preach that God was behind the sinner with a double-edged sword, ready to hew him down. I have got done with that. I preach now that God is behind the sinner with love, and he is running away from the God of love.

"Tuesday night came, and we thought surely he had exhausted the text, and that he would take another, but he preached the sixth sermon from that wonderful text. 'God so loved the world, that he gave his only begotten Son, that whosoever believeth in him should not perish, but have'—not going to have when you die, but have it right here, now—'everlasting life.' Although many years have rolled away, his hearers never have forgotten it.

"The seventh night came, and he went into the pulpit. Every eye was upon him. All were anxious to know what he was going to preach about. He said: 'My friends, I have been hunting all day for a new text, but I cannot find one as good as the old one; so we will go back to the third chapter of John and the sixteenth verse,' and he preached the seventh sermon from that wonderful text. I remember the closing up of that sermon. Said he:

"'My friends, for a whole week I have been trying to tell you how much God loves you, but I cannot do it with this poor stammering tongue. If I could borrow Jacob's ladder, and climb up into heaven, and ask Gabriel, who stands in the presence of the Almighty, if he could tell me how much love the Father has for the world, all he could say would be: "God so loved the world, that he gave his only begotten Son, that whosoever believeth in him should not perish, but have everlasting life."'"

It was a revelation to Mr. Moody of the inexhaustibility of Scripture such as he had never dreamed of. From that time, he became a more diligent student of the Bible. He asked Moorehouse how to study, and invited friends to his Chicago home for the first "Bible readings" that were held in America.

The only other place of special interest that Mr. Moody visited on this trip was Paris, whither he went with his wife for a week in order to avoid the trying English climate. He preached a few times with the help of interpreters, but spent most of the time in sightseeing. The Paris Exposition was then in progress.

He left a permanent impress upon English religious life by establishing a noon prayer-meeting at the Aldersgate Street Y.M.C.A. similar to the Chicago noon prayer-meeting. "I have sent you an account of the daily noon prayer-meeting I have at last got started here," he wrote his mother. "It is a great success, and they are starting them in different parts of the city. I am in hopes great good will come of it. They are also starting them in different parts of the kingdom."

HOW MOODY AND SANKEY FIRST CAME TOGETHER

Mr. Moody's name is, throughout the world, associated with that of Ira D. Sankey more than any other of his fellow-laborers in the gospel. By many, "Moody and Sankey" are thought of as one person.

They met for the first time in the year 1870, at the International Convention of the Young Men's Christian Association, held at Indianapolis, Indiana.

They had heard of each other, but had never met. Mr. Sankey was already known for his ability to win souls by his singing of hymns, but neither figured very prominently as leaders of the exercises at the convention.

At that time Mr. Sankey was a government officer in New Castle, Pennsylvania, holding commission in the Internal Revenue Service. He was thirty years old, having been born, of English and Scotch-Irish stock, at Edinburgh, Lawrence County, Pennsylvania, on August 28, 1840. He was a member of the Methodist Episcopal Church, but his religious work had been conducted only during leisure hours, and from an early age had been in the direction of singing.

He had heard enough of Mr. Moody to make him curious to see him and hear him talk, and when he went to the Indianapolis convention he immediately commenced to look for the young man from Chicago.

Their first meeting did not occur until a day or so after their arrival, and then only under rather novel circumstances.

It was announced that "Mr. Moody from Chicago" would conduct a prayer-meeting on Sunday morning at six o'clock, in a Baptist church some distance away from the Academy of Music, where the convention was held. Notwithstanding the early hour, Mr. Sankey determined to take advantage of the opportunity to see and hear the man whom until that time he had been unable to find.

The distance to the church was much greater than he had anticipated, and the service was half through when he arrived and took a seat near the door.

At the conclusion of a lengthy prayer, a friend, Rev. Robert McMillen, urged Mr. Sankey to start right in with a hymn, as there seemed to be no one in charge of the singing. Without waiting for further invitation, Mr. Sankey rose and sang:

"'There is a fountain filled with blood,
Drawn from Immanuel's veins;
And sinners plunged beneath that flood
Lose all their guilty stains.'"

The congregation joined in heartily.

When the meeting was brought to a close, Mr. McMillen asked Mr. Sankey to step forward, and he would introduce him to Mr. Moody.

As he drew near, Mr. Moody, recognizing the one who had led the singing, took his hand, and said:

"Where are you from?"

"Pennsylvania," replied Mr. Sankey.

"Married?"

"Yes. I have a wife and two children."

"What do you do for a living when you are at home?"

"I am in the government service."

All this time Mr. Moody had been holding Mr. Sankey's hand. Looking into his face with his keen eyes, he said:

"Well, you'll have to give up business."

Mr. Sankey stood amazed, and was at a loss to understand just what Mr. Moody meant by telling him he would have to give up what was to him a good position, and one affording a comfortable living. He was so taken aback for a few seconds that he could make no reply. Mr. Moody, however, explained what he meant.

"You'll have to give up your government position, and come with me. You are the man I have been looking for for the last eight years. I want you to come and help me in my work in Chicago."

Mr. Sankey had by this time partly recovered from his surprise, but the thought of giving up a good position for an uncertainty was too much, and he begged for time in which to consider the matter. Mr. Moody asked him if he would pray over the question, and out of politeness he said he would.

That was Sunday. All that day and night Mr. Sankey thought over Mr. Moody's words, but the next morning found him still inclined to stick to the government position, with his salary assured every month.

Just at a moment when he was inclined to be wavering, a card was brought to him. It was from Mr. Moody, asking him to meet him that evening at six o'clock at a certain street corner to sing.

Mr. Sankey wrote an acceptance upon the back of the card, and returned it to Mr. Moody, saying he would be there. Together with a few friends he went to the appointed place at the hour named, and in a few moments Mr. Moody came along.

Without even stopping, he walked into a store and asked for the use of a large store box for a pulpit. Permission being given, he rolled the box out to the street corner, and climbing upon it, asked Mr. Sankey to sing a hymn.

After one or two hymns had been sung, Mr. Moody commenced to preach. The workingmen were just on their way home from the mills and factories, and in a short time a large crowd had gathered. Mr. Sankey said that Mr. Moody preached that evening from that box as he had never heard any one preach before.

The crowd stood spellbound as the words flowed from his lips with wonderful force and rapidity. After he had talked for about fifteen minutes, he leaped down from the box, announced that he was going to hold a meeting at the Academy of Music, and invited the crowd to accompany him there. Mr. Sankey and his friends marched down the street four abreast, singing "Shall We Gather at the River?"

It took but a few minutes to pack the lower floor of the Academy of Music. Mr. Moody saw that the men in their working clothes were seated before he ascended the platform to speak.

His second address was as captivating as the one delivered on the street corner, and it was not until the delegates had arrived for the evening session of the convention that the meeting was brought to a close.

Mr. Sankey was still undecided when Mr. Moody again brought up the question of their going together. However, the impression made on his mind by those two services was so great that after a period of several months he accepted an invitation to spend a week with Mr. Moody in Chicago, and before that week was over he had sent his commission to the Secretary of the Treasury.

From that time to the day of Mr. Moody's death they continued their labors in unbroken harmony and accord.

Mr. Moody's opinion as to the value of singing in religious services was very decided. Not long ago he said:

"I feel sure the great majority of people do like singing, and I purpose to make it a prominent feature of all my services. It helps to build up your audience—even if you do preach a dry sermon. If you have singing that reaches the heart, it will fill the church every time."

He used to say that there is more said in the Bible about praise than about prayer, and that music and song not only accompanied all Scripture revivals, but were essential in deepening spiritual life. "We owe some of our best hymns to seasons like those, when in the family and church, in the factory and street, the great truths of the gospel are heard in song. Singing does at least as much as preaching to impress the Word of God upon people's minds. During the forty years since God first called me, the importance of praise expressed in song has grown upon me." It was his constant effort to promote good, lively singing in the church, and also in the home.

THE CHICAGO FIRE, AND AFTER

The year 1871 was critical to Mr. Moody's career. He realized more and more how little he was fitted by personal acquirements for his work. An intense hunger and thirst for spiritual power were aroused in him by the action of three holy women, who used to attend his meetings and sit on the front seat. He could see by the expression on their faces that they were praying. At the close of services they would say to him:

"We have been praying for you."

"Why don't you pray for the people?" he would ask.

"Because you need the power of the Spirit," they said.

"I need the power! Why," said Mr. Moody, speaking of it in after years, "I thought I had power. I had the largest congregation in Chicago, and there were many conversions. I was in a sense satisfied. But right along, those three godly women kept praying for me, and their earnest talk about anointing for special service set me to thinking. I asked them to come and talk with me, and we got down on our knees. They poured out their hearts that I might receive the filling of the Holy Spirit. There came a great hunger into my soul. I did not know what it was. I began to cry as I never did before. The hunger increased. I really felt that I did not want to live any longer if I could not have this power for service."

While he was in this mental and spiritual condition, Chicago was laid in ashes. The great fire commenced on October 8, 1871, and swept out of existence both Farwell Hall and Illinois Street Church. He had been preaching a series of sermons on the life of Christ in Farwell Hall for five Sabbath nights. He took the Savior from the cradle and followed Him up to the judgement hall, and that night made what he considered was as great a blunder as he ever made in his life. The courthouse bell was sounding an alarm of fire, but he paid no attention to it. They were accustomed to hear the fire-bell often, and it did not disturb them much when it sounded.

He finished his sermon upon, "What shall I do with Jesus?" and said to the audience:

"Now, I want you to take the question with you and think it over, and next Sunday I want you to come back and tell me what you are going to do with Him."

"What a mistake!" he said afterward; "it seems as if Satan was in my mind when I said this. Since then I have never dared to give an audience a week to think of their salvation. If they were lost they might rise up in judgement against me.

"I remember Mr. Sankey singing, and how his voice rang when he came to that pleading verse:

"'Today the Savior calls,
For refuge fly!
The storm of Justice falls,
And death is nigh!'"

After the meeting, as Mr. Moody went homeward, he saw the glare of flames, and knew it meant ruin to Chicago. About one o'clock Farwell Hall was burned. Soon his church went down. Everything was scattered. About midnight the fierceness of the fire seemed to be waning and they thought the fire department would gain the upper hand, as they had done the night before. The family retired, but within an hour a loud call was made to all the residents of their street to hasten their escape. The fire had crossed the river, and was rapidly advancing.

It was too late to think of saving much more than could be carried in the hands. A neighbor took Mr. Moody's two children in his already crowded carriage, and made his escape north. A few articles of silver and some valued tokens of friendships were hastily placed in a baby-cart. But there was one article Mrs. Moody's heart was set upon saving. This was a portrait in oil of her husband by the artist Healy, that hung on the wall of their parlor. It was a gift from the artist, presented to Mrs. Moody after the return from the first trip to Europe in 1867, when a free lease of this home, completely furnished, was presented to Mr. Moody by his Chicago friends. This portrait Mrs. Moody prized above anything the home contained.

A stranger who had entered the house assisted in taking it from the wall. Calling Mr. Moody, his wife urged him to save it for her.

No entreaty could prevail on him, but the canvas was hastily knocked out of the heavy gold frame, and carried off by Mrs. Moody herself.

A black eye and a bruised face was part of the price paid for this effort, for once on the street it was a constant struggle between the bearer of the panel and the terrific wind that was blowing for possession of the prize. Love won, but only after a continuous battle.

When they were safe, he said:

"Wouldn't it have been amusing for me to take my own picture! Suppose I was met on the street by friends in the same plight as ourselves, and they said: 'Hello, Moody, glad you have escaped; what's that you have saved and cling to so affectionately?'—wouldn't it have sounded fine to reply, 'Oh, I've got my own picture'?"

This portrait now hangs on the walls of the Northfield home, bringing to mind that night of fiery ordeal that tried many a man's soul.

As soon as his wife and family were safe with friends, Mr. Moody devoted himself to relief work. Before long he left for the East to raise money for the homeless, and also for a new church. George H. Stuart and John Wanamaker, of Philadelphia, and other friends raised three thousand dollars, and a temporary building, seventy-five by one hundred feet, was immediately reared on a lot not far from the site of the former church. On December 24, 1871, just two months and fifteen days after the fire, this building, known as the North Side Tabernacle, was dedicated.

But that Eastern visit was productive of greater blessing in Mr. Moody's life. The hunger for more spiritual power was still upon him. The fire did not dismiss the yearning. "My heart was not in the work for begging," he said. "I could not appeal. I was crying all the time that God would fill me with His Spirit. Well, one day, in the City of New York—ah, what a day!—I cannot describe it, I seldom refer to it, it is almost too sacred an experience to name—Paul had an experience of which he never spoke for fourteen years—I can only say God revealed Himself to me, and I had such an experience of His love that I had to ask Him to stay His hand. I went to preaching again. The sermons were not different; I did not present any new truths; and yet hundreds were converted. I would not now be placed back where I was before that blessed experience if you should give me all the world; it would be as the small dust of the balance."

When he returned to Chicago, his mission work at the new Tabernacle went forward successfully. Revival fires were kindled anew and blazed long and bright.

Within a year steps were taken to erect a permanent building. The lot on which the present church stands was secured. Contributions came in from all quarters, thousands of Sabbath-school children contributing five cents each to buy bricks. For two years the basement of the present building was roofed over temporarily, and used for meetings, and finally, as a subsequent chapter will explain, means were provided for the completion of the structure, which has since been known as the Chicago Avenue Church, or "Moody's" Church.

SECOND VISIT TO ENGLAND, 1872

While the audiences at the North Side Tabernacle were large and the meetings fruitful in results, it was impossible for Mr. Moody to do any visitation work, as there were no homes within reach. The fire had laid the city in ashes for a large area surrounding the Tabernacle. Where the people came from to attend the meetings was a mystery. Those who were building shanties among the ruins were constantly moving.

Finding, therefore, that he could be spared from Chicago, and desiring to learn more of the Bible at the feet of English Bible students, Mr. Moody determined to cross the sea again. He started in June, 1872.

This visit demands special consideration on account of one incident that undoubtedly marked another turning point in his career.

He was determined not to get into work if he could help it; but one day he went into the Old Baily prayer-meeting, and at the close of the service the Rev. Mr. Lessey, pastor of a church in the north of London, asked him to preach for him the next Sabbath. Mr. Moody consented.

The place seemed very dead and cold at the morning service. The people did not appear to be very much interested. It seemed to him as if he had been beating against the air. He felt as if it was a lost morning.

The next service was at half-past six in the evening, and while he was preaching it seemed as if the very atmosphere was charged with the Spirit of God. There came a hush from heaven upon the people, which showed that God was searching their hearts. He had not been much in prayer that day, and could not understand it.

When he had finished preaching, he asked all who would like to become Christians to rise, so that he might pray for them. They rose by the hundreds all over the house; it seemed as if the whole audience was getting up.

Mr. Moody said to himself: "These people did not understand me. They did not know what I meant when I asked them to rise."

He had never seen so many rise in America, and did not know what to make of it, so he put the test again.

"Now," he said, "all of you that want to become Christians just step into the inquiry-room."

They went in and crowded the room so that they had to take in extra chairs to seat them all. The minister was surprised, and so was

Mr. Moody. Neither had expected such a blessing. They had not faith to believe that God can save by hundreds and thousands as well as by ones and twos.

When Mr. Moody again asked those that really wanted to become Christians to rise, up rose the whole audience. What to do he did not know, so he told all who were really in earnest to meet the pastor there the next night.

Next day he went over to Dublin, but on Tuesday morning he got a dispatch urging him to return, and saying there were more inquirers on Monday than on Sunday. He went back and held meetings for ten days, and four hundred were taken into that church.

After some time the secret of this marvelous manifestation of the Spirit's working was revealed. There were two sisters that belonged to that church. One was strong, the other was bedridden. One day, as the sick woman was bemoaning her condition, the thought came to her that she could pray, and she began to pray God to revive the church of which she was a member. Day and night, her prayer went up to God, but the church still remained cold and dead.

Before long she read in a paper an account of some meetings Mr. Moody had held in America, and, though she did not know him, she began to pray God to send him to her church.

Her sister came home that Sunday after he had preached, and said:

"Well, who do you think preached this morning?" She guessed the names of a good many with whom her pastor was in the habit of exchanging.

Finally her sister said, "It was Mr. Moody, from America."

The bedridden saint turned pale, and said:

"I know what that means. God has heard my prayer."

She spent that afternoon in fasting and prayer, and in the evening the answer came in fire from heaven. Mr. Moody believed that that revival brought him back to England the next year. As a result of it, he received invitations from Rev. William Pennefather, rector of St. Jude's, Mildmay Park, London, and a Mr. Bainbridge, a prominent Methodist layman of Newcastle-on-Tyne, to hold meetings. But he had not come prepared for a long stay, and so returned to America after three months and rejoined his family, being urgently invited, however, to return to England next year.

GREAT ENGLISH CAMPAIGN WITH MR. SANKEY, 1873–75

Mr. Moody decided to accept the invitation that had been

pressed upon him, and waited for the funds they promised to send him for the expense of the ocean voyage. He arranged with Mr. Sankey, who was at that time chorister of his church and Sabbath-school, to accompany him.

Steamship passage was engaged for both families, but weeks went by and the promised funds did not arrive. He could not understand it. Finally, believing that God's leading was distinctly toward England, he was obliged to go to a friend with whom he had just deposited about four hundred and fifty dollars to invest during his absence, and get back this money. Another friend, quite unconscious of the real situation, handed him a check for five hundred dollars the day before he left Chicago. The greater portion of these two sums was expended in paying for ocean passage for the party.

They arrived at Queenstown in due time. There Mr. Moody received word that explained the non-receipt of the promised money. The two cordial and devoted Christian friends on whom he was relying for moral and financial support had both died.

After reading the letter through, he turned to Mr. Sankey and said:

"God seems to have closed the door. We will not open any ourselves. If He opens the door we will go in; otherwise we will return at once to America."

On landing at Liverpool, June 17, 1873, they went directly to the Northwestern Hotel. Three gentlemen, who had noticed their names in the list of arrivals, called upon them at the hotel for a short time. During the evening Mr. Moody discovered in one of his pockets an unopened letter which he had received, just before leaving New York, from the secretary of the Y.M.C.A. at York, England, saying that he had heard of his work among the young men in America, and that he hoped if he ever came to England he would come and speak at their Association.

Mr. Moody at once remarked: "This door is only ajar, but we will consider the letter as God's hand leading to York, and we will go there."

After spending one night in Liverpool, Mr. Moody, with his wife and children, took the train for London, and Mr. Sankey and his wife went to Manchester to the home of the one man he knew in England—Harry Moorehouse. Three days later they met again at York and commenced to hold meetings.

The ministers at first were strongly inclined to look upon the newcomers with suspicion and disfavor, and consequently held themselves aloof. The attendance was small to begin with. But gradually the meetings grew in interest, the ministers cooperated, the hymns took hold of the people, and both preaching and singing became the subject of public conversation throughout the community. The preaching was for believers rather than for the unconverted.

"Yes, thank God, I know Mr. Moody," wrote Rev. F. B. Meyer, of Christ Church, London, not long ago; "I have known him ever since a memorable Monday morning in 1873. I can now see him standing up to lead the first noon prayer-meeting in a small ill-lit room in Coney Street, York, little realizing that it was the seed-germ of a mighty harvest, and that a movement was beginning that would culminate in a few months in Free Assembly Hall, Edinburgh, and ultimately in the Agricultural Hall and the Royal Opera-house, London. It was the birth-time of new conceptions of ministry, new methods of work, new inspirations and hopes."

After five weeks of meetings in York, resulting in the professed conversions of several hundred people, they passed on to the seaport town of Sunderland. Here their meetings were still more largely attended. A better spirit was evident, and much larger numbers professed conversion. The chapel in which their first meetings were held soon became too small for the audience, necessitating the use of one of the largest halls in the north of England. The town had been placarded, in advance of their coming, with posters that read:

"Moody will preach the gospel
Sankey will sing the gospel"

—thus giving birth to the latter expression, which is now so current.

After six weeks spent in Sunderland and outlying districts, they were invited to Newcastle-on-Tyne. They had now gained the sympathy of nearly all the ministers of all denominations except those of the Established Church, who, learning that they were both unordained men, refused in any way to countenance them. After a few weeks of very successful meetings, the editor of the *Newcastle Chronicle,* a Mr. Cowan, then a member of Parliament for that district, wrote about the meetings in his paper, speaking of them as a "wonderful religious phenomenon." On the whole, it was a friendly review and criticism of the work.

It was a very unusual thing then for such a prominent secular paper to discuss religious matters, and Mr. Cowan's article created a profound impression throughout England. Invitations to hold services began to pour in from all sides.

The fame of the Newcastle revival reached Edinburgh, and ministers and laymen went to investigate. The result was an invitation from a large and representative committee to hold meetings in that city. They accepted, and the most interesting and wonderful meetings they had yet took place.

Special preparatory prayer-meetings had been organized. Everything was done to insure success. But there was much prejudice and criticism to overcome. Mr. Sankey's singing was contrary to Scottish ideas. His organ was called a "kist fu' o' whistles," and was regarded as an abomination. Mr. Moody's fiery speech and actions stood out in peculiar contrast with the staid demeanor and solemn spirit of the ordinary Scotch divine. But his simple and Scriptural style of preaching soon won them. The interest was intense from the first, and the crowds enormous. No one building could accommodate the people, and three or four overflow meetings were held at the same time. The newspapers gave ample reports of the meetings, and soon the news of the revival was telegraphed all over the country.

Withal, there was a solemn stillness in the meetings, and a complete absence of emotional excitement.

All classes of society were influenced. Dr. Horatius Bonar declared his belief that there was scarcely a Christian household in the whole city in which one or more persons had not been converted. People came in from miles around to attend the meetings, or to get someone to come to their town or hamlet and tell of the wonderful work, thus spreading the fires throughout the land. It was while organizing services for students there that Mr. Moody first met Henry Drummond, himself a student. Recognizing his ability, Mr. Moody attached him to himself, and got him to devote the next year or two to work among young men in the cities they visited.

After spending three months in Edinburgh, the evangelists went to Dundee, and then for a four months' campaign to Glasgow. "The career of these men has been like the rolling of a snowball," wrote the minister who had invited them to Sunderland; "it gathers as it goes; at first a handful, then a hill." One of the closing meetings at Glasgow was for converts, of whom three thousand five hundred were admitted by ticket. So great was the crowd on the last Sabbath evening—estimated at fifty thousand—that Mr. Moody did not go inside the Kibble Crystal Palace, where the meeting was advertised to be held, but preached to the multitude in the open air, standing on the box of a carriage. Mr. Sankey conducted the meeting in the palace.

Similar scenes of revival interest followed as the evangelists visited other towns as far north as John o' Groats. Scotland was stirred to its depths in a degree never known before. Mr. Moody has visited that country two or three times since then, with Mr. Sankey, and has always received an enthusiastic welcome, with good spiritual results. Well might Lord Overtoun telegraph on the occasion of his death:

"All Scotland mourns."

In September, 1874, Messrs. Moody and Sankey began to hold meetings in Belfast, Ireland. That first Sunday, it is estimated that four times as many people gathered as could get into the building. Other centers were visited in Ireland, the tour culminating in immense meetings in the great Exhibition Palace in Dublin. The evangelists had made almost as deep an impression upon Ireland as upon Scotland.

Returning to England, they visited Manchester, Sheffield, Birmingham, Liverpool, and other towns, with the usual demonstrations of the Spirit and of power. Finally, on March 9, 1875, they entered upon their great London campaign, which lasted until July 12.

The immense size and population of London made it necessary to strike successively at different points so as to reach the whole. The city and suburbs were therefore divided into four quarters, for each of which a secretary was appointed. Local committees were also formed, subordinate to the central committee. The enthusiasm was intense throughout. Greater crowds than ever attended. The Agricultural Hall, North London, was constantly overcrowded, although the capacity was variously estimated from fifteen to twenty thousand. The Royal Opera-house, in the fashionable West End, with seating capacity of five thousand, could have been filled three or four times over. The windows of all the bookstores hung with pictures of Moody and Sankey. The daily papers gave extended reports of the meetings. Penny editions of "Sacred Songs and Solos" were hawked in the streets. Not only was London itself stirred, but the revival became a world-wide wonder.

At this time Mr. Moody was only thirty-eight years old. Nobody was more surprised than he at the magnitude of the work initiated in York under such unpromising conditions two years before. From a little mission among the street [urchins] of Chicago, he had been led of God to make perhaps the deepest and most far-reaching religious impression that had as yet been made upon Great Britain and Ireland, and through these upon the whole English-speaking world.

Through it all, he remained perfectly humble before his God. "I am glad you have the papers," he once wrote to his mother. "It will be as good as a letter from me—in fact, better, for I would not like to have to write so much about myself."

Dr. R. W. Dale, one of the leading Nonconformists of England, sat and watched him for three or four days after he went to Birmingham, at different kinds of meetings, trying to discover the secret of his power. Then he told him that the work was most plainly of God, for he could see no relation between him personally and the work he was doing.

Mr. Moody laughed cheerily, and said he would be very sorry if it were otherwise.

Dr. Dale had a profound respect for Mr. Moody and considered that he had a right to preach the gospel, "Because," he said, "he could never speak of a lost soul without tears of Christly compassion in his eyes."

Some of the direct results of this English tour may be summarized as follows: Thousands of the unsaved and thousands of backslidden Christians were led into closer communion with God. A spirit of evangelism was awakened, and has never died down. A large number of city missions and other active aggressive organizations were established. Denominational differences were buried to a remarkable degree. Clergymen of all denominations were drawn into cooperation on a common platform, the salvation of the lost. Bibles were reopened, and Bible study received a wonderful impetus. Long-standing prejudices were swept away. New life was infused into all methods of Christian activity. No attempt was made to proselytize, and converts were passed over to existing churches for nurture and admonition in the Lord. Lord Shaftesbury once said that if Mr. Sankey had done no more than teach the people to sing the hymn "Hold the Fort," he had conferred an inestimable benefit on the British Empire. "Since Mr. Moody made his way across the ocean twenty-three years ago," wrote a prominent Scotch minister in 1896, "the American preacher has been a welcome visitor there."

The *New York Tribune* commented editorially on the work in England as follows:

"There can be but one opinion as to the sincerity of Messrs.

Moody and Sankey. They are not money-makers, they are not char-
latans. Decorous, conservative England, which reprobated both
their work and the manner of it, held them in the full blaze of
scrutiny for months, and could not detect in them a single motive
which was not pure."

After spending a few weeks with friends in Wales, speaking occasionally, Mr. Moody preached a farewell sermon in Liverpool on
August 3, 1875, and sailed for America the following day.

BIRTH OF THE MOODY AND SANKEY HYMN-BOOKS, 1873

Another episode that illustrated Mr. Moody's persistence and
faith was the birth and growth of the "Moody and Sankey Hymn-
Books." The great mission these books have had, not alone in
singing their way with gospel gladness into the hearts of millions
but also in singing up great institutions of education and Biblical
training, is one of the romances of religion and commerce.

When Mr. Moody and Mr. Sankey reached England, they
found a type of hymns in the churches different from what they had
been used to, and inappropriate for their purpose. A book of their
own American hymns was imperative.

No publisher could be found, however, to undertake the risk of
publication, as an American hymn-book previously issued had not
fulfilled expectations. Standing absolutely alone, and never flinch-
ing, Mr. Moody was obliged to print at his own risk and expense. He
invested all the money he had left (about one hundred dollars) in a
sixteen-page pamphlet of words and music, compiled by Mr.
Sankey, and sold at sixpence each. This was followed by a "words
only" edition that sold at one penny (two cents) per copy.

The supply was quickly exhausted. A publisher was now found
who agreed to pay a liberal royalty. This arrangement was accepted
by Mr. Moody, with the thought that it might in part pay expenses
for which he had obligated himself personally. So great was the
growing interest that little attention was paid to the matter of royalties, which were left to accumulate. In fact, it soon became a
problem what should be done with the sum due.

At the close of the London campaign and shortly before
Messrs. Moody and Sankey were to return home, the publishers'
statement showed that the sum standing to their credit on this royalty account was no less than thirty-five thousand dollars. They sent
word to the London committee that this amount was at their dis-
posal, to be used for Christian work as they should direct, as they

would not take a cent of the money for themselves. The committee refused to accept the fund, asserting that it belonged to them personally, and they did not propose to have them pay this large sum for the privilege of preaching.

Here was a peculiar case—money going begging for want of a receiver.

One of the officers of the Chicago Avenue Church, Chicago, who happened to be in London at the time, hearing of this predicament, suggested to the committee that the sum be forwarded to Chicago to complete the building of that church. Owing to the panic of 1873–74, pledges made for the erection of this building had become worthless. Work was stopped when only the first (or lecture-room) story was built. A temporary roof covered this, and here services had been held for two years.

The suggestion was adopted, the money paid over, and "Moody's Church" was completed.

So successful has been the sale of succeeding hymn-books that the amount realized in royalties in America alone has doubtless exceeded a million dollars; but not one cent of it has ever found its way into the pockets of either Mr. Moody or Mr. Sankey. It has all been administered by trustees for the benefit of Y.M.C.A.'s churches, and (of late years) Mr. Moody's schools at Northfield.

RETURN TO AMERICA,
THE GREAT MEETINGS IN THE SEVENTIES

It is beyond the truth to say, as some have said, that Great Britain "discovered" D. L. Moody. He was a widely known and widely honored Christian worker when he went abroad upon that momentous third visit to the motherland. But it undoubtedly is true that he returned to America with his fame greatly enhanced. The display of his powers, both natural and bestowed, upon a scene so conspicuous, and the magnitude of the results achieved, profoundly impressed the whole Christian world. Indeed, from that time dates his world-wide fame.

Naturally, his own countrymen followed his course through the three kingdoms most closely, and with deepest interest. The newspaper stories of the unprecedented meetings in London, Liverpool, Birmingham, Manchester, Glasgow, Belfast, and Dublin spread through the United States both the desire for and faith in a great revival whenever he should return to his native land. That expectation of blessing, as is well known to students of the history of revivals, creates the atmosphere favorable to the new birth.

Months before the close of the work in England, calls for his labors had been pouring in upon him, and the whole country was open before him. With his unfailing strategic insight he made his choice.

"Cities," he said, "are the centers of influence. Water runs downhill, and the highest hills in America are the great cities. If we can stir them we shall stir the whole country."

And so he began that series of meetings of unequaled numbers, power, and fruitage in the religious history of this country.

Into New York, Philadelphia, Baltimore, St. Louis, Cincinnati, Chicago, Boston, and later in the lesser of our great cities, he carried the gospel fire. Invariably he rallied about him the strongest laymen in the community. Men of great affairs gave not only of their means to the necessary expenses of the work, but gave themselves as well. They felt of kin to this strong dominant personality, and gladly followed his leadership.

To the very end of his life he retained the unbounded confidence of men of affairs. At a dinner in New York not a year before his death, a guest said to a great railway magnate who was present:

"How is it that while you and other like men are all but inaccessible, fenced in by closed doors and polite but immovable private secretaries, D. L. Moody sees you at any time?"

"He is one of us," was the reply.

In this series of meetings Mr. Moody's gifts were in full exercise. His methods combined the siege and the assault. Sometimes, as in Baltimore and St. Louis, he spent months in a place, studying the situation with unfailing sagacity, covering the entire city with meetings in which he utilized the ministers and lay workers, and often, especially toward the end, calling to his aid brother evangelists and singers from far and near. His objects were not only immediate results in conversion, though this, needless to say, held the first place, but also the permanent quickening of the life of the churches, and especially the promotion of Bible study.

Great stress was put upon this from the first. He usually gave the afternoon meetings to Bible readings, and no one who heard them will ever forget the impression of those fresh, original, and deeply spiritual expositions. But the meetings themselves were, after all, the most marvelous of all the manifestations of power in this memorable campaign.

No church or hall would seat the thousands who flocked to

hear. Resort was therefore to such vast roofed-in spaces as could be found. In New York, the immense building known as the Hippodrome was utilized for the meetings. Built originally for a railway station, and subsequently remodeled and filled with rising tiers of benches by P. T. Barnum for his circus, it was admirably adapted for such meetings as those of Moody and Sankey. Varying in minor detail in different places, the meetings were in essentials very much alike. The following interesting description, taken (by permission) from a recent article in the *Ladies' Home Journal* by Nathaniel P. Babcock, an eye-witness of the scenes in the Hippodrome, which he describes, may serve to give a truthful idea of Mr. Moody's work in the seventies:

"'To the Hippodrome!' was the cry of the Protestant religious world of New York during the early months of the year 1876. Twenty-one years ago, and yet the strangeness of those days, when over the great metropolis hung an atmosphere charged with the electricity of religious zeal, is fresh in my memory. 'To the Hippodrome!' The words were uttered from the pulpits of scores of churches—first as advice, then as a command—by ministers to congregations. 'To the Hippodrome!' You heard the phrase in the street-cars, in the hotels, sometimes upon the busy avenues. On early morning trains, steaming in from suburban points, you saw women by the hundreds, with luncheons in baskets, drawn to the city, not by the spring millinery of the stores, but by that shibboleth which echoed in myriad Christian hearts, 'To the Hippodrome!'

"Moody and Sankey, aided by a multitude of local clergymen and bands of volunteer Christian workers, had undertaken the task of setting New York on fire with enthusiasm for the cause of Christ. How great was the measure of their success may be judged by the fact that there were days between February 7th, the beginning of the revival, and April 19th, its close, when as many as sixty thousand persons found their way into the presence of the evangelists—one meeting following another from noon till quite late in the evening, with almost constantly assembling audiences of seven or eight thousand at each. A monster stage or platform in the main audience-room was built to hold a choir of six hundred voices, and still leave room for at least four hundred visiting clergymen or distinguished guests. Partitioned off at the extreme outer edge of this huge platform was the box—it could scarcely be called a pulpit—from which the exhorter was to speak. Strong needed to be the railing which fenced the front of this preacher's stand, for there were times, when the upheaving of the consciences of men began and the great evangelist with earnest eyes looked into the agonized faces of the multitude before him, that his strong frame bent heavily against the barrier, while his arms stretched forth as though to take the whole wide world of suffering sinners in a comforting embrace.

"This is how Mr. Moody looked, when to an eager, earnest, expectant audience he appeared through that small door at the back of the stage in the Hippodrome: a sturdy figure in a tightly fitting frock coat; a well-shaped head, made to look smaller than its actual size because of the broadness of the man's shoulders and shortness of the neck on which it was poised; a much bearded face, the black hair not only hanging down over his chest, but growing thickly up each cheek; a forehead seemingly low by reason of its projection beyond the line of the nose; keen eyes, with wrinkles running from their outer corners over ruddy cheeks, and a heavy black mustache hiding the mouth. In his hands, as he came for the first time into the presence of this mighty metropolitan audience, Mr. Moody carried a Bible, his fingers were interlaced about it, but as he passed through the narrow lane between the choir and the platform guests and reached the front of the stage, he shifted the book and lifted his right hand, palm downward, toward the vast audience. It was the signal for silence, and was heeded on the instant by every one.

"When in obedience to Mr. Moody's signal the music had ceased and the audience had become entirely attentive, the evangelist said:

"'Let us open the meeting by silent prayer.'

"These were the first words uttered by this remarkable man in his work in the chief city of America in that religious revival, the effects of which spread from end to end of the American continent. As he spoke he bowed his head on the railing at the platform's edge. Then among all that vast concourse heads were reverently bent, and absolute silence prevailed.

"How long this mute prayer continued I do not know. What is vividly before me is the singular commotion which followed at its close when Mr. Moody gave out the opening hymn. In all that assembly there were but few who were unprovided with hymnals, for from the date of the opening service in Brooklyn, on October 24, the Moody and Sankey Song Book had become universally popular. And now, when the command was given to 'join in singing' one of those inspiring melodies, the page number of which was announced by the evangelist, ten thousand hands began to turn the leaves of these books, making a rustling noise not unlike the wind in the trees before a storm. Meanwhile, Mr. Sankey seated himself at a small organ near the front of the platform, and assumed the direction of music.

"Down from the pulpit with outstretched hands came Mr. Moody, and as he passed through the aisles here and there, persons arose and with bowed heads walked away in the direction of doors that led to the apartments known as 'inquiry rooms.' Beyond these doors we may not follow them. I know that earnest men and women waited in those rooms to receive all whose agonized consciences led them there. I know that they knelt in prayer, and that words of love and sympathy were whispered in their ears, and I remember to have seen men come forth with countenances radiant; but of their personal experiences of converted sinners we are not speaking. It is the wonderful scene of a concourse stirred by something deeper than worldly enthusiasm, deeper than brotherly love, deeper than patriotism, that we are endeavoring to recall.

"Three meetings a day—sometimes, though not often, five—is the work these evangelists have laid out for themselves. In the afternoon of many days women only are admitted to the Hippodrome. They pack it solidly from the floor to the topmost seats, till their plumes brush the rafters. 'Pray for my husband!' 'Pray for my son!' 'Pray for my brother!' are the requests they make in faltering tones. 'Pray for me!' says one whose cheeks will perhaps never again be painted and whose feet will walk in a better path.

"At night the scene is still more wondrous, for then men—old men, young men, earnest men—have taken possession of the auditorium. At these meetings Mr. Moody is at his best. Eleven thousand men have been packed in that old Hippodrome at one of these night gatherings in March and April twenty-one years ago. The gas-lights shine in their eager faces. No political convention ever presented such a scene. Thousands arise and cry, 'I will! I will!' when asked to enlist; 'Amens!' sweep through the place like the rattling of musketry, and sometimes the ecstasy of religion becomes so manifest that long intervals of silent prayer are necessary in order to keep the sin-stricken within the bounds of needed self-restraint."

The numbers definitely brought to Christ in these meetings from 1876 to 1881 were never even estimated by Mr. Moody. He was intolerant of that kind of statistic. When a minister recently asked him how many souls had been saved under his preaching, he only answered:

"I don't know anything about that, Doctor. Thank God, I don't have to. I don't keep the Lamb's Book of Life."

[Fellow preacher and Bible teacher C. I. Scofield once described Moody the evangelist in] "D. L. Moody As An Evangelist: His Characteristics And Methods." Scofield wrote:

"It is the mark of weak men," Scofield noted, "that they break down under unusual responsibilities, of strong men that they are developed by them. The two Americans who in our generation had most in common, Lincoln and Grant, both came to the maturity of their powers under the pressure of immense labors and responsibilities. Both began with a modest estimate of their capacities; both came at last to a singularly humble self-confidence. So it may be said that under the testings of his great English campaign Mr. Moody came to the maturity of his powers. He grew in knowledge and in grace to the day of his death; but in mastery of assemblies, in readiness of resource, in capacity of leadership, in unfailing tact, and in strategic grasp and skill, he returned to America in the fullness of his great capacities.

"Doubtless, also, his character had ripened and matured. Three supreme testings await strong men in this life: the testing of poverty and obscurity; of prosperity and applause; and of suffering. Many who enter life conscious, even though dimly, of great latent capacities, turn sour and bitter under neglect, narrow circumstances, and lack of appreciation. Others who pass that first trial successfully are corrupted or enfeebled by success and adulation. Many who stand erect alike in obscurity and success, fail utterly under the testing of suffering. Mr. Moody, by God's grace, passed unscathed through them all. Perhaps it has happened to few men, suddenly lifted into the fellowship of the noble and famous of the earth, to be so little moved from the serenity of their minds, the even tenor of their ways.

"Doubtless this self-poise was in part an inheritance—the hilltown New Englander's habitual self-respect. But doubtless, too, Mr. Moody had so great a sense of the essential dignity of even the least of the sons of God, that he was little affected by earthly title or personal fame.

"At one of his great London meetings he was, as usual, superintending from the platform the seating of the immense audience. While so occupied, and at the moment when he was following with a rather anxious eye a couple of bewildered old ladies who were vainly seeking for front seats, a friend brought upon the platform a famous English earl.

"'Glad to see you, Lord,'" said Mr. Moody. 'Won't you please take a couple of chairs to those two old ladies down there?'

"This the earl proceeded to do, to the consternation of his rather obsequious introducer.

"On another occasion it was whispered to him, with some agitation, that a certain exalted personage had entered the hall.

"Mr. Moody quietly replied:

"'I hope she may be much blessed.'

"This independence, springing as it did from elevation and simplicity of character, and not at all from self-assertiveness, commended him to all classes in Great Britain. They found no subserviency . . . in this plain, strong Christian man.

"All these qualities, previously but partially apprehended by his countrymen, became known through newspaper reports, and did much to prepare in America the remarkable outburst of confidence and esteem with which his return was greeted. In a very real sense, Christian America rose to receive him.

"But the facts for once outran the rumor of them. It is not too much to say that as man, as preacher, as organizer, and as Christian strategist, the great 1876–1881 meetings revealed D. L. Moody as supreme.

"In the superficial view it was always his generalship, his mastery of vast numbers of men gathered in meetings, which first impressed the observer; and for this reason his grip of his audience was not due in the first instance to his power as a preacher. Other men, as Whitefield and Wesley and the great Welsh field-preachers, have drawn vast audiences, and have in the end powerfully swayed them, however turbulent or tumultuous they may have been when these great masters of the 'royal art of preaching' rose to address them. But D. L. Moody never began to preach until he had gathered his audience into almost perfect *rapport* with himself. This was his unique distinction among other equally great preachers.

"To accomplish this result he devised a method perfectly adapted to himself, but which in the hands of his imitators is by no means sure of success. Briefly, it was the conduct of a remarkably intense and spiritual preliminary service of song and prayer, interspersed with brief, pungent, characteristic sayings of his own. From the time he came before his great audiences to the moment when he rose to preach, he kept the entire body absorbingly occupied with something interesting. Singing by the great massed choir, by quartets, duetists, soloists, and by the whole assembly, never ceased, except for prayer. But it would be an utter misapprehension to suppose that either his purpose or the actual result achieved was the entertainment of the people. His own manner showed at once his tremendous earnestness, his profound concern for souls.

"The singing had a great and at times overpowering religious value. Before the evangelist rose, the throngs were already shaken, touched, persuaded. A great number of cases came to be known in which the momentous decision for Christ was actually made while Mr. Sankey was singing. Never was a more thoughtless criticism uttered than that Mr. Moody used music merely to attract.

"But simple and obvious as seemed the plan of his introductory service, it was soon found, when the host of imitators began to use it, that like any other method in evangelistic work, it was worth little simply as a method. Apart from the purpose, and above all the power, it accomplished little.

"When his almost unfailing spiritual discernment told him the time had come, he rose to preach.

"D. L. Moody as a preacher was much criticized from the standpoint of academic homiletics. Nor would any think of defending his preaching method on that ground. But that for thirty-five continuous years, in the centers of culture and of active practical thought in the English-speaking world, this self-taught preacher drew the greatest audiences which have fronted any modern speaker on any theme—this fact, one would say, should suggest to teachers of homiletics that possibly they might learn something from him.

"His method was devoid of mystery. Drawing his matter from the Scriptures, he utterly eschewed formal introduction, and plunged at once into the subject itself. That there were slips of grammar was most true; nor was there the slightest effort to suppress a nasal utterance. But he early came to the possession of a nervous Saxon vocabulary, and his strong sense taught him the value of the short sentence and of aphoristic forms.

"Of all this the man himself, as he stood before his audience, was utterly unconscious. He was tremendously in earnest, absolutely sincere, perfectly incapable of phrase-making. It was his supreme possession by the Spirit, united with his powerful understanding, which were his safeguards against bathos, turgid rhetoric, pose, and artifice. Like all natural orators, he made great and effective use of illustration. And yet, it is doubtful if he ever used even the most telling illustration purely for effect. He told an anecdote or referred to a Bible story or incident because it made his point clear.

"Among his natural gifts were humor, always refined, pathos, and a descriptive power which was due to his imagination. Few men ever equaled him in ability to summon before an audience the whole setting of a Bible incident. And he had the sovereign grace of brevity. He knew when to stop, and he never weakened his sermon at the close by recapitulation.

"That all these rare excellencies of public discourse might have been within the mastery of this man, and that he still might have failed utterly of his purpose apart from the mighty power of the baptizing Spirit, is wholly true; but it is right to say that in this humble servant of Jesus, the Spirit had the using of one of the great natural preachers of all time."

DAILY LIFE AT NORTHFIELD, AS CITIZEN AND NEIGHBOR

The career of a public man awakens interest in his manner of life behind the scenes. People want to know how the man whom they see on the platform or pulpit lives at home, and what his neighbors think of him.

No man's private life will stand scrutiny better than D. L. Moody's, whether you consider him in the role of parent, neighbor, or friend. Always and throughout everything, he was a true Christian, a true man.

His Chicago home had been burned in the fire of 1871. The winter following he slept in the North Side Tabernacle, while his wife and family stayed with friends. The missions in England occupied four years more, and when he returned to America he was still without a home.

Under these circumstances he went to Northfield to see his mother, and decided to make his permanent home there, in order to be near her when not engaged in evangelistic labors. He purchased an old homestead within a stone's-throw of his birthplace.

Northfield is a typical New England town, with a history running back more than two hundred years, beautifully situated on the banks of the Connecticut at the junction of the three States of Massachusetts, New Hampshire, and Vermont. From Mr. Moody's front porch a scene of great quiet beauty extends, embracing the rich valley of the Connecticut, with the Green Mountains beyond.

As the years went by Mr. Moody transformed the village into a veritable Mecca by establishing schools, conferences, and other enterprises, of which only brief mention can now be made.

Northfield Seminary for young women was formally opened on November 3, 1879.

Mount Hermon School for young men was projected in 1879, and opened for instruction on May 4, 1881.

The first General Conference for Christian Workers was held in 1880.

The Northfield Training School for women was opened in 1890.

The first Women's Conference was organized in 1893.

The magazine, *Northfield Echoes,* was established in 1894.

The General Eastern Depot of the Bible Institute Colportage Association of Chicago, was opened in 1895.

Camp Northfield, for men, was organized in 1896.

Of later years it was Mr. Moody's custom to spend the months from October to April (inclusive) in evangelistic work. With what pleasure his return to Northfield about May 1st was looked forward to by his students and family! There was no place he loved more than Northfield, and he always regretted to have to leave for even short absences during the summer months. Writing from New York City in December, 1896, he said:

"The city is no place for me. If it was not for the work I am called to do, I would never show my head in this city, or any other, again. It is a rush all the time, and a drive. Oh, the quiet days at Northfield, how I long for them!"

He was an early riser. He generally rose about day-break in summer, devoting the early hours to Bible study and communion with God. He used to say that one who followed this plan could not get more than twenty-four hours away from God.

It often happened, however, that some matter of business would demand attention before breakfast, and perhaps he would be found bursting into the kitchen at Mount Hermon School (four miles distant from his home) by seven o'clock, inspecting the food that was being prepared for breakfast, and tasting one dish and another to assure himself of their quality. Or perhaps he would drive up to his own garden to get some vegetables for breakfast.

Breakfast with the family at 7:30, and immediately afterward family prayers, which the house-servants and hired men also attended. Mr. Moody read a passage of Scripture and then prayed simply and earnestly.

While the schools were still in session, he usually conducted chapel exercises at the Seminary at 9 A.M. and at Mount Hermon School at noon. At these brief services, lasting about twenty minutes, he came into close heart relations with his students in spiritual things. He usually dealt with fundamental doctrines—intensely practical and personal talks, and quite informal. It was his supreme object to help his students into the deeper things of God, and he was always ready to meet those who were anxious about their spiritual condition.

The last mornings he spent with the students were occupied with the theme "Eternal Life."

Returning from chapel at Mount Hermon School, dinner was served at one o'clock. By this time the morning mail had been delivered.

His correspondence was quite large, and he made it a point to open every letter himself. Letters connected with the different schools were separated and given to subordinates, and general letters were usually handed to his secretary. In special cases he would indicate by brief notes what reply should be made. Letters received prompt attention—even those from religious and other cranks were usually courteously acknowledged.

The remaining hours of the day were filled in with an enormous amount of work and play. He gave personal attention to the innumerable details of the large institutions at Northfield, Mount Hermon, and Chicago; for it must be remembered that in addition to local interests he kept his hand on the Chicago Bible Institute, with its organizations for aggressive Christian work in prisons, in the army camps, as well as in the ordinary avenues in which his Colportage Association worked.

He gave careful attention to the planning of the summer conventions. It has often been remarked that one charm of these great gatherings is their freshness and spontaneity. This is true of the result, but the result is achieved by months of painstaking preparations and arrangement of details.

"In nothing, perhaps, is Mr. Moody's genius for command more manifest than in his capacity for detail," wrote a friend. "Nothing is too minute for his best thought, for he knows how much results depend on little things. Along with this genius for details goes remarkable quickness of insight and decision."

Mr. Moody used to perform the work of about ten men. How

he ever did it was a mystery until one realized (1) his absolute dependence upon God for guidance as to details, and his consequent freedom from anxiety as to the outcome; (2) his genius to command; (3) his faculty of doing promptly what had to be attended to personally, and of passing over to his subordinates and associates such details as they were competent to carry out.

How often he would say in some difficult case: "Oh, I wish I could see Christ face to face for five minutes and ask Him what He would do!"

All these matters were dealt with during his summer "rest"; but his real relaxation has not yet been mentioned. He thought that every man should have some hobby to divert his mind. Mr. Moody's hobby was his garden and his chickens. He must have LIFE; he loved to see things grow. "Send me a good farm letter," he would frequently write home.

A letter exists that would lead one to think that he was starting a farm instead of a boys' school at Mount Hermon twenty years ago:

"I bought twenty-five old sheep and twenty-five lambs for the boys' school," he wrote, "and turned the cows over there from my barn and Smith's, so we have eight cows over there now, and will have seventy-five hens there soon. One of the turkeys is setting. I am going to have some geese over there to make things lively. We have, or will have tomorrow night, seven boys. Am expecting more next week."

His garden was hardly conducted on a profitable basis. Here he experimented with asparagus and other vegetables, for the benefit of the schools. He tried to be first in the neighborhood with the different crops. He was greatly pleased to have peas from his garden in September. He kept a dozen or more families supplied daily with fresh vegetables during the summer months.

Feeding his chickens furnished him with an excuse for exercise, as he had to walk about half a mile and back twice daily to feed them. Each spring he hatched chickens by the hundred—sometimes by the thousand—in incubators.

The following is an estimate of D. L. Moody as a citizen and neighbor, taken by permission from the county paper:

"The old proverb 'A prophet is not without honor save in his own country' cannot be said of D. L. Moody, for surely no person could be more sincerely loved and honored by his townsmen than was he. Expressions of sorrow are heard from all classes of people in the town, and could each tribute be represented by a blossom on his grave, it would be piled high with flowers. His townsmen have been proud of him as a citizen, as a man, and as a religious worker. Although not all of them have endorsed his religious belief, they have thoroughly believed in his honesty of purpose and sincerity, and are convinced that the results of his life-work will be lasting and of inestimable value to future generations. They know that Northfield has been changed from a quiet farming town, with corresponding disadvantages, to a thrifty village with a steady growth; and that there and at Mount Hermon have been established two of the best fitting-schools in the State, all through the energy and perseverance of this man. Every effort has been made by him to bring these schools within the reach of the boys and girls of the town, and many an ambitious father and mother have been able to educate their children through his efforts.

"Last summer he was told of a woman who was supporting her family by taking in washing, that her daughter was ready for the Seminary, but she almost despaired of her ability to send her there. Mr. Moody instantly replied:

"'Tell the principal to put her on the free list, and find her a room in the building. The town girls must be helped first.'

"This is only one instance of many similar ones. Under certain provisions, a few years ago, he offered every Northfield and Gill boy free tuition for the first year at Mount Hermon, and several boys have availed themselves of this opportunity each year since.

"He was instantly alert and ready with money and work to forward any plans to benefit the town. At the time the Village Improvement Society was formed, he subscribed one hundred dollars to improve the street, knowing that it would be expended in a part of the village remote from the school and his residence. Every year since its formation he has given generously of money, and has also offered valuable advice and wise suggestions.

"He was very proud of the magnificent trees of the village, and nothing irritated him more than any attempt to injure them. He caused to be set a large number of trees and shrubs about his place and on the Seminary grounds. It must have been very gratifying for him to see Seminary Hill in all its June splendor, knowing that in his childhood it was considered one of the most barren places in town. One old man once said that that side-hill wouldn't bear white beans, when he was a boy.

"He was a kind neighbor, sickness and trouble finding him ready with sympathy and material help. The delicacies of his garden and fruit orchard found their way into many a humble home.

He encouraged his wife and daughter to interest themselves in helping the sick and needy in all parts of the town.

"During the autumn, when fruit was abundant, the Seminary girls were given free access to his orchard and grapery, to eat and carry baskets full to their rooms. Each fall he gave all the surplus apples on his own and the Seminary campus, and solicited from neighboring farmers to the extent of hundreds of bushels, which were distributed among the poor in Boston and New York.

"He had a strong aversion to committees. A few months ago an organization was being effected in the town hall, and a motion was made to appoint certain committees. Mr. Moody rose and said: 'We don't want committees. When you want anything done, tell Mr. So-and-so to do it, and you will accomplish something. One is enough to constitute any committee. If there had been a committee appointed, Noah's ark would never have been built.'"

He used to spend hours "puttering around" his hen-houses and garden (as he used to express it), but all the time his mind was ready to deal with more important things, and some fellow-worker or subordinate was frequently at his side, discussing plans.

He spent his evening with his family, when no meetings demanded his presence. He kept in touch with the progress of the world by reading the daily papers. He was no ascetic. No work was so important as to make him neglect his family duties and privileges. He took keen interest in the doings of his sons at school and college, and shared their joys and excitements. In his younger manhood he was a very swift runner, and could hold his own with his Chicago Sabbath-school scholars.

Rev. F. B. Meyer once called him the most fearless of whips. "Where have I not been in that buggy? It is the most natural thing in the world for the driver to leave the road, climb over a ditch and hedge, and make straight for the top of a grassy slope because he wanted to show you a view, or descend a plowed field into a glen to explain his method of raising water from the spring to Mount Hermon School."

VISIT TO THE HOLY LAND

A man of such energetic spirit as Mr. Moody found very little opportunity for holidays. He sacredly tried to observe one day in the seven as a Sabbath, but otherwise he was almost constantly occupied, except when journeying—and even then people recognized him and sought his spiritual advice, and were not denied. Of late years, with the multiplication of his schools, conferences, and other organizations for promoting the cause of Christ, there was less and less opportunity for withdrawing for any length of time from active participation in their control.

In the spring of 1892, Mr. Moody was able to take a well-deserved holiday and at the same time gratify an old longing to visit the Holy Land. The summer preceding, Dr. John Smith, of Edinburgh, had come to America with a huge roll of invitations from ministers of Scotland, asking Mr. Moody to visit that country again. He left America in October, 1891, and, with Mr. Sankey, held short meetings in ninety-nine towns in Scotland during the winter. This was his last visit to Scotland.

In April, 1892, he was invited by Mr. and Mrs. Peter McKinnon, of Scotland, to go to Palestine. From Paris he wrote to his mother, "I have a great desire to see the city of gold." Accompanied by his wife and his younger son Paul, he joined the McKinnons in Rome.

Mr. Moody's enjoyment of Rome was intense. Every place which could be verified as being in any way connected with the Apostle Paul (his greatest Bible hero, next to our Lord) was carefully sought out. The Appian Way was visited, and when the original pavement was reached he insisted on alighting from the carriage and going on foot over the stones which St. Paul had trodden. The ruins of Nero's palace on the Palatine Hill had far more attraction for him than St. Peter's or any of the spectacles of modern Rome.

The party sailed in one of Mr. McKinnon's liners, and landed at Port Said. It was necessary to sail down the Suez Canal as far as Ismailia, and thence take a train to Alexandria. Writing from Port Said, Mr. Moody said:

"We are now near where the children of Israel passed when they went out of Egypt. The country is sandy and barren, but the canal is a wonder, and it seems strange to be in this land of the Pharaohs, of Moses and Aaron and Joseph."

The day after his arrival in Jerusalem, which happened to be Easter Sunday, he spoke from the summit of the new (or Gordon) Calvary on the text: "As the mountains are round about Jerusalem, so the Lord is round about his people from henceforth even for ever"—pointing to Hermon, Olivet, and the mountains of Moab, all in sight from where he stood. It was afterward found that he had unwittingly spoken in the midst of a Mohammedan cemetery, and a little feeling was unfortunately aroused. It was not thought wise to repeat the mistake, so the following Sunday he preached in a recess in the side of the hill. Several hundreds of all races and creeds attended these meetings.

The week-days were spent in visiting places of interest in Jerusalem and the immediate vicinity. One day was devoted to Hebron. In Jerusalem all the sacred spots, like the Holy Sepulcher, were too uncertain or else too transformed by tawdriness to please. His favorite places were the Mount of Olives, to which he repeatedly returned, and the little village of Bethany, over the brow of the hill. Here, at any rate, he knew he was in the midst of scenes where his Master had often walked.

At Bethany he told his interpreter to ask if there were any Marys and Marthas among the children. The Arabic equivalents of these names were instantly claimed by a number, and nobody enjoyed the joke more than himself when it was explained that most of the "Miriams" and "Martas" were boys.

Being unable to ride horseback, Mr. Moody's travels in Palestine were limited; but he was an energetic sightseer.

The native children in Jerusalem amused him greatly. On his exit from the hotel he would invariably be surrounded by a crowd of ragged little Arabs, and he entertained himself by giving them baksheesh. The older natives also interested him, and he conversed with them constantly, questioning them as to their manner of living. By the end of the week he was well informed concerning the manner of life of the people, the condition of agriculture, the system of government, and a dozen and one other things.

Leaving Palestine, Mr. Moody and those with him went to Egypt. Several days were spent in Cairo, visiting the Pyramids and other points of interest, and in the first week of May the party left for Italy. May was spent in Naples and Florence, the Italian lakes and Switzerland, and by the end of the month he was again in England, having been absent for two months, probably the longest vacation he had taken since he entered business as a boy of seventeen. It was not an unbroken rest, however, for he had preached at Rome, Jerusalem, Cairo, Naples, and Paris, sometimes twice a day, besides having conducted numerous Bible readings, in compliance with the importunities of English and American friends, who recognized him wherever he went. Moreover, he used to lead the most unlikely on the most unlikely occasions into direct personal talk regarding their spiritual condition.

"Mr. Moody," said a titled lady to him, "no one ever talked to me like this before."

"Then it is quite time somebody did so," he replied; and they remained good friends thereafter.

His visit to the Holy Land remained a living memory with him. He constantly referred to it in private conversation and public discourse, regretting, on the one hand, the present mean condition of Palestine, which he believed was in accord with prophecy, and on the other hand looking forward with joy to its restoration, when the feet of the Messiah shall stand once more on Mount Olivet.

FACING DEATH ON THE ATLANTIC

On his return to England he again "got in harness," and preached in and around London. In August he crossed to Ireland, and preached in a number of centers there. Returning to America with his elder son in November, he had his memorable experience on board the North German Lloyd liner, the *Spree*, an experience as thrilling as any in the record of ocean accidents in Atlantic travel.

He took passage from Southampton, England, early in November. "My last day in London," said he, "was a pleasant one; a day of promise it might have been called, for the sun shone out brightly after some of those dark, foggy days so common in London. A company of friends gathered at the station to see me off, and I suggested that they should sing my favorite song, 'Then Shall My Heart Keep Singing,' but they said that they did not feel like singing that just then. I was the only one in the group who seemed to feel like singing.

"When about three days on our voyage, I remember, I was lying on my couch, as I generally do at sea, congratulating myself on my good fortune, and feeling very thankful to God. I considered myself a very fortunate man, for in all my extensive travels by land and sea I had never been in any accident of a serious nature.

"Suddenly I was startled by a terrible crash and shock, as if the vessel had been driven on a rock. I did not at first feel much anxiety—perhaps I was too ill to think about it. My son jumped from his berth, and rushed on deck. He was back again in a few moments, saying that the shaft was broken and the vessel sinking. I did not at first believe it could be so bad, but concluded to dress and go on deck. The report was only too true. The captain told the affrighted passengers, who had rushed on deck, that there was no danger, and some of the second-cabin passengers returned to their berths, only to be driven out again by the in-rushing water, leaving everything behind them.

"The officers and crew did all they could to save the vessel. But it was soon found that the pumps were useless, for the water poured into the ship too rapidly to be controlled. There was nothing more in the power of man to do. We were utterly, absolutely helpless. We could only stand still on the poor, drifting, sinking ship and look into our watery grave.

"All this time, unknown to the passengers, the officers were making preparations for the last resort. The life-boats were all put in readiness, provisions prepared, life-preservers in hand, the officers armed with revolvers to enforce their orders, and the question was evidently being debated in their mind whether to launch the boats at once, or wait. The sea was so heavy that the boats could hardly live in it. Two of the passengers had loaded revolvers ready to blow out their brains if the vessel should go down, preferring death by bullet to death by drowning.

"At noon the captain told us that he had the water under control, and was in hopes of drifting in the way of some passing vessel. The ship's bow was now high in the air, while the stern seemed to settle more and more. The sea was very rough, and the ship rolled from side to side with fearful lurches. If she had pitched violently but once, the bulkheads must have burst, and the end come. The captain tried to keep up hope by telling us we should probably drift in the way of a ship by three o'clock that Saturday afternoon, but the night closed upon us without sign of a sail.

"That was an awful night, the darkest in all our lives! Seven hundred men, women, and children waiting for the doom that was settling upon us! No one dared to sleep. We were all together in the saloon of the first cabin—Jews, Protestants, Catholics, and skeptics—although I doubt if at that time there were any skeptics among us. The agony and suspense were too great for words. With blanched faces and trembling hearts the passengers looked at one another, as if trying to read what no one dared to speak. Rockets flamed into the sky, but there was no answer. We were drifting out of the track of the great steamers. Every hour seemed to increase our danger.

"Sunday morning dawned without help or hope. Up to that time no suggestion of religious services had been made. To have done that would almost certainly have produced a panic. In the awful suspense and dread that prevailed a word about religion would have suggested the most terrible things to the passengers. But as that second night came on I asked General O. O. Howard, who was with us, to secure the captain's permission for a service in the saloon. The captain said:

"'Most certainly; I am that kind, too.'

"We gave notice of the meeting, and to our surprise nearly every passenger attended, and I think everybody prayed, skeptics and all.

"With one arm clasping a pillar to steady myself on the reeling vessel, I tried to read the ninety-first Psalm, and we prayed that God would still the raging of the sea and bring us to our desired haven. It was a new psalm to me from that hour. The eleventh verse touched me very deeply. It was like a voice of divine assurance, and it seemed a very real thing as I read: 'He shall give his angels charge over thee, to keep thee in all thy ways.' Surely He did it. I read also from Psalm 107:20–31. One lady thought those words must have been written for the occasion, and afterward asked to see the Bible for herself. A German translated verse by verse as I read, for the benefit of his countrymen.

"I was passing through a new experience. I had thought myself superior to the fear of death. I had often preached on the subject, and urged Christians to realize this victory of faith. During the Civil War I had been under fire without fear. I was in Chicago during the great cholera epidemic, and went around with the doctors visiting the sick and dying. Where they could go to look after the *bodies* of men I said I could go to look after their *souls*. I remember a case of smallpox where the flesh had literally dropped way from the backbone, yet I went to the bedside of that poor sufferer again and again, with Bible and prayer, for Jesus' sake. In all this I had no fear of death.

"But on the sinking ship it was different. There was no cloud between my soul and my Savior. I knew my sins had been put away, and that if I died there it would be only to wake up in heaven. That was all settled long ago. But as my thoughts went out to my loved ones at home—my wife and children, my friends on both sides of the sea, the schools and all the interests so dear to me—and as I realized that perhaps the next hour would separate me forever from all these, so far as this world was concerned, I confess it almost broke me down. It was the darkest hour of my life!

"I could not endure it. I must have relief, and relief came in prayer. God heard my cry, and enabled me to say, from the depth of my soul: 'Thy will be done!' Sweet peace came to my heart. Let it be 'Northfield or Heaven,' it made no difference now. I went to bed and almost immediately fell asleep, and never slept more soundly in all my life. Out of the depths I cried unto the Lord, and He heard me and delivered me from all my fears. I can no more doubt that God gave answer to my prayer for relief than I can doubt my own existence.

"About three o'clock at night I was aroused from my sound sleep by the voice of my son. 'Come on deck, father,' he said. I followed him, and he pointed to a far-off light, rising and sinking on the sea. It was a messenger of deliverance to us. It proved to be the light of the steamer *Lake Huron,* whose lookout had seen our flaming signals of distress, and supposed it was a vessel in flames. Oh, the joy of that moment, when those seven hundred despairing passengers beheld the approaching ship! Who can ever forget it?

"But now the question was, Can this small steamer tow the helpless *Spree* a thousand miles to Queenstown? Every moment was watched with the intensest anxiety and prayer. It was a brave and perilous undertaking. The two vessels were at last connected by two great cables. If a storm arose these would snap like a thread, and we must be left to our fate. But I had no fear. God would finish the work He had begun. The waves were calmed; the cables held; the steamer moved in the wake of the *Huron.* There were storms all about us, but they came not nigh our broken ship. Seven days after the accident, by the good hand of our God upon us, we were able to hold a joyous thanksgiving service in the harbor of Queenstown. The rescuing ship that God sent to us in our distress had just sufficient power to tow our ship and just enough coal to take her into port! Less would have been insufficient. Her captain also is a man of prayer, and he besought God's help to enable them to accomplish their dangerous and difficult task. God answered the united prayer of the distressed voyagers, and brought them to their desired haven.

"The nervous strain of those eight days and nights of suspense was something fearful. It was more than any one could long endure without help. The minds of several passengers gave way under the strain. A young Austrian, who had left his betrothed in Vienna, leaped overboard in despair, and was drowned before our eyes in spite of all we could do. It was a most pathetic sight to see a young mother with two beautiful children in dumb anguish during the first forty-eight hours, never taking her eyes off her little ones; and if the ship had gone down, I have no doubt she would have gathered them to her bosom and gone down with them in her arms. There was a Russian Jew, who had taken passage without the knowledge of his relatives at home. It was pitiful to see his distress, as he confessed his sin, beat his breast, and denounced himself as the Jonah of the company. Kneeling upon the deck, with tears streaming down his cheeks, he cried to Jehovah not to visit the punishment of his sin upon all those unfortunate people."

Mr. Moody always spoke with profound respect and gratitude of the courage and gallantry of the officers and crew of the *Spree*.

General O. O. Howard, who had faced danger and death many times during the Civil War, and who knew what courage meant, testified to the nerve and courage exhibited by Mr. Moody during those awful hours on the Atlantic.

Spending Saturday night in Queenstown, Mr. Moody sailed for America on the *Etruria* next day, and reached New York safely the following Saturday.

What a reception he got when he reached home at ten o'clock that night! As the train passed through Mount Hermon Station, three hundred students and teachers from that school swarmed in and around the train, with torches, music, and cheers to welcome their friend. At the next station he was met on alighting by another company of friends. The buildings of Northfield Seminary, as well as many private dwellings, were ablaze with innumerable lights in the windows. It seemed as if everyone who loved him meant to let him know it, and to give him an ovation on his rescue from the very jaws of death.

WITHIN THE FAMILY CIRCLE

"Has Grandpa gone to Jesus' house?"

"Yes."

"Where Dwight and Irene are?"

"Yes."

"Well, I want to go there, too, and I'll just hug Grandpa when I see him, and we'll all play together."

The questioning of a four-year-old little girl when she was told she would never see her grandfather any more down here, reveals a side of Mr. Moody's nature that was little known to the general public.

A new era began in his life with the marriage of his only daughter and elder son, both in 1894. Joys and sorrows, health and sickness, came hand in hand. In those last six years there were four births in his immediate family—four grandchildren; and four deaths—his mother, his wife's mother, and two of the grandchildren.

D. L. Moody was a loving, dutiful son. Hardly a week passed, from the time he left home in 1854, without his writing to his mother, or sending her newspaper clippings about his work. He settled in Northfield in 1875 so as to be near her. Every day, when he was in town, it was his delight to call upon her, generally bringing her some little delicacy, or some vegetables from his garden. He added to the old homestead a sunny room where she sat in her later years, a mother in Israel, glad because of the good works God was performing through her son.

Next to his wife, he consulted his mother more than any other living being.

One of the greatest joys of his life was to see his mother publicly confess Christ, and join the evangelical church. He was to preach that Sunday morning in 1876 in the old Congregational Church at Northfield. His subject was the fifty-first Psalm. "Religion is a personal matter," he said. "David prayed that God would wash *him,* not his clothes; and have mercy upon *him*." He sketched graphically the journey of life; some in the audience were nearing the top of the hill; others were already going down the other side. When he had finished preaching, he made a tender appeal to all to accept his Savior as their Savior. His mother sat near the front, and was one of the first to rise for prayer. When he saw her, tears of joy filled his eyes, his voice choked, and turning to B. F. Jacobs, of Chicago, who was sitting beside him on the platform, he asked him to pray, saying:

"That's my mother!"

Her birthday fell on the same day as his own (February 5), and his letters on successive anniversaries were peculiarly tender.

"You and I have now passed one more milestone on our way from earth to heaven. We have both reason to thank God for all His goodness to us."

"By the time you get this letter," he wrote from Perth, Scotland, in 1892, "you will be passing another milestone that will bring you nearer the Eternal City. I want to send you my best wishes for the new year you will be starting out on. I hope it will be full of joy and sunshine and peace."

The last birthday letter he wrote her was from San Antonio, Texas, on February 2, 1895:

"By the time this letter gets to you, you will have entered into your ninety-first year. Only think, when you entered this world, Napoleon was fighting his great battles! It seems a long time, as you look at the history that has been made. Nations have risen and fallen. Some have come and gone. Yet you live, and have all your faculties and good health. You have much to praise God for, and all your children rejoice to think you have been spared to us so long."

"Fifty years I have been coming back to Northfield," said he, "and have always been glad to get back. When I get within fifty miles of home I grow restless, and walk up and down the car. It seems as if the train will never get to Northfield. When I came back after dark, I always looked to see the light in Mother's window."

On January 26, 1896, she fell asleep. "Friends," said Mr. Moody at her funeral, "it is not a time of mourning. We are proud that we had such a mother. We have a wonderful legacy left us . . . God bless you, Mother; we love you still. Death has only increased our love. Good-bye for a little while."

The joy of being a grandparent had become his a few months previously, when Irene Moody was born on August 20, 1895, and Emma Fitt on December 16 following.

"Do you know I have a granddaughter? I am taking a present over to her," he shouted from his buggy to a summer visitor that August morning, pointing to a basket of doughnuts. He was happy as a schoolboy on a holiday, and told the news to everybody he met. Later that day he made a second trip to Mount Hermon to see the baby, this time bringing over an immense cauliflower, the best his garden had produced.

A letter he wrote to Emma a year later reveals his heart:
"December 10, 1896.

"In six days you will be one year old, and your grandmother will make you a cake, and have it all frosted over with white sugar, and they will put one tiny little candle in it . . . It will be one year ago next Tuesday night I was sitting up for your grandmother, and when it got past midnight I thought I would go up and see why she did not come home, and I heard you cry for the first time. The tears of joy came to my eyes, and I have thought a great deal of you ever since. Soon after, my mother died, and you seemed to come to take her place, and you have been a dear, good little girl . . .

"I am going to steal up to your home next summer and take you out riding before your parents get up. Only think, of some fine June morning, we can go up Lovers' Retreat. The birds will sing you a beautiful song. What times we will have together! I get real homesick thinking about it . . .

"And now, my dear Emma, I am praying for you that the Lord

will watch over you day and night, and keep you from all harm. You will never know how much your grandfather loves you. I shall be glad to get you into my arms again."

His playful nature is exhibited in the first letter he wrote to little Emma, on January 7, 1896, when she was three weeks old:

"This is my first letter to my dear little grandchild. I wanted to get a letter to you before you got your first tooth. Hurry up and get them all before the hot weather comes on, for I will get you some candy, and you will want teeth to eat it. I want you to hurry up and grow, so I can come early mornings and take you out riding when your father and mother are fast asleep. We will slip off over the river to see Irene, and have some good times. Your mother is so proud of you, and your nurse is so fussy. Only think, Emma, what your mother said the other day—I, your grandfather, could not kiss you on your lips! Did you ever hear anything like that! But I got a kiss on your lips all the same, and I will get a good many more when I get home."

A few months later he wrote:

"I have just heard that the milk you get at my house does not agree with you. Now I think the fault is not with the milk, but with the cooks. You know, or you should be old enough to know, that when you cook milk and put it in a bottle and put a black rubber nipple on it—you will be disgusted when you get a little older and know how your parents treated you! You must not blame my old cow, for she is as good as she can be. I do not want to turn you against your parents, but if they do not treat you right, slip down to my house and get some doughnuts and ice-cream."

And so his loving heart went out to his grandchildren, and they in return loved none better than him. In the summer months he would usually be seen with one or more of them seated beside him as he drove around town.

"He has learned to perfection the art of being a grandfather," wrote a friend. "I saw him one morning driving with his little four-year-old granddaughter into the yard of his house. The child had gone to sleep in the buggy, leaning against him. Rather than disturb her, he had the horse gently unharnessed and taken away, while they sat on. Presently he, too, was overcome with sleep."

But God had ordained something other than unbroken joy. His only grandson and namesake, who was born on November 7, 1897, was taken home on November 30, 1898, while he was absent in Colorado. Irene, his first grandchild, followed her baby brother on

August 22, 1899 (aged four years and two days), after a protracted and unusually persistent attack of pneumonia, which soon developed into consumption.

"Colorado Springs, Colo.

". . . I know Dwight is having a good time, and we should rejoice with him. What would the mansions be without children? And he has gone to help get things ready for his parents. You know the Master said: 'The last shall be first.' He was the last to come into our circle, and he is the first to go up there! So safe, so free from all the sorrow that we are passing through! I do thank God for such a life. It was nearly all smiles and sunshine. What a glorified body he will have, and with what joy he will await your coming! God does not give us such strong love for each other for a few days or years, but it is going to last forever, and you will have the dear little man with you for ages and ages, and love will keep increasing. The Master has need of him, or He would never have called him; and you should feel highly honored that you had anything in your home that He wanted.

"I cannot think of him as belonging to earth. The more I think of him the more I think he was only sent to us to draw us all closer to each other and up to the world of light and joy. I could not wish him back, if he could have all earth could give him. And then the thought that the Savior will take such good care of him! No going astray; no sickness; no death. Dear, dear, little fellow! I love to think of him, so sweet, so safe, and so lovely! His life was not only blameless, but faultless; and if his life here was so sweet, what will it be up there? I believe the only thing he took away from earth was that sweet smile, and I have no doubt that when he saw the Savior he smiled as he did when he saw you. My heart goes up to God often for you, and the word that keeps coming to my mind is this: 'It is well with the child.' Only think of his translation! Thank God, Dwight is safe at home, and we will all of us see him soon.

"Your loving father,

"D. L. Moody."

Just before the close of Irene's funeral service, Mr. Moody rose and spoke:

"I would like to say a few words, if I can trust myself. I have been thinking this morning about the aged prophet waiting in the Valley of the Jordan, so many years ago, for the chariot of God to take him home. The chariot of God came down to the Connecticut Valley yesterday morning about half-past six, and took our little Irene home. The one was taken at the end of years of active service;

the other at the early dawn of youth. But the service of the prophet was no more complete than that of the little handmaid of the Lord, for God called both, and He never interrupts the service of His own.

"Irene has finished her course. Her work was well wrought on earth. She has accomplished more than many in their threescore years and ten. We would not have her back, although her voice was the sweetest voice I ever heard on earth. She never met me once since she was three months old, until the last few days of pain, without a smile. But Christ had some service for her above. My life has been made much better by her ministry here on earth. She has made us all better.

"The last few days have been blessed days to me. I have learned many new and precious lessons. She was very fond of riding with me, and on Monday morning she asked me to take her driving, and at 6:30 we were out together. She never looked more beautiful. She was just ripening for heaven. She was too fair for this earth.

"I thank God this morning for the hope of immortality. I know I shall see her in the morning, more beautiful in her resurrection glory than she was here."

God filled up his cup once more when a fourth grandchild was born on November 13, 1899, four days before he broke down at Kansas City. "Thankful for the good news," he telegraphed his son; "may she become famous in the kingdom of heaven is the prayer of her grandfather"; and then he wrote:

"I am full of praise and thanksgiving today . . . Dear little child, I already feel my heart going out to her! Kiss the mother and the dear baby for me . . . Thank God for another grandchild!"

The same day he wrote his other surviving grandchild, Emma Fitt, one of those simple, loving letters that were so characteristic of him:

"My dear Emma: I am glad that you have a little cousin. Will you kiss her for me, and will you show her your grandfather's picture (referring to a newspaper clipping he enclosed)? I do not think she will know me, but you can tell her all about me, so she will know me when she gets older, and we will play together with her. I am going to send her a little kiss, just one little one.

"Your grandfather,

"D. L. Moody.

"I will put the kiss in a little box, and you can take it to her."

Little Mary, the new-born babe, was carried to her grandfather's home ten days later, but she will have to learn of his loving, playful, tender heart from the precious letters for whose possession the family are now so thankful.

LAST EVANGELISTIC MISSION

Mr. Moody left home for the last time on November 8, 1899. His family had no suspicion that he was not enjoying his usual health and strength.

He had engaged to conduct a week's meetings in Kansas City, Missouri. On his way thither he stopped over in Philadelphia, to see about a building they were erecting for him there for a series of meetings similar to his great meetings in 1875–76. He also stopped over at Chicago for a few hours, to attend to some business at the Bible Institute; and two addresses he delivered to the students were marked by unusual power.

He reached Kansas City a sick man. When some friends called on him at the hotel, he excused himself from rising, saying that he was tired. The first afternoon three of his old Mount Hermon students, C. M. Vining, Rev. D. Baines-Griffiths, and C. S. Bishop, took him on a drive around the city. He seemed in good spirits, but they saw that he was not quite himself.

The great auditorium in which the meetings were held is estimated to hold easily fifteen thousand people. They say that fully that number attended his first Sunday meeting, while thousands were unable to gain admittance. "It was a thrilling spectacle. The great arena, like a valley filled with upturned faces, and the balconies thronged like receding hillsides covered with a countless multitude—and a solemn silence hovering over them all! Alone in that great assemblage stood Mr. Moody, at the front end of the extended platform. His voice sounded as though he was talking confidentially to a man in the eight or tenth row, and without effort it carried to every part of the building." He said later that the building did not tax his efforts in preaching.

Before commencing with his sermon that first afternoon a characteristic incident happened. He raised in his hand a printed slip of hymns that had been distributed by the ushers, and said:

"Let everyone who has one of these slips hold it up."

Thousands of slips were raised aloft.

"Now sit on them," said he; and people laughed as they put the papers where their rustling should not disturb the meeting.

He preached both afternoon and evening on "Sowing and Reaping," from the text:

"Be not deceived; God is not mocked: for whatsoever a man soweth, that shall he also reap. For he that soweth to his flesh shall of the flesh reap corruption; but he that soweth to the Spirit, shall of the Spirit reap life everlasting" (Gal. 6:7, 8).

In conversation with Mr. Vining these few days, he talked of the institutions he had founded, and he said the work in Kansas City was, he believed, one of the greatest God had given him to do. He spoke of the bereavements that had occurred in his family during the past year, and picking up a copy of his book, "Thoughts from My Library," he read a selection that has a peculiar interest now. It comments on the text of Psalms 30:5: "Weeping may endure for a night, but joy cometh in the morning." The extract ends with the words:

"I have heard it in the Land of Light from which I come. There is a time approaching, steadily if not quickly, when the Lord will wipe away tears from all faces. This weary world shall obtain joy and gladness at last, and sorrow and sighing shall flee away. 'Wherefore comfort one another with these words.'"

Thursday, November 16th, was the day on which he preached for the last time.

On the afternoon of that day his subject was "Grace in a Three-fold Aspect":

"For the grace of God that bringeth salvation hath appeared to all men, teaching us that, denying ungodliness and worldly lusts, we should live soberly, righteously, and godly in this present world; looking for that blessed hope, and the glorious appearing of the great God and our Savior Jesus Christ, who gave himself for us, that he might redeem us from all iniquity, and purify unto himself a peculiar people, zealous of good works" (Titus 2:11–14).

That last night Convention Hall was well filled. Mr. Moody showed no signs of exhaustion.

His last sermon on earth was on "Excuses." He told the parable as found in Luke 14:16–24, beginning:

"Then said he unto him, A certain man made a great supper, and bade many: and sent his servant at supper time to say to them that were bidden, Come; for all things are now ready. And they all with one consent began to make excuse."

Had he known that this was to be his last sermon would he have made a more urgent and characteristic appeal in closing:

"Suppose we should write out tonight this excuse, how would it sound? 'To the King of Heaven: While sitting in Convention Hall, Kansas City, Mo., November 16, 1899, I received a very pressing invi-

tation from one of your servants to be present at the marriage supper of your only-begotten Son. I PRAY THEE HAVE ME EXCUSED.'

"Would you sign that, young man? Would you, mother? Would you come up to the reporter's table, take a pen and put your name down to such an excuse? You would say, 'Let my right hand forget its cunning, and my tongue cleave to the roof of my mouth, before I sign that.' I doubt if there is one here who would sign it. Will you, then, pay no attention to God's invitation? I beg of you, do not make light of it. It is a loving God inviting you to a feast, and God is not to be mocked. Go play with the forked lightening, go trifle with pestilence and disease, but trifle not with God.

"Just let me write out another answer. '*To the King of Heaven: While sitting in Convention Hall, Kansas City, Mo., November 16, 1899, I received a pressing invitation from one of your messengers to be present at the marriage supper of your only-begotten Son. I hasten to reply.* BY THE GRACE OF GOD I WILL BE PRESENT.'

"Who will sign that? Is there one here who will put his name to it? Is there no one who will say, 'By the grace of God I will accept the invitation now?' May God bring you to a decision now. If you would ever see the kingdom of God, you must decide this question one way or the other. What will you do with the invitation? I bring it to you in the name of my Master; will you accept or reject it? Be wise tonight, and accept the invitation. Make up your mind that you will not go away till the question of eternity is settled."

Day by day had passed in much the same way that week. Mr. Moody found it impossible to walk, although it did not trouble him to stand for an hour twice daily before those large audiences and preach. On Thursday he had quite a chill in the bathroom, and had to summon a doctor on Friday. Under the doctor's advice he decided to relinquish all further attempt to proceed with the mission. With this decision a burden rolled off his mind, and he began to gain. Steps were taken for his immediate return home.

A beautiful incident occurred on the homeward journey—illustrative of what used to happen very frequently of late years, north and south, east and west, wherever Mr. Moody went on his evangelistic missions.

When the train pulled into Detroit it was over an hour late, and unless at least half of this time should be made up, the eastern connection at Niagara for the through Boston train could not be made.

While the train was standing in the depot, waiting for the signal to start, some one told the engineer that Mr. Moody was on board.

"Where has he been?" came the question.

"He has been holding meetings in Kansas City, where he was taken ill, and now we are taking him home. We are about an hour late, and if we don't make up the time we won't make the proper connections for Boston."

"Look here," said the engineer, his voice choking as he spoke, "fifteen years ago I was converted by Moody, and I have lived a better and happier life ever since. I didn't know he was on board tonight, but if you want me to make up the time for you, I'll do it. Just tell him that one of his friends is at the throttle, and then hold your breath."

As soon as the train got clear of the city the engineer pulled open the throttle, and it is said that he made the fastest time ever made over his division. Including stops, he ran one hundred and thirty miles in exactly one hundred and thirty minutes. Connections were made all right, and when the party awakened the next morning they were on the Boston train.

The first intimation of sickness that his family had was a telegram: "Doctor thinks I need rest. Am on my way home." This was followed at short intervals by other telegrams: "Improving rapidly. Have not felt so well for a week"; and "Have had a splendid day; no fever; heart growing better all the time; no pain. Am taking good care of myself, not only for the loved ones, but for the work I think God still has for me to do on earth."

On reaching home, he telegraphed back to Kansas City as follows:

"Have reached home safely. Have traveled backward and forward for forty years, and never stood trip better. Regret exceedingly being forced to leave. Had I been with you tonight, I would have preached on 'thou art not far from the Kingdom.' My prayer is that many may be led into the Kingdom under Mr. Torrey's preaching. I want to thank the good people of Kansas City for their kindness and prayers."

He did not seem to think that he was drawing near his eternal home. He went upstairs that evening to get ready for supper, but the effort expended in climbing the stairs affected his heart so that he was completely exhausted; and he never came downstairs again.

From Sunday, November 19, until Friday, December 22, Mr. Moody was confined to the house. He never complained. Neither he nor his family anticipated the actual outcome. Once he asked if there was plenty of wood and coal in the cellar to carry the household through the winter. Another time he said to his wife that he had never expected a lingering sickness; that he thought his end would come suddenly, owing to heart-failure, while he was in full harness. As time wore slowly away—slowly to a man of such tremendous activity as he—he used to say that every night he longed for the morning. As he grew weaker, he said he now knew what that verse meant, "The grasshopper shall be a burden." But up to the day his spirit swept triumphantly within the gates of heaven, he talked and planned about the future, and never let others know it if he realized what actually did come to pass. His family understood that his heart was weak, but while they knew that the end was possible at any moment, they had no thought that it was probable.

The immediate physical cause of Mr. Moody's breakdown was undoubtedly the fact that he developed fatty degeneration of the heart. During the summer of 1899 circumstances were such that he did not exercise as much as usual, and he increased his weight by thirty pounds. This increase was fatal to a man of his build, whose heart was so weak. But his enormous vitality, his iron constitution, enabled him to stand a strain under which another would have gone down sooner. Despite the best expert medical assistance, he gradually became weaker and weaker, until the limit of nature was reached, and the Christian world was stunned by the sudden news that he was not, for God had taken him.

CORONATION DAY

To the world December 22 was the shortest day of all the year, but for D. L. Moody its dawn ushered in that day that knows no night. For forty-four years he had been a partaker of the divine life, and the transition from the seen to the unseen, from the sphere of the temporal to the eternal, was no interruption in his life. In other realms he continues to serve the same Master whose cause he loved with devotion and served with tireless energy. His one aim in his earthly life had been to do the will of God, and with characteristic readiness he responded to God's last summons.

Until within a few hours of the end, Mr. Moody shared with the family the conviction that he was improving. The day before he had seemed rather more nervous than usual, but spoke cheerfully about himself. In reply to an inquiry if he was comfortable, he said:

"Oh, yes! God is very good me—and so is my family."

No man loved his family and life-work more devotedly, and frequently he has been heard to say:

"Life is very sweet to me, and there is no position of power or wealth that could tempt me from the throne God has given me."

It was not that he was tired of life and wanted to be done with service that made him so ready to leave, for he knew such joy of Christian service as few have experienced.

The final summons came unexpectedly. During the first half of the night, A. P. Fitt, his son-in-law, had been on duty at his bedside. He slept the greater part of the time. At three in the morning his son, W. R. Moody, took the place as watcher in the sick-chamber. For several hours the patient was restless and unable to sleep, but about 6 A.M. he quieted down, and soon fell into a natural sleep.

He awoke in about an hour. His son suddenly heard him speaking in low and measured words, and he was saying:

"Earth recedes; heaven opens before me."

His son's first impulse was to try to arouse him from what he thought was a dream.

"No, this is no dream, Will," he said. "It is beautiful! It is like a trance! If this is death, it is sweet! There is no valley here! God is calling me, and I must go!"

Meanwhile the nurse was summoning the family and the physician, who had spent the night in the house. Mr. Moody continued to talk quietly on, and seemed to speak from another world his last messages to the loved ones he was leaving.

"I have always been an ambitious man," he said; "ambitious not to leave wealth or possessions, but to leave lots of work for you to do. You will carry on Mount Hermon; Paul will take up the Seminary, when he is older; Fitt will look after the Institute; and Ambert [his nephew] will help you all in the business details."

Then it seemed as though he saw beyond the veil, for he exclaimed:

"This is my triumph; this is my coronation day! I have been looking forward to it for years."

Then his face lit up, and he said, in a voice of joyful rapture, "Dwight! Irene! I see the children's faces!" referring to his two little grandchildren, whom God had taken home within the past year.

Then, as he thought he was losing consciousness, he said:

"Give my love to them all."

Turning to his wife, he added:

"Mamma, you have been a good wife to me!"

With this he became unconscious. Up to this time no drugs whatever had been administered.

It seemed to his family that he would never come back again, the sinking was so extreme. In half an hour, however, he revived under the effect of heart stimulants, and as he regained consciousness he feebly uttered these words: "No pain! No valley!"

Presently, as he rallied further, he added:

"If this is death, it's not bad at all! It's *sweet!*"

A little later, suddenly raising himself on his elbow, he exclaimed:

"What does all this mean? What are you all doing here?"

His wife explained that he had not been as well, and immediately it all seemed to be clear to him, and he said:

"This is a strange thing! I've been beyond the gates of death to the very portals of heaven, and here I am back again. It is very strange!"

Again he said: "This is my coronation day! It's glorious!" and talked about the work he was leaving behind, assigning to his two sons the Northfield schools, and to his daughter and her husband the Chicago Bible Institute. Asked what his wife's charge would be, he said:

"Oh, Mamma is like Eve, the mother of us all!"

To the urgent plea that he remain longer with his family he said:

"I'm not going to throw my life away. I'll stay as long as God wants me to; but if my time is come, I'm ready."

Something was soon said that showed how clear his mind was. He remarked, with deliberation:

"This is the twenty-second of December, isn't it? Five months ago today Irene died . . . and in this room!"

It was actually but four months (since August 22), but any one might make such a mistake.

Presently a new thought seemed to possess him, as he doubtless felt within him the rallied strength that often just precedes the end, and he exclaimed:

"I'm not at all sure but that God may perform a miracle and raise me up. I'm going to get up and sit in the chair. If God wants to heal me by a miracle that way, all right; and if not, I can meet death in my chair as well as here."

Turning to one who was applying warm cloths, he said:

"Here, take those away! If God is going to perform a miracle, we don't want them; and the first thing I suppose we should do will be to discharge you, Doctor."

He did not insist on this, however, but could not be dissuaded from getting up. He walked across the room to an easy-chair and sat down. A second sinking turn (which lasted only a few moments) left him exhausted, and he was willing to return to bed, where he remained quietly resting and sleeping for over an hour. Another sinking spell of brief duration intervened before the end.

To the very last he was thinking of those about him, and considering them. Turning to his wife, only a little while before he left, he said:

"This is terrible on you, Mamma; it's such a shock. I'm sorry to distress you in this way. Brace yourself. It is hard to be kept in such anxiety."

A few minutes before noon he was evidently sinking once again, and as the doctor approached to administer another hypodermic injection of nitroglycerine, Mr. Moody looked at him in a questioning and undecided way, and said, perfectly naturally:

"Doctor, I don't know about this. Do you think it wise?"

The doctor said he thought it would be all right.

"Well," Mr. Moody said, "it's prolonging the agony for the family!"

The doctor turned away, seeing that the patient's life could not be saved. In a few moments more another sinking turn came on, and from it Mr. Moody awoke in the presence of Him whom he loved and served so long and faithfully. It was not like death, for he fell asleep quietly and peacefully, and it was not hard to imagine his reception in that other world among the host of loved ones awaiting his coming. The whole occurrence was such, in the mercy of God, that the substance as well as the sting of death was removed.

A friend wired from a distant city: "Mr. Moody's love for music is at last satisfied this Christmas morning."

LAID AT REST

D. L. Moody was buried as he died—a victor. There was, indeed, no martial music or stately parade following a plumed hearse. In fact, there was no hearse, no funeral music, no tolling bells, no crape, no veils to hide faces suffused in tears. Tears there were in the eyes of every one of the large congregation that gathered to pay tribute to the dead. But there was no hopeless weeping. Everything was done in as near accord as could be imagined with what Mr. Moody himself would wish.

December 26, 1899, the day of the funeral, was a perfect day

—"one of the Lord's own days," a visitor called it. The sun rose clear over the mountain at whose feet Northfield nestles. In the distance, on the foothills of the Green Mountains, patches of snow appeared. The morning was frosty, but in the afternoon, as the friends gathered for the service, the temperature had risen several degrees.

At ten o'clock a brief service was held at the house, conducted by Dr. C. I. Scofield, pastor of the local Congregational church, and R. A. Torrey, pastor of the Chicago Avenue (Moody's) Church, Chicago. Dr. Scofield read the ninetieth Psalm and the fourth chapter of I Thessalonians, and Mr. Torrey offered prayer.

No signs of mourning appeared about the house; no crape was seen on the door. The window-blinds were all open.

Shortly after eleven o'clock the coffin was carried out of the house. It was a simple cloth-covered coffin, with quiet trimmings and a plate bearing the name and the dates of Mr. Moody's birth and decease:

DWIGHT L. MOODY 1837–1899

The coffin was placed upon a bier and lovingly carried by thirty-two Mount Hermon students to the Congregational church, half a mile away, where the body was laid in state.

Christmas greens festooned the galleries of the church. About the coffin were appropriate floral tributes from friends and from the trustees, faculties, and students of Mr. Moody's several institutions. At the head was a pillow, in which a crown had been worked in white, with a purple ribbon on which the words were sewn: "God is calling me." An open Bible, with "Victory. I Corinthians 15:55–57" on the left side, and "II Timothy 4:7, 8" on the other, rested at the foot. Palms, ferns, laurel, violets, cut-flowers, and callas were placed about the pulpit.

The public service was held at 2:30 P.M. Old associates, neighbors, and relatives had come from far and near. Simple tributes of love and joyous notes of triumphant praise were given by several friends.

In closing, that hymn which Mr. Moody so dearly loved was sung.

After the public service, the coffin was carried by the Mount Hermon students to Round Top, the Olivet of Northfield. A verse of "Jesus, Lover of My Soul" was sung, a brief prayer was offered, a last look was taken by his family at the beloved face of husband and father, and the precious form was lowered into the vault, just at the crown of the little hill.

From this resting place one may see his birthplace, a stone's throw to the south; his own home for the last twenty-five years, about as far to the west; the Seminary campus, directly north; Camp Northfield, half a mile up the mountain-side on the east; and the buildings of Mount Hermon School, about four miles distant down the Connecticut Valley.

A year or two ago, as Mr. Moody was walking one evening toward the Auditorium with a friend, he sat down on the grass of Round Top to rest. Looking out over the beautiful summer landscape spread before them, gilded with the glory of the westering sun, he said:

"I should like to be here when Christ comes back!"

His longing was not gratified during his life, but his earthly tabernacle rests there, awaiting the voice of the archangel and the trump of God.

2

WHY GOD USED D. L. MOODY
by R. A. Torrey

How was it that D. L. Moody had that power of God so wonderfully manifested in his life? Pondering this question, it seemed to me that there were seven things in the life of D. L. Moody that accounted for God's using him so largely as He did.

I. A FULLY SURRENDERED MAN

The first thing that accounts for God's using D. L. Moody so mightily was that *he was a fully surrendered man*. Every ounce of that 280-pound body of his belonged to God; everything he was and everything he had, belonged wholly to God. Now, I am not saying that Mr. Moody was perfect; he was not. If I attempted to, I presume I could point out some defects in his character. It does not occur to me at this moment what they were; but I am confident that I could think of some, if I tried really hard. I have never yet met a perfect man, not one. I have known perfect men in the sense in which the Bible commands us to be perfect, *i.e.*, men who are wholly God's, out-and-out for God, fully surrendered to God, with no will but God's will; but I have never known a man in whom I could not see some defects, some places where he might have been improved. No: Mr. Moody was not a faultless man. If he had any flaws in his character, and he had, I presume I was in a position to know them better than almost any other man, because of my very close association with him in the later years of his life; and, furthermore, I suppose that in his latter days he opened his heart to me more fully than to any one else in the world. I think he told me some things that he told no one else. I presume I knew whatever defects there were in his character as well as anybody. But while I recognized such flaws, nevertheless, I know that he was a man who belonged wholly to God.

The first month I was in Chicago, we were having a talk about something upon which we very widely differed, and Mr. Moody turned to me very frankly and very kindly and said in defense of his own position: "Torrey, if I believed that God wanted me to jump out of that window, I would jump." I believe he would. If he thought God wanted him to do anything, he would do it. He belonged wholly, unreservedly, unqualifiedly, entirely, to God.

Henry Varley, a very intimate friend of Mr. Moody in the earlier days of his work, loved to tell how he once said to him: "It remains to be seen what God will do with a man who gives himself up wholly to Him." I am told that when Mr. Henry Varley said that Mr. Moody said to himself: "Well, I will be that man." And I, for my part, do not think "it *remains* to be seen" what God will do with a man who gives himself up wholly to Him. I think it has been seen already in D. L. Moody. If you and I are to be used in our sphere as D. L. Moody was used in his, we must put all that we have and all that we are in the hands of God, for Him to use as He will, to send us where He will, for God to do with us what He will, and we, on our part, to do everything God bids us do. There are thousands and tens of thousands of men and women in Christian work, brilliant men and women, rarely gifted men and women, men and women who are making great sacrifices, men and women who have put all conscious sin out of their lives, yet who, nevertheless, have stopped short of absolute surrender to God, and therefore have stopped short of fullness of power. But Mr. Moody did not stop short of absolute surrender to God; he was a wholly surrendered man, and if you and I are to be used, you and I must be wholly surrendered men and women.

II. A MAN OF PRAYER

The second secret of the great power exhibited in Mr. Moody's life was that *Mr. Moody was, in the deepest and most meaningful sense, a man of prayer*. People oftentimes say to me: "Well, I went many miles to see and hear D. L. Moody and he certainly was a wonderful preacher." Yes, D. L. Moody certainly was a wonderful preacher; taking it all in all, the most wonderful preacher I have ever heard, and it was a great privilege to hear him preach as he alone could preach; but out of a very intimate acquaintance with him I wish to testify that he was a far greater *pray-er* than he was a preacher. Time and time again, he was confronted by obstacles that seemed insurmountable, but he always knew the way to surmount and to overcome all difficulties. He knew the way to bring to pass anything that needed to be brought to pass. He knew and believed in the deepest depths of his soul that "nothing was too hard for the Lord" and that prayer could do anything that God could do.

Oftentimes Mr. Moody would write me when he was about to undertake some new work, saying: "I am beginning work in such and such a place on such and such a day; I wish you would get the students together for a day of fasting and prayer," and often I have taken those letters and read them to the students in the lecture room and said: "Mr. Moody wants us to have a day of fasting and prayer, first for God's blessing on our own souls and work, and then for God's blessing on him and his work." Often we were gathered in the lecture room far into the night—sometimes till one, two, three, four, or even five o'clock in the morning, crying to God, just because Mr. Moody urged us to wait upon God until we received His blessing. How many men and women I have known whose lives and characters have been transformed by those nights of prayer and who have wrought mighty things in many lands because of those nights of prayer!

One day Mr. Moody drove up to my house at Northfield and said: "Torrey, I want you to take a ride with me." I got into the carriage and we drove out towards Lover's Lane, talking about some great and unexpected difficulties that had arisen in regard to the work in Northfield and Chicago, and in connection with other work that was very dear to him. As we drove along, some black storm-clouds lay ahead of us, and then suddenly, as we were talking, it began to rain. He drove the horse into a shed near the entrance to Lover's Lane to shelter the horse, and then laid the reins upon the dashboard and said: "Torrey, pray"; and then, as best I could, I prayed, while he in his heart joined me in prayer. And when my voice was silent he began to pray. Oh, I wish you could have heard that prayer! I shall never forget it, so simple, so trustful, so definite, and so direct and so mighty. When the storm was over and we drove back to town, the obstacles had been surmounted, and the work of the schools, and other work that was threatened, went on as it had never gone on before, and it has gone on until this day. As we drove back, Mr. Moody said to me: "Torrey, we will let the other men do the talking and the criticizing, and we will stick to the work that God has given us to do, and let Him take care of the difficulties and answer the criticism."

On one occasion Mr. Moody said to me in Chicago: "I have just found, to my surprise, that we are twenty thousand dollars behind in our finances for the work here and in Northfield, and we must have that twenty thousand dollars, and I am going to get it by prayer." He did not tell a soul who had the ability to give a penny of the twenty thousand dollars deficit, but looked right to God and said: "I need twenty thousand dollars for my work; send me that money in such a way that I will know it comes straight from Thee." And God heard that prayer. The money came in such a way that it was clear that it came from God, in direct answer to prayer. Yes, D. L. Moody was a man who believed in the God who answers prayer, and not only believed in Him in a theoretical way but believed in Him in a practical way. He was a man who met every difficulty that stood in his way—by prayer. Everything he undertook was backed up by prayer, and in everything, his ultimate dependence was upon God.

III. A DEEP AND PRACTICAL STUDENT OF THE BIBLE

The third secret of Mr. Moody's power, or the third reason why God used D. L. Moody, was because *he was a deep and practical student of the Word of God*. Nowadays, it is often said of D. L. Moody that he was not a student. I wish to say that he was a student; most emphatically he was a student. He was not a student of psychology, he was not a student of anthropology—I am very sure he would not have known what that word meant—he was not a student of biology, he was not a student of philosophy, he was not even a student of theology, in the technical sense of the term, but he was a student, a profound and practical student of the one Book that is more worth studying than all other books in the world put together; he was a student of the Bible. Every day of his life, I have reason for believing, he arose very early in the morning to study the Word of God, way down to the close of his life. Mr. Moody used to rise about four o'clock in the morning to study the Bible. He would say to me: "If I am going to get in any study, I have got to get up before the other folks get up," and he would shut himself up in a remote room in his house, alone with his God and his Bible.

I shall never forget the first night I spent in his home. He had invited me to take the superintendency of the Bible Institute and I had already begun my work, was on my way to some city in the East to preside at the International Christian Workers' Convention. He wrote me, saying: "Just as soon as the Convention is over, come up to Northfield." He learned when I was likely to arrive and drove over to South Vernon to meet me. That night he had all the teachers from the Mount Hermon School and from the Northfield Seminary come together at the house to meet me, and to talk over the problems of the two Schools. We talked together far on into the night, and then, after the principals and teachers of the Schools had gone home, Mr. Moody and I talked together about the problems a while longer. It was very late when I got to bed that night, but very early the next morning, about five o'clock, I heard a gentle tap on my door. Then I heard Mr. Moody's voice whispering: "Torrey, are you up?" I happened to be; I do not always get up at that early hour, but I happened to be up that particular morning. He said: "I want you to go somewhere with me," and I went down with him. Then I found out that he had already been up an hour or two in his room studying the Word of God.

Oh, you may talk about power; but, if you neglect the one Book that God has given you as the one instrument through which He imparts and exercises His power, you will not have it. You may read many books and go to many conventions and you may have your all-night prayer meetings to pray for the power of the Holy Ghost, but unless you keep in constant and close association with the one Book, the Bible, you will not have power. And if you ever had power, you will not maintain it except by the daily, earnest, intense study of that Book. *Ninety-nine Christians in every hundred are merely playing at Bible study; and therefore ninety-nine Christians in every hundred are mere weaklings, when they might be giants, both in their Christian life and in their service.*

It was largely because of his thorough knowledge of the Bible, and his practical knowledge of the Bible, that Mr. Moody drew such immense crowds. On "Chicago Day," in October 1893, none of the theaters of Chicago dared to open because it was expected that everybody in Chicago would go on that day to the World's Fair, and, in point of fact, something like four hundred thousand people did pass through the gates of the Fair that day. Everybody in Chicago was expected to be at that end of the city on that day. But Mr. Moody said to me: "Torrey, engage the Central Music Hall and announce meetings from nine o'clock in the morning till six o'clock at night." "Why," I replied, "Mr. Moody, nobody will be at this end of Chicago on that day; not even the theaters dare to open; everybody is going down to Jackson Park to the Fair; we cannot get anybody out on this day." Mr. Moody replied: "You do as you are told," and I did as I was told, and engaged the Central Music Hall for continuous meetings from nine o'clock in the morning till six o'clock at night. But I did it with a heavy heart; I thought there would be poor audiences. I was on the program at noon that day. Being very busy in my

office about the details of the campaign, I did not reach the Central
Music Hall till almost noon. I thought I would have no trouble getting in. But when I got almost to the Hall I found to my amazement
that not only was it packed but the vestibule was packed and the
steps were packed, and there was no getting anywhere near the
door; and if I had not gone round and climbed in a back window,
they would have lost their speaker for that hour. But that would not
have been of much importance, for the crowds had not gathered to
hear me; it was the magic of Mr. Moody's name that had drawn
them. And why did they long to hear Mr. Moody? Because they
knew that while he was not versed in many of the philosophies and
fads and fancies of the day, that he did know the one Book that this
old world most longs to know—the Bible.

I shall never forget Moody's last visit to Chicago. The ministers
of Chicago had sent me to Cincinnati to invite him to come to
Chicago and hold a meeting. In response to the invitation, Mr.
Moody said to me: "If you will hire the Auditorium for week-day
mornings and afternoons and have meetings at ten in the morning
and three in the afternoon, I will go." I replied: "Mr. Moody, you
know what a busy city Chicago is, and how impossible it is for business men to get out at ten o'clock in the morning and three in the
afternoon on working days. Will you not hold evening meetings and
meetings on Sunday?" "No," he replied, "I am afraid if I did, I would
interfere with the regular work of the churches."

I went back to Chicago and engaged the Auditorium, which at
that time was the building having the largest seating capacity of any
building in the city, seating in those days about seven thousand people, and announced week-day meetings, with Mr. Moody as the
speaker, at ten o'clock in the mornings and three o'clock in the afternoons. At once protests began to pour in upon me. One of them
came from Marshall Field, at that time the business king of Chicago. "Mr. Torrey," Mr. Field wrote, "we business men of Chicago wish
to hear Mr. Moody and you know perfectly well how impossible it
is for us to get out at ten o'clock in the morning and three o'clock in
the afternoon; have evening meetings." I received many letters of a
similar purport and wrote to Mr. Moody urging him to give us
evening meetings. But Mr. Moody simply replied: "You do as you
are told," and I did as I was told; that is the way I kept my job.

On the first morning of the meetings I went down to the Auditorium about half an hour before the appointed time, but I went
with much fear and apprehension; I thought the Auditorium would

be nowhere nearly full. When I reached there, to my amazement I found a queue of people four abreast extending from the Congress Street entrance to Wabash Avenue, then a block north on Wabash Avenue, then a break to let traffic through, and then another block, and so on. I went in through the back door, and there were many clamoring for entrance there. When the doors were opened at the appointed time, we had a cordon of twenty policemen to keep back the crowd, but the crowd was so great that it swept the cordon of policemen off their feet and packed eight thousand people into the building before we could get the doors shut. And I think there were as many left on the outside as there were in the building. I do not think that any one else in the world could have drawn such a crowd at such a time.

Why? Because though Mr. Moody knew little about science, or philosophy, or literature, in general, he did know the one Book that this old world is perishing to know and longing to know, and this old world will flock to hear men who know the Bible and preach the Bible as they will flock to hear nothing else on earth.

During all the months of the World's Fair in Chicago, no one else could draw such crowds as Mr. Moody. Judging by the papers, one would have thought that the great religious event in Chicago at that time was the World's Congress of Religions. One very gifted man of letters in the East was invited to speak at this Congress. He saw in this invitation the opportunity of his life, and prepared his paper, the exact title of which I do not now recall, but it was something along the line of "New Light on the Old Doctrines." He prepared the paper with great care, and then sent it around to his most trusted and gifted friends for criticisms. These men sent it back to him with such emendations as they had to suggest. Then he re-wrote the paper, incorporating as many of the suggestions and criticisms as seemed wise. Then he sent it around for further criticisms. Then he wrote the paper a third time, and had it, as he trusted, perfect. He went on to Chicago to meet this coveted opportunity of speaking at the World's Congress of Religions. It was at eleven o'clock on a Saturday morning (if I remember correctly) that he was to speak. He stood outside the door of the platform waiting for the great moment to arrive, and as the clock struck eleven walked on to the platform to face a magnificent audience of eleven women and two men! But there was not a building anywhere in Chicago that would accommodate the very same day the crowds that would flock to hear Mr. Moody at any hour of the day or night.

Oh, men and women, if you wish to get an audience and wish to do that audience some good after you get them, *study*, study, STUDY the one Book, and *preach*, preach, PREACH the one Book, and *teach*, teach, TEACH the one Book, the Bible, the only Book that contains God's Word, and the only Book that has power to gather, and hold, and bless the crowds for any great length of time.

IV. A HUMBLE MAN

The fourth reason why God continuously, through so many years, used D. L. Moody was because *he was a humble man*. I think D. L. Moody was the humblest man I ever knew in all my life. He loved to quote the words of another: "Faith gets the most, love works the most, but *humility keeps the most*." He himself had the humility that keeps everything it gets. As I have already said, he was the most humble man I ever knew, *i.e.*, the most humble man when we bear in mind the great things he did, and the praise that was lavished upon him. Oh, how he loved to put himself in the background and put other men in the foreground. How often he would stand on a platform with some of us little fellows seated behind him and as he spoke he would say: "There are better men coming after me." As he said it, he would point back over his shoulder with his thumb to the "little fellows." I do not know how he could believe it, but he really *did* believe that the others that were coming after him were really better than he was. He made no pretense to a humility he did not possess. In his heart of hearts he constantly underestimated himself, and overestimated others. He really believed that God would use other men in a larger measure than he had been used.

Mr. Moody loved to keep himself in the background. At his conventions at Northfield, or anywhere else, he would push the other men to the front and, if he could, have them do all the preaching— McGregor, Campbell Morgan, Andrew Murray, and the rest of them. The only way we could get him to take any part in the program was to get up in the convention and move that we hear D. L. Moody at the next meeting. He continually put himself out of sight.

Oh, how many a man has been full of promise and God has used him, and then the man thought that he was the whole thing and God was compelled to set him aside! I believe more promising workers have gone on the rocks through self-sufficiency and self-esteem than through any other cause. I can look back for forty years, or more, and think of many men who are now wrecks or derelicts who at one time the world thought were going to be something great.

But they have disappeared entirely from the public view. Why? Because of overestimation of self. Oh, the men and women who have been put aside because they began to think that they were somebody, that they were "IT," and therefore God was compelled to set them aside.

I remember a man with whom I was closely associated in a great movement in this country. We were having a most successful convention in Buffalo, and he was greatly elated. As we walked down the street together to one of the meetings one day, he said to me: "Torrey, you and I are the most important men in Christian work in this country" (or words to that effect). I replied: "John, I am sorry to hear you say that; for as I read my Bible I find man after man who had accomplished great things whom God had to set aside because of his sense of his own importance." And God set that man aside also from that time. I think he is still living, but no one ever hears of him, and has not heard of him for years.

God used D. L. Moody, I think, beyond any man of his day, but it made no difference how much God used him; he never was puffed up. One day, speaking to me of a great New York preacher, now dead, Mr. Moody said: "He once did a very foolish thing, the most foolish thing that I ever knew a man, ordinarily so wise as he was, to do. He came up to me at the close of a little talk I had given and said: 'Young man, you have made a great address tonight.'" Then Mr. Moody continued: "How foolish of him to have said that; it almost turned my head." But, thank God, it did *not* turn his head, and even when pretty much all the ministers in England, Scotland, and Ireland, and many of the English bishops were ready to follow D. L. Moody wherever he led, even then it never turned his head one bit. He would get down on his face before God, knowing he was human, and ask God to empty him of all self-sufficiency. And God did.

Oh, men and women! Especially young men and young women, perhaps God is beginning to use you; very likely people are saying: "What a wonderful gift he has as a Bible teacher, what power he has as a preacher, for such a young man!" Listen: get down upon your face before God. I believe here lies one of the most dangerous snares of the devil. When the devil cannot discourage a man, he approaches him on another tack, which he knows is far worse in its results: he puffs him up by whispering in his ear: "You are the leading evangelist of the day. You are the man who will sweep everything before you. You are the coming man. You are the D. L. Moody of the day," and if you listen to him, he will ruin you. The entire

shore of the history of Christian workers is strewn with the wrecks
of gallant vessels that were full of promise a few years ago, but these
men became puffed up and were driven on the rocks by the wild
winds of their own raging self-esteem.

V. HIS ENTIRE FREEDOM FROM THE LOVE OF MONEY

The fifth secret of D. L. Moody's continual power and usefulness was *his entire freedom from the love of money*. Mr. Moody might
have been a wealthy man, but money had no charms for him. He
loved to gather money for God's work: he refused to accumulate
money for himself. He told me during the World's Fair that if he had
taken, for himself, the royalties on the hymn books which he had
published, they would have amounted, at that time, to a million dollars. But Mr. Moody refused to touch the money. He had a perfect
right to take it, for he was responsible for the publication of the
books, and it was his money that went into the publication of the
first of them. Mr. Sankey had some hymns that he had taken with
him to England and he wished to have them published. He went to
a publisher (I think Morgan & Scott) and they declined to publish
them, because, as they said, Philip Phillips had recently been over
and published a hymn book and it had not done well. However, Mr.
Moody had a little money and said that he would put it into the publication of these hymns in cheap form and he did. The hymns had
a most remarkable and unexpected sale; they were then published
in book form and large profits accrued. The financial results were
offered to Mr. Moody, but he refused to touch them. "But," it was
urged on him, "the money belongs to you," but he would not touch
it. Mr. Fleming H. Revell was at the time treasurer of the Chicago
Avenue Church, commonly known as the Moody Tabernacle. Only
the basement of this new church had been completed, funds having
been exhausted. Hearing of the hymn-book situation Mr. Revell
suggested, in a letter to friends in London, that the money be given
for completion of this building, and it was. Afterwards, so much
money came that was given, by the committee into whose hands
Mr. Moody put the matter, to various Christian enterprises.

In a certain city to which Mr. Moody went in the latter years of
his life, and where I went with him, it was publicly announced that
Mr. Moody would accept no money whatever for his services. Now,
in point of fact, Mr. Moody was dependent, in a measure, upon
what was given him at various services, but when this announcement was made, Mr. Moody said nothing, and left that city without

a penny's compensation for the hard work he did there and, I think, paid his own hotel bill. And yet a minister in that very city came out with an article in a paper, which I read, in which he told a fairy tale of the financial demands that Mr. Moody made upon them, which story I knew personally to be absolutely untrue. Millions of dollars passed into Mr. Moody's hands, *but they passed through;* they did not stick to *his* fingers.

This is the point at which many an evangelist makes shipwreck, and his great work comes to an untimely end. The love of money on the part of some evangelists has done more to discredit evangelistic work in our day, and to lay many an evangelist on the shelf, than almost any other cause. While I was away on my recent tour I was told by one of the most reliable ministers in one of our eastern cities of a campaign conducted by one who has been greatly used in the past. (Do not imagine, for a moment, that I am speaking of Billy Sunday, for I am not; this same minister spoke in the highest terms of Mr. Sunday and of a campaign which he conducted in a city where this minister was a pastor.) This evangelist of whom I now speak came to a city for a united evangelistic campaign and was supported by fifty-three churches. The minister who told me about the matter was himself chairman of the Finance Committee. The evangelist showed such a longing for money and so deliberately violated the agreement he had made before coming to the city and so insisted upon money being gathered for him in other ways than he had himself prescribed in the original contract, that this minister threatened to resign from the Finance Committee. He was however persuaded to remain to avoid a scandal. "As the total result of the three weeks' campaign there were only twenty-four clear decisions," said my friend, "and after it was over the ministers got together and by a vote with but one dissenting voice, they agreed to send a letter to this evangelist telling him frankly that they were done with him and with his methods of evangelism forever, and that they felt it their duty to warn other cities against him and his methods and the results of his work." Let us lay the lesson to our hearts and take warning in time.

VI. HIS CONSUMING PASSION
FOR THE SALVATION OF THE LOST

The sixth reason why God used D. L. Moody was because of *his consuming passion for the salvation of the lost.* Mr. Moody made the resolution, shortly after he, himself, was saved, that he would never let twenty-four hours pass over his head without speaking to at least one person about his soul. His was a very busy life, and sometimes he would forget his resolution until the last hour, and sometimes he would get out of bed, dress, go out and talk to some one about his soul in order that he might not let one day pass without having definitely told at least one of his fellow-mortals about his need and the Savior who could meet it.

One night Mr. Moody was going home from his place of business. It was very late, and it suddenly occurred to him that he had not spoken to one single person that day about accepting Christ. He said to himself: "Here's a day lost. I have not spoken to anyone today and I shall not see anybody at this late hour." But as he walked up the street he saw a man standing under a lamp-post. The man was a perfect stranger to him, though it turned out afterwards the man knew who Mr. Moody was. He stepped up to this stranger and said: "Are you a Christian?" The man replied: "That is none of your business, whether I am a Christian or not. If you were not a sort of a preacher, I would knock you into the gutter for your impertinence."

Mr. Moody said a few earnest words and passed on. The next day that man called upon one of Mr. Moody's prominent business friends and said to him: "That man Moody of yours over on the north side is doing more harm than he is good. He has got zeal without knowledge. He stepped up to me last night, a perfect stranger, and insulted me. He asked me if I were a Christian, and I told him it was none of his business and if he were not a sort of a preacher, I would knock him into the gutter for his impertinence. He is doing more harm than he is good. He has got zeal without knowledge." Mr. Moody's friend sent for him and said: "Moody, you are doing more harm than you are good; you've got zeal without knowledge; you insulted a friend of mine on the street last night. You went up to him, a perfect stranger, and asked him if he were a Christian, and he tells me if you had not been a sort of a preacher, he would have knocked you into the gutter for your impertinence. You are doing more harm than you are good; you have got zeal without knowledge."

Mr. Moody went out of that man's office somewhat crestfallen. He wondered if he were not doing more harm than he was good, if he really *had* zeal without knowledge. (Let me say, in passing, it is far better to have zeal without knowledge than it is to have knowledge without zeal. Some men and women are as full of knowledge as an egg is of meat; they are so deeply versed in Bible truth that they can sit in criticism on the preachers and give the preachers pointers, but they have so little zeal that they do not lead one soul to Christ in a whole year.) Weeks passed by. One night Mr. Moody was in bed when he heard a tremendous pounding at his front door. He jumped out of bed and rushed to the door. He thought the house was on fire. He thought the man would break down the door. He opened the door and there stood this man. He said: "Mr. Moody, I have not had a good night's sleep since that night you spoke to me under the lamp-post, and I have come around at this unearthly hour of the night for you to tell me what I have to do to be saved."

Mr. Moody took him in and told him what to do to be saved. Then he accepted Christ, and when the Civil War broke out, he went to the front and laid down his life fighting for his country.

Another night, Mr. Moody got home and had gone to bed before it occurred to him that he had not spoken to a soul that day about accepting Christ. "Well," he said to himself, "it is no good getting up now; there will be nobody on the street at this hour of the night." But he got up, dressed, and went to the front door. It was pouring rain. "Oh," he said, "there will be no one out in this pouring rain." Just then he heard the patter of a man's feet as he came down the street, holding an umbrella over his head. Then Mr. Moody darted out and rushed up to the man and said: "May I share the shelter of your umbrella?" "Certainly," the man replied. Then Mr. Moody said: "Have you any shelter in the time of storm?" and preached Jesus to him. Oh, men and women, if we were as full of zeal for the salvation of souls as that, how long would it be before the whole country would be shaken by the power of a mighty, God-sent revival?

One day in Chicago—the day after the elder Carter Harrison was shot, when his body was lying in state in the City Hall—Mr. Moody and I were riding up Randolph Street together in a street car right alongside of the City Hall. The car could scarcely get through because of the enormous crowds waiting to get in and view the body of Mayor Harrison. As the car tried to push its way through the crowd, Mr. Moody turned to me and said: "Torrey, what does this mean?" "Why," I said, "Carter Harrison's body lies there in the City Hall and these crowds are waiting to see it." Then he said, "This will never do, to let these crowds get away from us without preaching to them; we must talk to them. You go and hire Hooley's Opera House (which was just opposite the City Hall) for the whole day." I did so. The meetings began at nine o'clock in the morning, and we had one continuous service from that hour until six in the evening, to reach those crowds.

Mr. Moody was a man on fire for God. Not only was he always

"on the job" himself, but he was always getting others to work as well. He once invited me down to Northfield to spend a month there with the schools, speaking first to one school and then crossing the river to the other. I was obliged to use the ferry a great deal; it was before the present bridge was built at that point. One day he said to me: "Torrey, did you know that that ferryman that ferries you across every day was unconverted?" He did not tell me to speak to him, but I knew what he meant. When some days later it was told him that the ferryman was saved, he was exceedingly happy.

Once, when walking down a certain street in Chicago, Mr. Moody stepped up to a man, a perfect stranger to him, and said: "Sir, are you a Christian?" "You mind your own business," was the reply. Mr. Moody replied: "This is my business." The man said: "Well, then, you must be Moody." Out in Chicago they used to call him in those early days "Crazy Moody," because day and night he was speaking to everybody he got a chance to speak to about being saved. One time he was going to Milwaukee, and in the seat that he had chosen sat a traveling man. Mr. Moody sat down beside him and immediately began to talk with him. "Where are you going?" Mr. Moody asked. When told the name of the town he said: "We will soon be there; we'll have to get down to business at once. Are you saved?" The man said that he was not, and Mr. Moody took out his Bible and there on the train showed him the way of salvation. Then he said: "Now, you must take Christ." The man did; he was converted right there on the train.

Most of you have heard, I presume, the story President Wilson used to tell about D. L. Moody. Ex-President Wilson said that he once went into a barber shop and took a chair next to the one in which D. L. Moody was sitting, though he did not know that Mr. Moody was there. He had not been in the chair very long before, as ex-President Wilson phrased it, he "knew there was a personality in the other chair," and he began to listen to the conversation going on, and he heard Mr. Moody tell the barber about the Way of Life, and President Wilson said, "I have never forgotten that scene to this day." When Mr. Moody was gone, he asked the barber who he was, and he was told that it was D. L. Moody, and President Wilson said: "It made an impression upon me I have not yet forgotten."

On one occasion in Chicago Mr. Moody saw a little girl standing on the street with a pail in her hand. He went up to her and invited her to his Sunday School, telling her what a pleasant place it was. She promised to go the following Sunday, but she did not do so. Mr. Moody watched for her for weeks, and then one day he saw her on the street again, at some distance from him. He started towards her, but she saw him too and started to run away. Mr. Moody followed her. Down she went one street, Mr. Moody after her, up she went another street, Mr. Moody after her, through an alley, Mr. Moody still following, out on another street, Mr. Moody after her, then she dashed into a saloon and Mr. Moody dashed after her. She ran out the back door and up a flight of stairs, Mr. Moody still following; she dashed into a room, Mr. Moody following, and threw herself under the bed and Mr. Moody reached under the bed and pulled her out by the foot, and led her to Christ.

He found that her mother was a widow who had once seen better circumstances, but had gone down until now she was living over this saloon. She had several children. Mr. Moody led the mother and all the family to Christ. Several of the children were prominent members of the Moody Church until they moved away, and afterwards became prominent in churches elsewhere. This particular child, whom he pulled from underneath the bed, was, when I was the pastor of the Moody Church, the wife of one of the most prominent officers in the church. Only two or three years ago, as I came out of a ticket office in Memphis, Tennessee, a fine looking young man followed me. He said: "Are you not Dr. Torrey?" I said, "Yes." He said: "I am so and so." He was the son of this woman. He was then a traveling man, and an officer in the church where he lived. When Mr. Moody pulled that little child out from under the bed by the foot, he was pulling a whole family into the Kingdom of God, and eternity alone will reveal how many succeeding generations he was pulling into the Kingdom of God.

D. L. Moody's consuming passion for souls was not for the souls of those who would be helpful to him in building up his work here or elsewhere; his love for souls knew no class limitations. He was no respecter of persons; it might be an earl or a duke or it might be an [uneducated] boy on the street, it was all the same to him; there was a soul to save and he did what lay in his power to save that soul. A friend once told me that the first time he ever heard of Mr. Moody was when Mr. Reynolds of Peoria told him that he once found Mr. Moody sitting in one of the squatters' shanties that used to be in that part of the city towards the lake, which was then called "The Sands," with a colored boy on his knee, a tallow candle in one hand and a Bible in the other, and Mr. Moody was spelling out the words (for at that time he could not read very well) of certain verses of Scripture, in an attempt to lead that ignorant colored boy to Christ. Oh, young men and women and all Christian workers, if you and I were on fire for souls like that, how long would it be before we had a revival? Suppose that tonight the fire of God falls and fills our hearts, a burning fire that will send us out all over the country, and across the water to China, Japan, India, and Africa, to tell lost souls the way of salvation?

VII. DEFINITELY ENDUED WITH POWER FROM ON HIGH

The seventh thing that was the secret of why God used D. L. Moody was that *he had a very definite enduement with power from on high, a very clear and definite baptism with the Holy Ghost.* Mr. Moody knew he had "the baptism with the Holy Ghost"; he had no doubt about it. In his early days he was a great hustler, he had a tremendous desire to do something, but he had no real power. He worked very largely in the energy of the flesh. But there were two humble Free Methodist women who used to come over to his meetings in the Y.M.C.A. One was "Auntie Cook" and the other Mrs. Snow. (I think her name was not Snow at that time.) These two women would come to Mr. Moody at the close of his meetings and say: "We are praying for you." Finally, Mr. Moody became somewhat nettled and said to them one night: "Why are you praying for me? Why don't you pray for the unsaved?" They replied: "We are praying that you may get the power." Mr. Moody did not know what that meant, but he got to thinking about it, and then went to these women and said: "I wish you would tell me what you mean," and they told him about the definite baptism with the Holy Ghost. Then he asked that he might pray with them and not they merely pray for him.

Auntie Cook once told me of the intense fervor with which Mr. Moody prayed on that occasion. She told me in words that I scarcely dare repeat, though I have never forgotten them. And he not only prayed with them, but he also prayed alone. Not long after, one day on his way to England, he was walking up Wall Street in New York (Mr. Moody very seldom told this and I almost hesitate to tell it) and in the midst of all the bustle and hurry of that city his prayer was answered; the power of God fell upon him as he walked up the street and he had to hurry off to the house of a friend and ask that he might have a room by himself, and in that room he stayed alone for hours; and the Holy Ghost came upon him filling his soul with such joy that at last he had to ask God to withhold His hand, lest he die on the spot from very joy. He went out from that place with the power of the Holy Ghost upon him, and when he got to London (partly through the prayers of a bedridden saint in Mr. Lessey's church) the power of God wrought through him mightily in North London and hundreds were added to the churches, and that was what led to his being invited over to the wonderful campaign that followed in later years.

Time and again Mr. Moody would come to me and say: "Torrey, I want you to preach on baptism with the Holy Ghost." I do not know how many times he asked me to speak on that subject. Once, when I had been invited to preach in the Fifth Avenue Presbyterian Church, New York (invited at Mr. Moody's suggestion; had it not been for his suggestion the invitation would never have been extended to me), just before I started for New York, Mr. Moody drove up to my house and said: "Torrey, they want you to preach at the Fifth Avenue Presbyterian Church in New York. It is a great, big church, cost a million dollars to build it." Then he continued: "Torrey, I just want to ask one thing of you. I want to tell you what to preach about. You will preach that sermon of yours on 'Ten Reasons Why I Believe the Bible to Be the Word of God' and your sermon on 'The Baptism with the Holy Ghost.'" Time and again, when a call came to me to go off to some church, he would come up to me and say: "Now, Torrey, be sure and preach on the baptism with the Holy Ghost." I do not know how many times he said that to me. Once I asked him: "Mr. Moody, don't you think I have any sermons but those two: 'Ten Reasons Why I Believe the Bible to Be the Word of God; and 'The Baptism with the Holy Ghost'?" "Never mind that," he replied, "you give them those two sermons.". . .

I shall never forget the 8th of July, 1894, to my dying day. It was the closing day of the Northfield Students' Conference—the gathering of the students from the eastern colleges. Mr. Moody had asked me to preach on Saturday night and Sunday morning on the Baptism with the Holy Ghost. On Saturday night I had spoken about "The Baptism with the Holy Ghost, What It Is, What It Does, the Need of It and the Possibility of It." On Sunday morning I spoke on "The Baptism with the Holy Spirit, How to Get It." It was just exactly twelve o'clock when I finished my morning sermon, and I took out my watch and said: "Mr. Moody has invited us all to go up on the mountain at three o'clock this afternoon to pray for the power of the Holy Spirit. It is three hours to three o'clock. You do not need to wait. Go to your rooms, go out into the woods, go to your tent, go anywhere where you can get alone with God and have this matter out with Him." At three o'clock we all gathered in front of Mr. Moody's mother's house (she was then still living), and then began to pass down the lane, through the gate, up on the mountainside. There were four hundred and fifty-six of us in all; I know the number because Paul Moody counted us as we passed through the gate.

After a while Mr. Moody said: "I don't think we need to go any further; let us sit down here." We sat down on stumps and logs and on the ground. Mr. Moody said: "Have any of you students anything to say?" I think about seventy-five of them arose, one after the other, and said: "Mr. Moody, I could not wait till three o'clock; I have been alone with God since the morning service, and I believe I have a right to say that I have been baptized with the Holy Spirit." When these testimonies were over, Mr. Moody said: "Young men, I can't see any reason why we shouldn't kneel down here right now and ask God that the Holy Ghost may fall upon us just as definitely as He fell upon the apostles on the Day of Pentecost. Let us pray." And we did pray, there on the mountainside. As we had gone up the mountainside heavy clouds had been gathering, and just as we began to pray those clouds broke and the rain-drops began to fall through the overhanging pines. But there was another cloud that had been gathering over Northfield for ten days, a cloud big with the mercy and grace and power of God, and as we began to pray our prayers seemed to pierce that cloud and the Holy Ghost fell upon us. Men and women, that is what we all need—the Baptism with the Holy Ghost.

SECTION 2
MOODY CLASSICS

3

THE WAY TO GOD

The Gateway into the Kingdom

Except a man be born again, he cannot see the kingdom of God
—John 3:3.

There is perhaps no portion of the Word of God with which we are more familiar than this passage. I suppose if I were to ask those in any audience if they believed that Jesus Christ taught the doctrine of the new birth, nine-tenths of them would say: "Yes, I believe He did."

THE MOST IMPORTANT DOCTRINE: THE NEW BIRTH

Now, if the words of this text are true, they embody one of the most solemn questions that can come before us. We can afford to be deceived about many things rather than about this one thing: the new birth. Christ makes it very plain. He says, "Except a man be born again, he cannot see the kingdom of God"—much less inherit it. This doctrine of the new birth is therefore the foundation of all our hopes for the world to come. It is really the A B C of the Christian religion.

My experience has been this—that if a man is unsound on this doctrine, he will be unsound on almost every other fundamental doctrine in the Bible. A true understanding of this subject will help a man to solve a thousand difficulties that he may meet within the Word of God. Things that before seemed very dark and mysterious will become very plain. The doctrine of the new birth upsets all false religion—all false views about the Bible and about God. A friend of mine once told me that in one of his after-meetings, a man came to him with a long list of questions, written out for him to answer. He said: "If you can answer these questions satisfactorily, I have made up my mind to become a Christian."

"Do you not think," said my friend, "that you had better come to Christ first? Then you can look into these questions." The man thought that perhaps he had better do so. After he had received Christ, he looked again at his list of questions; but then it seemed to him as if they had all been answered.

Nicodemus came with his troubled mind, and Christ said to him, "Ye must be born again." He was treated altogether different from what he expected, but I venture to say that was the most blessed night in all his life. To be "born again" is the greatest blessing that will ever come to us in this world.

Notice how the Scripture puts it: "Except a man be born again [born from above]" (John 3:3). From amongst a number of other passages where we find this word "except," I would name just three. "Except ye repent, ye shall all likewise perish" (Luke 13:3, 5). "Except ye be converted, and become as little children, ye shall not enter into the kingdom of heaven" (Matthew 18:3). "Except your righteousness shall exceed the righteousness of the scribes and Pharisees, ye shall in no case enter into the kingdom of heaven" (Matthew 5:20). They all really mean the same thing.

I am so thankful that our Lord spoke of the new birth to this ruler of the Jews, this doctor of the law, rather than to the woman at the well of Samaria, or to Matthew the publican, or to Zaccheus. If He had reserved His teaching on this great matter for those three, or such as these, people would have said: "Oh yes, these publicans and harlots need to be converted: but I am an upright man; I do not need to be converted." I suppose Nicodemus was one of the best specimens of the people of Jerusalem; there was nothing on record against him.

I think it is scarcely necessary for me to prove that we need to be born again before we are fit for heaven. I venture to say that there is no candid man but would say he is not fit for the kingdom of God until he is born of another spirit. The Bible teaches us that man by nature is lost and guilty, and our experience confirms this. We know also that the best and holiest man, if he turn away from God, will very soon fall into sin.

WHAT REGENERATION IS NOT

Now, let me say what regeneration is not. It is not going to church. Very often I see people and ask them if they are Christians. "Yes, of course I am; at least, I think I am; I go to church every Sunday." Ah, but this is not regeneration. Others say, "I am trying to do what is right—am I not a Christian? Is not that a new birth?" No. What has that to do with being born again? There is yet another class—those who have "turned over a new leaf" and think they are regenerated. No; forming a new resolution is not being born again.

Nor will being baptized do you any good. Yet you hear people say, "Why, I have been baptized and I was born again when I was baptized." They believe that because they were baptized into the church, they were baptized into the kingdom of God. I tell you that it is utterly impossible. You may be baptized into the church, and yet not be baptized into the Son of God. Baptism is all right in its place, God forbid that I should say anything against it. But if you put that in the place of regeneration—in the place of the new birth—it is a terrible mistake. You cannot be baptized into the kingdom of God. "Except a man be *born again,* he cannot see the kingdom of God." If anyone reading this rests his hopes on anything else—on any other foundation—I pray that God may sweep it away.

Another class says, "I go to the Lord's Supper, I partake uniformly of the sacrament." Blessed ordinance! Jesus hath said that as often as you do it, you commemorate His death. Yet, that is not being "born again," that is not passing from death unto life. Jesus says plainly—and so plainly that there need not be any mistake about it—"Except a man be born . . . of the Spirit, he cannot enter into the kingdom of God." What has a sacrament to do with that? What has going to church to do with being born again?

Another man comes up and says, "I say my prayers regularly." Still I say that is not being born of the Spirit. It is a very solemn question, then, that comes up before us; and, oh, that every reader would ask himself earnestly and faithfully: "Have I been born again? Have I been born of the Spirit? Have I passed from death unto life?"

"WE DO NOT NEED TO BE CONVERTED"

There is a class of men who say that special religious meetings are very good for a certain class of people. They would be very good if you could get the drunkard there, or get the gambler there, or get other vicious people there—that would do a great deal of good. But "we do not need to be converted." To whom did Christ utter these words of wisdom, that "ye must be born again" (verse 7)? To Nicodemus. Who was Nicodemus? Was he a drunkard, a gambler, or a thief? No! No doubt he was one of the very best men in Jerusalem. He was an honorable counselor; he belonged to the Sanhedrin; he held a very high position; he was an orthodox man; he was one of the very soundest men.

And yet what did Christ say to him? "Except a man be born again, he cannot see the kingdom of God."

But I can imagine someone saying, "What am I to do? I cannot create life. I certainly cannot save myself." You certainly cannot; and we do not claim that you can. We tell you it is utterly impossible to make a man better without Christ; but that is what men are trying to do. They are trying to patch up this "old Adam" nature. *There must be a new creation.* Regeneration is a new creation; and if it is a new creation, it must be the work of God. In Genesis 1, man does not appear; there is no one there but God. Man is not there to take part. When God created the earth, He was alone. When Christ redeemed the world, He was alone.

"That which is born of the flesh is flesh; and that which is born of the Spirit is spirit" (John 3:6). The leopard cannot change his spots. You might as well try to make yourselves pure and holy without the help of God. A man might just as well try to leap over the moon as to serve God in the flesh. Therefore, "that which is born of the flesh is flesh; and that which is born of the Spirit is spirit."

HOW TO ENTER INTO THE KINGDOM OF GOD

In John 3 God tells us how we are to get into His kingdom. We are not to work our way in—though such salvation is worth working for. If there were rivers and mountains in the way, it would be well worthwhile to swim those rivers and climb those mountains. There is no doubt that salvation is worth all that effort; but we do not obtain it by our works. It is "to him that worketh not, but believeth" (Romans 4:5). We work because we are saved; we do not work to be saved. We work from the cross; but not toward it. It is written, "Work out your own salvation with fear and trembling" (Philippians 2:12). Why, you must have your salvation before you can work it out.

Suppose I say to my little boy, "I want you to spend that hundred dollars carefully."

"Well," he says, "let me have the hundred dollars; and I will be careful how I spend it."

I remember when I first left home and went to Boston. I had spent all my money, and I went to the post office three times a day. I knew there was only one mail a day from home, but I thought by some possibility there might be a letter for me. At last I received a letter from my little sister, and oh, how glad I was to get it. She had heard that there were a great many pickpockets in Boston, and a large part of that letter was to urge me to be very careful not to let anybody pick my pocket. Now I require to have something in my pocket before I could have it picked. So you must have salvation before you can work it out.

When Christ cried out on Calvary, "It is finished!" He meant what He said. All that men have to do now is just to accept the work of Jesus Christ. There is no hope for man or woman so long as they are trying to work out salvation for themselves.

I can imagine there are some people who will say, as Nicodemus possibly did, "This is a very mysterious thing." I see the scowl on that Pharisee's brow as he says, "How can these things be?" It sounds very strange to his ear. "Born again; born of the Spirit? How can these things be?" A great many people say, "You must reason it out; but if you do not reason it out, do not ask us to believe it." When you ask me to reason it out, I tell you frankly I cannot do it. "The wind bloweth where it listeth, and thou hearest the sound thereof, but canst not tell whence it cometh, and whither it goeth; so is every one that is born of the Spirit" (John 3:8). I do not understand everything about the wind. You ask me to reason it out. I cannot. It may blow due north here, and a hundred miles away due south. I may go up a few hundred feet, and find it blowing in an entirely opposite direction from where it is down here.

You ask me to explain these currents of the wind; but suppose that, because I cannot explain them, and do not understand them, I were to take my stand and assert, "Oh, there is no such thing as wind." I can imagine some little girl saying, "I know more about it than that man does; often I have heard the wind, and felt it blowing against my face." She might say: "Did not the wind blow my umbrella out of my hands the other day? And did I not see it blow a man's hat off in the street? Have I not seen it blow the trees in the forest, and the growing corn in the country?"

You might just as well tell me that there is no such thing as wind, as tell me there is no such thing as a man being born of the Spirit. I have felt the Spirit of God working in my heart, just as really and as truly as I have felt the wind blowing in my face. I cannot reason it out. I never could reason out the creation. I can see the world, but I cannot tell how God made it out of nothing. But almost every man will admit there was a creative power.

IMPOSSIBLE TO EXPLAIN EVERYTHING

There are a great many things that I cannot explain and cannot reason out, and yet I believe them. I heard a commercial traveler say that he had heard that the ministry and religion of Jesus Christ were matters of revelation and not of investigation. "When it pleased God . . . to reveal his Son in me," says Paul (Galatians 1:15–16).

A party of young men were together, going up the country, and on their journey they made up their minds not to believe anything they could not reason out. An old man heard them; and presently he said: "I heard you say you would not believe anything you could not reason out."

"Yes," they said, "that is so."

"Well," he said, "coming down on the train today, I noticed some geese, some sheep, some swine, and some cattle all eating grass. Can you tell me by what process that same grass was turned into hair, feathers, bristles, and wool? Do you believe it is a fact?"

"Oh yes," they said, "we cannot help believing that, though we fail to understand it."

"Well," said the old man, "I cannot help believing in Jesus Christ."

And I cannot help believing in the regeneration of man when I see men who have been reclaimed, when I see men who have been reformed. Have not some of the very worst men been regenerated— been picked up out of the pit, and had their feet set upon the Rock, and a new song put in their mouths? Their tongues were cursing and blaspheming, and now are occupied in praising God. Old things have passed away, and all things have become new. They are not reformed only—but *regenerated*—new men in Christ Jesus.

PRACTICAL RESULTS IN REAL LIFE

Down there in the dark alleys of one of our great cities is a poor drunkard. I think if you want to get near hell you should go to a poor drunkard's home. Go into the house of that poor, miserable drunkard. See the want and distress that reign there. But hark! A footstep is heard at the door, and the children run and hide themselves. The patient wife waits to meet the man. He has been her torment. Many a time she has borne about the marks of his blows for weeks. Many a time that strong right hand has been brought down on her defenseless head. And now she waits expecting to hear his oaths and suffer his brutal treatment.

He comes in and says to her, "I have been to the meeting, and I heard there that if I will, I can be converted. I believe that God is able to save me."

Go down to that house again in a few weeks, and what a change! As you approach you hear someone singing. It is not the song of a reveler, but the strains of that good old hymn, "Rock of Ages." The children are no longer afraid of the man, but cluster around his knee. His wife is near him, her face lit up with a happy glow. Is not that a picture of regeneration? I can take you to many such homes, made happy by the regenerating power of the religion of Christ. What men want is the power to overcome temptation, the power to lead a right life.

The only way to get into the kingdom of God is to be "born" into it. The law of this country requires that the president should be born in this country. When foreigners come to our shores they have no right to complain against such a law, which forbids them from ever becoming presidents. Now, has not God a right to make a law that all those who become heirs of eternal life must be "born" into His kingdom?

An unregenerate man would rather be in hell than in heaven. Take a man whose heart is full of corruption and wickedness, and place him in heaven among the pure, the holy, and the redeemed, and he would not want to stay there. Certainly, if we are to be happy in heaven we must begin to make a heaven here on earth. Heaven is a prepared place for a prepared people. If a gambler or a blasphemer were taken out of the street of New York and placed on the crystal pavement of heaven and under the shadow of the tree of life, he would say, "I do not want to stay here." If men were taken to heaven just as they are by nature, without having their hearts regenerated, there would be another rebellion in heaven. Heaven is filled with a company of those who have been twice born.

"WHOSOEVER"

In John 3:14–15, we read, "As Moses lifted up the serpent in the wilderness, even so must the Son of man be lifted up; that *whosoever* believeth in him should not perish, but have eternal life" (emphasis added).

Mark that! Let me tell you who are unsaved what God has done for you. He has done everything that He could do toward your salvation. You need not wait for God to do anything more. In one place He asked the question, What more could He have done? (Isaiah 5:4). He sent His prophets, and they killed them; then He sent His beloved Son, and they murdered Him. Now He has sent the Holy Spirit to convince us of sin and to show how we are to be saved.

In John 3 we are told how men are to be saved, namely, by Him who was lifted up on the cross. Just as Moses lifted up the brazen serpent in the wilderness, so must the Son of Man be lifted up, "that whosoever believeth in him should not perish, but have eternal life" (verse 15). Some men complain and say that it is very unreasonable that they should be held responsible for the sin of a man six thousand years ago. It was not long ago that a man was talking to me about this injustice, as he called it. If a man thinks he is going to answer to God in that way, I tell you it will not do him any good. If you are lost, it will not be on account of Adam's sin.

THE CASE ILLUSTRATED

Let me illustrate this, and perhaps you will be better able to understand it. Suppose I am dying of tuberculosis, which I inherited from my father or mother. I did not get the disease by any fault of my own, by any neglect of my health; I inherited it, let us suppose. A friend happens to come along, he looks at me, and says: "Moody, you have tuberculosis."

"I know it very well," I reply. "I did not want anyone to tell me that."

"But," he says, "there is a remedy."

"But, sir, I do not believe it. I have tried the leading physicians in this country and in Europe; and they tell me there is no hope."

"But you know me, Moody; you have known me for years."

"Yes, sir."

"Do you think, then, I would tell you a falsehood?"

"No."

"Well, ten years ago I was as far gone. I was given up by the physicians to die, but I took this medicine and it cured me. I am perfectly well; look at me." I tell him that his is a very strange case.

"Yes, it may be strange; but it is a fact. This medicine cured me. Take this medicine, and it will cure you. Do not make light of it, I beg of you."

"Well," I say, "I should like to believe you, but this is contrary to my reason."

Hearing this, my friend goes away and returns with another friend, and that one testifies to the same thing. I am still disbelieving; so he goes away, and brings in another friend, and another, and another, and another; and they all testify to the same thing. They say they were as bad as myself; that they took the same medicine that has been offered to me; and that it has cured them. My friend then hands me the medicine. I dash it to the ground; I do not believe in its saving power; I die.

The reason is, then, that I spurned the remedy. So, if you perish, it will not be because Adam fell, but because you spurned the remedy offered to save you. You will choose darkness rather than light. "How shall we escape, if we neglect so great salvation?" There is no hope for you if you neglect the remedy. It does no good to look at the wound. If we had been in the Israelite camp and had been bitten by one of the fiery serpents, it would have done us no good to look at the wound. Looking at the wound will never save anyone. What you must do is to look at the remedy—look away to Him who hath power to save you from your sin.

Behold the camp of the Israelites; look at the scene that is pictured to your eyes! Many are dying because they neglect the remedy that is offered. In that arid desert is many a short and tiny grave; many a child has been bitten by the fiery serpents. Fathers and mothers are bearing away their children. Over yonder they are just burying a mother; a loved mother is about to be laid in the earth. All the family, weeping, gather around the beloved form. You hear the mournful cries; you see the bitter tears. There is wailing going up all over the camp. Tears are pouring down for thousands who have passed away; thousands more are dying; and the plague is raging from one end of the camp to the other.

LIFE IN A LOOK

I see in one tent an Israelite mother bending over the form of a beloved boy just coming into the bloom of life, just budding into manhood. She is wiping away the sweat of death that is gathering upon his brow. Yet a little while, and his eyes are fixed and glassy, for life is ebbing fast away. The mother's heartstrings are torn and bleeding. All at once she hears a noise in the camp. A great shout goes up. What does it mean? She goes to the door of the tent. "What is the noise in the camp?" she asks those passing by. And someone says: "Why, my good woman, have you not heard the good news that has come into the camp?"

"No," says the woman. "Good news! What is it?"

"Why, have you not heard about it? God has provided a remedy."

"What! For the bitten Israelites? Oh, tell me what the remedy is!"

"Why, God has instructed Moses to make a brazen serpent and to put it on a pole in the middle of the camp; and He has declared that whosoever looks upon it shall live. The shout that you hear is the shout of the people when they see the serpent lifted up."

The mother goes back into the tent, and she says: "My boy, I have good news to tell you. You need not die! My boy, my boy, I have come with good tidings; you can live!" He is already getting stupefied; he is so weak he cannot walk to the door of the tent. She puts her strong arms under him and lifts him up. "Look yonder; look right there under the hill!" But the boy does not see anything. He says: "I do not see anything; what is it, Mother?" And she says: "Keep looking, and you will see it."

At last he catches a glimpse of the glistening serpent; and lo, he is well! And thus it is with many a young convert.

Some men say, "Oh, we do not believe in sudden conversions." How long did it take to cure that boy? How long did it take to cure those serpent-bitten Israelites? It was just a look, and they were well.

That Hebrew boy is a young convert. I can fancy that I see him now calling on all those who were with him to praise God. He sees another young man bitten as he was, and he runs up to him and tells him, "You need not die."

"Oh," the young man replies, "I cannot live; it is not possible. There is not a physician in Israel who can cure me." He does not know that he need not die.

"Why, have you not heard the news? God has provided a remedy."

"What remedy?"

"Why, God has told Moses to lift up a brazen serpent, and has said that none of those who look upon that serpent shall die."

I can just imagine the young man. He may be what you call an intellectual young man. He says to the young convert, "You do not think I am going to believe anything like that? If the physicians in Israel cannot cure me, how do you think that an old brass serpent on a pole is going to cure me?"

"Why, sir, I was as bad as yourself!"

"You do not say so!"

"Yes, I do."

"That is the most astonishing thing I ever heard," says the

young man. "I wish you would explain the philosophy of it."

"I cannot. I only know that I looked at that serpent, and I was cured: that did it. My mother told me the reports that were being heard through the camp; and I just believed what my mother said, and I am perfectly well."

"Well, I do not believe you were bitten as badly as I have been."

The young man pulls up his sleeve. "Look there! That mark shows where I was bitten; and I tell you I was worse than you are."

"Well, if I understood the philosophy of it, I would look and get well."

"Let your philosophy go; look and live!"

"But, sir, you ask me to do an unreasonable thing. If God had said, 'take that brass and rub it into the wound,' there might be something in the brass that would cure the bite. Young man, explain the philosophy of it." I have often seen people before me who have talked in that way.

But the young man calls in another, and takes him into the tent, and says, "Just tell him how the Lord saved you"; and he tells the same story; and he calls in others, and they all say the same thing.

The young man says it is a very strange thing. "If the Lord had told Moses to go and get some herbs, or roots, and stew them, and take the decoction as a medicine, there would be something in that. But it is so contrary to nature to do such a thing as look at the serpent, that I cannot do it."

At length, his mother, who has been out in the camp, comes in, and she says, "My boy, I have just the best news in the world for you. I was in the camp and I saw hundreds who were very far gone, and they are all perfectly well now."

"I should like to get well," the young man says. "It is a very painful thought to die; I want to go into the promised land, and it is terrible to die here in this wilderness. But the fact is, I do not understand the remedy. It does not appeal to my reason. I cannot believe that I can get well in a moment." And the young man dies in consequence of his own unbelief.

GOD'S REMEDY FOR SIN

God has provided a remedy for this bitten Israelite: "Look and live!" And there is eternal life for every poor sinner. Look, and you can be saved, my reader, this very hour. God has provided a remedy, and it is offered to all. The trouble is, a great many people are looking at the pole. Do not look at the pole; that is the church. You need not look at the church; the church is all right, but the church cannot save you. Look beyond the pole. Look at the Crucified One. Look to Calvary.

Bear in mind, sinner, that Jesus died for all. You need not look at ministers; they are just God's chosen instruments to hold up the remedy, to hold up Christ. And so, my friend, take your eyes off men; take your eyes off the church. Lift them up to Jesus, who took away the sin of the world, and there will be life for you from this hour.

Thank God, we do not require an education to teach us how to look. That little girl, that little boy, only four years old, who cannot read, can look. When the father is coming home, the mother says to her little boy, "Look! Look! Look!" and the little child learns to look long before he is a year old. And that is the way to be saved. It is to look at the Lamb of God "which taketh away the sin of the world," and there is life this moment for everyone who is willing to look.

HOW TO BE SAVED

Some men say: "I wish I knew how to be saved." Just take God at His word, and trust His Son this very day—this very hour—this very moment. He will save you if you will trust Him. I imagine I hear someone saying: "I do not feel the bite as much as I wish I did. I know I am a sinner, and all that; but I do not feel the bite enough." How much does God want you to feel?

When I was in Belfast I knew a doctor who had a friend, a leading surgeon there; and he told me that the surgeon's custom was, before performing any operation, to say to the patient, "Take a good look at the wound, and then fix your eyes on me; and do not take them off until I get through." I thought at the time that was a good illustration. Sinner, take a good look at your wound and then fix your eyes on Christ, and do not take them off. It is better to look at the remedy than at the wound. See what a poor wretched sinner you are; and then look at the Lamb of God who "taketh away the sin of the world." He died for the ungodly and for the sinner. Say, "I will take Him!"

And may God help you lift your eyes to the Man on Calvary. And as the Israelites looked upon the serpent and were healed, so may you look and live.

THE DYING SOLDIER

After the battle of Pittsburgh Landing I was in a hospital at Murfreesboro. In the middle of the night I was awakened and told that a man in one of the wards wanted to see me. I went to him and he called me "chaplain"—I was not the chaplain—and said he wanted me to help him die.

And I said, "I would take you right up in my arms and carry you into the kingdom of God, if I could, but I cannot do it. I cannot help you die!"

"Who can?" he asked.

"The Lord Jesus Christ can—He came for that purpose."

He shook his head, and said: "He cannot save me; I have sinned all my life."

"But He came to save sinners," I replied. I thought of his mother in the North, and I was sure that she was anxious that he should die in peace; so I resolved I would stay with him. I prayed two or three times, and repeated all the promises I could; for it was evident that in a few hours he would be gone.

I said I wanted to read him a conversation that Christ had with a man who was anxious about his soul. I turned to the third chapter of John. His eyes were riveted on me; and when I came to the fourteenth and fifteenth verses he caught up the words, "As Moses lifted up the serpent in the wilderness, even so must the Son of man be lifted up: that whosoever believeth in him should not perish, but have eternal life."

He stopped me and said: "It that there?" I answered yes, and he asked me to read it again; and I did so. He leaned his elbows on the cot and clasping his hands together, said, "That's good; won't you read it again?" I read it the third time and then went on with the rest of the chapter.

When I had finished, his eyes were closed, his hands were folded, and there was a smile on his face. Oh, how it was lit up! What a change had come over it! I saw his lips quivering, and, leaning over him, I heard in a faint whisper, "As Moses lifted up the serpent in the wilderness, even so must the Son of man be lifted up; that whosoever believeth in him should not perish, but have eternal life." He opened his eyes and said, "That's enough; don't read any more." He lingered a few hours, pillowing his head on those two verses and then went up in one of Christ's chariots, to take his seat in the kingdom of God.

Christ said to Nicodemus, "Except a man be born again, he cannot see the kingdom of God." You may see many countries; but there is one country—the land of Beulah, which John Bunyan saw in vision—that you shall never behold unless you are born again— regenerated by Christ. You can look abroad and see many beautiful trees; but the Tree of Life, you shall never behold, unless your eyes are made clear by faith in the Savior. You may see the beautiful rivers of the earth, but bear in mind that your eye will never rest upon the river that bursts out from the throne of God and flows through the upper kingdom unless you are born again. God has said it and not man. You will never see the kingdom of God except you are born again.

You may see the kings and lords of the earth, but the King of kings and Lord of lords you will never see except you are born again. When you are in London you may go to the Tower and see the Crown of England, which is worth thousands of dollars, and is guarded there by soldiers; but bear in mind that your eye will never rest upon the crown of life, except you are born again.

WHAT THOSE NOT BORN AGAIN SHALL MISS

You may hear the songs of Zion that are sung here, but one song—that of Moses and the Lamb—the unspiritual ear shall never hear; its melody will only gladden the ear of those who have been born again. You may look upon the beautiful mansions of earth, but bear in mind the mansions that Christ has gone to prepare you shall never see, unless you are born again. It is God who says it. You may see ten thousand beautiful things in this world, but the city that Abraham caught a glimpse of you shall never see, unless you are born again (Hebrews 11:8, 10–16). You may often be invited to marriage feasts here; but you will never attend the marriage supper of the Lamb, unless you are born again. It is God who says it, dear friend. You may be looking on the face of your sainted mother tonight, and feel that she is praying for you; but the time will come when you shall never see her more, unless you are born again.

A PROMISE MADE TO MOTHER

The reader may be a young man or a young lady who has recently stood by the bedside of a dying mother, and she may have said: "Be sure and meet me in heaven," and you made the promise. Ah! You shall never see her more, except you are born again. I believe Jesus of Nazareth sooner than those infidels who say you do not need to be born again. Parents, if you hope to see your children who have gone before, you must be born of the Spirit. Possibly you are a father or mother who has recently borne a loved one to the grave, and how dark your home seems! Never more will you see your child, unless you are born again. If you wish to be reunited to your loved one, you must be born again.

I may be addressing a father or a mother who has a loved one up yonder. If you could hear that loved one's voice, it would say, "Come this way." Have you a sainted friend up yonder? Young man or young lady, have you not a mother in the world of light? If you could hear her speak, would not she say, "Come this way, my son"; "Come this way, my daughter"? If you would ever see her more, you must be born again.

We all have an Elder Brother there. Nearly nineteen hundred years ago He crossed over, and from the heavenly shores He is calling you to heaven. Let us turn our backs upon the world. Let us give a deaf ear to the world. Let us look to Jesus on the cross, and be saved. Then we shall one day see the King in His beauty, and we shall go out no more.

Christ All and in All

Where there is neither Greek nor Jew, circumcision nor uncircumcision, Barbarian, Scythian, bond nor free: but Christ is all, and in all—Colossians 3:11.

Christ is *all* to us that we make Him to be. I want to emphasize that word *all*. Some men make Him to be "a root out of a dry ground . . . without form or comeliness." He is nothing to them; they do not want Him. Some Christians have a very small Savior, for they are not willing to receive Him fully, and let Him do great and mighty things for them. Others have a mighty Savior, because they make Him to be great and mighty.

A SAVIOR FROM SIN

If we would know what Christ wants to be to us, we must first of all know Him as our Savior from sin. When the angel came down from heaven to proclaim that He was to be born into the world, you remember he gave His name, "He shall be called Jesus [Savior], for he shall save his people from their sins." *Have we been delivered from sin?* He did not come to save us *in* our sins, but *from* our sins.

Now, there are three ways of knowing a person. Some people

you know only by hearsay, others you merely know by having been once introduced to them—you know them very slightly. Still others you know by having been acquainted with them for years—you know them intimately. So I believe there are three classes of people today in the Christian church and out of it: those who know Christ only by reading or by hearsay (those who have a historical Christ); those who have a slight personal acquaintance with Him; and those who thirst—as Paul did, to "know him, and the power of his resurrection." The more we know of Christ the more we shall love Him, and the better we shall serve Him.

Let us look at Him as He hangs upon the cross, and see how He has put away sin. He was manifested that He might take away our sins; and if we really know Him, we must first of all see Him as our Savior from sin. You remember how the angel said to the shepherds on the plains of Bethlehem, "Behold, I bring you good tidings of great joy, which shall be to all people. For unto you is born this day in the city of David a Saviour, which is Christ the Lord" (Luke 2:10–11). Then if you go clear back to Isaiah, seven hundred years before Christ's birth, you will find these words: "I, even I, am the Lord; and beside me there is no saviour" (43:11).

Again, in 1 John 4:14 we read: "We have seen and do testify that the Father sent the Son to be the Saviour of the world." All the heathen religions teach men to work their way up to God, but the religion of Jesus Christ is God coming down to men to save them, to lift them up out of the pit of sin. In Luke 19:10 we read that Christ Himself told the people what He had come for: "The Son of man is come to seek and to save that which was lost." So we start from the cross, not from the cradle. Christ has opened up a new and living way to the Father; He has taken all the stumbling blocks out of the way, so that every man who accepts Christ as his Savior can have salvation.

MORE THAN A SAVIOR

But Christ is not only a Savior. I might save a man from drowning and rescue him from an untimely grave; but I might probably not be able to do any more for him. Christ is something more than a Savior. When the children of Israel were placed behind the blood when the angel of death passed over them, that blood was their salvation; but they would still have heard the crack of the slave driver's whip, if they had not been delivered from the Egyptian yoke of bondage: then it was that God delivered them from the hand of the king of Egypt. I have little sympathy with the idea that God comes down to save us, and then leaves us in prison, the slaves of our besetting sins. No; He has come to deliver us, and to give us victory over our evil tempers, our passions, and our lusts.

Are you a professed Christian, but one who is a slave to some besetting sin? If you want to get victory over that temper or that lust, go on to know Christ more intimately. He brings deliverance for the past, the present, and the future. "Who delivered . . . and doth deliver . . . [who] will yet deliver" (2 Corinthians 1:10).

WHEN THINGS LOOK DARK

How often, like the children of Israel when they came to the Red Sea, have we become discouraged because everything looked dark before us, behind us, and around us, and we know not which way to turn. Like Peter, we have said: "To whom shall we go?" But God has appeared for our deliverance. He has brought us through the Red Sea right out into the wilderness and opened up the way into the Promised Land. But Christ is not only our Deliverer; He is our Redeemer. That is something more than being our Savior. He has bought us back. "Ye have sold yourselves for nought; and ye shall be redeemed without money" (Isaiah 52:3). We "were not redeemed with corruptible things, as silver and gold" (1 Peter 1:18). If gold could have redeemed us, could He not have created ten thousand worlds of gold?

When God had redeemed the children of Israel from the bondage of Egypt and brought them through the Red Sea, they struck out for the wilderness; and then God became to them their way. I am so thankful the Lord has not left us in darkness as to the right way. There is no living man who has been groping in the darkness but may know the way. "I am the way," says Christ. If we follow Christ, we shall be in the right way and have the right doctrine. Who could lead the children of Israel through the wilderness like the Almighty God Himself? He knew the pitfalls and dangers of the way, and guided the people through all their wilderness journey right into the Promised Land. It is true that if it had not been for their accursed unbelief, they might have crossed into the land at Kadesh-Barnea, and taken possession of it, but they desired something besides God's word; so they were turned back, and they had to wander in the desert for forty years.

I believe there are thousands of God's children wandering in the wilderness still. The Lord has delivered them from the hand of the Egyptian, and would at once take them through the wilderness right into the Promised Land, if they were only willing to follow Christ. Christ has been down here, and has made the rough places smooth, and the dark places light, and the crooked places straight. If we will only be led by Him and will follow Him, all will be peace, and joy, and rest.

BLAZING THE WAY

In the frontier, when a man goes out hunting he takes a hatchet with him and cuts off pieces from the bark of the trees as he goes along through the forest. This is called "blazing the way." He does it that he may know the way back, as there is no pathway through these thick forests. Christ has come down to this earth; He has "blazed the way"; and now that He has gone up on high, if we will but follow Him, we shall be kept in the right path.

I will tell you how you may know if you are following Christ or not. If someone has slandered you, or misjudged you, do you treat them as your Master would have done? If you do not bear these things in a loving and forgiving spirit, all the churches and ministers in the world cannot make you right. "If any man have not the Spirit of Christ, he is none of his" (Romans 8:9). "If any man be in Christ, he is a new creature: old things are passed away; behold, all things are become new" (2 Corinthians 5:17).

Christ is not only our way, He is the light upon the way. He says, "I am the light of the world" (John 8:12; 9:5; 12:46). He goes on to say, "He that followeth me shall not walk in darkness, but shall have the light of life." It is impossible for any man or woman who is following Christ to walk in darkness. If your soul is in the darkness, groping around in the fog and mist of earth, let me tell you it is because you have got away from the true light. There is nothing but light that will dispel darkness.

So let those who are walking in spiritual darkness admit Christ into their hearts: He is the light. I call to mind a picture of which I used at one time to think a good deal; but now I have come to look more closely, I would not put it up in my house except I turned the face to the wall. It represents Christ as standing at a door, knocking, and having a big lantern in His hand. Why, you might as well hang up a lantern to the sun as put one into Christ's hand. He is the Sun of Righteousness; and it is our privilege to walk in the light of an unclouded sun.

TRYING TO CATCH ONE'S SHADOW

Many people are hunting after light, and peace, and joy. We are nowhere told to seek after these things. If we admit Christ into our hearts, these will all come of themselves. I remember, when a boy, I used to try in vain to catch my shadow. One day I was walking with my face to the sun. As I happened to look around I saw that my shadow was following me. The faster I went, the faster my shadow followed; I could not get away from it. So when our faces are directed to the Sun of Righteousness, the peace and joy are sure to come.

A man said to me some time ago, "Moody, how do you feel?" It was so long since I had thought about my feelings, I had to stop and consider awhile, in order to find out. Some Christians are all the time thinking about their feelings, and because they do not feel just right, they think their joy is all gone. If we keep our faces toward Christ, and are occupied with Him, we shall be lifted out of the darkness and the trouble that may have gathered round our path.

I remember being in a meeting after the War of the Rebellion broke out. The war had been going on for about six months. The army of the North had been defeated at Bull Run; in fact, we had nothing but defeat, and it looked as though the republic was going to pieces. So we were much cast down and discouraged. At this meeting every speaker for awhile seemed as if he had hung his harp upon the willow; and it was one of the gloomiest meetings I ever attended.

Finally, an old man with beautiful white hair got up to speak, and his face literally shone. "Young men," he said, "you do not talk like sons of the King. Though it is dark just here, remember it is light somewhere else." Then he went on to say that if it were dark all over the world, it was light up around the throne.

RISE ABOVE THE CLOUDS

He told us he had come from the East, where a friend had described to him how he had been up a mountain to spend the night and see the sun rise. As the party was climbing up the mountain, and before they had reached the summit, a storm came on. This friend said to the guide, "I will give this up; take me back." The guide smiled and replied, "I think we shall get above the storm soon." On they went; and it was not long before they got up to where it was as calm as any summer evening. Down in the valley a terrible storm raged; they could hear the thunder rolling, and see the lightening's flash; but all was serene on the mountain-top.

"And so, my young friends," continued the old man, "though all is dark around you, come a little higher and the darkness will flee away." Often when I have been inclined to get discouraged, I have thought of what he said. Now if you are down in the valley amidst the thick fog and the darkness, get a little higher; get nearer to Christ, and know more of Him.

You remember the Bible says that when Christ expired on the cross, the light of the world was put out. God sent His Son to be the light of the world; but men did not love the light, because it reproved them of their sins. When they were about to put out this light, what did Christ say to His disciples? "Ye shall be witnesses unto me" (Acts 1:8). He has gone up yonder to intercede for us; but He wants us to shine for Him down here. "Ye are the light of the world" (Matthew 5:14). So our work is to shine; not to blow our trumpet so that people may look at us. What we want to do is to show forth Christ. If we have any light at all, it is borrowed light.

Someone said to a young Christian: "Converted! It is a moonshine!" Said he: "I thank you for the illustration; the moon borrows its light from the sun; and we borrow ours from the Sun of Righteousness." If we are Christ's, we are here to shine for Him; by and by He will call us home to our reward.

THE BLIND MAN AND THE LANTERN

I remember hearing of a blind man who sat by the wayside with a lantern near him. When he was asked what he had a lantern for, as he could not see the light, he said it was that people should not stumble over him. I believe more people stumble over the inconsistencies of professed Christians than from any other cause. What is doing more harm to the cause of Christ than all the skepticism in the world is this cold, dead formalism, this conformity to the world, this professing what we do not possess. The eyes of the world are upon us. I think it was George Fox who said every Quaker ought to light up the country for ten miles around him. If we were all brightly shining for the Master, those about us would soon be reached, and there would be a shout of praise going to heaven.

People say: "I want to know what is the truth." Listen, to know what the truth is, get acquainted with Christ. People also complain that they have not life. Many are trying to give themselves spiritual life. You may galvanize yourselves and put electricity into yourselves, so to speak; but the effect will not last very long. Christ alone is the author of life. If you would have real spiritual life, get to know Christ. Many try to stir up spiritual life by going to meetings. That may be well enough; but it will be of no use, unless they get into contact with the living Christ. Then their spiritual life will not be a spasmodic thing, but will be perpetual; flowing on and on, and bringing forth fruit to God.

CHRIST SHALL KEEP US

Many young disciples are afraid they will not hold out. "He that keepeth Israel shall neither slumber nor sleep" (Psalm 121:4). It is the work of Christ to keep us; and if He keeps us, there will be no danger of our falling. I suppose if Queen Victoria had to take care of the Crown of England, some thief might attempt to get access to it; but it is put away in the Tower of London and guarded night and day by soldiers. The whole English army would, if necessary, be called out to protect it. And we have no strength in ourselves. We are no match for Satan; he has had six thousand years' experience. But then we remember that the One who neither slumbers nor sleeps is our keeper. In Isaiah 41:10, we read, "Fear thou not; for I am with thee: be not dismayed; for I am thy God: I will strengthen thee; yea, I will help thee; yea, I will uphold thee with the right hand of my righteousness." In Jude 24 we are also told that He is able to keep us from falling. The Apostle John adds that "We have an advocate with the Father, Jesus Christ the righteous" (1 John 2:1).

OUR SHEPHERD AND PROTECTOR

But Christ is something more. He is our *Shepherd*. It is the work of the shepherd to care for the sheep, to feed them, and protect them. "I am the good Shepherd." "My sheep hear my voice." "I lay down my life for the sheep." In that wonderful tenth chapter of John, Christ uses the personal pronoun no less than twenty-eight times, in declaring what He is and what He will do. In verse 28 He says, "They shall never perish, neither shall any *man* pluck them out of my hand." But notice the word *man* is in italics. See how the verse really reads: "Neither shall any pluck them out of my hand"—no devil or man shall be able to do it. In another place the Scripture declares, "Your life is hid with Christ in God" (Colossians 3:3). How safe and how secure!

Christ says, "My sheep hear my voice . . . and they follow me"

(John 10:27). A gentleman in the East heard of a shepherd who could call all his sheep to him by name. He went and asked if this were true. The shepherd took him to the pasture where they were and called one of them by some name. One sheep looked up and answered the call, while the others went on feeding and paid no attention. In the same way he called about a dozen of the sheep around him. The stranger said, "How do you know one from the other? They all look perfectly alike."

"Well," said he, "you see that sheep toes in a little, that other one has a squint, one has a little piece of wool off, another has a black spot, and another has a piece out of its ear."

The man knew all his sheep by their flaws, for he had not a perfect one in the whole flock. I suppose our Shepherd knows us in the same way.

An Eastern shepherd was once telling a gentleman that his sheep knew his voice and that no stranger could deceive them. The gentleman thought he would like to put the statement to the test. So he put on the shepherd's frock and turban, and took his staff and went to the flock. He disguised his voice and tried to speak as much like the shepherd as he could, but he could not get a single sheep in the flock to follow him. He asked the shepherd if his sheep never followed a stranger. He was obliged to admit that if a sheep got sickly it would follow anyone.

So it is with a good many professed Christians. When they get sickly and weak in the faith, they will follow any teacher who comes along; but when the soul is in health, a man will not be carried away by errors and heresies. He will know whether the "voice" speaks the truth or not. He can soon tell that, if he is really in communion with God. When God sends a true messenger, His words will find a ready response in the Christian heart.

OUR TENDER SHEPHERD

Christ is a tender shepherd. You may sometimes think He has not been a very tender shepherd to you; you are passing under the rod. It is written, "Whom the Lord loveth he chasteneth, and scourgeth every son whom he receiveth" (Hebrews 12:6). That you are passing under the rod is no proof that Christ does not love you.

A friend of mine lost all his children. No man could ever have loved his family more; but the scarlet fever took one by one away; and so the whole four or five, one after another, died. The poor stricken parents went over to Great Britain and wandered from one place to another, there and on the continent. At length they saw an Eastern shepherd come down to a stream, and call his flock to cross. The sheep came down to the brink and looked at the water, but they seemed to shrink from it, and he could not get them to respond to his call. He then took a little lamb and put it under the other arm, and thus passed into the stream. The old sheep no longer stood looking at the water; they plunged in after the shepherd. In a few minutes the whole flock was on the other side, and the shepherd hurried them away to newer and fresher pastures.

The bereaved father and mother, as they looked on the scene, felt it taught them a lesson. They no longer murmur because the Great Shepherd had taken their lambs one by one into yonder world; and they began to look up and look forward to the time when they would follow the loved ones they had lost. If you have loved ones gone before, remember that your Shepherd is calling you to "set your affection on things above" (Colossians 3:2). Let us be faithful to Him, and follow Him, while we remain in this world. And if you have not taken Him for your Shepherd, do so this very day.

WONDERFUL DESCRIPTION OF CHRIST

Christ is not only all these things that I have mentioned; He is also our Mediator, our Sanctifier, our Justifier; in fact, it would take volumes to tell what He desires to be to every individual soul. While looking through some papers, I once read this wonderful description of Christ. I do not know where it originally came from, but it was so fresh to my soul that I should like to give it to you:

"Christ is our Way; we walk in Him. He is our Truth; we embrace Him. He is our Life; we live in Him. He is our Lord; we choose Him to rule over us. He is our Master; we serve Him. He is our Teacher, instructing us in the way of salvation. He is our Prophet, pointing out the future. He is our Priest, having atoned for us. He is our Advocate, ever living to make intercession for us. He is our Savior, saving to the uttermost. He is our Root; we grow from Him. He is our Bread; we feed upon Him. He is our Shepherd, leading us into green pastures. He is our true Vine; we abide in Him. He is the Water of Life; we slake our thirst from Him.

"He is the fairest among ten thousand; we admire Him above all others. He is 'the brightness of the Father's glory, and the express image of His person'; we strive to reflect His likeness. He is the upholder of all things; we rest upon Him. He is our Wisdom; we are guided by Him. He is our Righteousness; we cast all our imperfections upon Him. He is our Sanctification; we draw all our power for holy life from Him. He is our Redemption, redeeming us from all iniquity. He is our Healer, curing all our diseases. He is our Friend, relieving us in all our necessities. He is our Brother, cheering us in our difficulties."

Here is another beautiful extract; it is from Gotthold:

"For my part, my soul is like a hungry and thirsty child; and I need His love and consolation for my refreshment. I am a wandering and lost sheep; and I need Him as a good and faithful shepherd. My soul is like a frightened dove pursued by the hawk; and I need His wounds for a refuge. I am a feeble vine; and I need His cross to lay hold of, and to wind myself about. I am a sinner; and I need His righteousness. I am naked and bare; and I need His holiness and innocence for a covering. I am ignorant; and I need His teaching: simple and foolish; and I need the guidance of His Holy Spirit.

"In no situation, and at no time, can I do without Him. Do I pray? He must prompt, and intercede for me. Am I arraigned by Satan at the divine tribunal? He must be my Advocate. Am I in affliction? He must be my Helper. Am I persecuted by the world? He must defend me. When I am forsaken, He must be my support; when I am dying, my life: when moldering in the grave, my Resurrection.

"Well, then, I will rather part with all the world, and all that it contains, than with Thee, my Savior. And, God be thanked! I know that Thou, too, are neither able nor willing to do without me. Thou art rich; and I am poor. Thou hast abundance; and I am needy. Thou hast righteousness; and I sins. Thou hast wine and oil; and I wounds. Thou hast cordials and refreshments; and I hunger and thirst.

"Use me, then, my Savior, for whatever purpose, and in whatever way, Thou mayest require. Here is my poor heart, an empty vessel; fill it with Thy grace. Here is my sinful and troubled soul; quicken and refresh it with Thy love. Take my heart for Thine abode; my mouth to spread the glory of Thy name; my love and all my powers, for the advancement of Thy believing people; and never suffer the steadfastness and confidence of my faith to abate—so that at all times I may be enabled from the heart to say, 'Jesus needs me, and I Him; and so we suit each other.'"

4

MEN OF THE BIBLE

The Call of Moses

There is a great deal more room given in Scripture to the *call* of men to God's work than there is to their *end*. For instance, we don't know where Isaiah died, or how he died, but we know a great deal about the call God gave him, when he saw God on high and lifted up on His throne. I suppose that it is true today that hundreds of young men and women who are listening for a call and really want to know what their life's mission is, perhaps find it the greatest problem they ever had. Some don't know just what profession or work to take up, and so I should like to take the call of Moses, and see if we cannot draw some lessons from it.

You remember when God met Moses at the burning bush and called him to do as great a work as any man has ever been called to in this world, that

He Thought The Lord Had Made A Mistake,

that he was not the man. He said, "Who am I?" He was very small in his own estimation. Forty years before he had started out as a good many others have started. He thought he was pretty well equipped for service. He had been in the schools of the Egyptians, he had been in the palaces of Egypt, he had moved in the *bon ton* society. He had had all the advantages any man could have when he started out, undoubtedly, without calling on the God of Abraham for wisdom and guidance, yet he broke down.

How many men have started out in some profession and made a failure of it! They haven't heard the voice of God, they haven't waited upon God for instruction.

I suppose Moses thought that the children of Israel would be greatly honored to know that a prince of the realm was going to take up their cause, but you remember how he lost his temper and killed the Egyptian, and the next day, when he interfered in a quarrel between two Hebrews, they wanted to know who had made him judge and ruler over them, and he had to flee into the desert, and was there for forty years hidden away. He killed the Egyptian and lost his influence thereby. Murder for liberty; wrong for right; it was a poor way to reform abuses, and Moses needed training.

It was a long time for God to keep him in His school, a long time for a man to wait in the prime of his life, from forty to eighty. Moses had been brought up with all the luxuries that Egypt could give him, and now he was a shepherd, and in the sight of the Egyptians a shepherd was an abomination. I have an idea that Moses started out with a great deal bigger head than heart. I believe that is the reason so many fail; they have

Big Heads And Little Hearts.

If a man has a shriveled-up heart and a big head, he is a monster. Perhaps Moses looked down on the Hebrews. There are many people who start out with the idea that they are great and other people are small, and they are going to bring them up on the high level with themselves. God never yet used a man of that stamp. Perhaps Moses was a slow scholar in God's school, and so He had to keep him there for forty years.

But now he is ready; he is just the man God wants, and God calls him. Moses said, "Who am I?" He was very small in his own eyes—just small enough so that God could use him. If you had asked the Egyptians who he was, they would have said he was

The Biggest Fool In The World.

"Why," they would say, "look at the opportunity that man had! He might have been commander of the Egyptian army, he might have been on the throne, swaying the scepter over the whole world, if he hadn't identified himself with those poor, miserable Hebrews! Think what an opportunity he has lost, and what a privilege he has thrown away!"

He had dropped out of the public mind for forty years, and they didn't know what had become of him, but God had His eye upon him. He was the very man of all others that God wanted, and when he met God with that question, "Who am I?" it didn't matter who *he* was but who his God was. When men learn the lesson that they are nothing and God is everything, then there is not a position in which God cannot use them. It was not Moses who accomplished that great work of redemption, for he was only the instrument in God's hand. God could have spoken to Pharaoh without Moses. He could have spoken in the voice of thunder, and broken the heart of Pharaoh with one speech, if He had wanted to, but He condescended to take up a human agent, and to use him. He could have sent Gabriel down, but he knew that Moses was the man wanted above all others, so He called him. God uses men to speak to men: He works through mediators. He could have accomplished the exodus of the children of Israel in a flash, but instead He chose to send a lonely and despised shepherd to work out His purpose through pain and disappointment. That was God's way in the Old Testament, and also in the New. He sent His own Son in the likeness of sinful flesh to be the mediator between God and man.

Moses went on making excuses and said, "When I go down there, who shall I say has sent me?" I suppose he remembered how he went before he was sent that other time, and he was afraid of a failure again. A man who has made a failure once is always afraid he will make another. He loses confidence in himself. It is a good thing to lose confidence in ourselves so as to gain confidence in God.

The Lord said, "Say unto them, 'I AM hath sent me.'"

Some one has said that God gave him

A Blank Check,

and all he had to do was to fill it out from that time on. When he wanted to bring water out of the rock, all he had to do was to fill out the check; when he wanted bread, all he had to do was to fill out the check and the bread came; he had a rich banker. God had taken him into partnership with Himself. God had made him His heir, and all he had to do was to look up to Him, and he got all he wanted.

And yet he seemed to draw back, and began to make another excuse, and said:

"They will not believe me."

He was afraid of the Israelites as well as of Pharaoh: he knew how hard it is to get even your friends to believe in you.

Now, if God has sent you and me with a message, it is not for us to say whether others will believe it or not. *We* cannot make men believe. If I have been sent by God to make men believe, He will give me power to make them believe. Jesus Christ didn't have that power; it is the work of the Holy Ghost; we cannot persuade men and overcome skepticism and infidelity unless we are baptized with the Holy Ghost and with power.

God told Moses that they *would* believe him, that he would succeed, and bring the children of Israel out of bondage. But Moses seemed to distrust even the God who had spoken to him.

Then the Lord said, "What is that in thy hand?"

He had a rod or staff, a sort of shepherd's crook, which he had cut haphazard when he had wanted something that would serve him in the desert.

"It is only a rod."

"With that you shall deliver the children of Israel; with that rod you shall make Israel believe that I am with you."

When God Almighty linked Himself to that rod, it was worth more than all the armies the world had ever seen. Look and see how that rod did its work. It brought up the plagues of flies, and the thunder storm, and turned the water into blood. It was not Moses, however, nor Moses' rod that did the work, but it was the God of the rod, the God of Moses. As long as God was with him, he could not fail.

Sometimes it looks as if God's servants fail. When Herod beheaded John the Baptist, it looked as if John's mission was a failure. But was it? The voice that rang through the valley of the Jordan rings through the whole world today. You can hear its echo upon the mountains and the valleys yet, "He must increase, but I must decrease." He held up Jesus Christ and introduced Him to the world, and Herod had not power to behead him until his life work had been accomplished. Stephen never preached but one sermon that we know of, and that was before the Sanhedrin; but how that sermon has been preached again and again all over the world! Out of his death probably came Paul, the greatest preacher the world has seen since Christ left this earth. If a man is sent by Jehovah, there is no such thing as failure. Was Christ's life a failure? See how His parables are going through the earth today. It looked as if the apostles had made a failure, but see how much has been accomplished. If you read the book of Acts, you will see that every seeming failure in Acts was turned into a great victory. Moses wasn't going to fail, although Pharaoh said with contempt, "Who is God that I should obey Him?" He found out who God was. He found out that there was a God.

But Moses made another excuse, and said, "I am slow of speech, slow of tongue." He said he was

Not An Orator.

My friends, we have too many orators. I am tired and sick of your "silver-tongued orators." I used to mourn because I couldn't be an orator. I thought, Oh, if I could only have the gift of speech like some men! I have heard men with a smooth flow of language take the audience captive, but they came and they went, their voice was like the air, there wasn't any *power* back of it; they trusted in their eloquence and their fine speeches. That is what Paul was thinking of when he wrote to the Corinthians—"My speech and my preaching was not with enticing words of man's wisdom, but in demonstration of the Spirit and of power: that your faith should not stand in the wisdom of men, but in the power of God."

Take a witness in court and let him try his oratorical powers in the witness-box, and see how quickly the judge will rule him out. It is the man who tells the plain, simple truth that has the most influence with the jury.

Suppose that Moses had prepared a speech for Pharaoh, and had got his hair all smoothly brushed, and had stood before the looking-glass or had gone to an elocutionist to be taught how to make an oratorical speech and how to make gestures. Suppose that he had buttoned his coat, put one hand in his chest, had struck an attitude and begun:

"The God of our fathers, the God of Abraham, Isaac, and Jacob, has commanded me to come into the presence of the noble King of Egypt."

I think they would have taken his head right off! They had Egyptians who could be as eloquent as Moses. It was not eloquence they wanted. When you see a man in the pulpit trying to show off his eloquence he is making a fool of himself and trying to make a fool of the people. Moses was slow of speech, but he had a message, and what God wanted was to have him deliver the message. But he insisted upon having an excuse. He didn't want to go; instead of being eager to act as heaven's messenger, to be God's errand boy, he wanted to excuse himself. The Lord humored him and gave him an interpreter, gave him Aaron.

Now, if there is a stupid thing in the world, it is to talk through an interpreter. I tried it once in Paris. I got up into a little box of a pulpit with the interpreter—there was hardly room enough for one. I said a sentence while he leaned away over to one side, and then I leaned over while he repeated it in French. Can you conceive of a more stupid thing than Moses going before Pharaoh and speaking through Aaron!

But this slow-of-speech man became eloquent. Talk about Gladstone's power to speak! Here is a man one hundred and twenty years old, and he waxed eloquent, as we see in Deuteronomy 32:1–4:

> Give ear, O ye heavens, and I will speak;
> And hear, O earth, the words of my mouth.
> My doctrine shall drop as the rain,
> My speech shall distil as the dew,
> As the small rain upon the tender herb,
> And as the showers upon the grass:
> Because I will publish the name of the Lord:
> Ascribe ye greatness unto our God.
> He is the Rock, his work is perfect:
> For all his ways are judgment:
> A God of truth and without iniquity,
> Just and right is he.

He turned out to be one of the most eloquent men the world has ever seen. If God sends men and they deliver His message, He will be with their mouth. If God has given you a message, go and give it to the people as God has given it to you. It is a stupid thing for a man to try to be eloquent. Make

Your Message, And Not Yourself,

the most prominent thing. Don't be self-conscious. Set your heart on what God has given you to do, and don't be so foolish as to let your own difficulties or your own abilities stand in the way. It is said that people would go to hear Cicero and would come away and say, "Did you ever hear anything like it? Wasn't it sublime? Wasn't it grand?" But they would go and hear Demosthenes, and he would fire them so with the subject that they would want to go and fight at once. They forgot all about Demosthenes, but were stirred by his message; that was the difference between the two men.

Next Moses said: "O my Lord, send, I pray thee, by the hand of him whom thou wilt send."

Did you ever stop to think what Moses would have lost if God had taken him at his word, and said:

"Very well, Moses; you may stay here in the desert, and I will send Aaron, or Joshua, or Caleb!"

Don't seek to be excused if God calls you to some service. What would the twelve disciples have lost if they had declined the call of Jesus! I have always pitied those other disciples of whom we read that they went back and walked no more with Jesus. Think what Orpah missed and what Ruth gained by cleaving to Naomi's God! Her story has been

Told These Three Thousand Years.

Father, mother, sisters, brothers, the grave of her husband— she turned her back on them all. Ruth, come back, and tell us if you regret your choice! No: her name shines one of the brightest among all the women that have ever lived. The Messiah was one of her descendants.

Moses, you come back and tell us if you were afterwards sorry that God had called you? I think that when he stood in glorified body on the Mount of Transfiguration with Jesus and Elijah, he did not regret it.

My dear friends, God is not confined to any one messenger. We are told that He can raise up children out of stones. Some one has said that there are three classes of people, the "wills," the "won'ts," and the "can'ts"; the first accomplish everything, the second oppose everything, and the third fail in everything. If God calls you, consider it a great honor. Consider it a great privilege to have partnership with Him in anything. Do it cheerfully, gladly. Do it with all your heart, and He will bless you. Don't let false modesty or insincerity, self-interest, or any personal consideration turn you aside from the path of duty and sacrifice. If we listen for God's voice, we shall hear the call; and if He calls and sends us, there will be no such thing as failure, but success all along the line. Moses had glorious success because he went forward and did what God called him to do.

5

THE FAITH WHICH OVERCOMES

Humility

There is no harder lesson to learn than the lesson of humility. It is not taught in the schools of men, only in the school of Christ. It is the rarest of all the gifts. Very rarely do we find a man or woman who is following closely the footsteps of the Master in meekness and in humility. I believe that it is the hardest lesson which Jesus Christ had to teach His disciples while He was here upon earth. He said: "Learn of me; for I am meek and lowly in heart" (Matthew 11: 29). It looked at first as though He had failed to teach it to the twelve men who had been with Him almost constantly for three years.

I believe that if we are humble enough we shall be sure to get a great blessing. After all, I think that more depends upon us than upon the Lord; because He is always ready to give a blessing and give it freely, but we are not always in a position to receive it. He always blesses the humble; and, if we can get down in the dust before Him, no one will go away disappointed. It was Mary at the feet of Jesus, who had chosen the "better part."

Did you ever notice the reason Christ gave for learning of Him? He might have said: "Learn of Me, because I am the most advanced thinker of the age. I have performed miracles that no man else has performed. I have shown My supernatural power in a thousand ways." But no: the reason He gave was that He was "meek and lowly in heart."

We read of the three men in Scripture whose faces shone, and all three were noted for their meekness and humility. We are told that the face of Christ shone at His transfiguration; Moses, after he had been in the mount for forty days, came down from his communion with God with a shining face; and when Stephen stood before the Sanhedrin on the day of his death, his face was lighted up with glory. If our faces are to shine, we must get into the valley of humility; we must go down in the dust before God.

Bunyan says that it is hard to get down into the valley of humiliation, the descent into it is steep and rugged; but that it is very fruitful and fertile and beautiful once we get there. I think that no one will dispute that; almost every man, even the ungodly, admires meekness.

Some one asked Augustine, what was the first of the religious graces, and he said "Humility." He asked him what was the second, and he replied, "Humility." He asked him the third, and he said, "Humility." I think that if we are humble, we have all the graces.

Some years ago I saw what is called a sensitive plant. I happened to breathe on it, and suddenly it drooped its head; I touched it, and it shrank up. Humility is as sensitive as that; it cannot safely be brought out on exhibition. A man who is flattering himself that he is humble and is walking close to the Master is self-deceived. It consists not in thinking meanly of ourselves, but in not thinking of ourselves at all. Moses wished not that his face shone. If humility speaks of itself, it is gone.

It has been remarked that the grass is an illustration of this lowly grace. It was created for the lowliest service. Cut it, and it springs up again. The cattle feed upon it, and yet how beautiful it is.

The showers fall upon the mountain peaks, and very often leave them barren because they rush down into the meadows and valleys and make the lowly places fertile. If a man is proud and lifted up, rivers of grace may flow over him and yet leave him barren and unfruitful; while they bring blessing to the man who has been brought low by the grace of God.

A man can counterfeit love, he can counterfeit faith, he can counterfeit hope, and all the other graces; but it is very difficult to counterfeit humility. You soon detect mock humility. They have a saying in the East among the Arabs, that as the tares and the wheat grow they show which God has blessed. The ears that God has blessed bow their heads and acknowledge every grain, and the more fruitful they are the lower their heads are bowed. The tares which God has sent as a curse, lift up their heads erect, high above the wheat; but they are only fruitful of evil. I have a pear tree on my farm which is very beautiful; it appears to be one of the most beautiful trees I possess. Every branch seems to be reaching up to the light and stands almost like a wax candle; but I never get any fruit from it. I have another tree, which was so full of fruit last year that the branches almost touched the ground. If we only get down low enough, my friends, God will use every one of us to His glory.

"As the lark that soars the highest builds her nest the lowest; as the nightingale that sings so sweetly, sings in the shade when all things rest; as the branches that are most laden with fruit, bend lowest; as the ship most laden, sinks deepest in the water—so the holiest Christians are the humblest."

The newspapers some years ago told the story of a petition that was being circulated for signatures. It was a time of great excitement, and this petition was intended to have great influence in the House of Lords; but there was one word left out. Instead of reading, "We humbly beseech thee," it read, "We beseech thee." So it was ruled out. My friends, if we want to make an appeal to the God of heaven, we must humble ourselves; and if we do humble ourselves before the Lord, we shall not be disappointed.

As I have been studying some Bible characters that illustrate humility, I have been ashamed of myself. If you have any regard for me, pray that I may have humility. When I put my life beside the life of some of these men, I say, Shame on the Christianity of the present day! If you want to get a good idea of yourself, look at some of the Bible characters that have been clothed with meekness and humility, and see what a contrast is your position before God and man.

One of the meekest characters in history was John the Baptist. You remember when a deputation was sent to him and asked if he was Elias, or this prophet, or that prophet, he said, "No." Now he might have said some very flattering things of himself. He might have said:

"I am the son of the old priest Zacharias. Have you not heard of my fame as a preacher? I have baptized more people, probably, than any man living. The world has never seen a preacher like myself."

I honestly believe that in the present day most men standing in his position would do that. In the train, some time ago, I heard a man talking so loudly that all the people in the carriage could hear him. He said that he had baptized more people than any man in his denomination. He told how many thousand miles he had traveled, how many sermons he had preached, how many open-air services he had held, and this and that, until I was so ashamed that I had to hide my head. This is the age of boasting. It is the day of the great "I."

My attention was recently called to the fact that in all the

Psalms you cannot find any place where David refers to his victory over the giant Goliath. If it had been in the present day, there would have been a volume written about it at once; I do not know how many poems there would be telling of the great things that this man had done. He would have been in demand as a lecturer, and would have added a title to his name: G.G.K.—Great Giant Killer. That is how it is today: great evangelists, great preachers, great theologians, great bishops.

"John," they asked, "who are you?"

"I am nobody. I am to be heard, not to be seen. I am only a voice."

He had not a word to say about himself. I once heard a little bird faintly singing close by me; at last it got clear out of sight, and then its notes were still sweeter. The higher it flew the sweeter sounded its notes. If we can only get self out of sight, and learn of Him who was meek and lowly of heart, we shall be lifted up into heavenly places.

Mark tells us, in the first chapter and seventh verse, that John came and preached, saying, "There cometh one mightier than I after me, the latchet of whose shoes I am not worthy to stoop down and unloose." Think of that; and bear in mind that Christ was looked upon as a deceiver, a village carpenter, and yet here is John, the son of the old priest, who had a much higher position in the sight of men than that of Jesus. Great crowds were coming to hear him, and even Herod attended his meetings.

When his disciples came and told John that Christ was beginning to draw crowds, he nobly answered: "A man can receive nothing, except it be given him from heaven. Ye yourselves bear me witness that I said, I am not the Christ, but that I am sent before him. He that hath the bride is the bridegroom: but the friend . . . rejoiceth greatly because of the bridegroom's voice: this my joy therefore is fulfilled. He must increase, but I must decrease."

It is easy to read that, but it is hard for us to live in the power of it. It is very hard for us to be ready to decrease, to grow smaller and smaller, that Christ may increase. The morning star fades away when the sun rises.

"He that cometh from above is above all: he that is of the earth is earthly, and speaketh of the earth: he that cometh from heaven is above all. And what he hath seen and heard, that he testifieth; and no man receiveth his testimony. He that hath received his testimony hath set to his seal that God is true. For he whom God hath sent speaketh the words of God: for God giveth not the Spirit by measure unto him."

Let us now turn the light upon ourselves. Have we been decreasing of late? Do we think less of ourselves and of our position than we did a year ago? Are we seeking to obtain some position of dignity? Are we wanting to hold on to some title, and are we offended because we are not treated with the courtesy that we think is due to us? Some time ago I heard a man in the pulpit say that he should take offense if he was not addressed by his title. My dear friend, are you going to take that position that you must have a title, or you will be offended? John did not want any title, and when we are right with God, we shall not be caring about titles. In one of his early epistles Paul calls himself the "least of the apostles." Later on he claims to be "less than the least of all saints"; and again, just before his death, humbly declares that he is the "chief of sinners." Notice how he seems to have grown smaller and smaller in his own estimation. So it was with John. And I do hope and pray that as the days go by we may feel like hiding ourselves, and letting God have all the honor and glory.

"When I look back upon my own religious experience," says Andrew Murray, "or round upon the Church of Christ in the world, I stand amazed at the thought of how little humility is sought after as the distinguishing feature of the discipleship of Jesus. In preaching and living, in the daily intercourse of the home and social life, in the more special fellowship with Christians, in the direction and performance of work for Christ—alas! how much proof there is that humility is not esteemed the cardinal virtue, the only root from which the graces can grow, the one indispensable condition of true fellowship with Jesus."

See what Christ says about John. "He was a burning and a shining light." Christ gave him the honor that belonged to him. If you take a humble position, Christ will see it. If you want God to help you, then take a low position.

I am afraid that if we had been in John's place, many of us would have said: "What did Christ say?—I am a burning and a shining light." Then we would have had that recommendation put in the newspapers, and would have sent them to our friends, with that part marked in blue pencil. Sometimes I get a letter just full of clippings from the newspapers, stating that this man is more eloquent than John Gough, etc. And the man wants me to get him some church. Do you think that a man who has such eloquence would be looking for a church? No, they would all be looking for him.

My dear friends, is it not humiliating? Sometimes I think it is a wonder that any man is converted these days. Let another praise you. Do not be always praising yourself. If we want God to lift us up, let us get down. The lower we get, the higher God will lift us. It is Christ's eulogy of John, "Greater than any man born of woman."

There is a story told of Carey, the great missionary, that he was invited by the Governor-General of India to go to a dinner party at which were some military officers belonging to the aristocracy, and who looked down upon missionaries with scorn and contempt.

One of these officers said at the table: "I believe that Carey was a shoemaker, was he not, before he took up the profession of a missionary?"

Mr. Carey spoke up and said: "Oh, no, I was only a cobbler. I could mend shoes, and was not ashamed of it."

The one prominent virtue of Christ, next to His obedience, is His humility; and even His obedience grew out of His humility. Being in the form of God, He counted it not a thing to be grasped to be on an equality with God; but He emptied Himself, taking the form of a bond-servant, and was made in the likeness of men. And being found in fashion as a man, He humbled Himself, and became obedient unto death, yea, the death of the cross. In His lowly birth, His submission to His earthly parents, His seclusion during thirty years, His consorting with the poor and despised, His entire submission and dependence upon His Father, this virtue that was consummated in His death on the cross shines out.

One day Jesus was on His way to Capernaum, and was talking about His coming death and suffering, and about His resurrection, and He heard quite a heated discussion going on behind Him. When He came into the house at Capernaum, He turned to His disciples, and said:

"What was all that discussion about?"

I see John look at James, and Peter at Andrew—and they all seem ashamed. "Who shall be the greatest?" That discussion had wrecked party after party, one society after another—"Who shall be the greatest?"

The way Christ taught them humility was by putting a little child in their midst and saying: "If you want to be great, take that little child for an example; and he who wants to be the greatest, let him be servant of all."

To me, one of the saddest things in all the life of Jesus Christ was the fact that just before His crucifixion, His disciples should have been striving to see who should be the greatest, that night when He instituted the Supper, and they ate the Passover together. It was His last night on earth, and they never saw Him so sorrowful before. He knew Judas was going to sell Him for thirty pieces of silver. He knew that Peter would deny Him. And yet, in addition to this, when going into the very shadow of the cross, there arose this strife as to who should be the greatest. He took a towel and girded Himself like a slave, and He took a basin of water and stooped and washed their feet. That was another object lesson of humility. He said, "Ye call Me Lord, and ye do well. If you want to be great in my Kingdom, be servant of all. If you serve, you shall be great."

When the Holy Ghost came, and those men were filled, from that time on mark the difference: Matthew takes up his pen to write, and he keeps Matthew out of sight. He tells what Peter and Andrew did; but he calls himself Matthew "the publican." He tells how they left all to follow Christ, but does not mention the feast he gave. Jerome says that Mark's gospel is to be regarded as memoirs of Peter's discourses, and to have been published by his authority. Yet here we constantly find that damaging things are mentioned about Peter, and things to his credit are not referred to. Mark's gospel omits all allusion to Peter's faith in venturing on the sea, but goes into detail about the story of his fall and denial of our Lord. Peter put himself down, and lifted others up.

If the gospel of Luke had been written today, it would be signed by the great Dr. Luke, and you would have his photograph as a frontispiece. But you cannot find Luke's name; he keeps out of sight. He wrote two books, and his name is not to be found in either. John covers himself always under the expression—"the disciple whom Jesus loved." None of the four men whom history and tradition assert to be the authors of the Gospels, lay claim to the authorship in their writings. Dear man of God, I would that I had the same spirit, that I could just get out of sight—hide myself.

My dear friends, I believe our only hope is to be filled with the Spirit of Christ. May God fill us, so that we shall be filled with meekness and humility. Let us take the hymn, "Oh to Be Nothing, Nothing!" and make it the language of our hearts. It breathes the spirit of Him who said: "The Son can do *nothing* of himself!"

"Oh to be nothing, nothing!
Only to lie at his feet,
A broken and emptied vessel,
For the Master's use made meet.
Emptied, that He might fill me
As forth to his service I go;
Broken, that so unhindered,
His life through me might flow.
Broken, that so unhindered,
His life through me might flow."

6

SOWING AND REAPING

Forgiveness and Retribution

I can imagine some one saying, "I attend church, and have heard that if we confess our sin, God will forgive us; now I hear that I must reap the same kind of seed that I have sown. How can I harmonize the doctrine of forgiveness with the doctrine of retribution? 'All we like sheep have gone astray; we have turned every one to his own way, and the Lord hath laid on him the iniquity of us all.' And yet you say that I must reap what I have sown."

Suppose I send my hired man to sow wheat. When it grows up, there are thistles mixed with the wheat. There wasn't a thistle a year ago. I say to my man:

"Do you know anything about the thistles in the field?"

He says: "Yes, I do; you sent me to sow that wheat, and I was angry and mixed some thistles with the wheat. But you promised me that if I ever did wrong and confessed it, you would forgive me; now I hold you to that promise, and expect you to forgive me."

"Yes," I say, "you are quite right; I forgive you for sowing the thistles; but I will tell you what you must do—you must reap the thistles along with the wheat when harvest time comes."

Many a Christian man is reaping thistles with his wheat. Twenty years ago you sowed thistles with the wheat and are reaping them now. Perhaps it was an obscene story, the memory of which keeps coming back to distress you, even at the most solemn moments. Perhaps some hasty word or deed that you have never been able to recall.

I heard John B. Gough say that he would rather cut off his hand than have committed a certain sin. He didn't say what it was, but I have always supposed it was the way he treated his mother. He was a wretched, drunken sot in the gutter when his mother died;

the poor woman couldn't stand it, and died of a broken heart. God had forgiven him, but he never forgave himself. A great many have done things that they will never forgive themselves for to their dying day. "At this moment," said one, "from many a harlot's dishonored grave there arises a mute appeal for righteous retribution. From many a drunkard's miserable home, from heartbroken wife, from starving children, there rings up a terrible appeal into the ears of God."

I believe that God forgives sin fully and freely for Christ's sake; but He allows certain penalties to remain. If a man has wasted years in riotous living, he can never hope to live them over again. If he has violated his conscience, the scars will remain through life. If he has soiled his reputation, the effect of it can never be washed away. If he shatters his body through indulgence and vice, he must suffer until death. As Talmage says, "The grace of God gives a new heart, but not a new body."

"John," said a father to his son, "I wish you would get me the hammer."

"Yes, sir."

"Now a nail and a piece of pine board."

"Here they are, sir."

"Will you drive the nail into the board?"

It was done.

"Please pull it out again."

"That's easy, sir."

"Now, John," and the father's voice dropped to a lower key, "pull out the nail hole."

Every wrong act leaves a scar. Even if the board be a living tree the scar remains.

"For our worse sins there is plenteous redemption. My sin may become white as snow, and pass away altogether, in so far as it has power to disturb or sadden my relation to God. Yet our least sins leave in our lives, in our characters, in our memories, in our consciences, sometimes in our weakness, often in our worldly position, in our reputation, in our success, in our health, in a thousand ways leave their traces and consequences. God will not put out His little finger to remove these, but lets them stay.

"Let no man fancy that the Gospel which proclaims forgiveness can be vulgarized into a mere proclamation of impunity. Not so. It was to *Christian men* that Paul said, 'Be not deceived; God is not mocked: for whatsoever a man soweth, that shall he also reap.'

God loves us too well not to punish His children when they sin, and He loves us too well to annihilate (were it possible) the *secondary* consequences of our transgressions. The two sides of the truth must be recognized—that the deeper and (as we call them) the *primary* penalties of our evil, which are separation from God and the painful consciousness of guilt, are swept away; and also that other results are allowed to remain, which being allowed, may be blessed and salutary for the transgressors."

MacLaren says, "If you waste your youth, no repentance will send the shadow back upon the dial, or recover the ground lost by idleness, or restore the constitution shattered by dissipation, or give back the resources wasted upon vice, or bring back the fleeting opportunities. The wounds can all be healed, for the Good Physician, blessed be His name! has lancets and bandages, and balm and anodynes for the deadliest; but scars remain even when the gash is closed."

God forgave Moses and Aaron for their sins, but both suffered the penalty. Neither one was permitted to enter the Promised Land. Jacob became a "prince of God" at the ford of Jabbok, but to the end of his days he carried in his body the mark of the struggle. Paul's thorn in the flesh was not removed, even after most earnest and repeated prayer. It lost its sting, however, and became a means of grace.

Perhaps that is one reason why God does not remove these penalties of sin. He may intend them to be used as tokens of His chastening. "Whom the Lord loveth he chasteneth." And if the temporal consequences were completely removed, we would be liable to fall back again into sin. Then penalty is a continual reminder of our weakness, and of the need of caution and dependence upon God.

One night in Chicago at the close of a meeting in the Y.M.C.A. rooms, a young man sprang to his feet and said: "Mr. Moody, would you let me speak a few words?"

I said, "Certainly."

Then for about five minutes he pleaded with those men to break from sin. He said:

"If you have anyone who takes any interest in your spiritual welfare, treat them kindly, for they are the best friends you have. I was an only child, and my mother and father took great interest in me. Every morning at the family altar Father used to pray for me, and every night he would commend me to God. I was wild and reckless and didn't like the restraint of home. When my father died my mother took up the family worship. Many a time she came to me and said, 'Oh, my boy, if you would stay to family worship, I should be the happiest mother on earth; but when I pray, you don't even stay in the house.' Sometimes I would go in at midnight from a night of dissipation and hear my mother praying for me. Sometimes in the small hours of morning I heard her voice pleading for me. At last I felt that I must either become a Christian or leave home, and one day I gathered a few things together and stole away from home without letting my mother know.

"Some time after, I heard indirectly that my mother was ill. Ah, I thought, it is my conduct that is making her ill! My first impulse was to go home and cheer her last days; but the thought came that if I did I should have to become a Christian. My proud heart revolted and I said: 'No, I will not become a Christian.'"

Months rolled by, and at last he heard again that his mother was worse. Then he thought:

"If my mother should not live, I would never forgive myself."

That thought took him home. He reached the old village about dark, and started on foot for the home which was about a mile and a half distant. On the way he passed the graveyard, and thought he would go to his father's grave to see if there was a newly made grave beside it. As he drew near the spot, his heart began to beat faster, and when he came near enough, the light of the moon shone on a newly-made grave. With a great deal of emotion he said:

"Young men, for the first time in my life this question came over me—who is going to pray for my lost soul now? Father is gone, and Mother is gone, and they are the only two who ever cared for me. If I could have called my mother back that night and heard her breathe my name in prayer, I would have given the world if it had been mine to give. I spent all that night by her grave, and God, for Christ's sake, heard my mother's prayers, and I became a child of God. But I never forgave myself for the way I treated my mother, and never will."

"Where is my wandering boy tonight—
The boy of my tenderest care,
The boy that was once my joy and light
The child of my love and prayer?
Once he was pure as morning dew,
As he knelt at his mother's knee;
No face was so bright, no heart more true

And none was so sweet as he.
O, could I see you now, my boy,
As fair as in olden time,
When prattle and smile made home a joy,
And life was a merry chime.
Go for my wandering boy tonight,
Go, search for him where you will;
But bring him to me with all his blight,
And tell him I love him still."

My dear friends, God may forgive you, but the consequences of your sin are going to be bitter even if you are forgiven.

A few years ago I was preaching in Chicago on that text, "Arise, go up to Bethel, and dwell there." After the meeting a man asked to see me alone. I went into a private room. The perspiration stood in beads on his forehead. I said:

"What is it?"

He replied: "I am a fugitive from justice. I am in exile, in disguise. The government of my state has offered a reward for me. I have been hidden here for months. They tell me there is no hell, but it seems as though I have been in hell for months."

He had been a business man, and having, as he thought, plenty of money, he forged some bonds, thinking that he could give his check any time and call them in, but he got beyond his depth and fell.

He said, "I have been here for six months. I have a wife and three children, but I cannot write to them or hear from them." The poor man was in terrible mental agony.

I said, "Why don't you go back and give yourself up and face the law, and ask God to forgive you?"

He said, "I would take the first train tomorrow and give myself up, except for one thing. I have a wife and three children; how can I bring the disgrace upon them?"

I, too, have a wife and three children, and when he said that, the thing looked very different.

Ah! If we could do our own reaping, it would not be so bitter, but when we make our little children or the wife of our bosom, or our old gray-haired mother, or our old father reap with us, isn't the reaping pretty bitter? I don't fear any pestilence or any disease as much as I fear this. If God will only keep sin out of my family, I will praise Him in time and in eternity. The worst enemy that ever crossed a man's path is sin.

If a man comes to me for advice, I always try to put myself in the place of the one to whom I am talking, and then to give the best advice I can. I said to this man,

"I don't know what to say, but it is safe to pray."

After I had prayed, I urged him to pray; but he said:

"If I do, it means the penitentiary."

I asked him to come the next day at twelve. He met me at the appointed hour, and said:

"It is all settled; if I ever meet the God of Bethel, I must go through the prison to meet Him, and God helping me, I will give myself up. I am going back, and I should like to have you keep quiet until I give myself over into the hands of the law; then you may hold me up as a warning. Little did I think when I started out in life that I was coming to this! Little did I think when I married a girl from one of the first families in the state that I should bring such disgrace on her." At four o'clock that afternoon he went back to Missouri. He reached home a little past midnight, and spent a week with his family. In a letter he said that he didn't dare let his children know he was there, lest they should tell the neighbor's children. At night he would creep out and look at his children, but he couldn't take them into his arms or kiss them. Oh, there is the result of sin! Would to God we could every one of us just turn from sin today!

One day, when this man was in hiding, he heard his little boy say:

"Mamma, doesn't Papa love us any more?"

"Yes," his mother replied. "Why do you ask?"

"Why," the little fellow said, "he has been gone so long and he never writes us any letters and never comes to see us."

The last night he came out from hiding and took a long look at those innocent, sleeping children; then he took his wife and kissed her again and again, and leaving that once happy home he gave himself up to the sheriff. The next morning he pleaded guilty, and was sent to the penitentiary for nineteen years. I believe that God had forgiven him, but he couldn't forgive himself, and he had to reap what he sowed. I pleaded with the governor for mercy, and the man was pardoned.

Some time ago I was telling this story, and some one doubted it, but the governor who pardoned him happened to be in the meeting, and rose and said, "I pardoned that man myself." The governor pardoned him, and he lived a few years, but from the time he committed that sin he had to reap. Oh, I can imagine some one saying,

"I am glad Mr. Moody hasn't tried to scare us about the future state. I agree with him that we shall receive all our reward and punishment in this life."

If you think I believe that, you are greatly mistaken. One sentence from the lips of the Son of God in regard to the future state has forever settled it in my mind. *"If ye die in your sins, where I am, there ye cannot go."* If a man has not given up his drunkenness, his profanity, his licentiousness, his covetousness, heaven would be hell to him. Heaven is a prepared place for prepared people. What would a man do in heaven who cannot bear to be in the society of the pure and holy down here?

It is not true that all reward and punishment is reaped in this life. Look how many crimes are committed, and the perpetrators are never caught. It often happens that the worst criminal uses his experience to escape detection, while a more innocent hand is captured. A man ruins a girl. Does he always reap punishment here? No. He holds his head as high as ever in society, while the unfortunate victim of his lust, who, perhaps, was innocently beguiled into sin by him, becomes an outcast. His punishment, however, is, at the latest, only adjourned to another world.

7

THE PERIL OF UNBELIEF
AND THE DANGER OF DOUBT

The Danger of Doubt

I was preaching once in the north of Scotland, in one of those towns that have a church large enough to take the whole town in. They have some Presbyterian churches in the north of Scotland large enough to accommodate the whole churchgoing community. This town had a church large enough to hold 2,500. I don't think I ever heard in my life the Twenty-third Psalm sung as it was sung in that church—"The Lord is my shepherd, I shall not want." And I sat and heard it; and it seemed as if the whole town was there—men, women and children—all singing very heartily that beautiful old Psalm.

After I got through preaching, I thought I would put a test and see how many could sing it from the heart. I said: "I never heard the Twenty-third Psalm sung as at the opening of this meeting; and I was wondering how many sang it from the heart and could say the Lord was their Shepherd. Now, I will put a test: All who can sing it from the heart and who can claim Christ as your Shepherd, won't you rise and sing it?" About fifty to sixty got up—some not half-way up—and I felt as if I had never heard it sung so poorly in my life.

IMPEDIMENTS TO ASSURANCE

Assurance is another word for our subject this morning. I once read of a couple of men who had their property burned out. They were away from the town while the fire attacked both of their houses. One man, when he heard of it, went almost wild, while the other was as calm as the summer evening. What was the difference? One had his property insured for its full value, and the other had no insurance. One lost everything; the other was fully insured. And, do you know, I believe that assurance is going to give us peace and rest in the hour of trial and in the testing time; therefore I believe it is a very vital subject.

Now, before I speak further, I want to say that there are three classes of people in our churches who have not got assurance, and I don't think it's the mind of God that they should have assurance. The first class is the people who have united with the church, but have never been "born of God," "of the Spirit," and never "became partakers of the divine nature." They have united with the church, perhaps persuaded by some minister or by some friend and thinking it might lead to their conversion. They have not been "born of the Spirit," and they will never have the assurance, until they have been "born from above."

Second, those not willing to "confess Christ." "Ashamed of Christ and His Word." Romans 10:9–11 says: "If thou shalt confess with thy mouth the Lord Jesus, and shalt believe in thine heart that God hath raised him from the dead, thou shalt be saved. For with the heart, man believeth unto righteousness; and with the mouth confession is made unto salvation. For the scripture saith, Whosoever believeth on him shall not be ashamed." Now, if I believe with my heart, and yet am ashamed to confess Christ and to "take my stand," I surely will not have assurance. We have got to confess Christ. "If any man be my disciple, let him take up his cross and come and follow me."

When I was in London, I heard of a certain minister. Many people were joining the churches, and he was not in the movement but stood outside, and many of his own people were going and joining other churches and he did not like it. He gave out a notice stating that if there was anyone in his congregation who wanted to be taken into the church privately he would take them in; but no one came in. I wouldn't give the snap of my finger for ten thousand church members who would "join privately" and who were ashamed to confess Jesus Christ. Such a man isn't worthy of being a disciple of Jesus Christ. He may believe with the heart, but he must "confess Christ" with the mouth.

Third, there is the class who aren't willing to "go to work." A man may believe and may confess, but if he isn't willing to go out into the harvest field and go to work, he will not have assurance. I believe that's the reason many people go on all through life without assurance—because they are not willing to do some work for the Master.

HOW TO GET RID OF DOUBTS

Some one said to me: "Don't you ever have any doubts?" I said: "I don't have any time to doubt." Some people are full of doubts because they have nothing else to do—doubts in the morning and at the dinner table, and doubts at the tea table; they get up on doubts, and live on them, and sleep on them, and think "doubts," "doubts," "doubts" all the time. If you get engaged in the Lord's work, and see the Lord answering your prayers, away go your doubts! I think I'd as soon doubt my existence as doubt that God answered my prayers. How is one going to doubt when he sees a man getting out of the pit and standing for five, ten, twenty years? In some places you find leading citizens standing very high in the church and in the places of business. And people say they can't help but doubt. My friend, you can get rid of doubts if you'll take God's way. First, believe with your heart. Next, confess it. Next, don't be ashamed of it, but go to work. Away go your doubts! It is the privilege of every child of God to know, if he will take pains to hunt up the evidence. It is his privilege. I don't believe it is the will of God in this world that I should not know whether I am saved or not. I don't believe it's the will of God that I should go on with a terrible uncertainty whether I am a child of God or of the devil. I believe God gives certain landmarks. It is a privilege; but no one, no man or woman, is qualified for God's work who has not assurance of God's salvation. If I were in the river and didn't have a firm grip on something, I couldn't help anybody; but when I put my feet on the shore, I am the man to help somebody else. I've got to get a good hold for myself before I can help some one else. There's no liberty, peace, rest, joy, power, until we have assurance!

Now, you want to keep that in mind—when you are sure of your own salvation, you are the one to go to the help of some one else. If I were blind, I'd be the last man to help a blind man. We want to make sure that we've got salvation and are His, and then we are ready for His service.

THE GOSPEL GUARANTEE

There are three lines on which Satan works: First, he keeps a man from believing. Then, after a man does believe, he does all he can to fill that man with doubts and fears; and if he doesn't succeed in that, and the man still has a "ringing testimony," he casts some "lie" on that man and blackens his testimony and cripples his character, if he can. He works on these lines. And if a man is going to be a disciple of Christ, he has got to come out even if there be an "evil report" about him. Never mind. If a man takes his character—his reputation—to God, God will take care of it. There's no trouble with the reputation if the character be all right.

Let me read John 20:31: "These are written, that ye might believe that Jesus is the Christ, the Son of God; and that believing ye might have life through his name." That Gospel was written with just one thought in mind—to prove that Jesus Christ was divine. If I wanted to convince a man that Jesus Christ was divine, I'd go to the Gospel of John. Every chapter but two speaks of "believing." The word "believe" occurs ninety-eight times in that Gospel. That's the key to that Gospel. Turn over to John's Epistles, and you'll find what he wrote that epistle for: the thirteenth verse of the fifth chapter of the First Epistle of John: "These things have I written unto you that believe on the name of the Son of God; that ye may know that ye have eternal life, and that ye may believe on the name of the Son of God." The Gospel was written that we might believe in Jesus Christ, and this epistle was written that we might know that we are in His family and belong to the household of faith.

A man said to me: "Can you recommend to me a good book on assurance?" "Yes." "Where will I get it?" "There was a very fine book written by a man named John, the son of Zebedee." "An Englishman, the author?" "No; the son of Zebedee." "Where can I get it?" "Most any bookstore." "What shall I call for?" "It is bound up with some other books, called the Bible. It's better than all the infidel books that come out, and you better read it and study it; and if you will take a few weeks on that epistle, you'll find out whether you're in the kingdom of God or not."

1 John 3:4: "Whosoever committeth sin transgresseth also the law: for sin is the transgression of the law." Fifth verse: "And ye know that he was manifested to take away our sins; and in him is no sin." Sixth verse: "Whosoever abideth in him sinneth not: whosoever sinneth hath not seen him, neither known him."

Now notice that fifth verse: "He was manifested to take away our sins." That's the first thing—the starting point. There's no assurance until we see that's true; that Jesus Christ was manifested to take away the sins of the world by the sacrifice of Himself. He forever settles the question of sin by His own death, and we start from there. "We know he was manifested to take away our sins." The rest will follow. You can't atone for your sins. Your tears can't atone for them. But "Jesus Christ was manifested to take away our sins." Five things worth knowing: "Jesus Christ was manifested to take away our sins." There's no abiding peace until you see the finished work of Jesus Christ. And it is a thing settled: Jesus Christ has put away sin. Then, the next thing worth naming is: "Hereby we know that we are of the truth, and shall assure our hearts before him. For if our heart condemn us, God is greater than our heart." "Beloved, if our heart condemn us not, then have we confidence toward God."

THE TRUTH THAT MAKES US FREE

Now, notice. "Hereby know we the truth." People say: "It makes no difference what we believe, if we are sincere and honest." It is one of the greatest delusions of the enemy of souls that it makes no difference what the man believes or has as a creed, if he is sincere. I don't know how many times a man has said to me: "Mr. Moody, you don't have an idea that what a man believes makes any difference, does it? A man may be a Mohammedan, or a Mormon, or a Confucian; let him only hold on to it and stick to it, and he will be all right."

Suppose you go down to the First National Bank and put in a check for $10,000, and the cashier says: "Have you any money in this bank?" You answer: "Why, no." "Well, what are you drawing your check for, then?" "Earnestness," you say. Now no man is more earnest than I. But they would have me in the lunatic asylum before the sun was down if I did that. Believe a lie as well as the truth, and stick to it? Hold on to it? John says: "We know that we have the truth." It is the *truth that "makes us free."* Lies bring us into bondage, but the truth brings liberty. A man who believes truth can stand on his feet; he knows what he believes. I pity those men who live on "negatives," on what they "don't believe." I met a man some time ago, and he said he didn't believe this and he didn't believe that, and he told me forty things he "didn't believe." I said: "Will you tell me what you do believe?" And the poor fellow didn't know what he did believe! I'm tired and sick of that kind of thing. If it's the *truth*, my friends, stick to it; hold on to it; but if it's not true, give it up.

TWO MEN AND A BALLOON

I heard of two men arranging to go up in a balloon, and they thought the car was fastened to the balloon in two places. One of the men seized hold of the car, which wasn't well fastened to the balloon, and the other seized hold of the rope of the balloon. One went up toward heaven and the other was dashed to pieces when he came falling down. Man, keep hold of the truth, and it will make you free: you don't want to take this man's or that man's creed; go to the Book and see what the Lord Himself says.

We know that we are passed from death unto life, because we love the brethren. "He that hateth his brother, abideth in life." What's the matter? "Something gone wrong there, brother." I thought I would read the passage the way we live it, and see how it sounds. A lot of people do that. Some one has said to them that something has gone wrong, and they go to nursing themselves, and wondering why it is they haven't got assurance. Now, we'll read it the way John wrote it. "We know, because we love the brethren." "Because we love the brethren." "He that loveth not his brother abideth in death." I wouldn't give a penny for the most magnificent creed I know of on earth, if there's no life in it. What do I care for a man's creed that has no life in it? "We know that we have passed from death unto life." How? "Because we love the brethren."

Take an unrenewed man—a man never quickened by the Spirit of God, and in whose heart the Holy Ghost has never shed abroad the love of God—tell me, how can he pray for an enemy? He can't do it. But, not only that, but you can love the brethren. Love must be spontaneous, and it will be so when I've been born from above and become a partaker of the divine nature. "By this shall all men know that ye are my disciples, if ye have love to one another."

LOVE ESSENTIAL

I have never seen a man full of love in Europe or in this country who has doubts. It makes no difference where we find them. I believe a man's religion, if it hasn't love in it, isn't worth having. If I had my way, I'd sweep away every church out of existence that didn't manifest love. That's what makes infidels. That's what draws men away from Christ and Christianity; that form of church has alienated the workingmen. "By love shall all men know that ye are my disciples." Nihilism, atheism, and every form of evil would flee away, if we were baptized with love.

And then we wouldn't have to be urged to work. That's the kind of Christianity. One city needs it as much as every other city. We find men sitting down and discussing theology, and very often they don't know what theology is nor what they are talking about. Some say they believe what the Church believes. I ask what does the Church believe? "What I believe," they say. They don't know any difference!

Now, let us read that again. "We *know*"—we don't *guess;* we don't *hope,* but we *know*—"because we love the brethren." Now mark: It is not only those who "love me"; but those who love men who may not love me, and we are to do them a kindness. To heap coals of fire upon the head of a sinner—that takes the love of God. Have you got it? If you haven't, you should throw your hope to the four winds and come and get a better one. Your hope is no good if you haven't got love in your heart. "Because we love the brethren."

ANOTHER THING WORTH KNOWING

The next thing worth knowing is this: "He that hateth his brother, abideth in darkness." If a man cultivates hate, he is in trouble. That man hasn't got assurance. There has been a family feud down in the Kentucky mountains for many years, and how many do you suppose have been murdered? Forty people or more—families on both sides. Cultivated hate—don't you see? People say they can't tell a child of God from one who isn't. *You* can tell very quickly; you don't go to a minister to find that out; you get into their house and live with them, and you can soon tell. If you want to find out whether a man is a Christian, you needn't go to the minister, but go to his wife and his children, and see how he treats them. If he's a merchant, I would see his employees. That's the way to find out. Talk is very cheap now. Some one says—and it is a simple expression—"a good many talk cream, and live skim-milk." They talk all right, but they don't live right. What we want is to keep enmity and jealousy out of our hearts. Perfect love casts out all fear. There being no "fear," we shall be able to look up to the Lord and read our title to the heavenly mansions.

A BANKER AND A MERCHANT

Once when I was preaching in the South, I was trying to show that we can't be Christians without love. A man said: "There are some things true, and one is that you can't be a true gentleman without resenting. I'm a Christian and a gentleman." He stuck to it. Where does that argument lead to? I was in a town where there was a banker and a merchant who had a quarrel; the banker stood in the office one morning and he put his hand into his hip-pocket and he fired at the merchant, and the merchant fired back, but he missed him; but the son was coming down the street, and he saw his father shot at, and he pulled his revolver, and the son and the merchant and the banker were all dead inside of a minute. First families in the town! That's where this thing leads to. Got to be "resented"! Jesus taught nothing of the sort. If they smite you on the one cheek, turn them the other. You say you don't believe in that. That's what Christ taught and it's what we need now. We can love and no one can hinder us either. I would love a man whether he wants to be loved or not. *He* can't hinder me.

Now, if you keep at love, summer, winter, all the year round, love will tell. Love begets love. Hatred begets hatred. You can't drive them. That's the mistake people make now. We want to go to the kindly and tell them of the "better life." He that winneth souls is wise. Save by winning.

8

FINDING GOD

Seek the Lord

You will find my text in Isaiah 55:6: "Seek ye the Lord while he may be found, call ye upon him while he is near." Under this text, man is told to seek the Lord. Now, I have learned this during the past few years in dealing with men: there isn't much hope of their being saved until they seek the Lord with all their hearts. One reason that men do not find the Lord is that they don't seek for Him with all their hearts. Very often you meet people who say, "Well, I don't know as I have any objections to being saved." Well, I don't know as I ever knew of anyone who found Christ that had that spirit. You have to have something beyond that.

I said to a man, some time ago, "I can tell you the day you will be converted, although I am not a prophet, and although I don't pretend to be a prophet." "Well," said he, "I would like to have you tell me that; for I would like to know myself." "Well," I said, "you shall find Him when you seek for Him, and search for Him with all your heart." In Jeremiah 29:13 it says: "And ye shall seek me, and find me, when ye shall search for me with all your heart." I wish men would seek for Christ as they seek for wealth. I wish men would seek for Christ as they seek for position in this world. Man prepares his feast, and there is a great rush to see who will get there first. God prepares His feast, and the excuses come in: "I pray thee have me excused."

Supposing I should state that last night a man came to me and said, "Mr. Moody, I lost a very valuable diamond; it was a gift from my dying mother, and I am willing to give anyone who finds that diamond $20,000." I am sure there would be a great search. How many do you suppose would be searching for that diamond? A man might say: "I am poor; and if I could find that diamond, wouldn't that take me out of poverty and out of want?" You would wish you had a chance to find it. Isn't the salvation of your soul worth more than all the diamonds that the world has seen? Isn't it worth more than the whole world itself, and isn't it the best thing you can do now to seek the Lord?

Not only that, but it is a command to seek the Lord while He may be found, and call upon Him while He is near. It is just as much a command for you to seek the Lord as it is that you should not swear. It is just as much a command, as it is that you should not steal. It is a command. There are a great many commandments. Some people have an idea that there are only Ten Commandments in the Bible. There are thousands of them, and this is one of them. It is the voice of the Lord Himself. Seek Him with all your heart.

Now just see how men seek wealth. When the California fever —the gold fever—broke out, men left their wives, and left their children, and left their parents, and their homes and luxury, and went out to the Pacific Coast and slept out in the open air, and under tents, and endured want. What for? That they might get wealth. They could not make too great a sacrifice to get wealth; and when I was out there on business, I was amazed when news came that gold was found one hundred miles away. They would pack up—men, women, and children—and away they would go. A whole town would move, just to seek wealth. Then they went out to Australia, in the time of the gold fever in that country. They were willing to make almost any sacrifice. Look and see these politicians work. Let one of them be nominated for alderman, or for some position in the government, and how they will seek your vote! They will come around to your house early in the morning, just to get your vote. They don't sleep at night; they are willing to do everything they can do to accomplish their purpose.

Let us learn a lesson from that. If there is no reality in this gift of God, if it is all a myth, then let us dismiss it. If it is true, and we can find the Lord by seeking Him, let us seek Him. A man will go around this world for his health; he will cross oceans and climb steep mountains just to get his health. Thanks be to God that you do not have to go around the world to get salvation. "Ye shall find me when ye shall search for me with all your heart." Now there isn't anything a man values as he does his life. A man on a sinking ship may be worth a million, and if the only way he can save his life is to give up that million, he would do it as quick as a flash. Now the gift of God is eternal life; it is life without end.

Christ says, "What shall it profit a man, if he gain the whole world, and lose his own soul?" Now, is it true that a man can be saved now? Won't you just stop and think a moment? If it is true that the Lord is worth more than the whole world, and He can be found by seeking, why not seek for Him—not with half of a heart—but with all your heart?

If you want to get into the kingdom of God, you will seek your soul's salvation now. Be in earnest for once in your life, and seek the kingdom of God with all your heart; and you shall find it now. It will be the time of your salvation. It is a good time to seek the Lord while the Spirit of God is still striving with men. One night a brother came to my private room, and said, "I want to introduce you to someone"; and there stood his wife, her face lit up with joy. She wanted to tell me that her husband was converted. She said: "I have been praying for him these twenty years, and he has found the Lord." "Seek ye the Lord while he may be found, call ye upon him while he is near."

How many men were there that were converted in the great revival of 1857 and 1858? And yet some people cry out against revivals. They had rather be converted at any time than during a revival. It was not long after the revival of 1857 and 1858 that the nation was deluged with blood, and half a million men laid down their lives. The best thing they could have done was to seek the Lord then. It was my privilege to be in the army at that time. I was by their cots, and I saw them die. I never saw a man all through the war that regretted that he had become a Christian. The best thing they could do was to call upon the Lord. It was a great calamity, and came right home to the heart of the nation. I believe that judgements are going to happen upon this nation again. Grace always precedes judgement. A great revival is in progress all over the country.

So there was in Jerusalem a day of grace; but the opportunity was spurned. Jerusalem and the country took no heed to their ways, and soon Titus appeared with a great army and besieged it, and more than 1,100,000 people perished. Those men rejected the Gospel and the Word of God. So at the present day men won't call upon Christ when He may be found, or seek Him when He is near. All along in the history of the church before some great calamity has fallen upon the earth there has been a great day of grace, offering salvation to those who will accept it. Before God has punished people, He holds out before them a chance to repent and to escape His wrath.

And now we hear Jesus calling to repentance throughout all the land. It is time to be up and doing. Save yourselves; and then plead with your friends, and bring them to Jesus. Tell them the glad tidings, and bring them into the fold of the Good Shepherd. If we are faithful now and watch for souls, we shall see in every town and city thousands who will accept Christ. It is time for us to go out and say to our friends and relatives: "Come in; the Lord is coming, the Lord is at work. Jesus of Nazareth is passing through the city. Let us call upon Him while He may be found; let us implore Him to save us while He is near." The very text implies that the time is come when the world should throw off its sloth and wake to repentance. The text implies that God is near and pleads with His people, that the time and the Son of God are near now. Isn't it true that He is seeking for you when you seek for Him? Seek, then, the Lord while He may be found; call upon Him while He is near.

Mr. Sankey has a song about those virgins. We read that five sought to gain admission too late. There was a time that they might have called upon the Lord; there was a time when, had they sought, they would have found Him. But they slumbered and slept until it was too late. Then they cried, but the door was shut—the day of grace was over. And so it may be the same with you. The day of grace may be drawing to a close with you too. It may be that I am speaking to you for the last time. This may be the last year you may have on earth. The prophecy may be true in regard to you and me, "This year thou shalt die." Is it or isn't it a time to seek the kingdom of God—to seek His face while Christ is calling upon us to repent, while the Spirit of God is moving upon our hearts? Isn't it the very best time to seek the Lord while He may be found?

Those antediluvian people called upon Noah to open the door of the ark and take them in; but it was too late. God will shut the door against you, too. You will soon be without hope. Undoubtedly, these men, women, and children called upon God to save them on that terrible day; but the day of grace was over for them. The day of wrath then had come, and the day of judgement had fallen upon them. Oh, who shall stand in the day of wrath? When the Lord shall shake the earth, what shall then save the souls of men? The day of grace is here. Save yourselves. Wash yourselves in His precious blood and be redeemed. Oh, this very hour, let there be a cry for salvation!

In Romans 10 it is written: "For whosoever shall call upon the name of the Lord shall be saved." I heard of a man away off in the mining district, who had wandered from his house and got lost. In that region, the ground is full of holes, and some pretty deep ones too. But it was night, and he could not make his way along. Had he undertaken to move on, there were the holes before him; and every step might precipitate him into a cavern. He did not know what to do, and he could not stir a step. At last he commenced to cry out, "Help! help! help!" and his cry was heard. They came with lanterns, and brought him safely out of danger. The depths of sin are surrounding you; the next step may land you into darkness and death. Don't make light of this warning voice. "Seek the Lord while he may be found, call ye upon him while he is near."

Let me warn you against the next verse (Isaiah 55:7). A great many people put verse 7 ahead of verse 6. "Let the wicked forsake his way, and the unrighteous man his thoughts." If you would be saved, call upon God first, and then God will give you help; and by His power you can then turn away from sin and from your evil thoughts, and will receive pardon. But you haven't power to give up your evil courses until you call upon God, and until He gives you strength. After you have called upon the Lord, you must receive Him when He comes; you must make room for Him. He has gone to make room for you, and you must make room for Him.

I found a man in the inquiry-room who was puzzled to know how there would be room for the saved in heaven. I tell you as I told him, you needn't borrow trouble on that account. If He finds He will not have room for you, or me, or for any of His chosen people in the heaven He now has, He will make another. Can He not make another place of happiness as easily as He made the present one? The Lord God of heaven can make plenty of room for you. You must not give that as an excuse. The Lord can make all the room He wants. Now let me ask you this question. In all candor, why don't you settle the question now? Will the Son of God have more power than He has now? Will He be readier to use it for your salvation at any other time than He is now? Hasn't He said that all power is given unto Him, both in heaven and on earth? Has He not the power to save everyone? Hasn't He the power and hasn't He the will? Hasn't He said: "As I live, saith the Lord, I have no pleasure in the death of the wicked . . . turn ye, turn ye . . . why will ye die, O house of Israel?" If you turn now and call upon Him, He will forgive you your sins. He will forgive everyone all his sins, no matter how many there are. He will save you, if you truly repent, and write your name in the Book of Life. But you must call upon Him with the heart.

As Spurgeon remarks, the Bible does not say that you must have a new head, or that you must seek Him with your head; but it says you must have a new heart, and must seek Him with your heart. If it meant head, it would have said so. Seek ye the Lord, therefore, with your heart; and Christ will enter into your heart, and not into your head. Give Christ your whole heart, and He will enter into it. If your heart is all right, your head will be also; for out of the heart proceeds all evil. Let that reservoir of sin be broken up and emptied, and all the rest of you will come around right. Will you not cry out, "God be merciful to me, a sinner"? "Lord, have mercy upon me"? Why not call upon him? Why not seek the Lord now? Why not make up your mind that you will not put this book down until the great question of eternity is settled? It is commanded, "Seek the Lord while he may be found." Don't put it off until it is too late. Don't neglect salvation.

Some people say, "Why, what have I done?" I tell you, if you have done nothing but neglect salvation, you will go to death and ruin. Look at the man in his boat on the river; he is not rowing; he is making no effort. But he has his hands folded, and is letting his boat drift down the stream toward the rapids. The current is taking him on, without any help from him; he will soon go over the rapids into the jaws of death. All he has to do is to sit still and be lost. Yes, I tell you if you don't actually do any sin, yet if you neglect Christ and neglect salvation as a gift from God, you must perish.

I am told that there were two men seen above the falls of Niagara. They were drinking champagne and carousing. They had no thought of danger; they had no perception of the end that was awaiting them. They sang and they drank. But by and by a warning voice came to their ears. They looked at the friend on shore, but paid no attention. They even mocked him; they lifted up the bottle, drank to him, and shook the bottle at him. Some one farther on, seeing their danger, also undertook to warn them; but they treated his voice with laughter and derision. You may make light of solemn services, and ridicule the Word of God. These men mocked the danger also. They drifted a little farther on, when a third voice shouted to give them notice of the approaching rapids. But the men still mocked on; and the current still took them on every second nearer to the great fatal plunge. Then they saw the water going over the falls, and in wild desperation seized the oars. They battled against the current with all their strength. Too late! Too late! They had neglected it too long, and with a wild cry they were forever engulfed.

What a picture! And yet hundreds and thousands have died just the same way.

By and by will come the piercing cry, "It's too late!" Tonight I plead with you to neglect it no longer. You may hear the appeal for the last time. Oh, may the Holy Spirit open your eyes now! While we were in Europe, a man came into one of the meetings in the coal region; and when the audience was dismissed, he was seen to remain, standing against a post. One of the men approached him, and asked him why he remained. He said he had made up his mind not to leave that church until he found the kingdom of God. The elder remained with him for a long time, and at last the miner made a surrender. The next day he went into the coal pit, and before night the mine fell in and buried him. He was taken from the ruins just before life became extinct, and was heard to say: "It is a good thing I settled it last night." Wasn't it a good thing? What do you think?

When Mr. Sankey and I were in the north of England, I was preaching one evening, and before me sat a lady who was a skeptic. When I had finished, I asked all who were anxious to remain. Nearly all remained; she was among the number. I asked her if she were a Christian; and she said she was not, nor did she care to be. I prayed for her there. On inquiry, I learned that she was a lady of good social position, but very worldly. She continued to attend the meetings, and a week later I saw her in tears. After the sermon I went to her, and asked her if she was of the same mind as before. She replied that Christ had come to her, and she was happy. Last autumn I had a note from her husband, saying she was dead, that her love for her Master had continually increased. When I read that note, I felt paid for crossing the Atlantic. She worked sweetly after her conversion, and was the means of winning many of her fashionable friends to Christ. Oh, may you seek the Lord while He may be found, and will you call upon Him while you may?

9

THE OVERCOMING LIFE

Rest

Some years ago a gentleman came to me and asked which I thought was the most precious promise of all those that Christ left. I took some time to look them over, but I gave it up. I found that I could not answer the question. It is like a man with a large family of children—he cannot tell which he likes best; he loves them all. But if not the best, this is one of the sweetest promises of all: "Come unto me, all ye that labour and are heavy laden, and I will give you rest. Take my yoke upon you, and learn of me; for I am meek and lowly in heart: and ye shall find rest unto your souls. For my yoke is easy, and my burden is light."

There are a good many people who think the promises are not going to be fulfilled. There are some that you do see fulfilled, and you cannot help but believe they are true. Now remember that [some] promises are given with, and others without, conditions attached to them. For instance, it says, "If I regard iniquity in my heart, the Lord will not hear me." Now, I need not pray as long as I am cherishing some known sin. He will not hear me, much less answer me. The Lord says in the eighty-fourth Psalm, "No good thing will he withhold from them that walk uprightly." If I am not walking uprightly, I have no claims under the promise. Again, some of the promises were made to certain individuals or nations. For instance, God said that He would make Abraham's seed to multiply as the stars of heaven, but that is not a promise for you or me. Some promises were made to the Jews and do not apply to the Gentiles.

Then there are promises without conditions. He promised Adam and Eve that the world should have a Savior, and there was no power in earth or perdition that could keep Christ from coming at the appointed time. When Christ left the world, He said He would send us the Holy Spirit. He had only been gone ten days when the Holy Spirit came. And so you can run right through the Scriptures, and you will find that some of the promises are with, and some without, conditions; and if we don't comply with the conditions, we cannot expect them to be fulfilled.

I believe it will be the experience of every man and woman on the face of the earth, I believe that everyone will be obliged to testify in the evening of life, that if they have complied with the condition, the Lord has fulfilled His word to the letter. Joshua, the old Hebrew hero, was an illustration. After having tested God forty years in Egypt, forty years in the desert, and thirty years in the Promised Land, his dying testimony was: "Not one thing hath failed of all the good things which the Lord promised."

I believe you could heave the ocean easier than break one of God's promises. So when we come to a promise like the one we have before us now, I want you to bear in mind that there is no discount upon it. "Come unto me, all ye that labour and are heavy laden, and I will give you rest."

Perhaps you say, "I hope Mr. Moody is not going to preach on this old text." Yes I am. When I take up an album, it does not interest me if all the photographs are new; but if I know any of the faces, I stop at once. So with these old, well-known texts. They have quenched our thirst before, but the water is still bubbling up—we cannot drink it dry.

If you probe the human heart, you will find a want, and that want is rest. The cry of the world today is, "Where can rest be found?" Why are the theaters and places of amusement crowded at night? What is the secret of Sunday driving, of the saloons and brothels? Some think they are going to get rest in pleasure, others think they are going to get it in wealth, and others in literature. They are seeking and finding no rest.

WHERE CAN REST BE FOUND?

If I wanted to find a person who had rest, I would not go among the very wealthy. The man that we read of in the twelfth chapter of Luke thought he was going to get rest by multiplying his goods, but he was disappointed. "Soul, take thine ease." I venture to say that there is not a person in this wide world who has tried to find rest in that way and found it.

Money cannot buy it. Many a millionaire would gladly give millions if he could purchase it as he does his stocks and shares.

God has made the soul a little too large for this world. Roll the whole world in, and still there is room. There is care in getting wealth, and more care in keeping it.

Nor would I go among the pleasure seekers. They have a few hours' enjoyment, but the next day there is enough sorrow to counterbalance it. They may drink a cup of pleasure today, but the cup of pain comes on tomorrow.

To find rest I would never go among the politicians, or among the so-called great. Congress is the last place on earth that I would go. In the Lower House they want to go to the Senate; in the Senate they want to go to the Cabinet; and then they want to go to the White House; and rest has never been found there. Nor would I go among the halls of learning. "Much study is a weariness to the flesh." I would not go among the upper ten, the "bon ton," for they are constantly chasing after fashion. Have you not noticed their troubled faces on our streets? And the face is index to the soul. They have no hopeful look. Their worship of pleasure is slavery. Solomon tried pleasure and found bitter disappointment, and down the ages has come the bitter cry "All is vanity."

Now there is no rest in sin. The wicked know nothing about it. The Scriptures tell us the wicked "are like the troubled sea that cannot rest." You have, perhaps, been on the sea when there is a calm, when the water is as clear as crystal, and it seemed as if the sea were at rest. But if you looked, you would see that the waves came in and that the calm was only on the surface. Man, like the sea, has no rest. He has had no rest since Adam fell, and there is none for him until he returns to God again and the light of Christ shines into his heart.

Rest cannot be found in the world, and thank God the world cannot take it from the believing heart! Sin is the cause of all this unrest. It brought toil and labor and misery into the world. Now for something positive. I would go successfully to someone who has heard the sweet voice of Jesus and has laid his burden down at the cross. There is rest, sweet rest. Thousands could certify to this blessed fact. They could say, and truthfully:

"I heard the voice of Jesus say,
'Come unto me and rest.
Lay down, thou weary one, lay down,
Thy head upon my breast.'
I came to Jesus as I was,
Weary and worn and sad.
I found in Him a resting place,

And He hath made me glad."

Among all his writings, St. Augustine has nothing sweeter than this: "Thou hast made us for Thyself, O God, and our heart is restless till it rests in Thee."

Do you know that for four thousand years no prophet or priest or patriarch ever stood up and uttered a text like this? It would be blasphemy for Moses to have uttered a text like it. Do you think he had rest when he was teasing the Lord to let him go into the Promised Land? Do you think Elijah could have uttered such a text as this when, under the juniper tree, he prayed that he might die? And this is one of the strongest proofs that Jesus Christ was not only man, but God. He was God-Man, and this is heaven's proclamation, "Come unto me, and I will give you rest." He brought it down from heaven with Him.

Now, if this text was not true, don't you think it would have been found out by this time? I believe it as much as I believe in my existence. Why? Because I not only find it in the Book, but in my own experience. The "I wills" of Christ have never been broken and never can be.

I thank God for the word "give" in that passage. He doesn't sell it. Some of us are so poor that we could not buy it if it was for sale. Thank God, we can get it for nothing.

I like to have texts like this, because it takes us all in. "Come unto me all ye that labor." That doesn't mean a select few—refined ladies and cultured men. It doesn't mean good people only. It applies to saint and sinner. Hospitals are for the sick, not for healthy people. Do you think that Christ would shut the door in anyone's face and say, "I did not mean *all*. I only meant certain ones"? If you cannot come as a saint, come as a sinner. Only come!

A lady told me once that she was so hard-hearted she couldn't come.

"Well," I said, "my good woman, it doesn't say, 'All ye softhearted people come.' Black hearts, vile hearts, hard hearts, soft hearts, all hearts come. Who can soften your hard heart but Himself?"

The harder the heart, the more need you have to come. If my watch stops, I don't take it to a drugstore or to a blacksmith's shop, but to the watchmaker's to have it repaired. So if the heart gets out of order, take it to its keeper, Christ, to have it set right. If you can prove that you are a sinner, you are entitled to the promise. Get all the benefits you can out of it.

Now, there are a good many believers who think this text applies only to sinners. It is just the thing for them too. What do we see today? The church, Christian people, all loaded down with cares and troubles. "Come unto me all ye that labor." All! I believe that includes the Christian whose heart is burdened with some great sorrow. The Lord wants you to come.

CHRIST THE BURDEN-BEARER

It says in another place, "Casting all your care upon him, for he careth for you." We would have a victorious church if we could get Christian people to realize that. But they have never made the discovery. They agree that Christ is the sin-bearer, but they do not realize that He is also the burden-bearer. "Surely he hath borne our griefs and carried our sorrows." It is the privilege of every child of God to walk in unclouded sunlight.

Some people go back into the past and rake up all the troubles they ever had, and they then look into the future and anticipate that they will have still more trouble, and they go reeling and staggering all through life. They give you the cold chills every time they meet you. They put on a whining voice and tell you what "a hard time they have had." I believe they embalm [their troubles] and bring out the mummy on every opportunity. The Lord says, "Cast all your care on Me. I want to carry your burdens and your troubles." What we want is a joyful church, and we are not going to convert the world until we have it. We want to get this long-faced Christianity off the face of the earth. Take these people that have some great burden, and let them come into a meeting. If you can get their attention upon the singing or preaching, they will say, "Oh, wasn't it grand! I forgot all my cares." And they just drop their bundle at the end of the pew. But the moment the benediction is pronounced they grab the bundle again. You laugh, but you do it yourself. Cast your care on Him.

Sometimes they go into the closet and close the door, and they get so carried away and lifted up they forget their trouble; but they just take it up again the moment they get off their knees. Leave your sorrow now; cast all your care upon Him. If you cannot come to Christ as a saint, come as a sinner. But if you are a saint with some trouble or care, bring it to Him. Saint and sinner, come! He wants you all. Don't let Satan deceive you into believing that you cannot come if you will. Christ says, "Ye will not come unto me." With the command comes the power.

A man in one of our meetings in Europe said he would like to come, but he was chained and couldn't come.

A [Scotsman] said to him, "Aye, man, why don't you come chain and all?"

He said, "I never thought of that."

Are you cross and peevish, and do you make things unpleasant at home? My friend, come to Christ and ask Him to help you. Whatever the sin is, bring it to Him.

WHAT DOES IT MEAN TO COME?

Perhaps you say, "Mr. Moody, I wish you would tell us what it is to come." I have given up trying to explain it. I always feel like the minister who said he was going to *confound*, instead of *expound*, the chapter.

The best definition is just—come. The more you try to explain it, the more you are mystified. About the first thing a mother teaches her child is to look. She takes the baby to the window, and says, "Look, baby, Papa is coming!" Then she teaches the child to come. She props it up against a chair and says, "Come!" and by and by the little thing pushes the chair along to Mama. That's coming. You don't need to go to college to learn how. You don't need any minister to tell you what it is. Now will you come to Christ? He said, "Him that cometh unto me, I will in no wise cast out."

When we have such a promise as this, let us cling to it and never give it up. Christ is not mocking us. He wants us to come with all our sins and backslidings and throw ourselves upon His bosom. It is our sins God wants, not our tears only. They alone do no good. And we cannot come through resolutions. Action is necessary. How many times at church have we said, "I will turn over a new leaf," but the Monday leaf is worse than the Saturday leaf.

The way to heaven is straight as a rule, but it is the way of the cross. Don't try to get around it. Shall I tell you what the "yoke" referred to in the text is? It is the cross which Christians must bear. The only way to find rest in this dark world is by taking up the yoke of Christ. I do not know what it may include in your case, beyond taking up our Christian duties, acknowledging Christ, and acting as becomes one of His disciples. Perhaps it may be to erect a family altar; or to tell a godless husband that you have made up your mind to serve God; or to tell your parents that you want to be a Christian. Follow the will of God, and happiness and peace and rest will come. The way of obedience is always the way of blessing.

I was preaching in Chicago to a hall full of women one Sunday afternoon, and after the meeting was over a lady came to me and said she wanted to talk to me. She said she would accept Christ, and after some conversation she went home. I looked for her for a whole week but didn't see her until the following Sunday afternoon. She came and sat down right in front of me, and her face had such a sad expression. She seemed to have entered into the misery, instead of the joy, of the Lord.

After the meeting was over I went to her and asked her what the trouble was.

She said, "Oh, Mr. Moody, this has been the most miserable week of my life."

I asked her if there was anyone with whom she had trouble and whom she could not forgive.

She said, "No, not that I know of."

"Well, did you tell your friends about having found the Savior?"

"Indeed I didn't. I have been all the week trying to keep it from them."

"Well," I said, "that is the reason why you have no peace."

She wanted to take the crown but did not want the cross. My friends, you must go by the way of Calvary. If you ever get rest, you must get it at the foot of the cross.

"Why," she said, "if I should go home and tell my infidel husband that I had found Christ, I don't know what he would do. I think he would turn me out."

"Well," I said, "go out."

She went away, promising that she would tell him, timid and pale, but she did not want another wretched week. She was bound to have peace.

The next night I gave a lecture to men only, and in the hall there were eight thousand men and one solitary woman. When I got through and went into the inquiry meeting, I found this lady with her husband. She introduced him to me (he was a doctor and a very influential man) and said, "He wants to become a Christian."

I took my Bible and told him all about Christ, and he accepted Him. I said to her after it was all over, "It turned out quite differently from what you expected, didn't it?"

"Yes," she replied, "I was never so scared in my life. I expected he would do something dreadful, but it has turned out so well."

She took God's way and got rest.

I want to say to young ladies, perhaps you have a godless father or mother, a skeptical brother, who is going down through drink, and perhaps there is no one who can reach them but you. How many times a godly, pure young lady has taken the light into some darkened home! Many a home might be lit up with the Gospel if the mothers and daughters would only speak the word.

The last time Mr. Sankey and I were in Edinburgh, there were a father, two sisters, and a brother, who used every morning to take the morning paper and pick my sermon to pieces. They were indignant to think that the Edinburgh people should be carried away with such preaching. One day one of the sisters was going by the hall, and she thought she would drop in and see what class of people went there. She happened to take a seat by a godly lady, who said to her, "I hope you are interested in this work."

She tossed her head and said: "Indeed I am not. I am disgusted with everything I have seen and heard."

"Well," said the lady, "perhaps you came prejudiced."

"Yes, and the meeting has not removed any of it, but has rather increased it."

"I have received a great deal of good from them."

"There is nothing here for me. I don't see how an intellectual person can be interested."

To make a long story short . . . when the meeting broke up, just a little of the prejudice had worn away. She promised to come back again the next day, and then she attended three or four more meetings and became quite interested. She said nothing to her family until finally the burden became too heavy, and she told them. They laughed at her and made her the butt of their ridicule.

One day, the two sisters were together, and the other said, "Now what have you got at those meetings that you didn't have in the first place?"

"I have a peace that I never knew before. I am at peace with God, myself, and all the world." Did you ever have a little war of your own with your neighbors, in your own family? And she said: "I have self-control. You know, sister, if you had said half of the mean things before I was converted that you have said since, I would have been angry and answered back, but if you remember correctly, I haven't answered once since I have been converted."

The sister said, "You certainly have something that I have not." The other told her it was for her too, and she brought the sister to the meetings, where she found peace.

Like Martha and Mary, they had a brother, but he was a member of the University of Edinburgh. He be converted? He go to these meetings? It might do for women, but not for him. One night, they came home and told him that a chum of his own, a member of the University, had stood up and confessed Christ, and when he sat down his brother got up and confessed; and so with the third one.

When the young man heard it, he said, "Do you mean to tell me that he has been converted?"

"Yes."

"Well," he said, "there must be something in it."

He put on his hat and coat and went to see his friend Black. Black got him down to the meetings, and he was converted.

We went through to Glasgow and had not been there six weeks when news came that the young man had been stricken down and died.

When he was dying he called his father to his bedside and said, "Wasn't it a good thing that my sisters went to those meetings? Won't you meet me in heaven, Father?"

"Yes, my son, I am so glad you are a Christian. That is the only comfort that I have in losing you. I will become a Christian and will meet you again."

I tell this to encourage some sister to go home and carry the message of salvation. It may be that your brother may be taken away in a few months. My dear friends, are we not living in solemn days? Isn't it time for us to get our friends into the kingdom of God? Come, wife, won't you tell your husband? Come, sister, won't you tell your brother? Won't you take up your cross now? The blessing of God will rest on your soul if you will.

I was in Wales once, and a lady told me this little story: An English friend of hers, a mother, had a child that was sick. At first they considered there was no danger, until one day the doctor came in and said that the symptoms were very unfavorable. He took the mother out of the room and told her that the child could not live. It came like a thunderbolt. After the doctor had gone the mother went into the room where the child lay and began to talk to the child and tried to divert its mind.

"Darling, do you know you will soon hear the music of heaven? You will hear a sweeter song than you have ever heard on earth. You will hear them sing the song of Moses and the Lamb. You are very fond of music. Won't it be sweet, darling?"

And the little tired, sick child turned its head away, and said,

"Oh, Mama, I am so tired and so sick that I think it would make me worse to hear all that music."

"Well," the mother said, "you will soon see Jesus. You will see seraphim and cherubim and the streets all paved with gold"; and she went on picturing heaven as it is described in Revelation.

The little tired child again turned its head away, and said, "Oh, Mama, I am so tired that I think it would make me worse to see all those beautiful things!"

At last the mother took the child up in her arms, and pressed her to her loving heart. And the little sick one whispered, "Oh, Mama, that is what I want. If Jesus will only take me in His arms and let me rest!"

Dear friend, are you not tired and weary of sin? Are you not weary of the turmoil of life? You can find rest in the bosom of the Son of God.

10

THE FULLNESS OF THE GOSPEL

Faith

Watch ye, stand fast in the faith, quit you like men, be strong—
1 Corinthians 16:13.

Bishop Ryle has very well likened faith to a root whose flower is assurance. To have the latter, he says, it is necessary that there must first be the hidden source of faith. Faith is the simplest and most universal experience in the world. Call it by whatever name you may—confidence, trust, or belief—it is inseparable from the human race. The first sign of a dawning intelligence in the mind is the exercise of the infant's faith toward those it knows, and its fear toward those it does not know. We cannot even remember when we first began to have faith.

Faith is the foundation of business. It is an essential asset to every bank and mercantile house in existence. Many a thriving business and successful enterprise has been carried through dark days of reverse on no other capital; and without such capital the markets of the world would soon come to a standstill. I have known men whose ruin has been brought about by some little insinuation relative to their credit—the business equivalent for trustworthiness. The loss of public faith has brought the darkest reverses to the richest of corporations, and even nations have felt the ruin which it entails.

Faith is the bond which holds firmly with family. If once this bond is dissolved, there would exist a state of barbarism and anarchy like that which marked the close of the eighteenth century in Paris. With everyone distrusting his neighbor, and fearing his nearest friends, progress is impossible and civilization inconceivable.

To many people, the very term of faith, used in connection

with man's relation to God, implies something mysterious. They will speak of having implicit confidence in a friend, of trusting a servant with their last cent, or being willing to credit a customer with any amount, considering his word as good as his note; yet they do not realize that God simply asks of them the same trust and confidence, which they are using in the affairs of their everyday life.

I remember a conversation I once had with a young lady who was anxious about her spiritual welfare. I tried to show her that salvation came from simply believing in Christ as her personal Redeemer. I well remember her troubled and almost annoyed look, as she replied: "Believe! Why Mr. Moody, everybody tells me to believe. My pastor says 'believe.' My Sunday-school teacher says 'believe.' My mother says 'believe.' I believe everything, but still I am not a Christian." "Well, then," I said, "we will use another word. You have confidence in your friends, and you trust them, don't you? Well, it is simply trusting God and taking Him at His word." In that one word "trust" she found peace. She had been trying to bring herself into some extraordinary frame of mind in order to believe, instead of simply exercising the same act of faith, which she was in the habit of doing almost continually in her daily life. Faith is composed of three elements: knowledge, assent, and action. Knowledge and assent are necessary for the latter, but without action they avail nothing.

When President Lincoln signed the Proclamation of Emancipation to the slaves in the United States, copies of it were sent to all points along the Northern line, where they were posted. Now, supposing a slave should have seen a copy of that proclamation and should have learned its contents. He might have known the fact, he might have assented to its justice, but if he had still continued to serve his old master as a slave, his faith in the document would not have amounted to anything. And so it is with us. A mere knowledge of the historical events of Christ's life, or a simple intellectual assent to His teachings and His mission, will be of no help in a man's life, unless he adds to them a trustful surrender to the Lord's loving-kindness.

But it is a matter of grave importance upon whom you place your faith. It is a very common thing to hear men say that it does not make very much difference what you believe; we are all trying to go to heaven, and that being the case, our belief or unbelief has no effect.

A man once told me that it was absurd to say that a man's actions were affected by his belief. He confessed, however, in a few moments, that he would flee from the building in which we were conversing if some one, whom he believed, should tell him that the place was on fire. A man's life is entirely affected by what he believes. His faith is the magic power of his life. It is an all-important matter, then, to look well to what you believe. Sincerity in believing what is a lie will not make it a truth. It is utter nonsense to say that if we are only in earnest, it is all right. God has given the world a revelation of His Salvation, and He will not hold a man guiltless who despises His Word and tries to substitute earnestness, in what he likes to believe, for what he has been taught to be true.

In New York Harbor lie two steamers tied side by side at their respective wharves—the one a beautifully fitted boat with every luxury that modern invention and skill can devise; the other a less attractive boat, perhaps a little old-fashioned, but, nevertheless, a well-tested, seaworthy boat. The first is destined for some port upon Long Island Sound, but the second boat for some distant port to which I want to go. Now, suppose I should reason, as many a young person does, and embark upon the Long Island boat, and trust to my earnestness to bring me to the desired haven. As I leave the port I inquire of an officer when I may expect to arrive across the ocean. "Why, you are on the wrong boat," he would say. "We do not cross the ocean. We are only built for the coast service." "But I believe in you, and in spite of what people have told me, I am so much in earnest that you must land me in Europe." You would say that I was a fool, and rightly too. Yet this is exactly what people are doing. Their faith and earnestness in some worldly pursuit will never bring them to their desired haven, be their surroundings ever so much to their taste.

Some people have faith in a minister. That is good if it brings them to have faith in a Higher Power. I have known others whose faith was all in some visible form of the Church or in some special congregation. Others there are whose faith is all in some outward symbols and ceremonies. But a time comes in every life, when all human expedients are vain, and outward forms, and human ties themselves, may fail us. When the tempest of bereavement breaks upon the soul there is need, sore need, of a sure and unfailing anchorage.

When first entering Christian work, my one ambition was to be a man of faith. I prayed for faith; I worked for faith; I fasted for faith. All the useful men I had ever heard of had been men of faith, and I realized that it was a necessity for anyone who was to devote his life to God's service. I looked for some wonderful, miraculous gift that should suddenly come to me. One day I was reading the Epistle of Romans when I came to the verse: "So then faith cometh by hearing, and hearing by the word of God" (Roman 10:17). That one passage gives the only direction for receiving faith in Christ, and that is simply by reading about Him. Faith is not some mysterious feeling that we discover within ourselves, but simply the natural results of knowing Christ, both through the Scriptures, and in our lives. Faith is an outward look and not an inward view. It is not important to examine the nature of faith, but it is all-important to study the object of faith.

Many people complain that they are unable to believe what they cannot see, and do not realize that, even in making the statement, they contradict themselves. Faith that requires proof isn't faith at all. To believe a person, or a truth, implies that by experience we do not know it or cannot understand it, but accept it on the statement of another. I am not a chemist, and I do not know anything about the results of certain drugs upon my body. Yet if I should be advised to take a certain medicine, I would have to depend fully upon the wisdom of the man from whom I bought it. I would have to exercise faith in him. If, however, I had been trained in the business, and could assure myself of the purity of every ingredient of the prescription, I would then have no need to exercise my faith, for I would then know and see. Faith is simply believing in God, and acting upon one's trust in Him, appropriating His blessings individually.

There is a story told of Alexander the Great and his trust in his attendant physician. Some one who was jealous of the doctor's distinction, sought to bring about his ruin by arousing suspicion against him, and sent an anonymous letter to the King accusing the doctor of treason. In the letter the writer warned the King that on the following morning the doctor would mix some deadly poison with medicine which he would bring him. Alexander knew his friend too well to believe the accusation. When the doctor came the next morning, the King, taking the goblet containing the medicine in his hand, gave the doctor the warning letter, and then, without waiting for him to read it, he drank the prescribed medicine. By that act of fearless faith he showed his implicit confidence in his friend, and displayed a love that was beyond suspicion, that could think no evil, a faith that could not, and would not, be shaken, no matter what the tests to which it might be subjected.

Such is the faith that God would inspire in our hearts—a faith that would not tolerate suspicious doubts and fears; a faith that would trust Him implicitly, however dark may be the shadows that fall across the path where He would lead us.

Nor does the Master ask of us implicit faith without giving us good reason to trust Him. In all His dealings with man for six thousand years there has not failed one promise nor one prophecy. Even at the present time He is still fulfilling promises and prophecies made before the Christian era. His dealings with the patriarchs, as summarized by the Apostle Paul in his letter to the Hebrews, are illustrations of His bounty and favor toward those whose faith is in Him. An especially striking instance of God's faithfulness, is in the dying message of the old Hebrew leader Joshua. He relied fully upon God's promises, and in his parting message to the leaders of Israel he says: "Behold, this day I am going the way of all the earth:; and ye know in all your hearts and in all your souls, that not one thing hath failed of all the good things which the Lord your God spake concerning you" (Joshua 23:14). There would be joy and exultation among all the powers of darkness, if God's Word could be broken down in one respect; but it stands firm and eternal, because He who promises is ever faithful.

Let a man believe in God's promises and place himself under the direction of God's will, and he will care little for aught else. The reason why there are so many "trimmers," who are seeking to tone down Christ's teaching, is that there is so little faith among them. If they truly believed that Christ's words were true and powerful to convert, they would hew to the line. They would strive to apply His teachings to raise men up, rather than lower their meaning or discredit their power to make them more popular to those living in sin. With faith and courage God will use a servant anywhere, but without these virtues no servant can accomplish anything in the kingdom.

During our war there were leaders whose very presence inspired new strength and purpose in the troops. They were men who had faith and courage. In a church or a community, one person filled with faith and courage often is the means of the greatest blessings. It is not always the visible instrument in God's work that has been the means of a revival, or a spiritual quickening, in a Church. Often the minister or the preacher has been used by God in direct answer to the prayers of some dear servant who is debarred from even leaving the sick-chamber or the many household duties. God uses the weak things, being connected through the bond of faith to

His infinite power, to confound the great and learned. And so it is that all of us, no matter how few talents are entrusted to our care, nor how humble our circumstances are, may have a part in God's great work. By the exercise of faith we may pray for those who work, and by our courage strengthen those who are weak.

I believe that there has never been a time in our history when there has been so great a need of simple faith upon the part of the Church. Temptations surround us, and the most subtle errors and philosophies are continually coming up. But let a man build wisely upon the Rock of Ages, and his life will never be a failure. The shifting sands of human error offer a poor holding for even the short season of a human life, but God's promises are unfailing, and His mercy endureth for ever. Sometimes I tremble in my weakness, but the Rock upon which I stand remains eternally immovable.

"Have faith in God, press near His side—
Thy troubled soul trust Him to guide;
In life, in death, whate'er betide,
Have faith, have faith in God."

Hope

Looking for that blessed hope, and the glorious appearing of the great God and our Saviour Jesus Christ—Titus 2:13.

Although faith and hope are very closely connected, they should be clearly distinguished. Faith has work to perform today; hope cheers faith on the way, and points to rewards of service. The former comes by hearing, the Apostle Paul tells us, while the latter comes by experience. Faith accepts the gift of promise, and hope guards the sacred treasure.

Hope confidently expects the fulfillment of promises in the future. The Bible has much to say about hope, but never does it use the term to mean uncertainty or doubt. It is always employed in the sense of implicit confidence in the fulfillment of the promise upon which it rests. It is a wrong use of the scriptural term for anyone to hope that he is a Christian, even as it would be absurd for me to hope that I am an American. That is a fact. I do not hope to be something that I know I am. I may hope to ever be a loyal citizen of my country, and, in the sense of truly believing that my patriotism will keep me such, I am hoping rightly. Thus, while we know that we are Christians, we may hope through faith to be kept from the temptations which surround us, through Him who has redeemed us from sin.

There are three classes in the world in respect to their relations to hope; first, those who have no hope; second, those who have a false hope; and third, those who have a true hope.

It is providential that those who belong to the first class are not numerous. Hope is as essential to the human soul as faith is to society. A life without hope becomes an unendurable misery, a burden too grievous to be borne. When in the latter days of heathen Rome, men recognized in their gods the reflection of their own weak natures, and realized the emptiness of their hope, they gave themselves over to the dictates of their wanton hearts, and when wearied of life, were advised by many of their wisest teachers to drown their despair in the forgetfulness of suicide.

Even in our own day the great army of suicides is chiefly recruited from those who have no hope. Day by day the newspapers chronicle the wreck of some poor life driven by hopelessness upon the rocks of suicide. Oh! That men would look to the right source for hope; to Him who never turned a deaf ear to the cry of despair, or refused to aid the neediest who came to Him for help. He it was who came "not to destroy men's lives, but to save them." What we all need is a hope that will stand the test in the hour of adversity—when everything about us seems full of doubt and uncertainty.

The second class, or those who cherish false hopes, are unlike those first in that they are very numerous. They are not limited to the so-called dark corners of the earth, but they are to be found even in the most enlightened Christian communities. Now a false hope is worse than no hope at all. A man who is hopeless may be induced to accept a true hope, but one who has a false hope must be first shown that his hope is false, before he will accept a true one.

How carefully men examine titles to property that they may purchase, and how exacting they are regarding all the evidence given. You would say a man was mad, who invested his worldly possessions in property of which he was wholly ignorant. How much more unreasonable, then, to build your eternal hopes without a firm belief in the promises of your Redeemer.

During the war a boy in Pennsylvania was condemned to death. The boy expected to be pardoned, and was resting upon that hope. The papers were full of statements that Governor Curtin would pardon the boy. One day Governor Curtin met Mr. George H.

Stuart, the noted philanthropist, on the street, and said, "Stuart, you know this boy who is sentenced to death. He is entertaining a hope that I am going to pardon him, but I cannot do it. Now, go and tell him." Mr. Stuart afterward told me that it was the hardest duty he had ever performed, but it was an act of mercy. When he entered the cell the prisoner rushed to him and cried, "Mr. Stuart, you are a good man, I know you bring me a pardon." Mr. Stuart knew not what to answer, but he summoned courage and told the boy the truth. The boy fell in a faint at Mr. Stuart's feet when he found his false hope taken away, but it prepared the way to tell him where alone a true and lasting hope might be found.

False hopes are apparently all-sufficient until the testing time, when they fall. Many a man founds his hope on his neighbor's weakness or his own conceit. Men say to me, "I think I am as good as So-and-so," or, "I'm doing as well as I know how." They forget that a hope, to be real or true, must rest upon something outside of one's self. I am like a man trying to build a house without a foundation, if I think that anything about myself is a sufficiently secure or lasting ground upon which to found my hopes. There is not a thief but believes that he will escape detection; not a drunkard but builds on a false hope that he is strong enough to stop at any time; not a defaulter but believes he can repay what he has overdrawn. These are false hopes, because, not built upon a firm foundation, they are like the "foolish man which built his house upon the sand."

Many build their hopes upon the piety of their parents. But a man's relations to God are independent of all others. Eli's sons were punished through their own passions. It is a sacred birthright and a privilege not to be thought of lightly, to have godly parents, but not a firm ground upon which to hope. Even wisdom that does not have its foundation on the fear of God is nothing else but "vexation of spirit." Turn to the opinion of the King of Israel, whose wisdom has become proverbial, and whose fame is undimmed by the ages: "For in much wisdom is much grief: and he that increaseth knowledge increaseth sorrow" (Ecclesiastes 1:18).

Hope is the silver lining to every dark cloud in the Christian life, and brings with it the ever-radiant presence of the Sun of Righteousness. It is this fact which makes Christianity the religion of gladness. I remember hearing Dr. Andrew Bonar once make the statement that "everything before a child of God was to be glorious." At once I made a study of the Christian's future, and found the statement to be literally true. Peter tells us that already we are "partaker[s] of the glory that shall be revealed" (1 Peter 5:1), and Paul asserts that "when Christ, who is our life, shall appear, then shall ye also appear with him in glory" (Colossians 3:4). These bodies, now so full of infirmities, are to be raised again in glory and "be fashioned like unto his glorious body" (Philippians 3:21). Our future home, the "New Jerusalem," will have no night nor darkness, because the "glory of God" will abide in it. We shall then see Him face to face, "by whom also we . . . rejoice in hope of the glory of God" (Romans 5:2). There is, then, good reason for the Christian to live in brightest anticipation of future joy, as well as the assurance that here on earth all things are subject to a loving Heavenly Father, who directs everything for the best interests of those who trust Him.

Then some look to an opportunity for repentance beyond this life. Such a hope has no encouragement in Scripture. The Bible teaches that "now is the accepted time," and again that "when a wicked man dieth, his expectation shall perish: and the hope of unjust men perisheth."

Even hope in our church membership is vain. There was probably no more conspicuous church member in Jerusalem, than the Pharisee who made such a parade of his temple devotions. He thanked God that he was "not as other men," that he gave largely for the Lord's work, and was such an exemplary member of society. Had you asked him, he would have boasted of his ancestry and his church relations. Yet with all his religion he did not have a good ground for his hope, for it was not resting on a sound foundation. Any hope in a religion that does not keep a man from sinning is a false and dangerous one.

There is another hope, which I believe is one of the most subtle and deceitful which ever existed, and one which wrecks the happiness of many a young girl's life. I refer to the common delusion that a woman can best reform a man by marrying him. It is a mystery to me how people can be so blinded to the hundreds of cases, in every community, where tottering homes have fallen and innocent lives have been wrecked, because some young girl has persisted in marrying a scoundrel in the hope of saving him. I have never known such a union—and I have seen hundreds of them—result in anything but sadness and disaster. Let no young girl think, that she may be able to accomplish what a loving mother or sympathetic sisters have been unable to do. Before there is any contract of marriage there should be convincing proof that there has been real and thorough regeneration.

Let no Christian woman believe that she can disregard St. Paul's injunction, "Be ye not unequally yoked together with unbelievers" (2 Corinthians 6:14), for I have always noted that the husband loses respect for the wife's faith, and she, too, follows her Master "afar off," or wholly denies Him.

I cannot leave this subject without adding just one more word in regard to a woman's duty to society. She stands as the sacred guardian of future homes and our nation's prosperity, and to her must we look for true reforms. To her standard must society come. Let her be sure to place it high and keep it pure, and make it apply impartially to all people. Let her keep out those whom she knows fall short of her standard, and never condone in the stronger sex what she condemns in the weaker. Let her think not to elevate society by hiding or condoning the evils which surround her on every side, but only by shutting out those whom she has found it impossible to raise to her standard. Then future generations will arise to bless her for their heritage, instead of cursing her for their misery.

11

HEAVEN

Its Happiness

Eye hath not seen, nor ear heard, neither have entered into the heart of man, the things which God hath prepared for them that love him —1 Corinthians 2:9; see Isaiah 64:4.

If there is one word above another that will swing open the eternal gates, it is the name of Jesus. There are a great many passwords and bywords down here, but that will be the countersign up above. Jesus Christ is the "Open Sesame" to heaven. Anyone who tries to climb up some other way is a thief and a robber. But when we get in, what a joy above every other joy we can think of will it be to see Jesus Himself all the time and to be with Him continually.

Isaiah has given this promise of God to everyone who is saved through faith: "Thine eyes shall see the king in his beauty: they shall behold the land that is very far off" (33:17). Some of us may not be able to go around the world. We may not be able to see any of the foreign countries; but every Christian by and by is going to see a land that is very far off. This is our Promised Land. John Milton says of the saints who have gone already:

"They walk with God

High in Salvation, and the climes of bliss."

It is blissful climate up there. People down here look around a great deal to find a good climate where they will not be troubled by any of their pains or aches, but the climate of heaven is so fine that no pains or aches can hold out against it. There will be no room to find fault. We shall leave all our pains and aches behind us and find an everlasting health, such as earth can never know.

But you know the glory of Christ as reigning King of heaven would be something too much for *mortal* eyes to endure. In the sixth chapter of 1 Timothy, we read of Christ as:

"The blessed and only Potentate, the King of kings, and Lord of lords; who only hath immortality, dwelling in the light which no man can approach unto; whom no man hath seen, nor can see" (vv. 15–16).

As mortals, we cannot see that light. Our feeble faculties would be dazzled before such a blaze of glory.

In Ezekiel 1:28, we read of that prophet having a faint glimpse of it:

"As the appearance of the bow that is in the cloud in the day of rain, so was the appearance of the brightness round about. This was the appearance of the likeness of the glory of the Lord. And when I saw it, I fell upon my face."

We are amazed at ordinary perfection now. None of us can look the sun squarely in the face. But when this corruptible shall have put on incorruption, as Paul says, the power of the soul will be stronger. We shall be able to see Christ in His glory then. Though the moon be confounded and the sun ashamed, yet we shall see Him as He is. This is what will make heaven so happy. We all know that great happiness cannot be found on earth. Reason, revelation, and the experience of six thousand years all tell us that. No human creature has the power to give it. Even doing good fails to give it fully, for, owing to sin in the world, even the best have not perfect happiness here. They have to wait for heaven, although they may be so near it sometimes that they can see heralds of its joy and beauty, as Columbus saw the strange and beautiful birds hovering around his ships long before he caught sight of America.

All the joys we are to know in heaven will come from the presence of God. This is the leading thought in all that the Scripture has to say on the subject. What life on this earth is without health, life in heaven would be without the presence of God. God's presence will be the very light and life of the place. It is said that one translation of the words describing the presence of God is "a happy-making sight." It will be a sight like the return of a long-lost boy to his mother, or the first glimpse of your home after you have been a long time away. Some of you know how a little sunshine on a dark day, or the face of a kind friend in trouble, often cheers us up. Well, it will be something like that, only a thousand times better. Our perceptions of God will be clearer then, and that will make us love Him all the more.

The more we know of God, the more we love Him. A great

many of us would love God more if we only became better acquainted with Him. While on earth it gives Christians great pleasure to think of the perfection of Jesus Christ, but how will it be when we see Him as He is?

WE SHALL BE LIKE CHRIST

Someone once asked a Christian what he expected to do when he got to heaven. He said he expected to spend the first thousand years looking at Jesus Christ, and after that he would look for Peter, and then for James, and for John; and all the time he could conceive of would be joyfully filled with looking upon these great persons. But it seems to me that one look at Jesus Christ will more than reward us for all we have ever done for Him down here, for all the sacrifices we can possibly make for Him, just to see Him; only to see Him. But we shall become like Him when we once have seen Him, because we shall have His Spirit. Jesus, the Savior of the world, will be there, and we shall see Him face to face.

It will not be the pearly gates, nor the jasper walls, nor the streets paved with transparent gold that will make it heaven to us. These would not satisfy us. If these were all, we would not want to stay there forever. I heard of a child whose mother was very sick; and while she lay very low, one of the neighbors took the child away to stay with her until the mother should be well again. But instead of getting better, the mother died; and they thought they would not take the child home until the funeral was all over; and would never tell her about her mother being dead. So awhile afterward they brought the little girl home.

First, she went into the sitting room to find her mother; then she went into the parlor to find her mother there; and she went from one end of the house to the other and could not find her. At last she said, "Where is my mama?" And when they told her her mama was gone, the little thing wanted to go back to the neighbor's house again. Home had lost its attraction to her since her mother was not there any longer. No, it will not be the jasper walls and the pearly gates that will make heaven attractive. It is our being with God. We shall be in the presence of the Redeemer; we shall be for ever with the Lord.

There was a time when I used to think more of Jesus Christ than I did of the Father; Christ seemed to be so much nearer to me because He had become the arbiter between me and God. In my imagination I put God away on the throne as a stern judge, but

Christ had come in as the Mediator, and it seemed as if Christ was much nearer to me than God the Father. I got over that years ago, when God gave me a son, and for ten years I had an only son, and as I looked at the child as he grew up, the thought came to me that it took more love for God to give up His Son than it did for His Son to die. Think of the love that God had for this world when He gave Christ up!

If you will turn to Acts 7:55, you will find that when Stephen was being stoned he lifted up his eyes, and it seemed as if God rolled back the curtain of time and allowed him to look into the eternal city and see Christ standing at the right hand of God. When Jesus Christ went on high He led captivity captive and took His seat, for His work was done; but when Stephen saw Him He was standing up, and I can imagine He saw that martyr fighting, as it were, single-handed and alone, the first martyr, though many were to come after him. You can hear the tramp of the millions coming after him to lay down their lives for the Son of God. But Stephen led the way; he was the first martyr. And as he was dying for the Lord Jesus Christ he looked up. Christ was standing to give him a welcome, and the Holy Ghost came down to bear witness that Christ was there. How then can we doubt it?

A beggar does not enjoy looking at a palace. The grandeur of its architecture is lost upon him. Looking upon a royal banquet does not satisfy the hunger of a starving man. *But seeing heaven is also having a share in it*. There would be no joy there if we did not feel that some of it was ours. God unites the soul to Himself. We read in 2 Peter that we are made "partakers of the divine nature" (1:4). Now if you put a piece of iron in the fire, it very soon loses its dark color and becomes red and hot like the fire, but it does not lose its iron nature. So the soul becomes bright with God's brightness, beautiful with God's beauty, pure with God's purity, and warm with the glow of His perfect love, and yet remains a human soul. We shall be like Him, but remain ourselves.

There is a fable that a kindhearted king was once hunting in a forest and found a blind orphan boy, who was living almost like a beast. The king was touched with pity and adopted the boy as his own and had him taught all that can be learned by one who is blind. When he reached his twenty-first year, the king, who was also a great physician, restored the youth his sight and took him to his palace, where, surrounded by his nobles and all the majesty and magnificence of his court, he proclaimed him one of his sons and commanded all to give him their honor and love. The once friendless orphan thus became a prince and a sharer in the royal dignity and of all the happiness and glory to be found in the palace of a king. Who can tell the joy that overwhelmed the soul of that young man when he first saw the king, of whose beauty and goodness and power he had heard so much? Who can tell the happiness he must have felt when he saw his own princely attire and found himself adopted into the royal family—honored and beloved by all?

Now Christ is the great and mighty King who finds our souls in the wilderness of this sinful world. He finds us, as we read in the third chapter of Revelation, "wretched, and miserable, and poor, and blind, and naked" (v. 17). We read in the first chapter of the same book that He "washed us from our sins in his own blood" (v. 5); and again, in the sixty-first chapter of Isaiah, He has clothed us with a spotless robe of innocence, "with the garments of salvation": He has covered us "with the robe of righteousness, as a bridegroom decketh himself with ornaments, and as a bride adorneth herself with her jewels" (v. 10).

The mission of the Gospel to sinners, as we find it in the twenty-sixth chapter of Acts, was "to open their eyes, and to turn them from darkness to light, and from the power of Satan unto God, that they may receive forgiveness of sins, and inheritance among them which are sanctified by faith that is in me" (v. 18). This is what Christ has done for every Christian. He has adorned you with the gift of grace and adopted you as His child; and as it says in the third chapter of 1 Corinthians:

"All things are yours; whether Paul, or Apollos, or Cephas, or the world, or life, or death, or things present, or things to come; all are yours; and ye are Christ's; and Christ is God's (vv. 21–22)".

He has given you His own Word to educate you for heaven; He has opened your eyes so that now you see. By His grace and your own cooperation your soul is being gradually developed into a more perfect resemblance to Him.

Finally, your Heavenly Father calls you home, where you will see the angels and saints clothed with the beauty of Christ Himself, standing around His throne and hearing the word that will admit you into their society: "Well done, thou good and faithful servant . . . enter thou into the joy of thy lord" (Matthew 25:21). In the sixteenth chapter of John, Christ Himself says: "All things that the Father hath are mine: therefore . . . he shall take of mine, and shall shew it unto you" (v. 15). All will be yours. Ah, how poor and mean

do earthly pleasures seem by comparison! How true those lines of
a Scots poet:
>"The world can never give
>The bliss for which we sigh;
>'Tis not the whole of life to live,
>Nor all of death to die.
>Beyond this vale of tears
>There is a life above,
>Unmeasured by the flight of years,
>And all that life is love."

OVER THE RIVER

There is joy in heaven, we are told, over the conversions that
take place on earth. In Luke 15:7, we read: "I say unto you, that likewise joy shall be in heaven over one sinner that repenteth, more
than over ninety and nine just persons, which need no repentance."
When there is going to be an election for president of the United
States there is tremendous excitement—a great commotion. There
is probably not a paper from Maine to California that would not
have something on nearly every page about the candidates; the
whole country is excited; but I doubt if it would be noticed in heav-
en. If a monarch should leave his throne, there would be great
excitement throughout the nations of the earth; the whole world
would be interested in the event; it would be telegraphed around
the world; but it would probably be overlooked altogether in heav-
en. Yet if one little boy or girl, one man or woman, would repent of
his sins, this day and hour that would be noticed in heaven.

They look at things differently up there. Things that look very
large to us look very small in heaven; and things that seem very
small to us down here may be very great up yonder. Think of it! By
an act of our own, we may cause joy in heaven. The thought seems
almost too wonderful to understand. To think that the poorest sinner on earth, by an act of his own, can send a thrill of joy through
the hosts of heaven!

The Bible says: "There is joy in the presence of the angels"
(Luke 15:10); not that the angels rejoice, but it is "in the presence"
of the angels. I have studied over that a great deal and often wondered what it meant. "Joy in the presence of the angels"? Now it is
speculation; I admit it may be true, or it may not; but perhaps the
friends who have left the shores of time—they who have gone within the fold—may be looking down upon us; and when they see one

they prayed for while on earth repenting and turning to God, it sends a thrill of joy to their very hearts. Even now, some mother who has gone up yonder may be looking down upon a son or daughter, and if that child should say: "I will meet that mother of mine; I will repent; yes, I am going to join you, Mother," the news, with the speed of a sunbeam, reaches heaven, and that mother may then rejoice, as we read, "in the presence of the angels."

In Dublin, after one of the meetings, a man walked into the inquiry-room with his daughter, his only one, whose mother had died some time before, and he prayed: "O God, let this truth go deep into my daughter's heart, and grant that the prayers of her mother may be answered today—that she may be saved." As they rose up she put her arms about his neck and kissed him and said: "I want to meet my mother; I want to be a Christian." That day she accepted Christ. That man was a minister in Texas. The daughter died out there a little while ago, and is now with her mother in heaven. What a blessed and joyful meeting it must have been! It may be a sister, it may be a brother, who is beckoning you over:

"Over the river they beckon to me,
Loved ones who've crossed to the farther side;
The gleam of their snowy robes I see,
But their voices are drowned in the rushing tide.
There's one with ringlets of sunny gold,
And eyes, the reflection of heaven's own blue;
He crossed in the twilight gray and cold,
And the pale mist hid him from mortal view.
We saw not the angels who met him there,
The gates of the city we could not see;
Over the river, over the river,
My brother stands waiting to welcome me.
Whoever you are, do not delay."

The story is told of a father who had his little daughter out late in the evening. The night was dark, and they had passed through a thick wood to the brink of a river. Far away on the opposite shore a light twinkled here and there in the few scattered houses, and still farther off blazed the bright lights of a great city to which they were going. The little child was weary and sleepy, and the father held her in his arms while he waited for the ferryman, who was at the other side. At length they saw a little light; nearer and nearer came the sound of the oars, and soon they were safe in the boat.

"Father," said the little girl.

"Well, my child?"

"It's very dark, and I can't see the shore; where are we going?"

"The ferryman knows the way, little one; we will soon be over."

"Oh, I wish we were there, Father."

Soon in her home, loving arms welcomed her, and her fears and her tremor were gone. Some months pass by, and this little child stands on the brink of a river that is darker and deeper, more terrible still. It is the River of Death. The same loving father stands near her, distressed that his child must cross this river and he not able to go with her. For days and for nights he and her mother have been watching over her, leaving her bedside only long enough for their meals, and to pray for the life of their precious one. For hours she has been slumbering, and it seems as if her spirit must pass away without her waking again, but just before the morning watch she suddenly awakes with the eye bright, the reason unclouded, and every faculty alive. A sweet smile is playing upon her face.

"Father," she says, "I have come again to the riverside, and am again waiting for the ferryman to come and take me across."

"Does it seem as dark and cold as when you went over the other river, my child?"

"Oh, no! There is no darkness here. The river is covered with floating silver. The boat coming toward me seems made of solid light, and I am not afraid of the ferryman."

"Can you see over the river, my darling?"

"Oh, yes, there is a great and beautiful city there, all filled with light, and I hear music such as the angels make!"

"Do you see anyone on the other side?"

"Why yes, yes, I see the most beautiful form; and He beckons me now to come. Oh, ferryman, make haste! I know who it is! It is Jesus; my own blessed Jesus. I shall be caught in His arms. I shall rest on His bosom—I come—I COME."

And thus she crossed over the River of Death, made like a silver stream by the presence of the blessed Redeemer.

SOMETHING MORE

There is hardly an unconverted man anywhere, no matter how high up or how rich he may be, but will tell you, if you get his confidence, that he is not happy. There is something he wants that he cannot get, or there is something he has that he wants to get rid of. It is very doubtful if the ruler of Russia is a happy man, and yet he has about all he can get. Although the English queen has palaces and millions at her command, and has besides what most sovereigns lack, the love of her subjects, it is a question whether she gets great pleasure out of her position. If kings and queens love Jesus Christ and are saved, then they may be happy. If they know they will reach heaven like the humblest of their subjects, then they may rest secure. Paul, the humble tent-maker, will have a higher seat in heaven than the best and greatest sovereign that ever ruled the earth. If a ruler should meet John Bunyan, the poor tinker, up in heaven, he no doubt would find him the greater man.

The Christian life is the only happy one. Without it something is always wanting. When we are young we have grand enterprises, but we soon spoil them by being too rash. We want experience. When we get old we have the experience, but then all the power to carry out our schemes is gone. "Happy is that people, whose God is the Lord" (Psalm 144:15).

The only way to be happy is to be good. The man who steals from necessity sins because he is afraid of being unhappy, but for the moment he forgets all about how unhappy the sin is going to make him. Bad as he is, man is the best and noblest thing on earth, and it is easy to understand how he fails to find true happiness in anything lower than himself. The only object better than ourselves is God, and He is all we can ever be satisfied with. Gold, which is mere dross dug up out of the earth, does not satisfy man. Neither do the honor and praise of other men. The human soul wants something more than that. Heaven is the only place to get it. No wonder that the angels who see God all the time are so happy.

The publicans went to hunt up John the Baptist in the wilderness, to know what they should do. Some of the highest men in the land went to consult the hermit to know how to get happiness. "Whoso trusteth in the Lord, happy is he" (Proverbs 16:20). It is because there is *no* real happiness down here, that earth is not worth living for. It is because it is *all* above, that heaven is worth dying for. It is because there is all life and no death. In hell there is all death and no life. Here on earth there are both living and dying, which is between the two. If we are dead to sin here, we will live in heaven, and if we live in sin here, we must expect eternal death to follow.

Do you know that every Christian dies twice? He first becomes spiritually dead to sin—that is the renewed soul. He then begins to feel the joy of heaven. The joys of heaven reach down to earth as many and as sure as the rays of the sun. Then comes physical death, which makes the way for the physical heaven. Of course the old sinful body has to be changed. We cannot take that into heaven. It will be a glorified body that we will get at the resurrection, not a sinful body. Our bodies will be transfigured like Christ's.

There will be no temptation in heaven. If there were no temptation in the world now, God could not prove us. He wants to see if we are loyal. That is why He put the forbidden tree in Paradise; that accounts for the presence of the Canaanite in the land of Israel. When we plant a seed, after a time it disappears and brings forth a seed that looks much the same, but still it is a different seed. So our bodies and the bodies of those we know and love will be raised up, looking much the same—but still not all the same.

Christ took the same body into heaven that was crucified on the cross, unless He was transformed in the cloud after the disciples lost sight of Him. There must have been some change in the appearance of Christ after His resurrection, for Mary Magdalene, who was the first one who saw Him, did not know Him; neither did the disciples, who walked and talked with Him about Himself, and did not recognize Him until He began to ask a blessing at supper. Even Peter did not know Him when He appeared on the seashore. Thomas would not believe it was Christ until he saw the prints of the nails and the wound in His side. But we shall all know Him in heaven.

There are two things that the Bible makes as clear and certain as eternity. One is that we are going to see Christ, and the other is that we are going to be like Him. God will never hide His face from us there, and Satan will never show his.

There is not such a great difference between grace and glory after all. Grace is the bud, and glory the blossom. Grace is glory begun, and glory is grace perfected. It will not come hard to people who are serving God down here to do it when they go up yonder. They will change places, but they will not change employments.

HIGHER UP

The moment a person becomes heavenly minded and gets his heart and affections set on things above, then life becomes beautiful, the light of heaven shines across his pathway, and he does not have to be all the time lashing and upbraiding himself because he is not more like Christ. Someone asked a Scotsman if he was on the way to heaven, and he said: "Why man, I live there; I am not on the way." That is just it. We want to *live* in heaven; while we are walking in this world it is our privilege to have our hearts and affections there.

I once heard Mr. Moorehouse tell a story about a lady in London who found one of those poor, bedridden saints, and then she found a wealthy woman who was all the time complaining and murmuring at her lot. Sometimes I think people whom God does the most for in worldly things think the less of Him and care less about Him and are the most unproductive in His service. But this lady went around as a missionary visiting the poor, and she used to go and visit the poor, bedridden saint, and she said if she wanted to get cheered up and her heart made happy, she would go and visit her.

[There is a place in Chicago, and has been for years, where a great many Christians have always gone when they want to get their faith strengthened; they go there and visit one of these saints. And a friend told me that she thought that the Lord kept one of those saints in most of the cities to entertain angels as they passed over the cities on errands of mercy, for it seems that these saints are often visited by the heavenly host.] Well, this lady missionary had wanted to get this wealthy woman in contact with this saint, and she invited her to go a number of times; finally the lady consented to go. And when she got to the place, she went up the first flight of stairs, and it was not very clean and was dark.

"What a horrible place," the lady said; "why did you bring me here?"

The lady smiled and said: "It is better higher up."

And then they went up another flight, and it didn't grow any lighter and she complained again and the lady said, "It is better higher up." And then they went up another flight, and it was no lighter; still the missionary kept saying, "It is better higher up." And when they got to the fifth story they opened the door and entered a beautiful room, a room that was carpeted, with plants in the window. A little bird was in a cage singing, and there was that saint just smiling. And the first thing the complaining woman had to say to her was, "It must be very hard for you to be here and suffer."

"Oh, that is a very small thing; it is not very hard," she said, "it is better higher up."

And so if things do not go just right, if they do not go to suit us here, we can say, "It is better higher up, it is better farther on," and we can lift up our hearts and rejoice as we journey on toward HOME.

You know those beautiful lines:

"Beyond the smiling and the weeping,

I shall be soon;
Beyond the waking and the sleeping,
Beyond the sowing and the reaping,
I shall be soon.
Love, rest, and home!
Sweet Home!
Lord, tarry not, but come.
Beyond the rising and the setting,
I shall be soon;
Beyond the calming and the fretting,
Beyond remembering and forgetting,
I shall be soon.
Love, rest, and home!
Sweet Hope!
Lord, tarry not, but come."

12

THE WAY HOME

Christ's Boundless Compassion

And Jesus went forth, and saw a great multitude, and was moved with compassion toward them, and he healed their sick—Matthew 14:14.

It is often recorded in Scripture that Jesus was moved by compassion. We are told in this verse that after the disciples of John had come to Him and told Him that their master had been beheaded, that he had been put to a cruel death, He went out into a desert place, and the multitude followed Him, and that when He saw the multitude He had "compassion" on them, and healed their sick.

If He were here tonight in person, standing in my place, His heart would be moved as He looked down into your faces, because He could also look into your hearts and could read the burdens and troubles and sorrows you have to bear. They are hidden from my eye, but He knows all about them. When the multitude gathered round about Him, He knew how many weary, broken, and aching hearts there were there. And He is here tonight, although we can not see Him with the bodily eye, and there is not a sorrow, or trouble, or affliction which any of you is enduring but He knows all about it; and He is the same tonight as He was when here upon earth—the same Jesus, the same Man of compassion.

When He saw that multitude He had compassion on them, and healed their sick. I hope He will heal a great many sin-sick souls here, and will bind up a great many broken hearts. There is no heart so bruised and broken but the Son of God will have compassion upon you, if you will let Him. "He will not break a bruised reed, nor quench the smoking flax." He came into the world to bring mercy, and joy, and compassion, and love.

If I were an artist, I should like to draw some pictures tonight, and put before you that great multitude on which He had compassion. I would draw another painting of that man coming to Him full of leprosy, full of it from head to foot. There he was, banished from his home, banished from his friends, and he comes to Jesus with his sad and miserable story. And now, my friends, let us

Make The Bible Stories Real,

for that is what they are.

Think of that man. Think how much he had suffered. I don't know how many years he had been away from his wife and children and home; but there he was. He had put on a strange and particular garb, so that anybody coming near him might know that he was unclean. When he saw anyone approaching him, he had to raise the warning cry, "Unclean! Unclean! Unclean!" Aye, and if the wife of his bosom were to come out to tell him that a beloved child was sick and dying, he durst not come near her, he was obliged to fly. He might hear her voice at a distance, but he could not be there to see his child in its last dying moments. He was, as it were, in a living sepulcher; it was worse than death! There he was, dying by inches, an outcast from everybody and everything, and not a hand put out to relieve him. Oh, what a terrible life! Think of him coming to Christ, and when Christ saw him, the Bible says He was moved with compassion. He had a heart that beat in sympathy with the poor leper, He had compassion on him. The man came to Him, and said,

"Lord, if Thou wilt, Thou canst make me clean!"

He knew there was no one to do it but the Son of God Himself.

The great heart of Christ was moved with compassion towards him. Hear the gracious words that fell from His lips—

"I will; be thou clean!"

The leprosy fled, and the man was made whole immediately.

Look at him now on his way back home to his wife and children and friends! No longer an outcast, no longer a loathsome thing, no longer cursed with that terrible leprous disease, but going back to his friends rejoicing.

Now, my friends, you may say you pity a man who was that bad off, but did it ever strike you that you are a thousand times worse off? The leprosy of the soul is far worse than the leprosy of the body. I would rather a thousand times have my body full of leprosy than go down to hell with my soul full of sin. A good deal better that this right hand of mine were lopped off, that this right foot should decay, and that I should go halt and lame and blind all the days of my life, than be banished from God by the leprosy of sin. Hear the wailing and the agony and the woe that is going up from this earth caused by sin! If there is one poor sin-sick soul filled with leprosy here tonight, if you come to Christ, He will have compassion on you, and say, as He did to that man,

"I will; be thou clean."

THE DEAD RAISED

Well, now we come to the next picture that represents Him as moved with compassion.

Look into that little home at Nain. There is a poor widow sitting there. Perhaps a few months before she had buried her husband, but she has an only son left. How she dotes upon him! She looks to him to be her stay and her support and friend in her old age. She loves him far better than her own life-blood. But see, at last sickness enters the dwelling, and death comes with it, and lays his ice-cold hand upon the young man. You can see that widowed mother watching over him day and night; but at last those eyes are closed, and that loved voice is hushed, she thinks, forever. She will never see or hear him more after he is buried out of her sight.

And so the hour comes for his burial. Many of you have been in the house of mourning, and have been with your friends when they have gone to the grave and looked at the loved one for the last time. There is not one here, I dare say, who has not lost some beloved one. I never went to a funeral and saw a mother take the last look at her child but it has pierced my heart, and I could not keep back the tears at such a sight.

Well, the mother kisses her only son on that poor, icy forehead. It is her last kiss, her last look, and the body is covered up, and they put him on the bier and start for the place of burial. She had a great many friends. The little town of Nain was moved at the sight of the widow's only son being borne away.

I see that great crowd as they come pushing out of the gates. Over yonder are thirteen men—weary, and dusty, and tired—and they have to stand by the wayside to let this great crowd pass by. The Son of God is in this group, and the others with Him are His disciples.

He looked upon that scene, and saw the mother with her broken heart; He saw it bleeding, crushed, and wounded, and it touched His heart. Yes, the great heart of the Son of God was moved with compassion, and He came up and touched the bier, and said,

"Young Man, Arise!"

and the young man sat up.

I can see the multitude startled and astonished. I can see the widowed mother going back home rejoicing, with the morning rays of the resurrection shining in her heart. Yes, He had compassion on her indeed! And there is not a widow in this hall but Christ's voice will respond to your trouble and give you peace. Oh, dear friends, let me say to you whose hearts are aching, you need a friend like Jesus! He is just the friend the widow needs. He will have compassion on you, and will bind up your wounded, bleeding heart if you will only come to Him just as you are. He will receive you, without upbraiding or chastising, to His loving bosom, and say, "Peace, be still," and you can walk in the unclouded sunlight of His love from this night. Christ will be worth more to you than all the world besides. He is just the friend that all of you need; and I pray God you may every one of you know Him from this hour as your Savior and friend.

THE MAN WHO WAS ROBBED

The next picture which I shall show you to illustrate Christ's compassion is of the man that was going down to Jericho and fell among thieves.

They had taken away his coat. They took his money, and stripped him, and left him half dead. Look at him wounded, bleeding, dying! And now comes down the road a priest, and he looks upon the scene. His heart might have been touched, but he was not moved with compassion enough to help the poor man. He might have said, "Poor fellow!" but he passed by on the other side, and left him.

After him came down a Levite, and perhaps he said, "Poor man!" but he was not moved with compassion to help him.

Ah, there are a good many like that priest and Levite! Perhaps some of you coming down to this hall meet a drunkard reeling in the street, and just say "Poor fellow!" or it may be you laugh because he stammers out some foolish thing. We are very unlike the Son of God.

At last a Samaritan came down that way, and he looked on the man and had compassion on him! He got off his beast, took oil and poured it into the man's wounds, bound them up, took him out of the ditch, helpless as he was, placed him on his own beast, brought him to an inn, and took care of him!

That good Samaritan represents your Christ and mine. He came into the world to seek and to save that which was lost.

Young man, have you come to the city, and fallen in with bad companions? Have they taken you to theaters and places of vice, and left you bleeding and wounded? Oh, come tonight to the Son of God, and He will have compassion on you, and take you off from the dunghill, and transform you, and lift you up into His kingdom, into the heights of His glory, if you will only let Him! I do not care who you are. I do not care what your past life may have been. He said to the poor woman caught in adultery, "Neither do I condemn thee; go, and sin no more." He had compassion upon her, and He will have compassion on you. That man going down from Jerusalem to Jericho represents thousands in our large cities, and that good Samaritan represents the Son of God. Young man, Jesus Christ has set His heart on saving you! Will you receive His love and compassion? Do not have such hard thoughts about the Son of God. Do not think He has come to condemn you. He has come to save you.

AN UNGRATEFUL WRETCH

But I should like to draw another picture—that young man going away from his home that we read of in the 15th chapter of Luke; an ungrateful man, as ungrateful a wretch as ever one saw. He can not wait for his inheritance till his father is dead, he wants his share at once, and so he says to his father,

"Give me the goods that belong to me."

His good old father gives him the goods, and away he goes.

I can see him as he starts on his journey, full of pride, boastful and arrogant, going out to see life, off in grand style to some foreign country—say, going down to London. How many have gone to London, that being the far country to them, squandering all their money!

Yes, he is a popular young man as long as he has money. His friends last as long as his money lasts. A very popular young man, "hail-fellow-well-met" greets him everywhere. He always pays the liquor bill and cigars. Yes, he has plenty of friends! What grand folly!

But when his money was gone, where were his friends? Oh, you that serve the devil, you have a hard master! When the prodigal's money was all gone, of course they laughed at him, and called him a fool; and so he was.

What a blind, misguided young man he was! Just see what he

lost. He lost his father's home, his table and food, and testimony, and every comfort. He lost his work, except what he got down there while feeding swine. He was in an unlawful business. And that's just what the backslider is doing; he is

In The Devil's Pay.

You are losing your time and testimony. No one has any confidence in a backslider, for even the world despises such a character.

This young man lost his testimony. Look at him amongst the swine! Some one in that far country comes along, and, beholding him, says,

"Look at that miserable, wretched, dirty, barefoot fellow taking care of swine!"

"Ah," says the prodigal, "don't talk to me like that. Why, my father's a rich man, and has got servants better dressed than you are."

"Don't tell me that!" says the other; "if you had such a father as that, I know very well he wouldn't own you."

No one would believe him. No one believes a backslider. Let him talk about his enjoyment with God, nobody believes it. Oh, poor backslider, I pity you! You had better

Come Home Again.

Well, at last the poor prodigal comes to himself and says, "I will arise and go to my father," and now he starts for home. Look at him as he goes along, pale and hungry, with his head down! His strength is exhausted, perhaps he is diseased in his frame, and so shattered that no one would know him but his father. But love is keen to detect its object. The old man has often been longing for his return.

I can see him many a night up on the house-top looking out to catch a glimpse of him. Many a long night he has wrestled in prayer with God that his prodigal son might come back. Everything he had heard from that far country told him his boy was going to ruin as fast as he could go. The old man spent much time in prayer for him. At last, faith begins to arise, and he says,

"I believe God will send back my boy."

One day the old man sees afar off the long-lost boy. He does not know him by his dress, but he detects his gait, and he says to himself,

"Yes, that's my boy!"

I see him pass down the stairs, he rushes along the highway, he is running! Ah! That is just like God. Many a time in the Bible, God is represented as running; He is in great haste to meet the back-slider. Yes, the old man is running: he sees his son afar off, and he has compassion on him.

The boy wanted to tell him his story, what he had done, and where he had been, but the old man could not wait to hear him; his heart was filled with compassion, and he took him to his loving bosom. The boy wanted to go down into the kitchen with the servants, but the old man would not let him. No, but he bade the servants put shoes on his feet, and a ring on his finger, and kill the fatted calf, and make merry. The prodigal has come home, the wanderer has returned, and the old man rejoices over his return.

Oh, backslider, come home, and there will be joy in your heart and in the heart of God. May God bring the backsliders back tonight —this very hour! Say as the poor prodigal did, "I will arise and go to my father," and on the authority of God I tell you God will receive you. He will blot out your sins, and restore you to His love, and you shall walk again in the light of His reconciled countenance.

CHRIST WEEPING OVER JERUSALEM

But look again. Jesus comes to Mount Olivet. He is under the shadow of the cross. The city bursts upon him. Yonder is the temple. He sees it in all its grandeur and glory. The people are shouting, "Hosanna to the Son of David!" They are breaking off palm branches, and taking off their garments, and spreading them before Him, still shouting, "Hosanna to the Son of David!" and bowing down before Him. But He forgets it all. Yes, even Calvary with all its sorrow He forgets. Gethsemane lay there at the foot of the hill; He forgot it too. As He looked upon the city which He loved, the great heart of the Son of God was moved with compassion, and He cried aloud,

"O Jerusalem, Jerusalem, thou that killest the prophets, and stonest them which are sent unto thee, how often would I have gathered thy children together, even as a hen gathereth her chickens under her wings, and ye would not!"

My friends, look at Him there weeping over Jerusalem! What a wonderful city it might have been! How exalted to heaven it was! Oh, if they had only known about the day of their visitation, and had received instead of rejected their king, what a blessing He would have been to them! Oh, poor backslider, behold the Lamb of God weeping over you, and crying to you to come to Him, and receive shelter and refuge from the storm which has yet to sweep over this earth!

PETER'S DENIAL

Now look at poor Peter. He denied the Lord, and swore he never knew Him. If ever Jesus needed sympathy, if ever He needed His disciples round Him, it was that night when they were bringing false witnesses against Him, that He might be condemned to death; and there was Peter, one of His foremost disciples, swearing he never knew Him. He might have turned on Peter and said,

"Peter, is it true you don't know Me? Is it true you have forgotten how I cured and healed your wife's mother when she lay at the point of death? Is it true you have forgotten how I caught you up when you were sinking in the sea? Is it true, Peter, you have forgotten you were with Me on the Mount of Transfiguration, when heaven and earth came together, and you heard God's voice speaking from the clouds? Is it true you have forgotten that mountain scene when you wanted to build the three tabernacles? Is it true, Peter, you have forgotten Me?"

Yes, thus He might have taunted poor Peter; but instead of that He just gave him one look of compassion that broke his heart, and Peter went out and wept bitterly.

• THE PERSECUTING SAUL

Again, look at that old blasphemer and persecutor who is going to stamp out the early church, and is breathing out threatenings and slaughter, when Christ meets him on his way to Damascus. It is the same Jesus still. Listen, and hear what he says—

"Saul, Saul, why persecutest thou me?"

He could have smitten him to the earth with a look or a breath; but instead of that, the heart of the Son of God is moved with compassion, and He cries out,

"Saul, Saul, why persecutest thou me?"

If there is a persecutor here tonight, I would ask you, "Why persecute Jesus?" He loves you, sinner; He loves you, persecutor! You never received anything but goodness and kindness and love from Him.

Saul cried out, "Who art thou?"

And He answered, "I am Jesus whom thou persecutest; it is hard for thee to kick against the pricks. It is hard to fight against such a loving friend, to contend against one who loves you as I do."

Down went the proud, persecuting Saul upon his face, and he cried out,

"Lord, what wouldst Thou have me to do?"

And the Lord told him, and he went and did it.

May the Lord have compassion upon the infidel, and skeptic, and persecutor here! Let me ask you, my friend, Is there any reason why you should hate Christ, or why your heart should be turned against Him?

"WHY DON'T YOU LOVE JESUS?"

I remember a story about a teacher telling her scholars all to follow Jesus, and how they might all be missionaries, and go out to work for others. One day, one of the smallest came to her, and said,

"I asked such and such a one to come with me, and she said she would like to come, but her father was an infidel."

The young child wanted to know what an infidel was, and the teacher went on to explain it to her.

One day, when she was on her way to school, this infidel was coming out of the post-office with his letters in his hand, when the child ran up to him, and said,

"Why don't you love Jesus?"

He thought at first to push her aside, but the child pressed it home again—

"Why don't you love Jesus?"

If it had been a man, the infidel would have resented it; but he did not know what to do with the child. With tears in her eyes she asked him again,

"Oh! Please, tell me, why don't you love Jesus?"

He went on to his office, but he felt as if every letter he opened read—"Why don't you love Jesus?" He attempted to write, with the same result; every letter seemed to ask him, "Why don't you love Jesus?" He threw down his pen in despair, and went out of his office, but he could not get rid of the question; it was asked by a still small voice within. As he walked along it seemed as if the very ground and the very heavens whispered to him, "Why don't you love Jesus?"

At last he went home, and there it seemed as if his own children asked him the question, so he said to his wife, "I will go to bed early tonight," thinking to sleep it away; but when he laid his head on the pillow it seemed as if the pillow whispered to him. So he got up about midnight, and said,

"I can find out where Christ contradicts Himself, and I'll search it out and prove Him a liar."

Well, he got up, and turned to the Gospel of John, and read on from the beginning until he came to the words,

"God so loved the world, that he gave his only begotten Son, that whosoever believeth in him should not perish, but have everlasting life."

"What love!" he thought; and at last the old infidel's heart was stirred. He could find no reason for not loving Jesus, and down he went on his knees and prayed, and before the sun rose he was in the kingdom of God.

I will challenge anyone on the face of the earth to find any reason for not loving Christ. It is only here on earth men think they have a reason for not doing so. In heaven they know Him, and they sing, "Worthy is the Lamb that was slain!" Oh, sinner, if you knew Him you would have no wish to find a reason for not loving Him! He is "the chiefest among ten thousand, and altogether lovely."

A QUESTION

I can imagine some one saying, "I should like very much to become a Christian, and I should like to know how I can come to Him, and be saved."

Come to Him as a personal friend. For years I have made this a rule. Christ is just as habitually near, as personally present to me as any other person living; and when I have any troubles, trials, and afflictions, I go to Him with them. When I want counsel I go to Him, just as if I could talk face to face with Him. Twenty years ago God met me and took me to His bosom, and I would sooner give up my life tonight than give up Christ, or that I should leave Him, or that He should leave me, and that I should have no one to bear my burdens or tell my sorrows to. He is worth more than all the world besides. And tonight He will have compassion upon you as He had upon me. I tried for weeks to find a way to Him, and I just went and laid my burden upon Him, and then He revealed Himself to me, and I have ever since found Him a true and sympathizing friend, just the friend you need. Go right straight to Him! You need not go to this man or that man, to this church or that church. "I am the Way, the Truth, and the Life," said Jesus.

There is no name so dear to Americans as that of Abraham Lincoln. Do you want to know the reason why? I will tell you. He was a man of compassion. He was very gentle, and was noted for his heart of sympathy for the down-trodden and the poor. No one went to him with a tale of sympathy but he had compassion on them, no matter how far down they were in the scale of society. He always took an interest in the poor.

There was a time in our history when we thought he had too much compassion. Many of our soldiers did not understand army discipline, and a great many were not true to the army regulations. They intended to be, but they did not understand them. Many men consequently went wrong, and they were court-martialed and condemned to be shot; but Abraham Lincoln would always pardon them. At length the nation rose up against him, and said that he was too merciful, and ultimately they got him to give out that if a man was court-martialed he must be shot, that there would be no more reprieves.

A few weeks after this, news came that a young soldier had been sleeping at his post. He was court-martialed, and condemned to be shot. The boy wrote to his mother,

"I'd not want you to think that I do not love my country, but it came about in this way: My comrade was sick, and I went out on picket for him. The next night he ought to have come, but being still sick I went out for him again, and without intending it I fell asleep. I did not intend to be disloyal."

It was a very touching letter. The mother and father said there was no chance for him; there were to be no more reprieves. But there was a little girl in that home, and she knew that Abraham Lincoln had a little boy, and how he loved that boy; and she thought if Abraham Lincoln knew how her mother and father loved her brother he would never allow him to be shot. So she took the train to go and plead for her brother.

When she got to the president's mansion, the difficulty arose how she was to get past the sentinel. She told him her story, and the tears ran down his cheeks, and he let her pass. But the next trouble was how to get past the secretary and the other officials. However, she succeeded in getting, unobstructed, into Lincoln's private room, and there were the senators and ministers busy with state affairs.

The president saw the child, and called her to him, and said, "My child, what can I do for you?"

She told him her story. The big tears rolled down his cheeks. He was a father, and his heart was full; he could not stand it. He treated the girl with kindness, reprieved the boy, gave him thirty days furlough, and sent him home to see his mother. His heart was full of compassion.

Let me tell you, Christ's heart is more full of compassion than any man's. You are condemned to die for your sins; but if you go to

Him, He will say, "Loose him, and let him go." He will rebuke Satan. Go to Him as that little girl went to the president, and tell Him all. Keep nothing from Him, and He will say, "Go in peace."

THE TOUCH OF COMPASSION

Did you ever feel the touch of the hand of Jesus? If so, you will know it again, for there is love in it.

There is a story told in connection with our war of a mother who received a dispatch that her boy was mortally wounded. She went down to the front, as she knew that those soldiers told to watch the sick and wounded could not watch her boy as she would. So she went to the doctor, and said,

"Would you like me to take care of my boy?"

The doctor said, "We have just let him go to sleep, and if you go to him, the surprise will be so great it might be dangerous to him. He is in a very critical state. I will break the news to him gradually."

"But," said the mother, "he may never wake up. I should so dearly like to see him."

Finally the doctor said, "You can see him, but if you wake him up and he dies, it will be your fault."

"Well," she said, "I will not wake him up if I may only go to his dying cot and see him."

She went to the side of the cot. Her eyes had longed to see him. As she gazed upon him she could not keep her hand off that pallid forehead, and she laid it gently there. There was love and sympathy in that hand, and the moment the slumbering boy felt it, he said,

"Oh, Mother, have you come?"

He knew there was sympathy and affection in the touch of that hand. And if you, oh sinner, will let Jesus reach out His hand and touch your heart, you too will find there is sympathy and love in it. That every lost soul here may be saved, and come to the arms of our blessed Savior, is the prayer of my heart!

13

SECRET POWER

Witnessing in Power

The subject of witness-bearing in the power of the Holy Ghost is not sufficiently understood by the church. Until we have more intelligence on this point we are laboring under great disadvantage. Now, if you will take your Bible and turn to John 15:26, you will find these words: "But when the Comforter is come, whom I will send unto you from the Father, even the Spirit of truth, which proceedeth from the Father, he shall testify of me; and ye also shall bear witness, because ye have been with me from the beginning." Here we find what the Spirit is going to do, or what Christ said He would do when He came; namely, that He should testify of Him. And if you will turn over to the 2nd chapter of Acts, you will find that when Peter stood up on the day of Pentecost, and testified of what Christ had done, the Holy Spirit came down and bore witness to that fact, and men were convicted by hundreds and by thousands. So then, man can not preach effectively of himself. He must have the Spirit of God to give ability, and study God's Word in order to testify according to the mind of the Spirit.

WHAT IS THE TESTIMONY?

If we keep back the Gospel of Christ and do not bring Christ before the people, then the Spirit has not the opportunity to work. But the moment Peter stood up on the day of Pentecost and bore testimony to this one fact, that Christ died for sin, and that He had been raised again, and ascended into heaven—the Spirit came down to bear witness to the Person and work of Christ.

He came down to bear witness to the fact that Christ was in heaven, and if it were not for the Holy Ghost bearing witness to the preaching of the facts of the Gospel, do you think that the church

would have lived during these last eighteen centuries? Do you believe that Christ's death, resurrection, and ascension would not
have been forgotten as soon as His birth, if it had not been for the
fact that the Holy Spirit had come? Because it is very clear, that
when John made his appearance on the borders of the wilderness,
they had forgotten all about the birth of Jesus Christ. Just thirty
short years. It was all gone. They had forgotten the story of the
shepherds; they had forgotten the wonderful scene that took place
in the temple, when the Son of God was brought into the temple
and the older prophets and prophetesses were there; they had forgotten about the wise men coming to Jerusalem to inquire where
He was that was born King of the Jews. That story of His birth
seemed to have just faded away; they had forgotten all about it, and
when John made his appearance on the borders of the wilderness it
was brought back to their minds. And if it had not been for the Holy
Ghost coming down to bear witness to Christ, to testify of His death
and resurrection, these facts would have been forgotten as soon as
His birth.

GREATER WORK

The witness of the Spirit is the witness of power. Jesus said,
"The works that I do shall ye do also, and greater works than these
shall ye do because I go to the Father." I used to stumble over that.
I didn't understand it. I thought, what greater work could any man
do than Christ had done? How could anyone raise a dead man who
had been laid away in the sepulcher for days, and who had already
begun to turn back to dust; how with a word could he call him
forth? But the longer I live, the more I am convinced it is a great
thing to influence a man's will; a man whose will is set against God;
to have that will broken and brought into subjection to God's will—
or, in other words, it is a greater thing to have power over a living,
sinning, God-hating man, than to quicken the dead. He who could
create a world could speak a dead soul into life; but I think the
greatest miracle this world has ever seen was the miracle at Pentecost. Here were men who surrounded the apostles, full of prejudice,
full of malice, full of bitterness, their hands, as it were, dripping
with the blood of the Son of God, and yet an unlettered man, a man
whom they detested, a man whom they hated, stands up there and
preaches the Gospel, and three thousand of them are immediately
convicted and converted, and become disciples of the Lord Jesus
Christ, and are willing to lay down their lives for the Son of God. It

may have been on that occasion that Stephen was converted, the first martyr and some of the men who soon after gave up their lives for Christ. This seems to me the greatest miracle this world has ever seen. But Peter did not labor alone; the Spirit of God was with him; hence the marvelous results.

The Jewish law required that there should be two witnesses, and so we find that when Peter preached there was a second witness. Peter testified of Christ, and Christ says that when the Holy Spirit comes "He will testify of me." And they both bore witness to the verities of our Lord's incarnation, ministry, death, and resurrection, and the result was that a multitude turned as with one heart unto the Lord. Our failure now is, that preachers ignore the Cross, and veil Christ with sapless sermons and superfine language. They don't just present Him to the people plainly, and that is why I believe that the Spirit of God doesn't work with power in our churches. What we need is, to preach Christ and present Him to a perishing world. The world can get on very well without you and me, but the world can not get on without Christ, and therefore we must testify of Him, and the world, I believe, today is just hungering and thirsting for this divine, satisfying portion. Thousands and thousands are sitting in darkness, knowing not of this great Light, but when we begin to preach Christ honestly, faithfully, sincerely, and truthfully; holding Him up, not ourselves, exalting Christ and not our theories; presenting Christ and not our opinions; advocating Christ and not some false doctrine; then the Holy Ghost will come and bear witness. He will testify that what we say is true. When He comes He will confirm the Word with signs following. This is one of the strongest proofs that our Gospel is divine; that it is of divine origin; that not only did Christ teach these things, but when leaving the world He said, "He shall glorify me," and "He will testify of me." If you will just look at the 2nd chapter of Acts—to that wonderful sermon that Peter preached—the 36th verse, you will read these words: "Therefore let all the houses of Israel know assuredly, that God hath made that same Jesus, whom ye have crucified, both Lord and Christ." And when Peter said this the Holy Ghost descended upon the people and testified of Christ—bore witness in signal demonstration that all this was true. And again, in the 40th verse, "And with many other words did he testify and exhort, saying, Save yourselves from this untoward generation." With many other words did He testify, not only these words that have been recorded, but many other words.

THE SURE GUIDE

Turn to John 16:13, and read: "Howbeit, when he, the Spirit of truth, is come, he will guide you into all truth: for he shall not speak of himself; but whatsoever he shall hear, that shall he speak: and he will show you things to come." He will guide you into all truth. Now there is not a truth that we ought to know but the Spirit of God will guide us into it if we will let Him; if we will yield ourselves up to be directed by the Spirit, and let Him lead us, He will guide us into all truth. It would have saved us from a great many dark hours if we had only been willing to let the Spirit of God be our counselor and guide.

Lot never would have gone to Sodom if he had been guided by the Spirit of God. David never would have fallen into sin and had all that trouble with his family, if he had been guided by the Spirit of God.

There are many Lots and Davids nowadays. The churches are full of them. Men and women are in total darkness, because they have not been willing to be guided by the Spirit of God. "He will guide you into all truth: for he shall not speak of himself." He shall speak of the ascended, glorified Christ.

What would be thought of a messenger, entrusted by an absent husband with a message for his wife or mother who, on arrival, only talked of himself and his conceits, and ignored both the husband and the message? You would simply call it outrageous. What, then, must be the crime of the professed teacher who speaks of himself, or some insipid theory, leaving out Christ and His Gospel? If we witness according to the Spirit, we must witness of Jesus.

The Holy Spirit is down here in this dark world to just speak of the Absent One, and He takes the things of Christ and brings them to our mind. He testifies of Christ; He guides us into the truth about Him.

RAPPINGS IN THE DARK

I want to say right here, that I think in this day a great many children of God are turning aside and committing a grievous sin. I don't know as they think it is a sin, but if we examine the Scriptures, I am sure we will find that it is a great sin. We are told that the Comforter is sent into the world "to guide us into all truth," and if He is sent for that purpose, do we need any other guide? Need we hide in the darkness, consulting with mediums, who profess to call up the spirits of the dead? Do you know what the Word of God pronounces against that fearful sin? I believe it is one of the greatest sins we have to contend with at the present day. It is dishonoring to the Holy Spirit for me to go and summon up the dead and confer with them, even if it were possible.

I would like you to notice 1 Chronicles 10:13–14: "So Saul died for his transgression which he had committed against the Lord, even against the word of the Lord, which he kept not, and also for asking counsel of one that had a familiar spirit, to enquire of it; and enquired not of the Lord: therefore he slew him, and turned the kingdom unto David the son of Jesse."

God slew him for this very sin. Of the two sins that are brought against Saul here, one is that he would not listen to the Word of God, and the second is that he consulted a familiar spirit. He was snared by this great evil, and sinned against God.

Saul fell right here, and there are a great many of God's professed children today who think there is no harm in consulting a medium, who pretends to call up some of the departed to inquire of them.

But how dishonoring it is to God who has sent the Holy Spirit into this world to guide us "into all truth." There is not one thing that I need to know, there is not a thing that is important for me to know; there is not a thing that I ought to know but the Spirit of God will reveal it to me through the Word of God, and if I turn my back upon the Holy Spirit, I am dishonoring the Spirit of God, and I am committing a grievous sin. You know we read in Luke, where that rich man in the other world wanted to have some one sent to his father's house to warn his five brothers. Christ said: "They have Moses and the prophets, and if they will not hear them they will not hear one though he rose from the dead." Moses and the prophets, the part of the Bible then completed, that is enough. But a great many people now want something besides the Word of God, and are turning aside to these false lights.

SPIRITS THAT PEEP AND MUTTER

There is another passage which reads, "And when they shall say unto you, Seek unto them that have familiar spirits, and unto wizards that peep, and that mutter: should not a people seek unto their God? for the living to the dead?" [Isaiah 8:19] What is that but table rapping, and cabinet-hiding? If it were a message from God, do you think you would have to go into a dark room and put out all the lights? In secret my Master taught nothing. God is not in that movement, and what we want as children of God is to keep ourselves from this evil. And then notice the verse following, quoted so often out of its connection. "To the law and to the testimony: if they speak not according to this word, it is because there is no light in them." Any man, any woman who comes to us with any doctrine that is not according to the law and the testimony, let us understand that they are from the evil one, and that they are enemies of righteousness. They have no light in them. Now you will find these people who are consulting familiar spirits, first and last attack the Word of God. They don't believe it. Still a great many people say, you must hear both sides—but if a man should write me a most slanderous letter about my wife, I don't think I would have to read it; I should tear it up and throw it to the winds. Have I to read all the infidel books that are written, to hear both sides? Have I to take up a book that is slander on my Lord and Master, who has redeemed me with His blood? Ten thousand times "no"; I will not touch it.

"Now the Spirit speaketh expressly, that in the latter times some shall depart from the faith, giving heed to seducing spirits, and doctrines of devils" (1 Timothy 4:1). That is pretty plain language, isn't it? "Doctrines of devils." Again, "speaking lies in hypocrisy; having their conscience seared with a hot iron." There are other passages of Scripture warning against every delusion of Satan. Let us ever remember the Spirit has been sent into the world to guide us into all truth. We don't want any other guide; He is enough. Some people say, "Is not conscience a safer guide than the Word and the Spirit?" No, it is not. Some people don't seem to have any conscience, and don't know what it means. Their education has a good deal to do with conscience. There are persons who will say that their conscience did not tell them that they had done wrong until after the wrong was done; but what we want, is something to tell us a thing is wrong before we do it. Very often a man will go and commit some awful crime, and after it is done his conscience will wake up and lash and scourge him, and then it is too late, the act is done.

THE UNERRING GUIDE

I am told by people who have been over the Alps, that the guide fastens them, if they are going in a dangerous place, right to himself, and he just goes on before; they are fastened to the guide.

And so should the Christian be linked to His unerring Guide, and be safely upheld. Why, if a man was going through the Mammoth Cave, it would be death to him if he strayed away from his guide—if separated from him, he would certainly perish; there are pitfalls in that cave and a bottomless river, and there would be no chance for a man to find his way through that cave without a guide or a light. So there is no chance for us to get through the dark wilderness of this world alone. It is folly for a man or woman to think they can get through this evil world without the light of God's Word and the guidance of the divine Spirit. God sent Him to guide us through this great journey, and if we seek to work independent of Him, we shall stumble into the deep darkness of eternity's night.

But bear in mind the *words* of the Spirit of God; if you want to be guided, you must study the Word; because the Word is the light of the Spirit. In John 14:26, we read:

"But the Comforter, which is the Holy Ghost, whom the Father will send in my name, he shall teach you all things, and bring all things to your remembrance, whatsoever I have said unto you."

Again, in John 16:13:

"Howbeit when he, the Spirit of truth, is come, he will guide you into all truth: for he shall not speak of himself; but whatsoever he shall hear, that shall he speak: and he will show you things to come."

"He will show you things to come." A great many people seem to think that the Bible is out of date, that it is an old book, and they think it has passed its day. They say it was very good for the dark ages, and that there is some very good history in it; but that it was not intended for the present time; that we are living in a very enlightened age, and that men can get on very well without the old book; that we have outgrown it. They think we have no use for it, because it is an old book. Now you might just as well say that the sun, which has shone so long, is now so old that it is out of date, and that whenever a man builds a house he need not put any windows in it, because we have got a newer light and a better light; we have gaslight and this new electric light. These are something new; and I would advise people, if they think the Bible is too old and worn out, when they build their houses, not to put any windows in them, but just to light them with this new electric light; that is something new, and this is what they are anxious for. People talk about this Book as if they understood it; but we don't know much about it yet. The press gives us the daily news of what has taken place. This Bible, however, tells us what is about to take place. This *is* new; we have the news here in this Book; this tells us of the things that will surely come to pass; and that is a great deal newer than anything in the newspapers. It tells us that the Spirit shall teach us all things; not only guide us into all truth, but teach us all things; He teaches us how to pray, and I don't think there has ever been a prayer upon this sin-cursed earth that has been indited by the Holy Spirit but was answered. There is much praying that is not indited by the Holy Spirit. In former years I was very ambitious to get rich; I used to pray for one hundred thousand dollars; that was my aim, and I used to say, "God does not answer my prayer; He does not make me rich." But I had no warrant for such a prayer; yet a good many people pray in that way; they think that they pray, but they do not pray according to the Scriptures. The Spirit of God has nothing to do with their prayers, and such prayers are not the product of His teaching.

It is the Spirit that teaches us how to answer our enemies. If a man strikes me, I should not pull out a revolver and shoot him. The Spirit of the Lord doesn't teach me revenge; He doesn't teach me that it is necessary to draw the sword and cut a man down in order to defend my rights. Some people say, You are a coward if you don't strike back. Christ says, Turn the other cheek to him who smites. I would rather take Christ's teaching than any other. I don't think a man gains much to loading himself down with weapons to defend himself. There has been life enough sacrificed in this country to teach men a lesson in this regard. The Word of God is a much better protection than the revolver. We had better take the Word of God to protect us, by accepting its teaching, and living out its precepts.

AN AID TO MEMORY

It is a great comfort to us to remember that another office of the Spirit is to bring the teaching of Jesus to our remembrance. This was our Lord's promise, "He shall teach you all things, and bring all things to your remembrance" (John 14:26).

How striking that is! I think there are many Christians who have had that experience. They have been testifying, and found that while talking for Christ the Spirit has just brought into mind some of the sayings of the Lord Jesus Christ, and their mind was soon filled with the Word of God. When we have the Spirit resting upon us, we can speak with authority and power, and the Lord will bless our testimony and bless our work. I believe the reason why God makes use of so few in the church is because there is not in them the power that God can use. He is not going to use our ideas, but we must have the Word of God hid in our hearts, and then, the Holy Spirit inflaming us, we will have the testimony which will be rich, and sweet, and fresh, and the Lord's Word will vindicate itself in blessed results. God wants to use us; God wants to make us channels of blessing; but we are in such a condition He does not use us. That is the trouble; there are so many men who have no testimony for the Lord; if they speak, they speak without saying anything, and if they pray, their prayer is powerless; they do not plead in prayer; their prayer is just a few set phrases that you have heard too often. Now what we want, is to be so full of the Word, that the Spirit coming upon us shall bring to mind—bring to our remembrance—the words of the Lord Jesus.

In 1 Corinthians 2:9, it is written: "Eye hath not seen, nor ear heard, neither have entered into the heart of man, the things which God hath prepared for them that love him."

We hear that quoted so often in prayer—many a man weaves it into his prayer and stops right there. And the moment you talk about heaven, they say, "Oh, we don't know anything about heaven; it hath not entered into the heart of man; eye hath not seen; it is all speculation; we have nothing to do with it"; and they say they quote it as it is written. "Eye hath not seen, nor ear heard; neither have entered into the heart of man, the things which God hath prepared for them that love him." What next—"But God hath revealed them unto us by his Spirit." You see the Lord hath revealed them unto us: "For the Spirit searcheth all things, yea, the deep things of God." That is just what the Spirit does.

LONG AND SHORT SIGHT

He brings to our mind what God has in store for us. I heard a man, some time ago, speaking about Abraham. He said: "Abraham was not tempted by the well-watered plains of Sodom, for Abraham was what you might call a long-sighted man; he had his eyes set on the city which had a foundation—'whose Builder and Maker is God.'" But Lot was a short-sighted man; and there are many people in the church who are very short-sighted; they only see things right around them they think are good. Moses was long-sighted, and he left the palaces of Egypt and identified himself with God's people— poor people, who were slaves: but he had something in view yonder; he could see something God had in store. Again there are some people who are sort of long-sighted and short-sighted, too. I have a friend who has one eye that is long-sighted and the other is short-sighted; and I think the church is full of this kind of people. They want one eye for the world and the other for the kingdom of God. Therefore everything is blurred, one eye is long and the other is short, all is confusion, and they "see men as trees walking." The church is filled with that sort of people. But Stephen was long-sighted; he looked clear into heaven; they couldn't convince him even when he was dying, that Christ had not ascended to heaven. "Look, look yonder," he says, "I see Him over there; He is on the throne, standing at the right hand of God"; and he looked clear into heaven; the world had no temptation for him; he had put the world under his feet. Paul was another of those long-sighted men; he had been caught up and seen things unlawful for him to utter; things grand and glorious. I tell you when the Spirit of God is on us the world looks very empty; the world has a very small hold upon us, and we begin to let go our hold of it. When the Spirit of God is on us we will just let go the things of time and lay hold of things eternal. This is the church's need today; we want the Spirit to come in mighty power, and consume all the vile dross there is in us. Oh! That the Spirit of fire may come down and burn everything in us that is contrary to God's blessed Word and will.

In John 14:16, we read of the Comforter. This is the first time He is spoken of as the Comforter. Christ had been their Comforter. God had sent Him to comfort the sorrowing. It was prophesied of Him, "The Spirit of the Lord is upon me, because he hath anointed me to preach the gospel to the poor; he has sent me to heal the brokenhearted." You can't heal the broken-hearted without the Comforter; but the world would not have the first Comforter, and so they rose up and took Him to Calvary and put Him to death; but on going away He said, "I will send you another Comforter; you shall not be comfortless; be of good cheer, little flock; it is the Father's good pleasure to give you the kingdom." All these sweet passages are brought to the remembrance of God's people, and they help us to rise out of the fog and mist of this world. Oh, what a Comforter is the Holy Spirit of God!

THE FAITHFUL FRIEND

The Holy Spirit tells a man of his faults in order to lead him to a better life. In John 16:8, we read: "He will reprove the world of sin." Now, there are a class of people who don't like this part of the Spirit's work. Do you know why? Because He convicts *them* of sin; they don't like that. What they want is some one to speak comforting words and make everything pleasant; keep everything all quiet; tell them there is peace when there is war; tell them it is light when it is dark, and tell them everything is growing better; that the world is getting on amazingly in goodness; that it is growing better all the time; that is the kind of preaching they seek for. Men think they are a great deal better than their fathers were. That suits human nature, for it is full of pride. Men will strut around and say, "Yes, I believe that; the world is improving; I am a good deal better man than Father was; my father was too strict; he was one of those old Puritanical men who was so rigid. Oh, we are getting on; we are more liberal; my father wouldn't think of going out riding on Sunday, but we will; we will trample the laws of God under our feet; we are better than our fathers."

That is the kind of preaching which some dearly love, and there are preachers who tickle such itching ears. When you bring the Word of God to bear upon them, and when the Spirit drives it home, then men will say: "I don't like that kind of preaching; I will never go to hear that man again"; and sometimes they will get up and stamp their way out of church before the speaker gets through; they don't like it. But when the Spirit of God is at work He convicts men of sin. "When he is come, he will reprove the world of sin, and of righteousness, and of judgment: of sin"—not because men swear and lie and steal and get drunk and murder—"of sin, because they believe not on me."

THE CLIMAX SIN

That is the sin of the world. Why, a great many people think that unbelief is a sort of misfortune, but do not know, if you will allow me the expression, it is the damning sin of the world today; that is what unbelief is, the mother of all sin. There would not be a drunkard walking the streets, if it were not for unbelief; there would not be a harlot walking the streets, if it were not for unbelief; there would not be a murderer, if it were not for unbelief; it is the term of all sin. Don't think for a moment that it is a misfortune, but just bear in mind it is an awful sin, and may the Holy Spirit convict every reader that unbelief is making God a liar. Many a man has been knocked down on the streets because some one has told him he was a liar. Unbelief is giving God the lie; that is the plain English of it. Some people seem to boast of their unbelief; they seem to think it is quite respectable to be an infidel and doubt God's Word, and they will vainly boast and say, "I have intellectual difficulties; I can't believe." Oh, that the Spirit of God may come and convict men of sin! That is what we need—His convicting power, and I am so thankful that God has not put that into our hands. We have not to convict men; if we had, I would get discouraged, and give up preaching, and go back to business within the next forty-eight hours. It is my work to preach and hold up the Cross and testify of Christ; but it is His work to convict men of sin and lead them to Christ. One thing I have noticed, that some conversions don't amount to anything; that if a man professes to be converted without conviction of sin, he is one of those stony-ground hearers who don't bring forth much fruit. The first little wave of persecution, the first breath of opposition, and the man is back in the world again. Let us pray, dear Christian reader, that God may carry on a deep and thorough work, that men may be convicted of sin so that they can not rest in unbelief. Let us pray God it may be a thorough work in the land. I would a great deal rather see a hundred men thoroughly converted, truly born of God, than to see a thousand professed conversions where the Spirit of God has not convicted of sin. Don't let us cry: "Peace, peace, when there is no peace." Don't go to the man who is living in sin, and tell him all he has to do is to stand right up and profess, without any hatred for sin. Let us ask God first to show every man the plague of his own heart, that the Spirit may convict them of sin. Then will the work in our hands be real, deep, and abide the fiery trial which will try every man's labor.

Thus far, we have found the work of the Spirit is to impart life, to implant hope, to give liberty, to testify of Christ, to guide us into all truth, to teach us all things, to comfort the believers, and to convict the world of sin.

14

TO THE WORK

Enthusiasm

"Awake thou that sleepest, and arise from the dead, and Christ shall give thee light" (Ephesians 5:14). I want to apply these words to the children of God. If the lost are to be reached by the Gospel of the Son of God, Christianity must be more aggressive than it has been in the past. We have been on the defensive long enough; the time has come for us to enter on a war of aggression. When we as children of God wake up and go to work in the vineyard, then those who are living in wickedness all about us will be reached; but not in any other way. You may go to mass meetings and discuss the question of "How to reach the masses," but when you have done with discussion you have to go back to personal effort. Every man and woman who loves the Lord Jesus Christ must wake up to the fact that he or she has a mission in the world, in this work of reaching the lost.

A man may talk in his sleep, and it seems to me that there is a good deal of that kind of thing now in the Lord's work. A man may even preach in his sleep. A friend of mine sat up in his bed one night and preached a sermon right through. He was sound asleep all the time. Next morning his wife told him all about it. He preached the same sermon in his church the next Sabbath morning; I have it in print, and a good sermon it is. So a man may not only talk but actually preach in his sleep. There are many preachers in these days who are fast asleep.

There is one thing, however, that we must remember; a man can not *work* in his sleep. There is no better way to wake up a church than to set it to work. One man will wake up another in waking himself up. Of course the moment we begin a work of aggression, and declare war with the world, the flesh, and the devil, some wise head will begin to shake, and there will be the cry, "Zeal without knowledge!" I think I have heard that objection ever since I commenced the Christian life. I heard of some one who was speaking the other day of something that was to be done, and who said he hoped zeal would be tempered with moderation. Another friend wisely replied that he hoped moderation would be tempered with zeal. If that were always the case, Christianity would be like a red hot ball rolling over the face of the earth. There is no power on earth that can stand before the onward march of God's people when they are in dead earnest.

In all ages God has used those who were in earnest. Satan always calls idle men into his service. God calls active and earnest—not indolent men. When we are thoroughly aroused and ready for His work, then He will take us up and use us. You remember where Elijah found Elisha; he was plowing in the field—he was at work. Gideon was at the threshing floor. Moses was away in Horeb looking after the sheep. None of these eminent servants of God were indolent men; what they did, they did with all their might. We want such men and women nowadays. If we cannot do God's work with all the knowledge we would like, let us at any rate do it with all the zeal that God has given us.

Mr. Taylor says: "The zeal of the Apostles was seen in this—they preached publicly and privately; they prayed for all men; they wept to God for the hardness of men's hearts; they became all things to all men, that they might gain some; they traveled through deeps and deserts; they endured the heat of the Syrian sun and the violence of Euroclydon, winds and tempests, seas and prisons, mockings and scourgings, fastings and poverty, labor and watching; they endured of every man and wronged no man; they would do any good, and suffer any evil, if they could but hope to prevail upon a soul; they persuaded men meekly, they entreated them humbly, they convinced them powerfully; they watched for their good, but meddled not with their interest; and this is the Christian zeal—the zeal of meekness, the zeal of charity, the zeal of patience."

A good many people are afraid of the word *enthusiasm*. Do you know what the word means? It means "In God." The person who is "in God" will surely be fired with enthusiasm. When a man goes into business filled with fire and zeal, he will generally carry all before him. In the army, a general who is full of enthusiasm will fire up his men, and will accomplish a great deal more than one who is not stirred with the same spirit. People say that if we go on in that way many mistakes will be made. Probably there will. You never saw any boy learning a trade who did not make a good many mistakes. If you do not go to work because you are afraid of making mistakes, you will probably make one great mistake—the greatest mistake of your life—that of doing nothing. If we all do what we can, then a good deal will be accomplished.

How often do we find Sabbath-school teachers going into their work without any enthusiasm. I had just as soon have a lot of wooden teachers as some that I have known. If I were a carpenter, I could manufacture any quantity of them. Take one of those teachers who has no heart, no fire, and no enthusiasm. He comes into the schoolroom perhaps a few minutes after the appointed time. He sits down, without speaking a word to any of the scholars, until the time comes for the lessons to begin. When the Superintendent says it is time to begin the teacher brings out a Question Book. He has not been at the trouble to look up the subject himself, so he gets what some one else has written about it. He takes care not only to get a Question Book, but an Answer Book.

Such a teacher will take up the first book and he says: "John, who was the first man?" (looking at the book)—"Yes, that is the right question." John replies, "Adam." Looking at the Answer Book the teacher says: "Yes, that is right." He looks again at the Question Book and he says: "Charles, who was Lot?" "Abraham's nephew." "Yes, my boy, that is right." And so he goes on. You may say that this is an exaggerated description, and of course I do not mean to say it is literally true; but the picture is not so much overdrawn as you would suppose. Do you think a class of little boys full of life and fire is going to be reached in that way?

I like to see a teacher come into the class and shake hands with the scholars all round. "Johnnie, how do you do? Charlie, I am glad to see you! How's the baby? How's your mother? How are all the folks at home?" That is the kind of a teacher I like to see. When he begins to open up the lesson all the scholars are interested in what he is going to say. He will be able to gain the attention of the whole class, and to train them for God and for eternity. You cannot find me a person in the world who has been greatly used of God, who has not been full of enthusiasm. When we enter on the work in this spirit it will begin to prosper, and God will give us success.

As I was leaving New York to go to England in 1867, a friend said to me: "I hope you will go to Edinburgh and be at the General Assembly this year. When I was there a year ago I heard such a speech as I shall never forget. Dr. Duff made a speech that set me all on fire. I shall never forget the hour I spent in that meeting." Shortly after reaching England I went to Edinburgh and spent a week there, in hopes that I might hear that one man speak. I went to work to find the report of the speech that my friend had referred to, and it stirred me wonderfully. Dr. Duff had been out in India as a missionary. He had spent twenty-five years there preaching the Gospel and establishing schools. He came back with a broken-down constitution. He was permitted to address the General Assembly, in order to make an appeal for men to go into the mission field. After he had spoken for a considerable time, he became exhausted and fainted away. They carried him out of the hall into another room. The doctors worked over him for some time, and at last he began to recover. When he realized where he was, he roused himself and said: "I did not finish my speech; carry me back and let me finish it." They told him he could only do it at the peril of his life. Said he: "I will do it if I die." So they took him back to the hall. My friend said it was one of the most solemn scenes he ever witnessed in his life.

They brought the white-haired man into the Assembly Hall, and as he appeared at the door every person sprang to his feet; the tears flowed freely as they looked upon the grand old veteran. With a trembling voice, he said: "Fathers and mothers of Scotland, is it true that you have no more sons to send to India to work for the Lord Jesus Christ? The call for help is growing louder and louder, but there are few coming forward to answer it. You have the money put away in the bank, but where are the laborers who shall go into the field? When Queen Victoria wants men to volunteer for her army in India, you freely give your sons. You do not talk about their losing their health, and about the trying climate. But when the Lord Jesus is calling for laborers, Scotland is saying: 'We have no more sons to give.'"

Turning to the President of the Assembly, he said: "Mr. Moderator, if it is true that Scotland has no more sons to give to the service of the Lord Jesus Christ in India; although I have lost my health in that land, if there are none who will go and tell those heathen of Christ, then I will be off tomorrow, to let them know that there is one old Scotsman who is ready to die for them. I will go back to the shores of the Ganges, and there lay down my life as a witness for the Son of God."

Thank God for such a man as that! We want men today who

are willing, if need be, to lay down their lives for the Son of God. Then we shall be able to make an impression upon the world. When they see that we are in earnest, their hearts will be touched, and we shall be able to lead them to the Lord Jesus Christ.

I did not agree with Garibaldi's judgement in all things, but I must confess I did admire his enthusiasm. I never saw his name in the papers, or in a book, but I read all I could find about him. There was something about him that fired me up. I remember reading of the time when he was on the way to Rome in 1867, and when he was cast into prison. I read the letter he sent to his comrades: "If fifty Garibaldis are thrown into prison, let Rome be free!" He did not care for his own comfort, so long as the cause of freedom in Italy was advanced. If we have such a love for our Master and His cause that we are ready to go out and do His work whatever it may cost us personally, depend upon it the Lord will use us in building up His kingdom.

I have read of a man in the ninth century who came up against a king. The king had a force of thirty thousand men, and when he heard that this general had only five hundred men, he sent him a message that if he would surrender he would treat him and his followers mercifully. Turning to one of his followers, the man said: "Take that dagger and drive it to your heart." The man at once pressed the weapon to his bosom, and fell dead at the feet of his commander. Turning to another, he said: "Leap into yonder chasm." Into the jaws of death the man went; they saw him dashed to pieces at the bottom. Then turning to the king's messenger, the man said: "Go back to your king, and tell him that I have five hundred such men. Tell him that we may die but we never surrender. Tell him that I will have him chained with my dogs within forty-eight hours." When the king heard that he had such men arrayed against him, it struck terror to his heart. His forces were so demoralized that they were scattered like chaff before the wind. Within forty-eight hours the king was taken captive and chained with the dogs of his conqueror. When the people see that we are in earnest in all that we undertake for God, they will begin to tremble; men and women will be enquiring the way to Zion.

A fearful storm was raging, when the cry was heard, "Man overboard!" A human form was seen manfully breasting the furious elements in the direction of the shore; but the raging waves bore the struggler rapidly outward, and, ere the boats could be lowered, a fearful space separated the victim from help. Above the shriek of the storm and roar of the waters rose his rending cry. It was an agonizing moment. With bated breath and blanched cheek, every eye was strained to the struggling man. Manfully did the brave rowers strain every nerve in that race of mercy; but all their efforts were in vain. One wild shriek of despair, and the victim went down. A piercing cry, "Save him, save him!" rang through the hushed crowd; and into their midst darted an agitated man, throwing his arms wildly in the air, shouting, "A thousand pounds for the man who saves his life!" but his starting eye rested only on the spot where the waves rolled remorselessly over the perished. He whose strong cry broke the stillness of the crowd was the Captain of the ship from whence the drowned man fell, and was *his brother*. This is the feeling we want to have in the various ranks of those bearing commission under the great Captain of our salvation. "Save him! He is my brother!"

The fact is, men do not believe in Christianity because they think we are not in earnest about it. In [the Second Letter of Paul to the Corinthians] the apostle says we are to be living epistles of Christ, "known and read of all men" [3:2]. I never knew a time when Christian people were ready to go forth and put in the sickle, but there was a great harvest. Wherever you put in the sickle you will find the fields white. The trouble is there are so few to reap.

God wants men and women; that is something far better than institutions. If a man or a woman be really in earnest, they will not wait to be put on some committee. If I saw a man fall into the river, and he was in danger of drowning, I would not wait until I was placed on some committee before I tried to save him. Many people say they cannot work because they have not been formally appointed. They say: "It is not my parish." I asked a person one day, during our last visit to London, if he would go and work in the inquiry-room. The reply was: "I do not belong to this part of London." Let us look on the whole world as our parish, as a great harvest field. If God puts anyone within our influence, let us tell them of Christ and heaven. The world may rise up and say that we are mad. In my opinion no one is fit for God's service until he is willing to be considered mad by the world. They said Paul was mad. I wish we had many more who were bitten with the same kind of madness. As some one has said: "If we are mad, we have a good Keeper on the way and a good Asylum at the end of the road."

One great trouble is that people come to special revival meetings, and for two or three weeks, perhaps, they will keep up the fire, but by and by it dies out. They are like a bundle of shavings with kerosene on the top—they blaze away for a little, but soon there is nothing left. We want to keep it all the time, morning, noon, and night. I heard of a well once that was said to be very good, except that it had two faults. It *would* freeze up in the winter and it *would* dry up in the summer. A most extraordinary well, but I am afraid there are many wells like it. There are many people who are good at certain times; as some one has expressed it, they seem to be good "in spots." What we want is to be red hot all the time. Do not wait till some one hunts you up. People talk about striking while the iron is hot. I believe it was Cromwell who said that he would rather strike the iron and make it hot. So let us keep at our post, and we will soon grow warm in the Lord's work.

Let me say a few words specially to Sabbath-school teachers. Let me urge upon you not to be satisfied with merely pointing the children a way to the Lord Jesus Christ. There are so many teachers who go on sowing the seed, and who think they will reap the harvest by and by; but they do not look for the harvest now. I began to work in that way, and it was years before I saw any conversions. I believe God's method is that we should sow with one hand and reap with the other. The two should go on side by side. The idea that children must grow into manhood and womanhood before they can be brought to Jesus Christ is a false one. They can be led to Christ now in the days of their youth, and they can be kept, so that they may become useful members of society, and be a blessing to their parents, to the Church of God, and to the world. If they are allowed to grow up to manhood and womanhood before they are led to Christ, many of them will be dragged into the dens of vice; and instead of being a blessing they will be a curse to society.

What is the trouble throughout Christendom today, in connection with the Sabbath-school? It is that so many when they grow up to the age of sixteen or so, drop through the Sabbath-school net, and that is the last we see of them. There are many young men now in our prisons who have been Sabbath scholars. The cause of that is that so few teachers believe the children can be converted when they are young. They do not labor to bring them to a knowledge of Christ, but are content to go on sowing the seed. Let a teacher resolve that, God helping him, he will not rest until he sees his whole class brought into the kingdom of God; if he thus resolves he will see signs and wonders inside of thirty days.

I well remember how I got waked up on this point. I had a large Sunday-school with a thousand children. I was very much pleased with the numbers. If they only kept up or exceeded that number, I was delighted; if the attendance fell below a thousand, I was very much troubled. I was all the time aiming simply at numbers. There was one class held in a corner of the large hall. It was made up of young women, and it was more trouble than any other in the school. There was but one man who could ever manage it and keep it in order. If he could manage to keep the class quiet, I thought it was about as much as we could hope for. The idea of any of them being converted never entered my mind.

One Sabbath this teacher was missing, and it was with difficulty that his substitute could keep order in the class. During the week the teacher came to my place of business. I noticed that he looked very pale, and I asked what was the trouble. "I have been bleeding at the lungs," he said, "and the doctor tells me I cannot live. I must give up my class and go back to my widowed mother in New York State." He fully believed he was going home to die. As he spoke to me his chin quivered, and the tears began to flow. I noticed this and said: "You are not afraid of death, are you?" "Oh, no, I am not afraid to die, but I will meet God, and not one of my Sabbath-school scholars is converted. What shall I say?" Ah, how different things looked when he felt he was going to render an account of his stewardship.

I was speechless. It was something new to me to hear anyone speak in that way. I said: "Suppose we go and see the scholars and tell them about Christ." "I am very weak," he said, "too weak to walk." I said I would take him in a carriage. We took a carriage and went round to the residence of every scholar. He would just be able to stagger across the sidewalk, sometimes leaning on my arm. Calling the young lady by name, he would pray with her and plead with her to come to Christ. It was a new experience for me. I got a new view of things. After he had used up all his strength I would take him home. Next day he would start again and visit others in the class. Sometimes he would go alone, and sometimes I would go with him. At the end of ten days he came to my place of business, his face beaming with joy, and said: "The last one has yielded her heart to Christ. I am going home now; I have done all I can do; my work is done." I asked when he was going, and he said: "Tomorrow night." I said: "Suppose I ask these young friends to have a little gathering, to meet you once more before you go." He said he would be very glad. I sent out the invitations and they all came together. I had never spent such a night up to that time. I had never met such a large number of young converts, led to Christ by his influence and mine. We prayed for each member of the class, for the Superintendent, and for the teacher. Every one of them prayed; what a change had come over them in a short space of time. We tried to sing—but we did not get on very well—

"Blest be the tie that binds
Our hearts in Christian love."

We all bade him good-bye; but I felt as if I must go and see him once more. Next night, before the train started, I went to the station, and found that, without any concert of action, one and another of the class had come to bid him good-bye. They were all there on the platform. A few gathered around us—the fireman, engineer, brakeman, and conductor of the train, with the passengers. It was a beautiful summer night, and the sun was just going down behind the western prairies as we sang together—

"Here we meet to part again,
But when we meet on Canaan's shore,
There'll be no parting there."

As the train moved out of the station, he stood on the outside platform, and, with his finger pointing heaven-ward, he said: "I will meet you yonder"; then he disappeared from our view.

What a work was accomplished in those ten days! Some of the members of that class were among the most active Christians we had in the school for years after. Some of them are active workers today. I met one of them at work away out on the Pacific Coast, a few years ago. We had a blessed work of grace in the school that summer; it took me out of my business and sent me into the Lord's work. If it had not been for the work of those ten days, probably I should not have been an evangelist today.

Let me again urge on Sunday-school teachers to seek the salvation of your scholars. Make up your mind that within the next ten days you will do all you can to lead your class to Christ. Fathers, mothers, let there be no rest till you see all your family brought into the kingdom of God. Do you say that He will not bless such consecrated effort? What we want today is the spirit of consecration and concentration. May God pour out His Spirit upon us, and fill me with a holy enthusiasm.

15

PREVAILING PRAYER

Answered Prayers

In the fifteenth chapter of John and the seventh verse, we find who have their prayers answered—"If ye abide in me, and my words abide in you, ye shall ask what ye will, and it shall be done unto you." Now in the fourth chapter of James, in the third verse, we find some spoken of whose prayers were not answered: "Ye ask, and receive not, because ye ask amiss." There are a great many prayers not answered because there is not the right motive; we have not complied with the Word of God; we ask amiss. It is a good thing that our prayers are not answered when we ask amiss.

If our prayers are not answered, it may be that we have prayed without the right motive; or that we have not prayed according to the Scriptures. So let us not be discouraged, or give up praying, although our prayers are not answered in the way we want them.

A man once went to George Mueller and said he wanted him to pray for a certain thing. The man stated that he had asked God a great many times to grant him his request, but He had not seen fit to do it. Mr. Mueller took out his notebook, and showed the man the name of a person for whom, he said, he had prayed for twenty-four years. The prayer, Mr. Mueller added, was not answered yet; but the Lord had given him assurance that that person was going to be converted, and his faith rested there.

We sometimes find that our prayers are answered right away while we are praying; at other times the answer is delayed. But especially when men pray for mercy, how quickly the answer comes! Look at Paul, when he cried, "O Lord, what wilt thou have me to do?" The answer came at once. Then the publican who went up to the temple to pray—he got an immediate answer. The thief on the cross prayed, "Lord, remember me when thou comest into thy kingdom!" and the answer came immediately—then and there. There are many cases of a similar kind in the Bible, but there are also others who prayed long and often. The Lord delights in hearing His children make their requests known unto Him—telling their troubles all out to Him; and then we should wait for His time. We do not know when that is.

There was a mother in Connecticut who had a son in the army, and it almost broke her heart when he left, because he was not a Christian. Day after day she lifted up her voice in prayer for her boy. She afterward learned that he had been taken to the hospital, and there died, but she could not find out anything about how he had died. Years passed, and one day a friend came to see some member of the family on business. There was a picture of the soldier boy upon the wall. He looked at it, and said, "Did you know that young man?" The mother said, "That young man was my son. He died in the late war." The man replied, "I knew him very well; he was in my company." The mother then asked, "Do you know anything about his end?" The man said, "I was in the hospital, and he died a most peaceful death, triumphant in the faith." The mother had given up hope of ever hearing of her boy; but before she went hence she had the satisfaction of knowing that her prayers had prevailed with God.

I think we shall find a great many of our prayers that we thought unanswered answered when we get to heaven. If it is the true prayer of faith, God will not disappoint us. Let us not doubt God. On one occasion, at a meeting I attended, a gentleman pointed out an individual and said, "Do you see that man over there? That is one of the leaders of an infidel club." I sat down beside him, when the infidel said, "I am not a Christian. You have been humbugging these people long enough, and making some of these old women believe you get answers to prayer. Try it on me." I prayed, and when I got up, the infidel said with a good deal of sarcasm, "I am not converted; God has not answered your prayer!" I said, "But you may be converted yet." Some time afterwards I received a letter from a friend, stating that he had been converted and was at work in the meetings.

Jeremiah prayed, and said, "Ah, Lord God! behold, thou hast made the heaven and the earth by thy great power and stretched out arm, and there is nothing too hard for thee." Nothing is too hard for God; that is a good thing to take for a motto. I believe this is a time of great blessing in the world, and we may expect great things.

While the blessing is falling all around, let us arise and share in it. God has said, "Call unto me, and I will answer thee, and show thee great and mighty things, which thou knowest not." Now let us call on the Lord; and let us pray that it may be done for Christ's sake— not our own.

ALWAYS ASK "FOR CHRIST'S SAKE"

At a Christian convention a number of years ago, a leading man got up and spoke—his subject being "For Christ's Sake"—and he threw new light upon that passage. I had never seen it in that way before. When the war broke out the gentleman's only son had enlisted, and he never saw a company of soldiers but his heart went right out after them. They started a Soldiers' Home in the city where the gentleman lived, and he gladly went on the committee, and acted as President. Some time afterward he said to his wife, "I have given so much time to these soldiers that I have neglected my business," and he went down to his office with the fixed determination that he would not be disturbed by any soldiers that day. The door opened soon after, and he saw a soldier entering. He never minded him, but kept on writing; and the poor fellow stood for some time. At last the soldier put down an old soiled piece of paper on which there was writing. The gentleman observed that it was the handwriting of his son, and he seized the letter at once and read it. It was something to this effect: "Dear Father, this young man belongs to my company. He has lost his health in defense of his country, and he is on his way home to his mother to die. Treat him kindly for Charlie's sake." The gentleman at once dropped his work and took the soldier to his house, where he was kindly cared for until he was able to be sent home to his mother; then he took him to the station, and sent him home with a "God bless you, for Charlie's sake!"

Let our prayers, then, be for Christ's sake. If we want our sons and daughters converted, let us pray that it be done for Christ's sake. If that is the motive, our prayers will be answered. If God gave up Christ for the world, what will He not give us? If He gave Christ to the murderers and blasphemers, and the rebels of a world lying in wickedness and sin, what would He not give to those who go to Him for Christ's sake? Let our prayer be that God may advance His work, not for our glory—not for our sake—but for the sake of His beloved Son whom He hath sent.

So let us remember that when we pray we ought to expect an answer. Let us be looking for it. I remember at the close of a meeting in one of our Southern cities near the close of the war, a man came up to me weeping and trembling. I thought something I had said had aroused him, and I began to question him as to what it was. I found, however, that he could not tell a word of what I had said. "My friend," said I, "what is the trouble?" He put his hand into his pocket, and brought out a letter, all soiled, as if his tears had fallen on it. "I got that letter," he said, "from my sister last night. She tells me that every night she goes on her knees and prays to God for me. I think I am the worst man in all the Army of the Cumberland. I have been perfectly wretched today." That sister was six hundred miles away, but she had brought her brother to his knees in answer to her earnest, believing prayer. It was a hard case, but God heard and answered the prayer of this godly sister, so that the man was as clay in the hands of the potter. He was soon brought into the kingdom of God—all through his sister's prayers.

I went off some thirty miles to another place, where I told this story. A young man, a lieutenant in the army, sprang to his feet and said, "That reminds me of the last letter I got from my mother. She told me that every night as the sun went down she prayed for me. She begged of me, when I got her letter, to go away alone, and yield myself to God. I put the letter in my pocket, thinking there would be plenty of time." He went on to say that the next news that came from home was that that mother was gone. He went out into the woods alone, and cried to his mother's God to have mercy upon him. As he stood in the meeting with his face shining, that lieutenant said: "My mother's prayers are answered; and my only regret is that she did not live to know it; but I will meet her by and by." So, though we may not live to see the answer to our prayers, if we cry mightily to God, the answer will come.

In Scotland, a good many years ago, there lived a man with his wife and three children—two girls and a boy. He was in the habit of getting drunk, and thus losing his situation. At last, he said he would take Johnnie, and go off to America, where he could be away from his old associates, and where he could commence life over again. He took the little fellow, seven years old, and went away. Soon after he arrived in America, he went into a saloon and got drunk. He got separated from his boy in the streets, and he has never been seen by his friends since. The little fellow was placed in an institution, and afterward apprenticed in Massachusetts. After he had been there some time, he became discontented, and went off to sea; finally, he came to Chicago to work on the lakes. He had been a roving spirit, had gone over sea and land, and now he was in Chicago. When the vessel came into port one time, he was invited to a Gospel meeting. The joyful sound of the Gospel reached him, and he became a Christian.

After he had been a Christian a little while, he became very anxious to find his mother. He wrote to different places in Scotland, but could not find out where she was. One day he read in the Psalms—"No good thing will he withhold from them that walk uprightly." He closed his Bible, got down on his knees, and said: "Oh, God, I have been trying to walk uprightly for months past; help me to find my mother." It came into his mind to write back to the place in Massachusetts from which he had run away years before. It turned out that a letter from Scotland had been waiting for him there for seven years. He wrote at once to the place in Scotland, and found that his mother was still living; the answer came back immediately. I would like you to have seen him when he got that letter. He brought it to me; and the tears flowed so that he could scarcely read it. His sister had written on behalf of the mother; she had been so overcome by the tidings of her long-lost boy that she could not write.

The sister said that all the nineteen years he had been away, his mother had prayed to God day and night that he might be saved, and that she might live to know what had become of him, and see him once more. Now, said the sister, she was so overjoyed, not only that he was alive, but that he had become a Christian. It was not long before the mother and sister came out to Chicago to meet him.

I mention this incident to show how God answers prayer. This mother cried to God for nineteen long years. It must have seemed to her sometimes as though God did not mean to give her the desires of her heart; but she kept praying, and at last the answer came.

The following personal testimony was publicly given at one of our meetings lately held in London, and may serve to help and encourage readers of these pages.

A PRAYER-MEETING TESTIMONY

"I want you to understand, my friends, that what I state is not what I did, but what God did. God only could have done it! I had given it up as a bad job, long before. But it is of God's great mercy that I am standing here tonight, to tell you that Christ is able to save to the uttermost all that come to God through Him.

"The reading of those 'requests' for the salvation of inebriates touched me very deeply indeed. They seemed to be an echo of many a request for prayer which has been made for me. And, from my knowledge of society generally, and of human nature, I know that in a very great number of families there is need of some such request.

"Therefore if what I may tell you will cheer any Christian heart, encourage any godly father and mother to go on praying for their sons, or assist any man or woman who has felt himself or herself beyond the reach of hope, I shall thank God for it.

"I had very good opportunities. My parents love the Lord Jesus, and did their best to train me up in the right path; and for some time I thought myself that I should be a Christian. But I got away from Christ, and turned further and further away from God and all good influences.

"It was at a public school where I first learned to drink. Many a time at seventeen I drank to excess, but I had an amount of self-respect that kept me from going thoroughly to the bad till I was about twenty-three; but from then till I was twenty-six, I went steadily downhill. At Cambridge I went on further and further in drinking until I lost all self-respect, and voluntarily chose the worst of companions.

"I strayed further and further from God, until my friends, those who were Christians and those who were not, considered, and told me that there was very little hope for me. I had been pleaded with by all sorts of people, but I 'hated reproof.' I hated everything that savored of religion, and I sneered at every bit of good advice, or any kind word offered me in that way.

"My father and mother both died without seeing me brought to the Lord. They prayed for me all the time they lived, and at the very last my mother asked me if I would not follow her to be with her in heaven. To quiet and soothe her, I said I would. But I did not mean it; and I thought, when she had passed away, that she knew now my real feelings. After her death I went from bad to worse, and plunged deeper and deeper into vice. Drink got a stronger hold on me, and I went lower and lower down. I was never 'in the gutter,' in the acceptation in which that term is generally understood; but I was as low in my soul as any man who lives in one of the common lodging-houses.

"I went from Cambridge first to a town in the north, where I was articled to a solicitor; and then to London. While I was in the north, Messrs. Moody and Sankey came to the town I lived in; and

an aunt of mine, who was still praying for me after my mother's death, came and said to me, 'I have a favor to ask of you.' She had been very kind to me, and I knew what she wanted. She said, 'It is to go and hear Messrs. Moody and Sankey.' 'Very good,' I said; 'it is a bargain. I will go and hear the men; but you are never to ask me again. You will promise that?' 'Yes,' she said, 'I do.' I went, and kept, as I thought, most religiously my share of the bargain.

"I waited until the sermon was over, and I saw Mr. Moody coming down from the pulpit. Earnest prayer had been offered for me, and there had been an understanding between my aunt and him that the sermon should apply to me, and that he would come and speak to me immediately afterward. We met Mr. Moody in the aisle, and I thought that I had done a very clever thing when I walked round my aunt, before Mr. Moody could address me, and out of the building.

"I wandered further from God after that; and I do not think that I bent my knees in prayer for between two and three years. I went to London, and things grew worse and worse. At times I tried to pull up. I made any number of resolutions. I promised myself and my friends not to touch the drink. I kept my resolutions for some days, and, on one occasion, for six months; but the temptation came with stronger force than ever, and swept me further and further from the pathway of virtue. When in London I neglected my business and everything I ought to have done, and sank deeper into sin.

"One of my boon companions said to me, 'If you don't pull up, you will kill yourself.' 'How is that?' I asked. 'You are killing yourself, for you can't drink so much as you used to.' 'Well,' I replied, 'I can't help it, then.' I got to such a state that I did not think there was any possible help for me.

"The recital of these things pains me; and as I relate them, God forbid that I should feel anything but shame. I am telling you these things because we have a Savior; and if the Lord Jesus Christ saved even me, He is able also to save you.

"Affairs went on in this manner until, at last, I lost all control over myself.

"I had been drinking and playing billiards one day, and in the evening I returned to my lodgings. I thought that I would sit there awhile, and then go out again, as usual. Before going out, I began to think, and the thought struck me, 'How will all this end?' 'Oh,' I thought to myself, 'what is the use of that? I know how it will end—

in my eternal destruction, body and soul!' I felt I was killing my-self—my body; and I knew too well what would be the result to my soul. I thought it impossible for me to be saved. But the thought came to me very strongly, 'Is there any way of escape?' 'No,' I said; 'I have made any number of resolutions. I have done all I could to keep clear of drink, but I can't. It is impossible.'

ALL THINGS ARE POSSIBLE WITH GOD

"Just at that moment the words came into my mind from God's own Word—words that I had not remembered since I was a boy: 'With men this is impossible, but with God all things are possible.' And then I saw, in a flash, that what I had just admitted, as I had done hundreds of times before, to be an impossibility, was the one thing that God had pledged Himself to do, if I would go to Him. All the difficulties came up in my way—my companions, my surround-ings of all sorts, and my temptations; but I just looked up and thought, 'It is possible with God.'

"I went down on my knees there and then, in my room, and be-gan to ask God to do the impossible. As soon as I prayed to Him, with very stammering utterance—I had not prayed for nearly three years—I thought, 'Now, then, God will help me.' I took hold of His truth, I don't know how. It was nine days before I knew how and be-fore I had any assurance, or peace and rest, to my soul. I got up, there and then, with the hope that God would save me. I took it to be the truth, and I ultimately proved it; for which I praise God.

"I thought the best thing I could do would be to go and get somebody to talk to me about my soul, and tell me how to be saved; for I was a perfect heathen, though I had been brought up so well. I went out and hunted about London; and it shows how little I knew of religious people and places of worship, that I could not find a Wes-leyan chapel. My mother and father were Wesleyans, and I thought I would find a place belonging to their denomination; but I could not. I searched an hour and a half; and that night I was in the most utter, abject misery of body and soul any man can think of or conceive.

"I came home to my lodgings and went upstairs and thought to myself, 'I will not go to bed till I am saved.' But I was so ill from drinking—I had not had my usual amount of food in the evening; and the reaction was so tremendous, that I felt I must go to bed (al-though I dared not), or I should be in a very serious condition in the morning.

"I knew how I should be in the morning, thinking, 'What a fool

I was last night!' then I would wake up moderately fresh, and go off to drink again, as I had often done. But again I thought, 'God can do the impossible. He will do that which I cannot do myself.' And I prayed to the Lord to let me wake up in much the same condition as that in which I went to bed, feeling the weight of my sins and my misery. Then I went to sleep. The first thing in the morning, as soon as I remembered where I was, I thought, 'Has the conviction left me?' No; I was more miserable than before, and—it seemed strange, though it was natural—I got up, and thanked the Lord because He had kept me anxious about my soul.

"Have you ever felt like that? Perhaps after some meeting or conversation with some Christian, or reading the Word of God, you have gone to your room miserable and 'almost persuaded.'

"I went on for eight or nine days seeking the Lord. On the Saturday morning I had to go and tell the clerks. That was hard. I did it with tears running down my cheeks. A man does not like to cry before other men. Anyway, I told them I wanted to become, and meant to become, a Christian. The Lord helped me with that promise, 'With God all things are possible.'

"A skeptic dropped his head, and said nothing. Another fellow, with whom I played billiards, said, 'I wish I had the pluck to say so myself!' My words were received in a different way from what I thought they would be. But the very man who had told me that I was killing myself with drink, spent an hour and a half trying to get me to drink, saying that I 'had the blues, and was out of sorts; and that a glass of brandy or whiskey would do me good.' He tried to get me to drink; and I turned upon him at last, and said, 'You remember what you said to me; I am trying to get away from drink, and not to touch it again.' When I think of that I am reminded of the words of God Himself: 'The tender mercies of the wicked are cruel.'

"And now the Lord drew me on until the little thread became a cable, by which my soul could swing. He drew me nearer; until I found that He was my Savior. Truly He is 'able to save to the uttermost all that come unto God by him.'

"I must not forget to tell you that I went down before God in my misery, my helplessness, and my sin, and owned to Him that it was impossible that I should be saved; that it was impossible for me to keep clear of drink; but from that night to this moment, I have never had the slightest desire for drink.

"It was a hard struggle indeed to give up smoking. But God in His great wisdom knew that I must have come to grief if I had to fight single-handed against the overwhelming desire I had for drink; and He took that desire, too, clean away. From that day to this, the Lord has kept me away from drink, and made me hate it most bitterly. I simply said that I had not any strength; nor have I now; but it is the Lord Jesus who 'is able to save them to the uttermost that come unto God by Him.'

"If there is any one hearing me who has given up all hope, come to the Savior! That is His name, for 'He shall save His people from their sins.' Wherever I have gone, since then, I have found Him to be my Savior. God forbid that I should glory! It would be glorying in my shame. It is to my shame that I speak thus of myself; but oh, the Savior is able to save, and He will save!

"Christian friends, continue to pray. You may go to heaven before your sons are brought home. My parents did; and my sisters prayed for me for years and years. But now I can help others on their way to Zion. Praise the Lord for all His mercy to me!

"Remember, 'with God all things are possible.' And then you may say like St. Paul, 'I can do all things through Christ which strengtheneth me'" (Philippians 4:13).

16

SOVEREIGN GRACE

✑

Law and Grace

In his epistle to the Romans, Paul writes, "For as by one man's disobedience many were made sinners, so by the obedience of one shall many be made righteous. Moreover, the law entered, that the offence might abound. But where sin abounded, grace did much more abound: that as sin hath reigned unto death, even so might grace reign through righteousness unto eternal life by Jesus Christ our Lord."

Moses was the representative of the law. You remember that he led the children of Israel through the wilderness, and brought them to Jordan, but there he left them. He could take them up to the river, which is a type of death and judgement; but Joshua (which means Jesus—Savior) led them right through death and judgement—through the Jordan into the Promised Land. Here we have the difference between Law and Grace; between the law and the Gospel.

Take another illustration. John the Baptist was the last prophet of the old dispensation—the last prophet under the law. You remember that before Christ made His appearance at the Jordan, the cry of John day by day was, "Repent: for the kingdom of God is at hand!" He thundered out the law. He took his hearers down to the Jordan and baptized them. He put them in the place of death; and that was as far as he could take them. But there was One coming after him who could take them into the Promised Land. As Joshua led the people through the Jordan into Canaan—so Christ went down into the Jordan of death, through death and judgement, on to resurrection ground.

If you run all through Scripture, you will find that the law brings us to death. "Sin reigned unto death." A friend was telling me lately that an acquaintance of his, a minister, was once called upon to officiate at a funeral, in the place of a chaplain of one of Her Majesty's prisons, who was absent. He noticed that only one solitary man followed the body of the criminal to the grave. When the grave had been covered, this man told the minister that he was an officer of the law whose duty it was to watch the body of the culprit until it was buried out of sight; that was "the end" of the British law.

And that is what the law of God does to the sinner: it brings him right to death, and leaves him there. I pity deep down in my heart those who are trying to save themselves by the law. It never has; it never will; and it never can—save the soul. When people say they are going to try and do their best, and so save themselves by the law, I like to take them on their own ground. Have they ever done their very best? Granting that there *might* be a chance for them if they had, was there ever a time when they could not have done a little better? If a man wants to do his best, let him accept the grace of God; that is the best thing that any man or woman can possibly do.

But you will ask, What is the law given for? It may sound rather strange, but it is given that it may stop every man's mouth. "We know that what things soever the law saith, it saith to them who are under the law: that every mouth may be stopped, and all the world may become guilty before God. Therefore by the deeds of the law there shall no flesh be justified in his sight: for by the law is the knowledge of sin." The law shuts my mouth; grace opens it. The law locks up my heart; grace opens it—and then the fountain of love begins to flow out. When men get their eyes opened to see this glorious truth, they will cease their constant struggle. They will give up trying to work their way into the kingdom of God by the deeds of the law. They will give themselves up for lost, and take salvation as a free gift.

Life never came through the law. As some one has observed, when the law was given, three thousand men lost life; but when grace and truth came at Pentecost, three thousand obtained life. Under the law, if a man became a drunkard, the magistrates would take him out and stone him to death. When the prodigal came home, grace met him and embraced him. Law says, Stone him!—grace says, Embrace him! Law says, Smite him!—grace says, Kiss him! Law went after him, and bound him; grace said, loose him and let him go! Law tells me how crooked I am; grace comes and makes me straight.

I pity those who are always hanging around Sinai, hoping to get life there. I have an old friend in Chicago who is always lingering at Sinai. He is a very good man; but I think he will have a different story to tell when he gets home to heaven. He thinks I preach free grace too much; and I must confess I do like to speak of the free grace of God. This friend of mine feels as though he has a kind of mission to follow me; and whenever he gets a chance he comes in with the thunders of Sinai. I never yet met him but he was thundering away from Horeb. The last time I was in Chicago, I said to him, "Are you still lingering around Sinai?" "Yes," said he, "I believe in the law." I have made inquiries, and I never heard of anyone being converted under his preaching; the effects have always dwindled and died out. If the law is the door to heaven, there is no hope for any of us. A perfect God can only have a perfect standard. He that offends in one point is guilty of all; so "all have sinned, and come short of the glory of God."

Paul says to the Galatians: "Is the law then against the promises of God? God forbid: for if there had been a law given which could have given life, verily righteousness should have been by the law. But the scripture hath concluded all under sin, that the promise by faith of Jesus Christ might be given to them that believe. But before faith came, we were kept under the law, shut up unto the faith which should afterwards be revealed. Wherefore the law was our schoolmaster to bring us unto Christ, that we might be justified by faith. But after that faith is come, we are no longer under a schoolmaster. For ye are all the children of God by faith in Christ Jesus."

THE SOFTENING POWER OF GRACE

So we see that the law cannot give life; all it can do is to bring us to Him who is the life. The law is said to be "a schoolmaster." Perhaps some of you do not know what a schoolmaster is. If you had been under the same schoolmaster as I was when a boy, you would have known. He had a good cane and it was frequently in use. In the little country district where I went to school, there were two parties; for the sake of illustration we may call the one the "law" party and the other the "grace" party. The law party said that boys could not possibly be controlled without the cane; and they kept a schoolmaster there who acted on their plan. The struggle went on, and at last, on one election day, the law party was put out, and the grace party ruled in their stead. I happened to be at the school that time; and I remember we said to each other that we were going to have a grand time that winter. There would be no more corporal punishment, and we were going to be ruled by love.

I was one of the first to break the rules of the school. We had a lady teacher, and she asked me to stay behind. I thought the cane was coming out again; and I was going to protest against it. I was quite in a fighting mood. She took me alone. She sat down and began to talk to me kindly. I thought that was worse than the cane; I did not like it. I saw that she had not got any cane. She said: "I have made up my mind that if I can not control the school by love, I will give it up. I will have no punishment; and if you love me, try and keep the rules of the school." I felt something right here in my throat. I was not one to shed many tears; but they would come—I could not keep them back. I said to her, "You will have no more trouble with me"; and she did not. I learned more that winter than in the other three put together.

That was the difference between law and grace. Christ says, "If you love me, keep my commandments." He takes us out from under the law, and puts us under grace. Grace will break the hardest heart. It was the love of God that prompted Him to send His only begotten Son into the world that He might save it. I suppose the thief had gone through his trial unsoftened. Probably the law had hardened his heart. But on the cross no doubt that touching prayer of the Savior, "Father, forgive them!" broke his heart, so that he cried, "Lord, remember me!" He was brought to ask for mercy. I believe there is no man so far gone but the grace of God will melt his heart.

It is told of Isaac T. Hopper, the Quaker, that he once encountered a profane colored man, named Cain, in Philadelphia, and took him before a magistrate, who fined him for blasphemy. Twenty years after, Hopper met Cain, whose appearance was much changed for the worse. This touched the Friend's heart. He stepped up, spoke kindly, and shook hands with the forlorn being. "Dost thou remember me," said the Quaker, "how I had thee fined for swearing?"

"Yes, indeed, I do: I remember what I paid as well as if it was yesterday."

"Well, did it do thee any good?"

"No, never a bit; it made me mad to have my money taken from me."

Hopper invited Cain to reckon up the interest on the fine, and paid him principal and interest too. "I meant it for thy good, Cain; and I am sorry I did thee any harm."

Cain's countenance changed; the tears rolled down his cheeks. He took the money with many thanks, became a quiet man, and was not heard to swear again.

PEACE, GRACE, AND GLORY

So there is a great deal of difference between law and grace. "Being justified by faith, we have peace with God through our Lord Jesus Christ: by whom also we have access by faith into this grace wherein we stand, and rejoice in hope of the glory of God." There are three precious things here: peace for the past; grace for the present; and glory for the future. There is no *peace* until we see the finished work of Jesus Christ—until we can look back and see the cross of Christ between us and our sins. When we see that Jesus was "the end of the law for righteousness"; that He "tasted death for every man"; that He "suffered the just for the unjust"—then comes peace. Then there is "the *grace* wherein we now stand." There is plenty of grace for us as we need it—day by day, and hour by hour.

Then there is *glory* for the time to come. A great many people seem to forget that the best is before us. Dr. Bonar says that everything before the true believer is "glorious." This thought took hold of my soul; and I began to look the matter up, and see what I could find in Scripture that was glorious hereafter. I found that the kingdom we are going to inherit is glorious; our crown is to be a "crown of glory"; the city we are going to inhabit is the city of the glorified; the songs we are to sing are the songs of the glorified; we are to wear garments of "glory and beauty"; our society will be the society of the glorified; our rest is to be "glorious"; the country to which we are going is to be full of "the glory of God and of the Lamb." There are many who are always looking on the backward path, and mourning over the troubles through which they have passed; they keep lugging up the cares and anxieties they have been called on to bear, and are forever looking at them. Why should we go reeling and staggering under the burdens and cares of life when we have such prospects before us?

If there is nothing but glory beyond, our faces ought to shine brightly all the time. If a skeptic were to come up here and watch the countenances of the audience he would find many of you looking as though there was anything but glory before you. Many a time it seems to me as if I were at a funeral, people look so sad and downcast. They do not appear to know much of the joy of the Lord. Surely if we were looking right on to the glory that awaits us, our faces would be continually lit up with the light of the upper world. We can preach by our countenances if we will. The nearer we draw to that glory-land, where we shall be with Christ—the more peace, and joy, and rest we ought to have. If we will but come to the throne of grace, we shall have strength to bear all our troubles and trials. If you were to take all the afflictions that flesh is heir to and put them right on any one of us, God has grace enough to carry us right through without faltering.

Some one has compiled the following, which beautifully describes the contrast between law and grace:

THE LAW was given by Moses.

GRACE and truth came by Jesus Christ.

THE LAW says—This do, and thou shalt live.

GRACE says—Live, and then thou shalt do.

THE LAW says—Pay me what thou owest.

GRACE says—I frankly forgive thee all.

THE LAW says—The wages of sin is death.

GRACE says—The gift of God is eternal life.

THE LAW says—The soul that sinneth, it shall die.

GRACE says—Whosoever believeth in Jesus, though he were dead, yet shall he live; and whosoever liveth and believeth in Him shall never die.

THE LAW pronounces—Condemnation and death.

GRACE proclaims—Justification and life.

THE LAW says—Make you a new heart and a new spirit.

GRACE says—A new heart will I give you, and a new spirit will I put within you.

THE LAW says—Cursed is every one that continueth not in all things which are written in the book of the law to do them.

GRACE says—Blessed is the man whose iniquities are forgiven, whose sin is covered; blessed is the man to whom the Lord will not impute iniquity.

THE LAW says—Thou shalt love the Lord thy God with all thy heart, and with all thy mind, and with all thy strength.

GRACE says—Herein is love; not that we love God, but that He loved us, and sent His Son to be the propitiation for our sins.

THE LAW speaks of what man must do for God.

GRACE tells of what Christ has done for man.

THE LAW addresses man as part of the old creation.

GRACE makes a man a member of the new creation.

THE LAW bears on a nature prone to disobedience.

GRACE creates a nature inclined to obedience.

THE LAW demands obedience by the terror of the Lord.

GRACE beseeches men by the mercies of God.

THE LAW demands holiness.

GRACE gives holiness.

THE LAW says—Condemn him.

GRACE says—Embrace him.

THE LAW speaks of priestly sacrifices offered year by year continually, which could never make the comers thereunto perfect.

GRACE says—But this *Man,* after he had offered *one* sacrifice for sins forever . . . by one offering hath perfected forever them that are sanctified.

THE LAW declares—That as many as have sinned in the Law, shall be judged by the Law.

GRACE brings eternal peace to the troubled soul of every child of God, and proclaims *God's* salvation in defiance of the accusations of the adversary. "He that heareth my word, and believeth on him that sent me, hath everlasting life, and shall not come into condemnation; but is passed from death unto life."

17

THE EMPTY TOMB

The Fifteenth Chapter of First Corinthians

I think this is one of the grandest chapters in the writings of Paul. It is especially grand to those who have lost friends. No sooner do loved ones pass away than the question arises—Shall we meet them again? Paul answers this question, and gives a consolation we can find so clearly stated nowhere else. What a consolation to know, as we lay our friends away, that we shall meet them again in a little while!

As I go into a cemetery I like to think of the time when the dead shall rise from their graves. We read part of this chapter in what we call the "burial service." I think it is an unfortunate expression. Paul never talked of "burial." He said the body was *sown* in corruption, *sown* in weakness, *sown* in dishonor, *sown* a natural body. If I *bury* a bushel of wheat, I never expect to see it again, but if I *sow* it, I expect results. Thank God, our friends are not buried; they are only sown! I like the Saxon name for the cemetery—"God's acre."

The Gospel preached by the apostles rested upon four pillars. The first was the atoning death of Christ, the second was His burial and resurrection, the third was His ascension, the fourth His coming again. These four doctrines were preached by all the apostles, and by them the Gospel must stand or fall.

In the opening verses of this chapter in Corinthians we get a clear statement from Paul, that the doctrine of the resurrection is a part of the Gospel. He defines the Gospel as meaning that Christ died for our sins, but not that only—He was buried and rose again the third day. Then he summons witnesses to prove the resurrection: "He was seen of Cephas (that is, Simon Peter), then of the twelve:

after that, he was seen of above five hundred brethren at once; of whom the greater part remain unto this present, but some are fallen asleep. After that, he was seen of James; then of all the apostles. And last of all he was seen of me also, as of one born out of due time."

Now that is pretty clear testimony, strong enough to satisfy a candid inquirer. But the Greeks had no belief in the possibility of the resurrection, and these converts at Corinth had all been reared in that unbelief. And so Paul puts the question: "Now if Christ be preached that he rose from the dead, how say some among you that there is no resurrection from the dead?" It was one of the false doctrines that had crept into the church at Corinth, because no orthodox Jew would ever think of questioning it.

To deny the resurrection is to say that we will never see more of the loved ones whose bodies have been committed to the clay. If Christ has not risen, this life is the only one, and we are as the brutes. How cruel it is to have anyone love you if this be true! How horrible that they should let the tendrils of your heart twine around them, if, when they are torn away in death, it is to be the end. I would rather *hate* than *love* if I thought there will be no resurrection, because then I would feel no pangs at losing the hated thing. Oh, the cruelty of unbelief! It takes away our brightest hopes. "If in this life only we have hope in Christ, we are of all men most miserable."

IMMORTALITY

Mankind has naturally "yearnings after the infinite." Among the most primitive peoples philosophers have detected what has been well called "an appetite for the infinite," which belies the teaching that death ends all. It is one of the points of difference between man and beast. The birds of the air, the beasts of the field, are much the same today as they were in Eden. They eat and sleep and pass their life from sun to sun in unvarying monotony. Their desires are the same, their needs the same. But man is always changing. His desires are always enlarging. His mind is always planning ahead. No sooner does he reach one goal, then he presses towards the next, and not even death itself can arrest him. A well-known infidel once said: "The last enemy that shall be destroyed is not death, but the belief of man in his own immortality."

This presentiment of a future life has been beautifully illustrated by the feeling which grows within the bird when winter approaches, impelling it to travel towards the south—"an impulse mysterious and undefined, but irresistible and unerring": or to the longing of southern plants, taken to a northern climate and planted in a northern soil. They grow there, but they are always failing of their flowers. The poor exiled shrub dreams of a splendid blossom which it has never seen, but which it is dimly conscious that it ought somehow to produce. It feels the flower which it has not strength to make in the half-chilled but still genuine juices of its southern nature. "That is the way in which the thought of a future life haunts us all."

Philosophers have many facts to prove this universal reaching-forward to the life beyond the grave. It is supposed that many funeral rites and ceremonies, for instance, are due to it. If the body is once more to be occupied by its spirit, it at once suggests itself that it must be protected from harm. Accordingly we find that graves are concealed lest enemies should dig up the remains and dishonor them. Livingstone tells how a Bechuana chief was buried in his own cattle-pen. Then the cattle were driven about for some hours until all trace of the grave was obliterated. But the body must be protected not alone from ill-usage, but also, as far as possible, from decay; and the process of embalming is an endeavor in this direction. Sometimes, indeed, resurrection would be undesirable, and so we find that dead bodies are thrown into the water to drown the spirit. Modern Egyptians turn the body round and round, it is said, to make the spirit giddy and therefore unable to retrace its steps; while certain aboriginal Australians take off the nails of the hands lest the reanimated corpse should scratch its way out of its narrow cell.

When the conception of a second life as a continuation of the present life is held, we find the custom of burying inanimate things, such as weapons and instruments. The dead man will require everything beyond—as he did this side of—death. Not alone inanimate things, but animals are killed in order that their ghost may accompany the ghost of the dead man. The Bedouins slaughter his camel over the grave of their dead comrade: indispensable in this world, it will be the same in the next. From this, one step leads to the immolation of human beings. Wives follow their husbands; slaves are slain that they may continue to serve their masters. In the words of Tennyson:

"They that in barbarian burials killed the slaves and slew the wife;
Felt within themselves the sacred passion of the second life."

THE DOCTRINE OF THE
RESURRECTION IN THE OLD TESTAMENT

We only catch glimpses of the doctrine of the resurrection now
and then in the Old Testament, but the saints of those days evidently believed in it. Nearly two thousand years before Christ, Abraham
rehearsed His sacrifice on Mt. Moriah when he obeyed God's call to
offer up Isaac. Referring to this, Paul writes: "accounting that God
was able to raise (Isaac) up, even from the dead; from whence also
he received him in a figure." Five hundred years later we find God
saying unto His servant Moses: "I kill, and I make alive." Isaiah
wrote—"He will swallow up death in victory; and the Lord God will
wipe away tears from off all faces": and again—"Thy dead men shall
live, together with my dead body shall they arise. Awake and sing,
ye that dwell in dust: for thy dew is as the dew of herbs, and the
earth shall cast out the dead." Ezekiel's vivid description of the resurrection of dry bones, setting forth in prophecy the restoration of
Israel, is other evidence. When David lost his child, he said he could
not call the little one back to him, but that he would go and be with
the child. At other times he wrote—"As for me, I will behold thy face
in righteousness: I shall be satisfied, when I awake, with thy likeness"; and—"God will redeem my soul from the power of the grave:
for he shall receive me."

The patriarch Job comforted himself with the same glorious
hope in the hour of his deep sorrow. He who had asked—"What is my
strength, that I should hope? and what is mine end, that I should pro-
long my life?"—said, "I know that my redeemer liveth, and that he
shall stand at the latter day upon the earth: and though after my skin
worms destroy this body, yet in my flesh shall I see God; whom I shall
see for myself, and mine eyes shall behold, and not another." Job
must have firmly believed that his body was to be raised to life again,
hereafter but not on earth, for "there is hope of a tree," he said again,
"if it be cut down, that it will sprout again, and the tender branch
thereof will not cease. Though the root thereof wax old in the earth,
and the stalk thereof die in the ground; yet through the scent of water it will bud, and bring forth boughs like a plant. But man dieth,
and wasteth away: yea, man giveth up the ghost, and where is he? As
the waters fail from the sea, and the flood decayeth and drieth up: so
man lieth down, and riseth not: till the heavens be no more, they
shall not awake, nor be raised out of their sleep."

In Hosea the Lord declares: "I will ransom them from the power of the grave; I will redeem them from death: O death, I will be thy plagues: O grave, I will be thy destruction."

In the last chapter of Daniel we have another glimpse of the same truth: "They that be wise shall shine as the brightness of the firmament; and they that turn many to righteousness as the stars for ever and ever." And his book closes with these words: "Go thou thy way till the end be: for thou shalt rest, and stand in thy lot at the end of the days."

And typically, too, resurrection was set forth in the Old Testament. By the firstfruits offered the day after the Passover-Sabbath as a pledge of the whole harvest, the children of Israel were taught in type of the Messiah who should be "the firstfruits of them that slept." Some one has said that the very first employment of Israel in Canaan was preparing the type of the Savior's resurrection, and their first religious act was holding up that type of a risen Savior.

AND IN THE NEW TESTAMENT

But what was referred to only at long intervals in the Old Testament became in the New Testament a prominent matter of fact and teaching. The word "resurrection" occurs forty-two times in the New Testament. Many times during His ministry did our Lord refer to the general resurrection of the dead. The Sadducees once came to Him with a difficult question about the marriage relation hereafter, and Jesus said: "As touching the resurrection of the dead, have ye not read that which was spoken unto you by God, saying, I am the God of Abraham, and the God of Isaac, and the God of Jacob? God is not the God of the dead, but of the living." On another occasion Christ said: "When thou makest a dinner or a supper, call not thy friends, nor thy brethren, neither thy kinsmen, nor thy rich neighbours; lest they also bid thee again, and a recompense be made thee. But when thou makest a feast, call the poor, the maimed, the lame, the blind: and thou shalt be blessed; for they cannot recompense thee: for thou shalt be recompensed at the resurrection of the just." When Lazarus died, Jesus spake the consoling words to his sisters: "Thy brother shall rise again." Martha replied: "I know that he shall rise again in the resurrection at the last day." Jesus said unto her: "I am the resurrection and the life."

A SPLENDID GUESS

We see then that the belief in a future life did not begin with Christ, and nowhere is the claim made that immortality is His gift.

We get that from the Creator.

But though the idea existed before Christianity, it was at best only "a splendid guess." The natural man cannot look across the narrowest grave and see what is beyond. Strain his eyes as he will, he cannot pierce the veil of death. It is ever before him, blighting his hopes, checking his plans, thwarting his purposes, a barrier that nothing can break down. Ever since sin entered the world, death has reigned, making the earth one huge graveyard. He has not rested for a moment. In every age and every country, "Dust thou art and to dust thou shalt return" has been the sentence overhanging mankind. All the generations of men as they pass across the earth do but follow their dead.

Many unexpected things happen to us in this life, but death is not among them. We do not know *how or when* it will come, but come it will, if the Lord tarry. We have heard of doctors who have performed wonderful cures, but all their skill and knowledge has been unable to undo the work of death. In all these six thousand years since death entered this sin-cursed earth, human means have failed to win back a single trophy from death. Advancing civilization, increased education, progress in commerce and art—none of these things make us superior to the most degraded savages. Death always triumphs in the end. The flow is always in one direction, onward and never backward.

BROUGHT TO LIGHT BY CHRIST

What was unknown by the wisest men on earth was revealed by Christ. He did not create immortality, but He "abolished death, brought life and immortality to light through the gospel." "That undiscovered country," spoken of by the poet, "from whose realm no traveler returns," is *not* an undiscovered country to the believer. Our Lord explored it. He entered the lists against death in His own territory and came off more than conqueror. The scepter of death is universal still, but it is broken, and shall one day crumble into dust. The Christian need no longer speculate about the future: certainty is reached beside the empty tomb of Christ. "Now is Christ risen from the dead, and become the firstfruits of them that slept." We can see the trace of His returning footprints.

TRIUMPH

And so we can join in the triumphant strain, "Death is swallowed up of victory." The sting of death is sin, and God has given us the victory through our Lord Jesus Christ. They which have fallen asleep in Christ have *not* perished, but we shall one day see them face to face.

What a Gospel of joy and hope we have, compared to that of unbelief! "The heathen sorrowed without hope," wrote Dr. Bonar; "To them death connected itself with no hope, no brightness, no triumph. It was not *sunset* to them, for that bids us be on the look-out for another sun, as bright as that which set. It was not *autumn or winter,* for these speak of returning spring and summer. It was not *seed* cast into rough soil, for that predicts the future tree or flower, more beautiful than the seed. It was pure and simple darkness, all cloud, shadow, desolation. A shattered pillar, a ship gone to pieces, a race lost, a harp lying on the ground with snapped strings and all its music lost, a flower-bud crushed—these were the sad utterances of their hopeless grief. The thought that death was the gate of life came not in to cheer the parting and brighten the sepulcher. The truth that the grave was the soil and the body the seed sown by God's own hand to call out the latent life; that the race was not lost, but only a little earlier won: that the column was not destroyed but transferred to another building and another city to be 'a pillar in the house of God' that the bud was not crushed, but transplanted for fuller expansion to a kindlier soil and air; that the harp was not broken, but handed to a truer minstrel who will bring out all the rich compass of its hidden music: these were things that had no place in their theology, hardly in their dreams."

AN ESSENTIAL DOCTRINE

Some people claim that the question of a risen Savior is not essential. Hear what Paul says: "If Christ be not risen, then is our preaching vain, and your faith is also vain. Yea, and we are found false witnesses of God; because we have testified of God that he raised up Christ: whom he raised not up, if so be that the dead rise not. For if the dead rise not, then is not Christ raised: and if Christ be not raised, your faith is vain; ye are yet in your sins." I tell you it is very essential. It is not a mere speculative question that we are dealing with: it is of the greatest practical importance. The resurrection is the keystone of the arch on which our faith is supported.

If Christ has not risen, we must impeach all those witnesses of lying.

If Christ has not risen, we have no proof that the crucifixion of Jesus differed from that of the two thieves who suffered with Him.

If Christ has not risen, it is impossible to admire His atoning death as accepted. Some one has said that the power of Christ's death to take away sin is always conditioned in the New Testament with the fact of His resurrection.

If Christ has not risen, it is impossible to admire His words and character. He made the resurrection a test-truth of His divinity. The Jews once asked for a sign, and He answered—"Destroy this temple, and in three days I will raise it up"—referring to the temple of His body. On another occasion He gave the sign of the prophet Jonah: "As Jonas was three days and three nights in the whale's belly; so shall the Son of man be three days and three nights in the heart of the earth." Paul says, "Declared to be the Son of God with power . . . by the resurrection from the dead." "If He had not been divine," says one, "the sins of anyone of us would have been a grave-stone too heavy for Him to throw off; the claims of Jehovah's justice would have been bands of death too strong for Him to burst."

What would Christianity be without the resurrection? It would descend to the level of any of the other religious systems of the world. If Christ never rose from the dead, how do His words differ from those of Plato? Other men besides Christ have lived beautiful lives and have left behind them beautiful precepts to guide their followers. We should have to class Christ with these.

18

WEIGHED AND WANTING

Tenth Commandment

Thou shalt not covet thy neighbour's house, thou shalt not covet thy neighbour's wife, nor his manservant, nor his maidservant, nor his ox, nor his ass, nor any thing that is thy neighbour's."

In the twelfth chapter of Luke our Savior lifted two danger signals. "Beware ye of the leaven of the Pharisees, which is hypocrisy . . . Take heed, and beware of covetousness."

The greatest dupe the devil has in the world is the hypocrite; but the next greatest is the covetous man, "for a man's life consisteth not in the abundance of the things which he possesseth."

I believe this sin is much stronger now than ever before in the world's history. We are not in the habit of condemning it as a sin. In his epistle to the Thessalonians Paul speaks of "the cloak of covetousness." Covetous men use it as a cloak, and call it prudence, and foresight. Who ever heard it confessed as a sin? I have heard many confessions, in public and private, during the past forty years, but never have I heard a man confess that he was guilty of this sin. The Bible does not tell of one man who ever recovered from it, and in all my experience I do not recall many who have been able to shake it off after it had fastened on them. A covetous man or woman generally remains covetous to the very end.

We may say that covetous desire plunged the human race into sin. We can trace the river back from age to age until we get to its rise in Eden. When Eve saw that the forbidden fruit was good for food and that it was desirable to the eyes, she partook of it, and Adam with her. They were not satisfied with all that God had showered upon them, but coveted the wisdom of gods which Satan deceitfully told them might be obtained by eating the fruit. She saw—she desired— then she took! Three steps from innocence into sin.

A SEARCHING COMMANDMENT

It would be absurd for such a law as this to be placed upon any human statute book. It could never be enforced. The officers of the law would be powerless to detect infractions. The outward conduct may be regulated, but the thoughts and intents of a man are beyond the reach of human law.

But God can see behind outward actions. He can read the thoughts of the heart. Our innermost life, invisible to mortal eye, is laid bare before Him. We cannot deceive Him by external conformity. He is able to detect the least transgression and shortcoming, so that no man can shirk detection. God cannot be imposed upon by the cleanness of the outside of the cup and the platter.

Surely we have here another proof that the Ten Commandments are not of human origin, but must be divine.

This commandment, then, did not even on the surface, confine itself to visible actions as did the preceding commandments. Even before Christ came and showed their spiritual sweep, men had a commandment that went beneath public conduct and touched the very springs of action. It directly prohibited—not the wrong act, but the wicked desire that prompted the act. It forbade the evil thought, the unlawful wish. It sought to prevent—not only sin, but the desire to sin. In God's sight it is as wicked to set covetous eyes, as it is to lay thieving hands, upon anything that is not ours.

And why? Because if the evil desire can be controlled, there will be no outbreak in conduct. Desires have been called "actions in the egg." The desire in the heart is the first step in the series that ends in action. Kill the evil desire, and you successfully avoid the ill results that would follow upon its hatching and development. Prevention is better than cure.

We must not limit covetousness to the matter of money. The commandment is not thus limited; it reads, "Thou shalt not covet . . . anything . . ." That word "anything" is what will condemn us. Though we do not join in the race for wealth, have we not sometimes a hungry longing for our neighbor's goodly lands—fine houses, beautiful clothes, brilliant reputation, personal accomplishments, easy circumstances, comfortable surroundings? Have we not had the desire to increase our possessions or to change our lot in accordance with what we see in others? If so, we are guilty of having broken this law.

GOD'S THOUGHTS ABOUT COVETOUSNESS

Let us examine a few of the Bible passages that bear down on this sin, and see what are God's thoughts about it.

"Know ye not that the unrighteous shall not inherit the kingdom of God? Be not deceived: neither fornicators, nor idolaters, nor adulterers, nor effeminate, nor abusers of themselves with mankind, nor thieves, nor covetous, *nor drunkards, nor revilers, nor extortioners, shall inherit the kingdom of God"* (1 Corinthians 6:9–10).

Notice that the covetous are named between thieves and drunkards. We lock up thieves, and have no mercy on them. We loathe drunkards, and consider them great sinners against the law of God as well as the law of the land. Yet there is far more said in the Bible against covetousness than against either stealing or drunkenness.

Covetousness and stealing are almost like Siamese twins— they go together so often. In fact we might add lying, and make them triplets. "The covetous person is a thief *in* the shell. The thief is a covetous person *out* of the shell. Let a covetous person see something that he desires very much; let an opportunity of taking it be offered; how very soon he will break through the shell and come out in his true character as a thief." The Greek word translated "covetousness" means an inordinate desire of getting. When the Gauls tasted the sweet wines of Italy, they asked where they came from, and never rested until they had overrun Italy.

"For this ye know, that no whoremonger, nor unclean person, nor covetous man, who is an idolater, hath any inheritance in the kingdom of Christ and of God" (Ephesians 5:5). There we have the same truth repeated: but notice that covetousness is called idolatry. The covetous man worships Mammon, not God.

"Moreover thou shalt provide out of all the people able men, such as fear God, men of truth, hating covetousness; *and place such over them, to be rulers of thousands, and rulers of hundreds, rulers of fifties, and rulers of tens"* (Exodus 18:21).

Isn't it extraordinary that Jethro, the man of the desert, should have given this advice to Moses? How did he learn to beware of covetousness? We honor men today if they are wealthy and covetous. We elect them to office in church and state. We often say that they will make better treasurers just because we know them to be covetous. But in God's sight, a covetous man is as vile and black as any thief or drunkard. David said: "The wicked boasteth of his heart's desire, and blesseth the covetous, whom the Lord abhorreth" (Psalm

10:3). I am afraid that many who profess to have put away wickedness also speak well of the covetous.

A SORE EVIL

"He that loveth silver shall not be satisfied with silver; nor he that loveth abundance with increase: this is also vanity. When goods increase, they are increased that eat them: and what good is there to the owners thereof, saving the beholding of them with their eyes? The sleep of the labouring man is sweet, whether he eat little or much: but the abundance of the rich will not suffer him to sleep. There is a sore evil which I have seen under the sun, namely, riches kept for the owners thereof to their hurt" (Ecclesiastes 5:10–13).

Isn't that true? Is the covetous man ever satisfied with his possessions? Aren't they vanity? Does he have peace of mind? Don't selfish riches always bring hurt?

The folly of covetousness is well shown in the following extract: "If you should see a man that had a large pond of water, yet living in continual thirst, nor suffering himself to drink half a drought for fear of lessening his pond; if you should see him wasting his time and strength in fetching more water to his pond, always thirsty, yet always carrying a bucket of water in his hand, watching early and late to catch the drops of rain, gaping after every cloud, and running greedily into every mire and mud in hopes of water, and always studying how to make every ditch empty itself into the pond; if you should see him grow grey in these anxious labors, and at last end a thirsty life by falling into his own pond, would you not say that such a one was not only the author of his own disquiet, but was foolish enough to be reckoned among madmen? But foolish and absurd as this character is, it does not represent half the follies and absurd disquiets of the covetous man."

I have read of a millionaire in France, who was a miser. In order to make sure of his wealth, he dug a cave in his wine cellar so large and deep that he could go down into it with a ladder. The entrance had a door with a spring lock. After a time, he was missing. At last his house was sold, and the purchaser discovered this door in the cellar. He opened it, went down, and found the miser lying dead on the ground, in the midst of his riches. The door must have shut accidentally after him, and he perished miserably.

A TEMPTATION AND A SNARE

"They that will be (that is, desire to be) *rich fall into temptation and a snare, and into many foolish and hurtful lusts, which drown men in destruction and perdition"* (1 Timothy 6:9).

The Bible speaks of the deceitfulness of two things—"the deceitfulness of *sin*" and "the deceitfulness of *riches*." Riches are like a mirage in the desert, which has all the appearance of satisfying, and lures on the traveler with the promise of water and shade; but he only wastes his strength in the effort to reach it. So riches never satisfy; the pursuit of them always turns out a snare.

Lot coveted the rich plains of Sodom, and what did he gain? After twenty years spent in that wicked city, he had to escape for his life, leaving all his wealth behind him.

What did the thirty pieces of silver do for Judas? Weren't they a snare?

Think of Balaam. He is generally regarded as a false prophet, but I do not find that any of his prophecies that are recorded are not true; they have been literally fulfilled. Up to a certain point his character shone magnificently, but the devil finally overcame him by the bait of covetousness. He stepped over a heavenly crown for the riches and honors that Balak promised him. He went to perdition backwards. His face was set toward God, but he backed into hell. He wanted to die the death of the righteous, but he did not live the life of the righteous. It is sad to see so many who know God, miss everything for riches.

Then consider the case of Gehazi. There is another man who drowned in destruction and perdition by covetousness. He got more out of Naaman than he asked for, but he also got Naaman's leprosy. Think how he forfeited the friendship of his master Elisha, the man of God! So today lifelong friends are separated by this accursed desire. Homes are broken up. Men are willing to sell out peace and happiness for the sake of a few dollars.

Didn't David fall into foolish and hurtful lusts? He saw Bathsheba, Uriah's wife, and she was "very beautiful to look upon," and David became a murderer and an adulterer. The guilty longing hurled him into the deepest pit of sin. He had to reap bitterly as he had sowed.

I heard of a wealthy German out West, who owned a lumber mill. He was worth nearly two millions of dollars, but his covetousness was so great that he once worked as a common laborer carrying railroad ties all day. It was the cause of his death.

"And Achan answered Joshua, and said, Indeed I have sinned against the Lord God of Israel, and thus and thus have I done: When I saw among the spoils a goodly Babylonish garment, and two hundred shekels of silver, and a wedge of gold of fifty shekels weight, then I coveted them, and took them; and, behold, they are hid in the earth in the midst of my tent, and the silver under it" (Joshua 7:20–21).

He saw—he coveted—he took—he hid! The covetous eye was what led Achan up to the wicked deed that brought sorrow and defeat upon the camp of Israel.

We know the terrible punishment that was meted out to Achan. God seems to have set danger signals at the threshold of each new age. It is remarkable how soon the first outbreaks of covetousness occurred. Think of Eve in Eden, Achan just after Israel had entered the Promised Land, Ananias and Sapphira in the early Christian Church.

A ROOT EXTRACTOR

"For the love of money is the root of all evil: which while some coveted after, they have erred from the faith, and pierced themselves through with many sorrows" (1 Timothy 6:10).

The Revised Version translates it—"a root of all kinds of evil." This tenth commandment has therefore been aptly called a "root-extractor," because it would tear up and destroy this root. Deep down in our corrupt nature it has spread. No one but God can rid us of it.

Matthew tells us that the deceitfulness of riches chokes the Word of God. Like the Mississippi River, which chokes up its mouth by the amount of soil it carries down. Isn't that true of many business men today? They are so engrossed with their affairs that they have not time for religion. They lose sight of their soul and its eternal welfare in their desire to amass wealth. They do not even hesitate to sell their souls to the devil. How many a man says, "We must make money, and if God's law stands in the way, brush it aside."

The word "lucre" occurs five times in the New Testament, and each time it is called *"filthy* lucre."

"A root of all kinds of evil." Yes, because what will not men be guilty of when prompted by the desire to be rich? Greed for gold leads men to commit violence and murder, to cheat and deceive and steal. It turns the heart to stone, devoid of all natural affection, cruel, unkind. How many families are wrecked over the father's will! The scramble for a share of the wealth smashes them to pieces. Covetous of rank and position in society, parents barter sons and daughters in ungodly marriage. Bodily health is no consideration. The uncontrollable fever for gold makes men renounce all their settled prospects, and undertake hazardous journeys—no peril can drive them back. It destroys faith and spirituality, turning men's minds and hearts away from God. It disturbs the peace of the community by prompting to acts of wrong. Covetousness has more than once led nation to war against nation for the sake of gaining territory or other material resources. It is said that when the Spaniards came over to conquer Peru, they sent a message to the king, saying, "Give us gold, for we Spaniards have a disease that can only be cured by gold."

Dr. Boardman has shown how covetousness leads to the transgression of every one of the commandments, and I cannot do better than quote his words: "Covetousness tempts us into the violation of the first commandment, worshiping Mammon in addition to Jehovah. Coveting tempts us into a violation of the second commandment, or idolatry. The apostle Paul expressly identifies the covetous man with an idolater: 'covetousness, which is idolatry.' Again: Coveting tempts us into violation of the third commandment, or sacrilegious falsehood: for instance, Gehazi, lying in the matter of his interview with Naaman the Syrian, and Ananias and Sapphira, perjuring themselves in the matter of the community of goods. Again: Coveting tempts us into the violation of the fourth commandment, or Sabbath-breaking. It is covetousness which encroaches on God's appointed day of sacred rest, tempting us to run trains for merely secular purposes, to vend tobacco and liquors, to hawk newspapers. Again: Coveting tempts us into the violation of the fifth commandment, or disrespect for authority; tempting the young man to deride his early parental counsels, the citizen to trample on civic enactments. Again: Covetousness tempts us into violation of the sixth commandment, or murder. Recall how Judas' love of money lured him into the betrayal of his Divine Friend into the hand of His murderers, his lure being the paltry sum of—say—fifteen dollars. Again: Covetousness tempts us into the violation of the seventh commandment, or adultery. Observe how Scripture combines greed and lust. Again: Covetousness tempts us into the violation of the eighth commandment, or theft. Recall how it tempted Achan to steal a goodly Babylonish mantle, and two hundred shekels of silver, and a wedge of gold for fifty shekels weight. Again: Covetousness tempts us into the violation of the ninth commandment, or

bearing false witness against our neighbor. Recall how the covetousness of Ahab instigated his wife Jezebel to employ sons of
Belial to bear blasphemous and fatal testimony against Naboth,
saying, 'Thou didst curse God and the king.'"

HOW TO OVERCOME

You ask me how you are to cast this unclean spirit out of your
heart? I think I can tell you.

In the first place, make up your mind that by the grace of God
you will overcome the spirit of selfishness. You must overcome it,
or it will overcome you. Paul said: "Mortify therefore your members
which are upon the earth; fornication, uncleanness, inordinate affection, evil concupiscence, and covetousness, which is idolatry: for
which things' sake the wrath of God cometh on the children of disobedience" (Colossians 3:5–6).

I heard of a rich man who was asked to make a contribution on
behalf of some charitable object. The text was quoted to him—"He
that hath pity upon the poor lendeth unto the Lord; and that which
he hath given will he pay him again." He said that the security might
be good enough, but the credit was too long. He was dead within two
weeks. The wrath of God rested upon him as he never expected.

If you find yourself getting very miserly, begin to scatter, like a
wealthy farmer in New York State I heard of. He was a noted miser,
but he was converted. Soon after, a poor man who had been burned
out and had no provisions, came to him for help. The farmer
thought he would be liberal and give the man a ham from his smoke
house. On his way to get it, the tempter whispered to him: "Give
him the smallest one you have."

He had a struggle whether he would give a large or a small
ham, but finally he took down the largest he could find.

"You are a fool," the devil said.

"If you don't keep still," the farmer replied, "I will give him
every ham I have in the smoke house."

Mr. Durant told me he woke up one morning to find that he
was a rich man, and he said that the greatest struggle of his life then
took place as to whether he would let money be his master, or he be
master of money, whether he would be its slave, or make it a slave
to him. At last he got the victory, and that was how Wellesley College came to be built.

In the next place, cultivate the spirit of contentment. "Let your
conversation be without covetousness; and be content with such

things as ye have: for he hath said, I will never leave thee, nor forsake thee. So that we may boldly say, The Lord is my helper, and I will not fear what man shall do unto me" (Hebrews 13:5–6).

Contentment is the very opposite of covetousness, which is continually craving for something it does not possess. "Be content with such things as ye have," not worrying about the future, because God has promised never to leave or forsake you. What does the child of God want more than this? I would rather have that promise than all the gold of the earth.

Would to God we might all be able to say with Paul—"I have coveted no man's silver or gold, or apparel." The Lord had made him partaker of His grace, and he was soon to be a partaker of His glory, and earthly things looked very small. "Godliness with contentment is great gain," he wrote to Timothy; "having food and raiment let us be therewith content." Observe that he puts godliness first. No worldly gain can satisfy the human heart. Roll the whole world in, and still there would be room.

May God tear the scales off our eyes if we are blinded by this sin. Oh, the folly of it, that we should set our heart's affections upon anything below! "For we brought nothing into this world, and it is certain we can carry nothing out. . . . Be not thou afraid when one is made rich, when the glory of his house is increased; for when he dieth he shall take nothing away: his glory shall not descend after him" (1 Timothy 6:7; Psalm 49:16–17).

19

PLEASURE AND PROFIT IN BIBLE STUDY

How to Study the Bible

Someone has said that there are four things necessary in studying the Bible: Admit, submit, commit, and transmit. First, admit its truth; second, submit to its teachings; third, commit it to memory; and fourth, transmit it. If the Christian life is a good thing for you, pass it on to someone else.

Now I want to tell you how I study the Bible. Every man can not fight in Saul's armor; and perhaps you cannot follow my methods. Still I may be able to throw out some suggestions that will help you. Spurgeon used to prepare his sermon for Sunday morning on Saturday night. If I tried that, I would fail.

FEED YOURSELF

The quicker you learn to feed yourself the better. I pity down deep in my heart any men or women who have been attending some church or chapel for, say, five, ten, or twenty years, and yet have not learned to feed themselves.

You know it is always regarded a great event in the family when a child can feed itself. It is propped up at the table, and at first perhaps it uses the spoon upside down, but by and by it uses it all right, and mother, or perhaps sister, claps her hands and says, "Just see, baby's feeding himself!" Well, what we need as Christians is to be able to feed ourselves. How many there are who sit helpless and listless, with open mouths, hungry for spiritual things, and the minister has to try to feed them, while the Bible is a feast prepared, into which they never venture.

There are many who have been Christians for twenty years who have still to be fed with an ecclesiastical spoon. If they happen to have a minister who feeds them, they get on pretty well; but if they have not, they are not fed at all. This is the test as to your being a true child of God—whether you love and feed upon the Word of God. If you go out to your garden and throw down some sawdust, the birds will not take any notice; but if you throw down some crumbs, you will find they will soon sweep down and pick them up. So the true child of God can tell the difference, so to speak, between sawdust and bread. Many so-called Christians are living on the world's sawdust, instead of being nourished by the Bread that cometh down from heaven. Nothing can satisfy the longings of the soul but the Word of the living God.

THE LAW OF PERSEVERANCE

The best law for Bible study is the law of perseverance. The Psalmist says, "I have *stuck* unto thy testimonies." Application to the Word will tend to its growth within and its multiplication without. Some people are like express-trains; they skip along so quickly that they see nothing.

I met a lawyer in Chicago who told me he had spent two years in studying one subject; he was trying to smash a will. He made it his business to read everything on wills he could get. Then he went into court and he talked two days about that will; he was full of it; he could not talk about anything else but wills. That is the way with the Bible—study it and study it, one subject at a time, until you become filled with it.

Read the Bible itself—do not spend all your time on commentaries and helps. If a man spent all his time reading up the chemical constituents of bread and milk, he would soon starve.

THREE BOOKS REQUIRED

There are three books which I think every Christian ought to possess.

The first, of course, is the Bible. I believe in getting a good Bible, with a good plain print. I have not much love for those little Bibles which you have to hold right under your nose in order to read the print; and if the church happens to be a little dark, you can not see the print, but it becomes a mere jumble of words. Yes, but some one will say you cannot carry a big Bible in your pocket. Very well, then, carry it under your arm; and if you have to walk five miles, you will just be preaching a sermon five miles long. I have known a man convicted by seeing another carrying his Bible under his arm. You are not ashamed to carry hymn-books and prayer-books, and the Bible is worth all the hymn-books and prayer-books in the world put together. If you get a good Bible, you are likely to take better care of it. Suppose you pay ten dollars for a good Bible: the older you grow the more precious it will become to you. But be sure you do not get one so good that you will be afraid to mark it. I don't like gilt-edged Bibles that look as if they had never been used.

Then next I would advise you to get a Cruden's Concordance. I was a Christian about five years before I ever heard of it. A skeptic in Boston got hold of me. I didn't know anything about the Bible and I tried to defend the Bible and Christianity. He made a mis-quotation and I said it wasn't in the Bible. I hunted for days and days. If I had had a concordance, I could have found it at once. It is a good thing for ministers once in awhile to tell the people about a good book. You can find any portion or any verse in the Bible by just turning to this concordance.

Thirdly, a topical text book. These books will help you to study the Word of God with profit. If you do not possess them, get them at once; every Christian ought to have them.

[This would include] *The Bible Text Cyclopedia,* a complete classification of Scripture texts in the form of an alphabetical list of subjects. . . .

SUNDAY-SCHOOL QUARTERLIES AND THE BIBLE

I think Sunday-school teachers are making a woeful mistake if they don't take the whole Bible into their Sunday-school classes. I don't care how young children are, let them understand it is one book, that there are not two books—the Old Testament and the New are all one. Don't let them think that the Old Testament doesn't come to us with the same authority as the New. It is a great thing for a boy or girl to know how to handle the Bible. What is an army good for if they don't know how to handle their swords?

I speak very strongly on this, because I know some Sabbath-schools that don't have a single Bible in them. They have question books. There are questions and the answers are given just below; so that you don't need to study your lesson. They are splendid things for lazy teachers to bring along into their classes. I have seen them come into the class with a question book, and sometimes they get it wrong side up while they are talking to the class, until they find out their mistake, and then they begin over again. I have seen an ex-amination take place something like this:

"John, who was the first man?"

"Methuselah."

"No; I think not; let me see. No, it is not Methuselah. Can't you guess again?"

"Elijah."

"No."

"Adam."

"That's right, my son; you must have studied your lesson hard."

Now, I would like to know what a boy is going to do with that kind of a teacher, or with that kind of teaching. That is the kind of teaching that is worthless, and brings no result. Now, don't say that I condemn helps. I believe in availing myself of all the light you can get. What I want you to do, when you come into your class, is to come prepared to explain the lesson without the use of a concordance. Bring the Word of God with you; bring the old Book.

You will often find families where there is a family Bible, but the mother is so afraid that the children will tear it that she keeps it in the spare room, and once in a great while the children are allowed to look at it. The thing that interests them most is the family record—when John was born, when Father and Mother were married.

I came up to Boston from the country and went into a Bible class where there were a few Harvard students. They handed me a Bible and told me the lesson was in John. I hunted all through the Old Testament for John, but couldn't find it. I saw the fellows hunching one another, "Ah, greenie from the country." Now, you know that is just the time when you don't want to be considered green. The teacher saw my embarrassment and handed me his Bible, and I put my thumb in the place and held on. I didn't lose my place. I said then that if I ever got out of that scrape, I would never be caught there again. Why is it that so many young men from eighteen to twenty cannot be brought into a Bible class? Because they don't want to show their ignorance. There is no place in the world that is so fascinating as a live Bible class. I believe that we are to blame that they have been brought up in the Sunday-school without Bibles and brought up with quarterlies. The result is, the boys are growing up without knowing how to handle the Bible. They don't know where Matthew is, they don't know where the Epistle to the Ephesians is, they don't know where to find Hebrews or any of the different books of the Bible. They ought to be taught how to handle the whole Bible and it can be done by Sunday-school teachers taking the Bible into the class and going right about it at once.

You can get a Bible in this country for almost a song now. Sunday-schools are not so poor that they cannot get Bibles. Some time ago there came up in a large Bible class a question, and they thought they would refer to the Bible, but they found that there was not a single one in the class. A Bible class without a Bible! It would be like a doctor without medicine; or an army without weapons. So they went to the pews, but could not find one there. Finally they went to the pulpit and took the pulpit Bible and settled the question. We are making wonderful progress, aren't we? Quarterlies are all right in their places, as helps in studying the lesson, but if they are going to sweep the Bibles out of our Sunday-schools, I think we had better sweep them out.

20

BIBLE CHARACTERS

John the Baptist

The contemplation of no Bible character quickens me more than the life and character of John the Baptist. I never touch that life but I get a blessing. I used to think that I should liked to have lived in his day, and in the times of some of the prophets; but I have given up that idea long ago: for when a prophet appears, it is when the priests have been unfaithful, religion is at a low ebb, and everything is in disorder and confusion. When John appeared it was as black as midnight. The Old Testament had been sealed up by Malachi's proclamation of the Lord's coming, and of the forerunner who should introduce Him.

With Malachi, prophecy ceased for four hundred years; then John came, preaching repentance and preparing the way for the dispensation of the grace of God. The word "John" means the grace and mercy of God. He looked back upon the past, and looked forward to the future. I will not dwell upon his birth, although it is interesting to read in Luke 1, the conversation of Gabriel with Zachariah, John's father, when he was executing the priest's office before God, and what took place when John was born. As in the case of Jesus, his name and his birth were announced beforehand. When John was born there was considerable stir but it soon died out. The death of Christ would have died out of men's recollection but for the Holy Ghost.

Notwithstanding the wonders attending John's birth, for thirty years he dropped out of sight. Many events had taken place during that period. The Roman Emperor had died; Herod, who had sought the lives of the young children when he heard that Jesus was born King of the Jews, was dead; the shepherds were gone; Simeon and Anna, the prophet and prophetess, were gone; the father of John the

Baptist was gone; and all the rumors that were afloat at the time of John's birth had died out and were forgotten, when all at once he burst upon the scene like the flashing of a meteor. There was a voice heard in the wilderness, and the cry came, "Repent: for the kingdom of heaven is at hand!" There had been a long line of prophets. He was the last prophet of the Law; he was to close up that dispensation; he stood upon the threshold of the new age, with one foot upon the old and the other upon the new dispensation. He told them what had taken place in the past, and what would take place in the future.

All the evangelists speak of John. Matthew says, "In those days came John the Baptist, preaching in the wilderness of Judea." Mark says, "The voice of one crying in the wilderness, Prepare ye the way of the Lord, make his paths straight." In Luke we read, "The word of God came unto John, the son of Zacharias in the wilderness." And John, the beloved, says, "There was a man sent from God, whose name was John." That is the way in which these four men introduce him.

Another thing that stirred the people and moved them was his dress. It was like Elijah's, which was of camel's hair, with a leather girdle. His preaching was like that of Elijah. No name could arouse the nation like Elijah's name. And when the news began to spread from town to town, and at last reached Jerusalem, that one had risen like unto Elijah in appearance and dress; that the eloquence of heaven and the power of God were upon him; that he was a Nazarite from his birth—when these strange rumors got abroad, the people flocked to hear him. It is remarkable that he never performed one miracle nor gave one sign, and yet he moved the whole nation!

People tell us that they do not believe in revivals. There never was a country moved so suddenly and awakened so quickly as was Judea under the preaching of John and Jesus Christ. Talk about sensational preaching! If by that term you mean preaching designed merely to impress the outward senses, then their preaching was not sensational; but if you mean preaching calculated to produce a striking effect, then it was indeed sensational. The greatest sensation that any nation ever witnessed was brought about by these mighty preachers. Some great patriarchs, prophets, and kings —some wonderful men had arisen; but now the Jewish world was about to gaze upon its greatest. It was moved from center to circumference. I am amused to hear some people talk against revivals.

If you take up history, you will see that every church has sprung out of revivals. This was the mightiest work the church had seen. It was sudden. It was not long before you could hear the tramp of thousands flocking from the towns into the desert to hear a man who had no commission from his fellow-men; who had gone through no seminary nor college; who had not been brought up in the temple among the sons of Levi; who belonged to no sect or party; who had no D.D., LL.D., or any handle to his name, but simply John; a heaven-sent man, with a heaven-given name. He had no *prestige* in Jerusalem, nor any influential committee meetings. He was simply John the Baptist, preaching in the wilderness! And away went the crowd to hear him, and many believed him. Why? Because he was sent from God.

In New York, or London, or any large city, any man of note can gather a large audience; but let him go away into the desert and see if he can draw the inhabitants from the large cities to hear him, as John did. Like Elijah, he was intrepid and uncompromising. He did not preach to please the people for he denounced their sins. When the Pharisees and Sadducees came to his baptism, he cried out, "O generation of vipers, who hath warned you to flee from the wrath to come?" And to the Jews, who prided themselves on belonging to the seed of Abraham, he said, "Think not to say within yourselves, We have Abraham to our father; for I say unto you, that God is able of these stones to raise up children unto Abraham." He tore off the mask of their hypocrisy, warned them against trusting in their self-righteousness, and told them "to bring forth fruits meet for repentance." There was not pandering to their prejudices, nor truckling to their tastes or wishes. He delivered his message as he had received it from God; he asked no favors; he talked plainly, and called things by their right names.

We have in Matthew just a glimpse, a specimen, of his courageousness. He brought the law right down upon those who boasted of themselves. "And now," said he, "the axe is laid unto the root of the trees: therefore every tree which bringeth not forth good fruit is hewn down, and cast into the fire." And in Luke we read that the people asked him, "What shall we do then?" They had an inquiry-meeting right there!

That is the beginning; but he did not leave them there. You may bring down the law, and cry "Reform! Reform!" "Repent! Repent!" but that leaves a man outside the kingdom of God; that does not bring him to Christ; and it will not be long before he goes back to his sins. In every one of his sermons John alluded to the coming Messiah.

The bank of the Jordan was his pulpit, the desert his home; when his message was delivered he retired again into the wilderness. His food was locusts and wild honey; there was not a beggar who did not fare better than he. He did not shun to declare the whole counsel of God. He kept back nothing.

We read: "Then went out to him Jerusalem, and all Judea, and all the region round about Jordan." Think of the whole population going out into the wilderness to hear this wonderful open-air preacher, to be "baptized of him in Jordan, confessing their sins." John was a preacher of *repentance*. Perhaps no one ever rang out the word "Repent!" like John the Baptist. Day after day, as he came out of the desert and stood on the banks of that famous river, you could hear his voice rolling out, "Repent! for the kingdom of heaven is at hand." We can almost now hear the echoes of his voice as they floated up and down the Jordan. Many wonderful scenes had been witnessed at that stream. Naaman had washed away his leprosy there; Elijah and Elisha had crossed it dry-shod; Joshua had led through its channel the mighty host of the redeemed on their journey from Egypt into the Promised Land, but it had never seen anything like this: men, women, and children, mothers with babes in their arms, Scribes, Pharisees, and Sadducees, publicans and soldiers, flocked from Judea, Samaria, and Galilee, to hear this lonely wilderness prophet.

What excited them most was not his cry, "Repent," nor that they were to be baptized, confessing their sins, in order to the remission of their sins; but it was this, "He that cometh after me is mightier than I." How it must have thrilled the audience when they heard him proclaim!—"There is One coming after me; I am only the herald of the coming King." You know that when kings travel in Eastern countries they are preceded by heralds who shout, "The king is coming!" and they clear the highways, repair the bridges, and remove the stumbling-blocks. John announced that he was only His fore-runner; and that He Himself was nigh at hand. Perhaps at the after-meetings some would inquire, "When is He coming?" "He is coming unexpectedly, suddenly, and we shall see the Spirit of God descending and remaining upon Him. He may be here tomorrow." And as John preached His first coming, so we preach the second coming of Christ. It is always safe, for He said that He was coming again; and none can hinder it. We are told to "watch"—for death?

No; for the second coming of the Lord.

At length the time came when John still more mightily moved his hearers by declaring, "He is among us. He is in our midst." For four thousand years had the Jews been watching for the event which it was the immediate mission of the Baptist to predict. It had been a long time to be looking into the mists of the future for the Seed of the woman that should bruise the head of the serpent; but the mists had rolled away at last.

One day there came down from Jerusalem a very influential committee, appointed by the chief priests, to ask that wilderness preacher whether he were the Messiah or Elijah, or who or what he was. In John, we read that they made their appearance when he was in the very zenith of his popularity, preaching perhaps to twenty thousand people. Pushing their way up to where he was, they said, "We have been sent to inquire who you are. Are you the long-looked-for Messiah?" What an opportunity he had to pass himself off as the Christ. All were musing as to who he was. Some said that he really was the long-looked-for One. He was one of the grandest characters that ever trod this earth. Instead of elevating, he humbled himself. The great tendency with men is to make themselves out a little bigger than they are, to make it appear that there is more of them than there really is. Most men, as you get nearer to them, grow smaller and smaller. But John grows larger and larger! Why? Because he is nothing in his own sight. So he replied to the Committee, "Take back word to those who sent you: I am Mr. Nobody. I am a voice to be heard, and not to be seen. I am here to proclaim the coming of Him whose shoe latchet I am not worthy to unloose." That is a grand character! He confessed, "I am not the way; I am a finger-post pointing to the way. Walk in it. Do not follow me, but Him that is coming. I have found the way, and have come to herald the glad tidings." I wish all Christian workers would have the spirit of John, and get behind the cross, and be a mere sign-post pointing out Christ. John the Baptist was very little in his own estimation, but the angel had said before his birth, "He shall be great in the sight of the Lord." And this was his greatness, that he cried, "Behold the Lamb of God! I am nothing; He is all in all." Let that be our testimony.

"And this is the record of John, when the Jews sent priests and Levites from Jerusalem to ask him, Who art thou? And he confessed, and denied not; but confessed, I am not the Christ. And they asked him, What then? Art thou Elias [Elijah]? And he saith, I am not. Art thou that prophet? And he answered, No. Then said they unto him, Who art thou? that we may give an answer to them that sent us. What sayest thou of thyself? He said, I am the voice of one crying in the wilderness, Make straight the way of the Lord, as said the prophet Esaias," quoting Scripture; for Isaiah had prophesied that there should be a voice heard in the wilderness, "Prepare ye the way of the Lord."

Do you know what happened the next day? One of the most exciting things that ever took place on this earth. The next day the deputation, who waited upon this desert preacher, had perhaps returned to Jerusalem, or they may have been still on the banks of the Jordan. I think I see the crowds of men and women leaning forward with breathless eagerness to catch every word as it falls from the lips of John. He pauses suddenly in the middle of a sentence, his appearance changes, the eye that has been so keen quails, the bold rugged man shrinks back, and, as he stands silent and amazed, every eye is upon him.

Suppose at some great gathering I should stop preaching for a minute, the congregation would not know what had happened. They would ask, "Has he lost the thread of his discourse?" "Is sickness stealing over him?" "Has death laid his icy hand upon him?" But John stops. The people wonder what it means. The eye of the Baptist is fixed; and the crowd gives way before a Man of no very extraordinary mien, who approaches the Jordan, and addressing John, asks to be baptized. "Baptize you?" He remonstrates. It was the first man whom he had hesitated to baptize. The people are asking, "What does this mean?" John says, "I have need to be baptized of Thee, and comest Thou to me? I am not worthy to baptize *Thee*." The Master said, "Suffer it to be so now: for thus it becometh us to fulfil all righteousness"; and they both went down into the Jordan, and Jesus was baptized by John. The Master commanded, and John obeyed. It was simple obedience on his part.

Canon Farrar, in his "Life of Christ," thus describes this wonderful scene:

"To this preaching, to this baptism, in the thirtieth year of His age, came Jesus from Galilee. John was His kinsman by birth, but the circumstances of their life had entirely separated them. John, as a child, in the house of the blameless priest, his father, had lived at Juttah, in the far south of the tribe of Judah, and not far from Hebron. Jesus had lived in the deep seclusion of the carpenter's shop in the valley of Galilee. When He first came to the banks of the Jordan, the great forerunner, according to his own emphatic and twice-repeated testimony, "knew Him not." Though Jesus was not yet revealed as the Messiah to His great herald prophet, there was something in His look, something in the sinless beauty of His ways, something in the solemn majesty of His aspect, which at once over-awed and captivated the soul of John. To others he was the uncompromising prophet; kings he could confront with rebuke; Pharisees he could unmask with indignation; but before this presence all his lofty bearing falls. As when some unknown dread checks the flight of the eagle, and makes him settle with hushed scream and drooping plumage on the ground, so before the purity of sinless life, the wild prophet of the desert becomes like a submissive and timid child. The battle-brunt which legionnaires could not daunt, the lofty manhood before which hierarchies trembled and princes grew pale, resigns itself, submits, adores before moral force which is weak in every external attribute, and armed only in an invisible mail.

John bowed to the simple, stainless manhood before he had been inspired to recognize the Divine commission. He earnestly tried to forbid the purposes of Jesus. He who had received the confessions of all others now reverently and humbly makes his own: "I have need to be baptized of thee, and comest thou to me?" The response contains the second recorded utterance of Jesus, and the first word of His public ministry: "Suffer it to be so now: for thus it becometh us to fulfil all righteousness."

Do you tell me that the immense throng are not moved? Every man is holding his breath. And as they came out of the water, the Spirit descended like a dove and abode upon Him, and the voice of Jehovah, which had been silent on earth for centuries, was heard saying from heaven, "This is my beloved Son, in whom I am well pleased." From the time of the disobedience of the first Adam, God could not say that He was well pleased in man; but He could say so now. As Jesus came up out of the water, the silence of heaven was broken: God Himself bore witness that He was well pleased with His beloved Son.

What a day that must have been! You have seen the moon shining in the early morning; but as the sun ascends the moon fades away. So now John fades away. The moon's light is borrowed. All it can do is to reflect the light of the sun. That is what John did. He reflected the light of the Sun of Righteousness now that He had risen "with healing in His wings." From that day John changes his text. He had preached, "Repent;" but now his text is, "Behold the Lamb of God, who taketh away the sins of the world." "Behold the Sin-bearer of the world; God's Son come down into this world to bear away its sin. I am nothing now. He is everything."

Let us notice the testimony that John bore to Christ. The following was the substance of it:—"He that cometh after me is mightier than I; whose shoes I am not worthy to bear; there standeth One among you whom ye know not; He it is who, coming after me, is preferred before me. He shall baptize with the Holy Ghost and with fire. He is the Judge; His fan is in His hand; and He will thoroughly purge His floor and gather His wheat into the garner; but He will burn up the chaff with unquenchable fire. I knew Him not; but He that sent me to baptize with water the same said unto me, Upon whom thou shall see the Spirit descending, and remaining on Him, the same is He who baptizeth with the Holy Ghost. And after all the people had been baptized in the Jordan, confessing their sins, He came from Galilee to be baptized by me. But I said, I have need to be baptized of Thee, and comest Thou to me? And He answered me, Suffer it to be so now for thus it becometh us to fulfill all righteousness. Then I suffered Him, and I baptized Him. As He went up out of the water He was praying, and the heaven was opened, and the Holy Ghost descended in a bodily shape like a dove upon Him, and a voice came from heaven, which said, 'Thou art my beloved Son in whom I am well pleased.' And I saw and bear record that this is the Son of God."

The next day after Jesus had been baptized, John saw Him coming to him and said, "Behold the Lamb of God, which taketh away the sin of the world." Yesterday He had been baptized in the same river of judgement, where all the people had been baptized, confessing their sins, and today John points Him out as the Sin-bearer. And again, the next day, John was standing with two of his disciples, and, looking upon Jesus as He walked, he said, "Behold the Lamb of God!" He did not need to add the words he used the day before. His disciples knew that the Lamb of God was the antitype of all the sacrifices, from Abel's offering to the lamb laid that morning on the altar of burnt-offering. The two disciples heard him speak; they did not ask him what he meant, but they followed Jesus; went home with Him, and abode with Him that day, and became two of His intimate disciples and friends.

John continued effacing, denying himself, and testifying more and more of Jesus. "I am not the Christ: I am sent before Him. He is the Bridegroom, and I the Bridegroom's friend: I rejoice greatly, because of the Bridegroom's voice. Thus my joy, therefore, is fulfilled. He must increase, but I must decrease. He cometh from above; He is above all. And what He hath heard in heaven that He testifieth. But no one receives His testimony. He that hath received His testimony hath set to his seal that God is true. For God hath sent Him, and He speaketh the words of God. For God giveth not the Spirit by measure unto Him. The Father loved the Son, and hath given all things into His hand. He that believeth in the Son hath everlasting life; and he that believeth not the Son shall not see life, but the wrath of God is abiding on him."

Yes: "He that cometh from heaven is above all." No prophet, priest, nor king, ever lived to compare with Him. Jesus Christ had no peer. We ought to bear this in mind, and never put Him on a level with any other man. When Moses and Elijah appeared on the Mount of Transfiguration, Peter said to Jesus, "Let us make here three tabernacles, one for thee, and one for Moses, and one for Elias." But while he yet spoke a bright cloud overshadowed them. And when they had lifted up their eyes, they saw no man save Jesus only. Jesus was left alone to show the superiority of the new dispensation, which was represented by Him, over the old dispensation, represented by Moses and Elijah. God's voice said, "This is my beloved Son; hear Him." Christ has no equal. He is above all; He is sent by God; yea, He is God; all things were made by Him; He speaks the words of God; and the Spirit is given to Him without measure.

It was not long, however, before jealousy began to rankle in the breasts of John's disciples. One of the worst things with which Christian people have to contend is jealousy. It is a most accursed viper, and I would to God that it were cast out of all our hearts. This is one of the devils that need to be cast out. It were, indeed, well if we all possessed the feeling which animated Moses when Joshua asked him to forbid Eldad and Medad from prophesying in the camp: "And Moses said unto him, Enviest thou for my sake? would God that all the Lord's people were prophets, and that the Lord would put his spirit upon them." If ever there were two men who had reason to be jealous, they were Jonathan and John the Baptist; but the one stripped himself of the robe that was upon him, and gave it to David; and the other, when his disciples sought to arouse John's jealousy of Him of whom he came to bear witness, on account of the great crowds who flocked to His ministry, answered and said, "A man can receive nothing, except it be given him from heaven. Ye yourselves bear me witness, that I said, I am not the Christ, but that I am sent before him."

I do not know of anything, in all Scripture, more sublime than that one thing. As if John had said, "My joy is fulfilled. I could not be happier. I am the friend of the Bridegroom. I came to introduce Him. I want all my disciples to follow Him. I must decrease, He must increase." I once heard Dr. Bonar remark that he could tell whether a Christian were growing. In proportion to his growth in grace he would elevate his Master, talk less of what he was doing, and become smaller and smaller in his own esteem, until, like the morning star, he faded away before the rising sun. Jonathan was willing to decrease, that David might increase; and John the Baptist showed the same spirit of humility.

It took a great deal of grace for a man who, like John, had had such vast crowds following him out of the cities into the wilderness, to listen to his preaching, to declare that his mission was accomplished, and that he must retire into obscurity. He gloried in it. As a friend of the Bridegroom, he rejoiced to hear His voice, and that the Stone that smote the image would become a great mountain, and fill the whole earth.

I think that John showed more unselfishness than any man that ever lived. He did not know what selfishness was. If we could analyze our feelings, we should find that self is mixed up with almost everything we do; and that this is the reason why we have so little power as Christians. Oh, that this awful viper may be cast out! If we preached down ourselves and exalted Christ, the world would soon be reached. The world is perishing today for the want of Christ. The church could do without our theories and pet views, but not without Christ; and when her ministers get behind the cross, so that Christ is held up, the people will come flocking to hear the Gospel. Selfishness is one of the greatest hindrances to the cause of Christ. Every one wants the chief seat in the synagogue. One prides himself that he is pastor of this church, and another of that. Would to God we could get all this out of the way and say, "He must increase, but I must decrease." We cannot do it, however, except we get down at the foot of the cross. Human nature likes to be lifted up; the grace of God alone can humble us.

I have no sympathy with those who think that John lost confidence in his Master. From the earliest times a great difference of opinion has existed among ecclesiastical writers as to the question which John from the prison sent his two disciples to ask of Jesus.

The difficulty has been stated thus: "If John the Baptist had recognized in our Lord the Eternal Son of God, the Divine Lamb, and the Heavenly Bridegroom, is it possible to believe that he could, within a few months, question whether Jesus was the Christ; and that he should, with a simple desire for information, have asked, 'Art Thou He that should come, or do we look for another?'"

Some have thought that it was so, and have accounted for John's declension from his former testimony to Jesus, by supposing that the prophetic gift of the Holy Spirit had departed from him. Others have indignantly refused to believe this, and have eagerly defended John by maintaining that he simply sought by sending them to Jesus to remove the doubts of the disciples themselves. I have strongly urged this view myself in preference to the other, for I can not believe that this noble man, who was filled with the Holy Ghost from his mother's womb, and who had been His appointed forerunner, became discouraged by a few months in prison, and gave up his confidence in Jesus as the promised Messiah.

I think, however, that Dr. Reynolds, in his "lectures on John the Baptist," has thrown much light on this subject, and has shown that John may quite consistently have sent to ask this question; he says:

"Until the death, resurrection, and ascension of Jesus had taken place, until the descent of the Spirit, John's prophecies were not completely fulfilled. He may, nay he must, have had ideas of the Coming One which Jesus had not yet realized. There is nothing, therefore, unworthy of John's character, nothing incompatible with John's testimonies, in the supposition that he did not see the whole of his ideal embodied in the ministry of Jesus . . . There were elements of the 'Coming One' which were clearly a part of that type of Messiah which entered into John's predictions, and he was specially tempted or moved to ask, 'Art Thou the Coming One, or must we expect another of a different kind from Thyself, to fulfill the larger hope that is throbbing in the heart of Israel?'"

After these disciples had left, it was then that Christ gave His testimony of John. It was, "Verily I say unto you, Among them that are born of women there hath not arisen a greater than John the Baptist." What a tribute for the Son of God to pay! That must have sounded strange in the ears of the Jews. What! Greater than Abraham the father of the faithful? than Moses, the law-giver? than Elijah and Elisha? than Isaiah, Daniel, and all the prophets? Yes, none in all the world, born of women, greater than John. That is the eulogy which was pronounced on him. Truly he that humbleth himself shall be exalted. John had humbled himself before the Master, and now the Master exalts His faithful servant.

But this testimony of Jesus to his forerunner must not be regarded exclusively or chiefly as relating to his personal character. "There hath not risen a greater prophet than John the Baptist; but he that is least in the kingdom of God is greater than he." No prophet under the old dispensation had so great a testimony to bear as John. None before him could say, "There stands among you He that baptizes with the Holy Ghost. Behold the Lamb of God!" But the least disciple in the new dispensation has a still greater testimony. He can declare accomplished salvation: for the essence of the Gospel is "Jesus and the resurrection."

John was beheaded for his testimony, the first martyr for the Gospel's sake. He sealed his testimony with his blood. He rebuked the king, and told him that it was not lawful for him to live in adultery. He was not ashamed to deliver God's message just as it had been given to him. And no man has lived from the time of John but has enemies, if he be a disciple of Christ. Christ said this, "For John came neither eating nor drinking, and they say, He hath a devil. The Son of man came eating and drinking, and they say, Behold a man gluttonous and a winebibber, a friend of publicans and sinners." Think of saying that John the Baptist had a devil! Such a man! That is the world's estimate. They hated him. Why? Because he rebuked sin.

He, the last of a long line of prophets, was beheaded for his testimony, and buried in the land of Moab, just outside the Promised Land, near to where Moses, the first law-giver, was buried. His ministry was very short. It lasted only two years. But he had finished his course; he had done his work.

Dear friend, you and I may not have that time to work. Let us consecrate ourselves and get the world and self beneath our feet; and let Christ be all and in all. We must "stoop to conquer." Let us be nothing, and Christ everything. Let the house of Saul wax weaker and weaker, and the house of David wax stronger and stronger. Let us get to the end of self, and adopt as our motto, "He must increase, but I must decrease."

21

THE WAY OF LIFE

Obedience

*And being made perfect, he became the author of eternal salva-
tion unto all them that obey him*—Hebrews 5:9.

My subject is one that you will not like very well, but I found out
a long time ago that the medicine we don't like is the best medicine for us. If there is anything that throws a coldness over a
meeting, it is to talk about obedience. You can talk about love and
heaven and other things, and people get so warmed that they shout;
but when you talk about obedience, there is a sort of coldness over
the meeting. Like a man I heard of during the time of slavery. He
was preaching with great power (he was a slave), and his master
heard of it and said, "I understand you are preaching, and they tell
me you are preaching with great power."

"Yes," said the slave.

"Well, now," said the master, "I will give you all the time you
want, and you prepare a sermon on the commandments and preach
on the commandments, and bear down on stealing, for there is a
great deal of stealing on the plantation." The man's countenance fell
at once. He said he wouldn't like to do that; there wasn't the warmth
in it there was in some things.

And I have always noticed when you come right down to such
matters, people don't like to be told about them, because it comes a
little too near home. Once I heard about a young minister who took
the place of an old pastor, and he began to bear down pretty hard
upon the sins of the people. A man came to him afterwards and
said, "Look here, young man, if you expect to hold this pulpit, you
have got to stop that kind of preaching, for the people won't stand
it." There are a good many people who are delighted when you talk

about the sins of the patriarchs, and the sins of other Bible characters, but when you touch upon the sins of today, that is another thing. They say, "I don't like his style." No, nor his matter either, and perhaps you won't like this subject of obedience.

We are told that without faith it is impossible to please God, and you will find that it is impossible to please God without obedience. Your faith doesn't amount to much without obedience. "And being made perfect, he became the author of eternal salvation unto all them that obey him." Eternal salvation unto all them that *obey* Him; not all them that feel Him, talk to Him, that say, "Lord, Lord," but them that obey Him. Eternal salvation means eternal safety.

ALL BUT THE HEART OF MAN OBEYS GOD

Did you ever notice all but the heart of man obeys God? If you look right through history, you will find that this is true. In the beginning God said, "Let there be light," and there was light. "Let the waters bring forth," and the waters brought forth abundantly. And one of the proofs that Jesus Christ is God is that He spoke to nature, and nature obeyed Him. At one time He spoke to the sea, and the sea recognized and obeyed Him. He spoke to the fig tree, and instantly it withered and died. It obeyed literally and at once. He spoke to devils, and the devils fled. He spoke to the grave, and the grave obeyed Him and gave back its dead. But when He speaks to man, man will not obey Him; that is why man is out of harmony with God, and it will never be different until men learn to obey God. God wants obedience and He will have it, or else there will be no harmony. In the first Epistle of John, we read, "And the world passeth away, and the lust thereof: but he that doeth the will of God abideth for ever." He says in another place that if we keep His sayings we shall never die. The world is like a floating island and as surely as we anchor to it, we will be carried away by it.

NEAR TO GOD

Now, if you want to get near God, just obey Him; that is the quickest way to get near Him. He takes those into the nearest communion with Himself who obey Him. Once while Jesus talked to the people, behold, His mother and His brethren stood without, desiring to speak unto Him. "Then one said unto him, 'Behold, thy mother and thy brethren stand without, desiring to speak with thee.' But he answered, and said unto him that told him, 'Who is my mother? and who are my brethren?' And he stretched his hand toward his disciples, and said, 'Behold my mother and my brethren! For whosoever shall do the will of my Father which is in heaven, the same is my brother, and sister, and mother.' There is no friendship without obedience. The truest sign that we love God is that we obey Him.

"I do love God," a little girl said to her father one day, when he was speaking to her about loving God. "Perhaps you think you do, dear," said the father.

"But I do."

"Suppose you should come to me and say, 'Papa, I love you,' and then run off and disobey me, could I believe you?" The child said, "No."

"Well," continued the father, "how can I believe that you love God when I see you every day doing things that He forbids?" "If ye love me, keep my commandments."

It isn't a matter of feeling or picking out things we like to do, but it is doing what He commands us to do. Now notice, Adam lost everything by disobedience, and the second Adam gained everything by obedience. "For as by one man's disobedience many were made sinners, so by the obedience of one shall many be made righteous."

TO OBEY IS BETTER THAN SACRIFICE

Let me call your attention to another portion of Scripture. "And Samuel said, Hath the Lord as great delight in burnt offerings and sacrifices, as in obeying the voice of the Lord? Behold, to obey is better than sacrifice, and to hearken than the fat of rams." God doesn't want sacrifice, if there is disobedience. If we are living in disobedience to God, that is no sacrifice; it is sacrilege. If Adam and Eve had obeyed God, there would have been no need of sacrifices of any kind. Many men want to bring Him a sacrifice, instead of obeying Him. What does your work of charity amount to, if you are not obedient? Do you think that you can gain heaven by sacrificing your money or your time? "To obey is better than sacrifice."

Suppose a father sends his boy to school and he plays truant. He says, "I don't want to go to school," and he goes off and fishes all day. He knows his father is very fond of trout. He says, "I know I have been disobedient, but I can sell these trout for fifty cents, and I will just take them home to my father. It will be a great sacrifice, but it will please my father." Do you think that will please him? Not by a good deal. He wants obedience, and until his son obeys, his sacrifice is an abomination. The sacrifices of the wicked are an abomination to God and man. Don't let any man deceive himself and think he is going to please God by giving something to Him when he is living in disobedience.

Men say to me, "You talk against the gambler but he is very good to the poor," and they think he is going to merit heaven because he is good to the poor. "God will have to remember him." My dear friend, as long as he is living a disobedient life, he cannot do a thing to please God. That boy cannot please his father until he is willing to obey and do the very thing he was told to do. It is much easier to bring a lamb or bullock to the altar than it is to bring ourselves. Do you know it? I remember hearing a story about an Indian who wanted to come to the Lord. He brought his blanket, but the Lord wouldn't have it. He brought his gun, his dog, his bow and arrow, but the Lord wouldn't have them; but at last he brought himself and the Lord took him. The Lord wanted himself. What the Lord wants is not what you have got, but yourself, and you cannot do a thing to please God until you surrender yourself to Him.

Take the two Sauls. They lived about 1000 years apart. One started out well and ended poorly, and the other started out poorly and ended well. The first Saul got a kingdom and a crown; he had a lovely family (no father ever had a better son than Saul had in Jonathan); he had the friendship of Samuel, the best prophet there was on the face of the earth; and yet he lost the friendship of Samuel, lost his crown, his kingdom, and his life, all through an act of disobedience. God took the crown from his brow and put another man in his place. Why? Because he disobeyed. All his kingly dignity and power could not excuse him. Now take the Saul of the New Testament. When God called him he wasn't disobedient to the heavenly vision, and he was given a heavenly kingdom. One act of obedience, one act of disobedience. The act of obedience gained all, and the act of disobedience lost everything. And so you will find right through the Scriptures this is taking place constantly. I believe the wretchedness and misery and woe in our American cities today comes from disobedience to God. If they won't obey God as a nation, let us begin individually. Let us make up our minds that we will do it, cost us what it will, and you will have peace and joy.

A BLESSING OR A CURSE

In the book of Deuteronomy, we read, "Behold, I set before you this day a blessing and a curse; a blessing, if ye obey the commandments of the Lord your God, which I command you this day; and a curse, if ye will not obey the commandments of the Lord your God, but turn aside out of the way I command you this day, to go after other gods, which ye have not known." Isn't that enforced? A man who serves God, isn't the blessing of God resting upon him? There is great reward in keeping God's laws and statutes, but a great curse upon them that disobey God. A lawyer once gave a client instructions what to do, but the latter did not follow them and lost his case. When he complained to his lawyer, "Well," said he, "you did not do what I told you." Look at the wives and mothers that have gone right against the law of God and married ungodly men and drunkards. See what hells they are living in today! Just one act of disobedience. They are suffering tortures day by day, dying by inches.

The whole country is more or less cursed by this disobedience. A mother told me up in Minnesota that she had a little child who took a book and threw it out of the window. She told him to go and pick it up. The little boy said, "I won't." She said, "What?" He said again, "I won't." She said, "You will. You go and pick up that book." He said he couldn't do it. She took him out and she held him right to it. Dinner-time came and he hadn't picked up the book. She took him to dinner, and after it was over she took him out again. They sat there until tea-time. When tea-time came she took him in and gave him his supper, and then took him out and kept him there until bed-time. The next morning she went out again and kept him there until dinner-time. He found he was in for a life job, and he picked the book up. She said she never had any trouble with the child afterwards. Mothers, if you don't make your boy obey when he is young, he will break your heart.

You say, "Cannot God make a man obey?" I suppose He could but He does not work on those lines. He isn't going to force you against your will. He is going to draw you by the cords of love, but if you are not going to obey Him, then you are going to suffer. God made man neither obedient nor disobedient; and a man must choose for himself. As Dr. Parker says, "A child can treat God with sulkiness and silence. The tiniest knee can stiffen and refuse to bow before Him."

"Strive to enter in at the strait gate." "I will not."
"Look unto me, and be ye saved." "I will not."
"Come unto me, and I will give you rest." "I will not."
"Seek ye first the kingdom of God." "I will not."
"Repent." "I will not."

"Turn ye, turn ye, why will ye die?" "I will not."

"Follow me." "I will not."

"Believe in the Lord Jesus Christ." "I will not."

"Give me thine heart." "I will not."

"Go work in my vineyard." "I will not."

"Remember the Sabbath day to keep it holy." "I will not."

"Lay up for yourself treasures in heaven." "I will not."

So we might go through the Bible, and we would find that rebellious man refuses to obey His commandments, and follows the devices and desires of his own heart. God made man for His glory, but he joined the devil and became a rebel.

Now this is the question to be settled. The battle is fought on that one word of the will; the door hangs on that one hinge of the will. Will you obey? That is the question! Will you obey the voice of God and do as He commands you? No man can obey for you any more than he can eat and drink for you. You must eat and drink for yourself, and you must obey God for yourself.

God requires literal, prompt, cheerful obedience. Nothing less will do. If you changed the doctor's prescription only a little, you might turn it into rank poison. A Sunday-school teacher once asked her class, "How is the will of God done in heaven?" One child answered, "Cheerfully." Another, "By everybody." A third, "All the time." But the best answer was, "It is done *without asking any questions*."

DISOBEDIENCE BRINGS PUNISHMENT

Men don't seem to think that there is any thing in disobedience that needs to be punished. They shoot a soldier in the army for disobedience.

"Their's not to reason why,
Their's not to make reply,
Their's but to do or die."

It is said that an officer of engineers once told the Duke of Wellington it was impossible to carry out some orders he had given. "Sir," replied the duke, "I did not ask your opinion. I gave you my orders and I expect them to be obeyed." God never gave a command that we cannot obey. Perhaps we don't know the reason—but God knows it.

Will not the farmer be punished if he disobeys the laws of nature? and does not the same hold as regards spiritual laws? The only way to reap happiness in the life to come is to obey God's commandments in the life that now is.

People say, "Well, don't you think it very unreasonable of God to punish Adam because he transgressed once?" Some years ago a superintendent telegraphed to a man not to turn the bridge over a certain river until a special train passed. He waited and waited and the man stood firm, until finally some one over him persuaded him and he opened the bridge. He thought he would have time to let the boats pass and swing the bridge back before the train came. But he hadn't got it more than opened before he heard the coming of the quick train. He hadn't time to get the bridge back, and there was a tremendous accident and lives were lost. The man went out of his mind and was sent to a madhouse, and his cry for years, until death released him, was: "If I only had! if I only had!" If he only had what? If he had only obeyed, those lives would not have been lost. In England, not long ago, a switchman just turned the switch at the wrong time, and twenty men were hurled into eternity, and a good many were maimed and hurt for life. He only just disobeyed once.

SIMPLE OBEDIENCE

There is a story told about Girard, one of the first millionaires this country ever had. A green Irishman came over to this country, and he had been walking round the streets of Philadelphia for a long time, unable to get anything to do. One day he went into Girard's office and asked him if he couldn't give him something to do to keep soul and body together. Girard said, "Yes; do you see that pile of bricks down there?" "Yes." "Well, pile it up at the other end of the yard." The Irishman went to work. Night came on and he had the work all done, and he went into the office, touched his hat, got his pay, and asked if Girard had any work for him the next morning. Girard told him he had. The next morning he came along. Girard said, "You go and carry that pile of bricks back to where you found it." The Irishman went at the work without a word. Night came on, he got his pay and wanted to know if there would be work for him the next morning. Girard kept him marching up and down there for a number of days, until he found he was just the man he wanted. One day he said, "You go down and bid that sugar off." When the auctioneer put the sugar up, here was a green Irishman bidding. The people laughed and made sport of him, and finally it was knocked off to him. The auctioneer said in a gruff tone, "Who is going to pay for this sugar?" "Girard, sir." "You are Girard's agent? Mighty man then!" Girard had found a man he could trust; God wants to find a man He can trust to obey Him.

BLESSED BY OBEDIENCE

Do you know every man who was blessed while Christ was on earth was blessed in the act of obedience? Ten lepers came to Him, and He said, "Go and show yourselves to the priest." They might have said, "What good is that going to do us? It was the priest that sent us away from our families." But they said nothing; and it came to pass, that, as they went, they were healed. Do you want to get rid of the leprosy of sin? Obey God. You say you don't feel like it. Did you always feel like going to school when you were a boy? Supposing a man only went to business when he felt like it; he would fail in a few weeks. Jesus said to another man, "Go to the Pool of Siloam and wash," and as he washed, he received his sight. He was blessed in the act of obedience. The prophet said to Naaman, "Go and dip seven times in Jordan," and while he was dipping he was healed. Simple obedience. You don't need to go to any theological seminary to find out how to obey, need you? Old Matthew Henry used to say, "If you live by the Gospel precepts, you may live on the Gospel promises." To know the truth and not to obey it is unprofitable. It is said over fifty times of Moses that he did "as the Lord commanded him." That was why Moses had the confidence of God.

ETERNAL SALVATION

If you want eternal salvation, you can have it now. The terms are right here. What are they? Obedience.

"This is his commandment, That we should believe on the name of his Son, Jesus Christ."

"He that believeth on him is not condemned: but he that believeth not is *condemned already*, because he hath not believed in the name of the only begotten Son of God." If you disobey, you shut the only door of hope. You may have a profession of Christianity, you may join the church, you may know the doctrine, but unless you hearken unto God's commandments, it will all be of no avail.

Will you obey? You have got to settle this thing in your mind. Just make up your mind that you are going to obey. Nothing very mysterious about it. You needn't go to any old musty library to read up on obedience, need you? If God tells you to repent, then repent. This will be the grandest day you have ever seen if you make up your mind to obey Him. Will you do it?

Reader, decide now. In olden times, when a Roman ambassador came to a king who was not allied to the Empire, he said,

"Will you have peace with Rome or not?" If the king asked for time to think it over, the ambassador used, with his rod, to draw a ring around the man, and say, "You must decide before you step out of that circle; for if you do not say 'peace' before you cross the line, Rome will crush you with her armies." Do not trespass any longer on God's mercy. "Choose you this day whom ye will serve."

This life will not last forever. The trumpet will one day sound and call you forth from your narrow bed. The graves will be opened and you will be summoned forth to meet your God. The proud heart that scoffs at religion down here will be compelled to listen to the judgement sentence of God. The ears that will not obey the sound of the church-going bell will be compelled to obey the sound of the last trumpet. The eyes that behold evil here shall one day gaze upon the spotless throne of God. Do not forever disobey. May God help you to submit without delay your proud will in loving, child-like obedience to Himself.

SECTION 3
ANTHOLOGIES

22

CALVARY'S CROSS

The Blood—New Testament

Without shedding of blood is no remission—Hebrews 9:22.

I remember when Mr. Sankey and myself came back to this country in '75, I got a letter from a lady stating that she had read about our work in Europe and was greatly encouraged, and thought we were going to be used in this country, but she had read one of my sermons on the atonement and had given up hope. She said: "Where did Jesus Christ ever teach men they were saved by His death and suffering? Never, never did He teach it." Do you know what I do when I get this kind of a letter? I get my concordance and topical text book and go right at it, and I begin to preach more on the atonement than ever; and if I get into any town where they don't believe it, I preach it more than ever. The idea that Christ never taught it! If you will read the Gospels carefully, you will find He didn't teach anything else regarding the way of salvation.

Look at the beginning of His ministry, when He went down to be baptized of John in the Jordan. When He made His appearance, what did John say? "Behold the Lamb of God, which taketh away the sin of the world!" Bible students tell us that from the institution of the Passover not less than a quarter of a million lambs were slain annually by the Jews for the Passover supper; yet you never find them spoken of as "lambs," always "the lamb." For fifteen hundred years God had been educating the Jews up to that point, and when John burst upon the nation he cried: "Behold the Lamb of God, which taketh away the sin of the world."

What did Christ teach Nicodemus? "As Moses lifted up the serpent in the wilderness, even so must the Son of man be lifted up: that whosoever believeth in him should not perish; but have eternal life. For God so loved the world, that he gave his only begotten Son, that whosoever believeth in him should not perish, but have everlasting life." He never spoke, I believe, of His death but once when He didn't say He would rise again. A year before He was crucified, He was on His way to Capernaum, and He said to His disciples— you will find it in the 9th chapter of Mark and the 31st verse—"The Son of man is delivered into the hands of men, and they shall kill him; and after that he is killed, he shall rise the third day. But they understood not that saying, and were afraid to ask him." That was a year before His death. Then in the 10th chapter of Mark and the 32nd verse it says, "And they were in the way going up to Jerusalem; and Jesus went before them: and they were amazed; and as they followed, they were afraid. And he took again the twelve, and began to tell them what things should happen unto him, saying, Behold, we go up to Jerusalem; and the Son of man shall be delivered unto the chief priests, and unto the scribes; and they shall condemn Him to death, and shall deliver him to the Gentiles; and they shall mock him, and shall scourge him, and shall spit upon him, and shall kill him: and the third day he shall rise again." That doesn't look as if He died as a martyr, as if He didn't come into the world expecting to die for a special purpose. Mark too the account of the Transfiguration. That was the most important council ever held on earth. There were present Moses, the great law-giver, and Elijah, the great prophet, and Peter, James, and John that became the founders of the new church and the new dispensation, and Jesus, the Son of God, and God the Father. Mark and Matthew leave us in darkness; they don't tell us what they talked about, but Luke does. He says they spoke of "his decease which he should accomplish at Jerusalem." That was the theme that interested heaven, and I believe it is the most important thing to discuss in this world: what Jesus Christ came into this world to do, what He suffered, how He suffered, and what He suffered for.

NOT A MARTYR

Now I want to repudiate the statement that He died as a martyr. People say He laid down certain principles that finally took Him to the cross; that the cross was an accident, He couldn't help it, and He died as a martyr to His principles. Not a word of truth in it! Christ never died as a martyr, and the Bible doesn't say it anywhere. He laid His life down voluntarily. Do you want proof of it? Hear His own words:

"I lay down my life, that I might take it again. No man taketh it from me, but I lay it down of myself. I have power to lay it down, and I have power to take it again." Jesus Christ could have gone up on the other side of the cross just as well as this side. The law had no claim on Him. If He had broken the law, He would have had to die for His own sin, but He was a Lamb without spot or without blemish, and He died as our substitute voluntarily. That is the teaching of Jesus Christ.

When Peter drew his sword and cut off the servant's ear, the Lord rebuked him, and said He could call twelve legions of angels if it was necessary. One angel came and slew 85,000 men; what would 72,000 do? Do you think they had power to arrest the Son of God? Do you think they had power to take Him to Calvary and to His cross? With one wave of His hand He could send them to perdition, the whole of them. All Rome, hell, and earth combined couldn't take the life of the Son of God. "I lay down my life, and I take it up again." He voluntarily gave Himself up. He died as your substitute and mine, and that is my hope of heaven. I haven't any other hope; I don't want any other. When people accuse me of preaching an old Gospel, I thank God and take it as a compliment. I do preach an old Gospel. It is 6,000 years old. The Gospel I preach goes back there to Eden.

The 26th of Matthew, 28th verse: "For this is my blood of the new testament, which is shed for many for the remission of sins." Only two of the evangelists record Christ's birth, but all four of them speak of His death and sufferings. Mark says, the 14th chapter and 24th verse: "And he said unto them, This is my blood of the new testament, which is shed for many." Luke 22:20: "This cup is the new testament in my blood, which is shed for you."

Then after He had passed through the grave and had risen on the resurrection morn, it says in the 24th of Luke and 26th verse: "Ought not Christ to have suffered these things, and to enter into his glory? And beginning at Moses and all the prophets, he expounded unto them in all the scriptures the things concerning himself." It says in another place He quoted from the Psalms how He was to suffer and how He was to die.

REDEEMED WITH BLOOD

In 1 Peter 1:18, we read: "Forasmuch as ye know that ye were not redeemed with corruptible things, as silver and gold, from your vain conversation, received by tradition from your fathers; but with the precious blood of Christ, as of a lamb without blemish and without spot."

Silver and gold could not redeem our souls. As I have tried to show, life had been forfeited. Death had come into the world by sin, and nothing but blood could atone for the soul. Therefore, says Peter, "You are not redeemed with silver and gold." If gold and silver could have redeemed us, do you not think that God would have created millions of worlds full of gold? It would have been an easy matter for Him. But we are not redeemed by such corruptible things, but by the precious blood of Christ. Redemption means "Buying back"; we had sold ourselves for nought, and Christ redeemed us and bought us back.

"How can I be saved?" do you ask. Accept the Redeemer, the Lord Jesus Christ, and rest on His finished work. When Christ on Calvary said "It is finished," it was the shout of a conqueror. He had come to redeem the world, and now He had done it—done it without money! And His cry to the world comes ringing down the ages—"Ho, every one that thirsteth, come ye to the waters, and he that hath no money; come ye, buy, and eat; yea, come, buy wine and milk *without money and without price*."

A few years ago I was going with a friend to preach one Sunday morning, when a young man drove up in front of us. He had an aged woman with him.

"Who is that young man?" I asked.

"Do you see that beautiful meadow?" said my friend, "and that land there with the house upon it?"

"Yes."

"His father drank that all up," he said. Then he went on to tell all about him. His father was a great drunkard, squandered his property, died, and left his wife in the poor-house. "And that young man," he said, "is one of the finest young men I ever knew. He has toiled hard and earned money, and bought back the land. He has taken his mother out of the poor-house, and now he is taking her to church."

I thought, that is an illustration for me. The first Adam, in Eden, sold us for nought, but the Messiah, the second Adam, came and bought us back again. The first Adam brought us *to the poor-house*, as it were; the second Adam makes us kings and priests unto God. That is redemption. We get in Christ all that Adam lost, and more.

Men look on the blood of Christ with scorn and contempt, but the time is coming when the blood of Christ will be worth more than all the kingdoms of the world. Suppose you were going down to death's gates tonight, going down to the brink of the Jordan, without any hope in Christ. Suppose you were a millionaire, what would your millions be worth then? The blood of Christ would be worth more to you than all the silver and gold in the world.

TWO CRIES

The blood has two cries: it cries either for my condemnation (or if you will allow me to use a stronger word, for my damnation), or for my salvation. If I reject the blood of Christ, it cries out for my condemnation; if I accept it, it cries out for pardon and peace. The blood of Abel cried out against his brother Cain. So it was in the days of Christ.

When Pilate had Christ on his hands, he said to the Jews, "What shall I do with Him?" They cried out, "Away with Him! Crucify Him!" And when he asked which one he should release, Barabbas or Christ, they cried out, "Barabbas!" Then when he asked again, "What shall I then do with Him?" a universal shout went up from Jerusalem, "Let Him be crucified! Away with Him! We do not want Him." Pilate turned and washed his hands, and said, "I am innocent of this just man's blood," and they cried, "His blood be on us and on our children. We shall take the responsibility of it. We endorse the act. Crucify Him, and let His blood be on us and on our children."

Would to God that there might be a cry going up, "Let His blood be on us to save, not to condemn."

PEACE THROUGH THE BLOOD

Turn now to Colossians 1:20: "Having made peace through the blood of his Cross." I can tell you there is no peace in the world. There are many rich men, many great men in the world, who have got no peace. No; I have never seen a man who knew what peace was until he got it at Calvary. "Being justified by faith, we have peace with God through our Lord Jesus Christ" (Romans 5:1.). Sin covered—that brings peace. There is no peace for the wicked; they are like the troubled sea that cannot rest. Calvary is the place to find peace—peace for the past and grace for the present.

But there is something better still: "And rejoice in hope of the glory of God." Some people think that when they get to Calvary they have got the best; but there is something better in store—glory! I do not know how near it may be to us; it may be that some of us will be ushered very soon into the presence of the King. One gaze at Him will be enough to reward us for all we have had to bear. Yes, there is peace for the past, grace for the present, and glory for the future. These are three things that every child of God ought to have. When the angels came bringing the Gospel, they proclaimed, "Glory to God, peace on earth, and good will towards men." That is what the blood brings—sin covered and taken away, peace for the past, grace for the present, and glory for the future.

Would you now turn to John 19:34: "But one of the soldiers with a spear pierced his side, and forthwith came there out blood and water."

You know that in Zechariah it was foretold that there should be opened in the house of David a fountain for sin and for uncleanness. Now we have it opened. The Son of God has been pierced by that Roman soldier's spear. It seems to me that that was the crowning act of earth and hell—the crowning act of sin. Look at that Roman soldier as he pushed his spear into the very heart of the God-man. What a hellish deed! But what took place? Blood covered the spear! Oh! Thank God, the blood covers sin.

A usurper has got this world now, but Christ will have it soon. The time of our redemption draweth nigh. A little more suffering, and He returns to set up His kingdom and reign upon the earth. He will rend the heavens, and His voice will be heard again. He will descend from heaven with a shout. He will sway His scepter from the river to the ends of the earth. The thorn and the briar shall be swept away, and the wilderness shall rejoice. Let us rejoice also. We shall see better days. The dreary darkness and sin that sweep along our earth shall be done away with, the dark waves of death and hell shall be beaten back. Oh, let us pray to the Lord to hasten His coming!

Would you now turn to Romans 3:24: "Being justified freely by his grace through the redemption that is in Christ Jesus."

What God does He does freely, because He loves to do it. Mark these words, "Through the redemption that is in Christ Jesus." Then in the 5th chapter, 9th verse, we read, "Much more then, being now justified by his blood, we shall be saved from wrath through him." The sinner is justified with God by His matchless grace through the blood of His Son.

Justified, that means just as if he had never committed sin. What a wonderful thing; not one sin against him! It is as if he owed some one a debt, and when he went to pay it, was told:

"There is nothing against you; it is all settled."

"Why," he would say, "how is that? I got some things from you not long ago, and I want to pay the bill."

"There is nothing against you."

"But I am sure I got something here."

"There is nothing against you in my ledger; some one has come and paid it."

That is substitution. Now I know who paid my spiritual debts. It was the Lord Jesus Christ. God looks at His ledger, and there is nothing against us. Christ was raised up for our justification. It is a good deal better to be justified than pardoned. Suppose I was arrested for stealing $1,000, tried, and found guilty; but suppose the judge had mercy on me and pardoned me; I would come out of prison, but it would be with my head down. I had been found guilty, I could never face the world again. But suppose I was accused of stealing and it could not be proven, and when the case came on, it was found I had not done anything of the kind; then I would be *justified*. It would make all the difference in the world. Now God *justifies* us by the blood of His Son. That is what the blood does—sin covered, put out of the way, and nothing against us. Is not that good news?

Revelation 1:5: "Unto him that loved us, and washed us from our sins in his own blood." There are a great many people who wish to be saved, but who think they cannot be saved until they get a little better. If you are going to wait till you get rid of your sins, you will never be saved. You can not get rid of one sin. Instead of getting better you will get worse. But thanks be to God, He loves us even in our sins, even before He saves us from our sins. "He loved us and washed us from our sins in His own blood." *Loved us* first, then washed us. If we attempt to wash ourselves, we will make wretched work of it. The blood will cover it all up if we only trust ourselves to Christ. Who shall lay anything to the charge of God's elect? If He has justified me, it is enough.

HYMNS THAT LIVE

Why do we like to sing that old hymn—
"There is a fountain filled with blood
Drawn from Immanuel's veins."
Why will it live as long as the Church lives on earth? Why do you hear it sung all over Christendom? I remember how it used to thrill my soul even before I was converted. I could not tell why. Thank God, every sin is lost in that fountain. You will find that all

these hymns with the scarlet thread in them will live. There is that grand old hymn—

"Rock of Ages, cleft for me,
Let me hide myself in Thee;
Let the water and the blood,
From Thy riven side that flowed,
Be of sin the double cure,
Cleanse me from its guilt and power."

That speaks of the crucified Christ; it will never get worn out. Then there is—

"Just as I am, without one plea,
But that Thy blood was shed for me,
And that Thou bidst me come to Thee
O Lamb of God, I come."

That is another hymn that will live; you will never tire of it. It will be sung on and on, as long as the Church is on earth. I tell you why these are so precious; it is because they tell us about the blood.

Look at Hebrews 9:22: "And without shedding of blood is no remission." I would like to ask these men who do not believe in the blood, What are you going to do with your sins? Would you insult the Almighty by offering Him the fruit of your body to atone for them? Can a *man* atone for sin? If there is a scoffer here, a man who makes light of the blood, I want to know what he is going to do.

A gentleman once came to me and said, "If you are right, I am wrong; and if I am right, you are wrong."

I saw he was a minister, and I said, "Well, I never heard you preach; if you have heard me, you can tell what the difference is. Where do we differ?"

"Well, you preach the death of Christ; I preach His life. I tell people His death has nothing to do with their salvation; you tell them His life has nothing to do with it, and that His death only will save them. I do not believe a word of it."

"Well," I said, "what do you do with this passage, 'Who His own self bare our sins in His own body on the tree'?"

"Well, I have never preached on that text."

"What do you do with this, then, 'Ye are not redeemed with corruptible things as silver and gold, but with the precious blood of Christ'?"

"I have never preached on that text either," was the reply.

"Well, what do you do with this, 'Without shedding of blood there is no remission'?"

"I have never spoken on that," he said.

"What do you do with this, 'He was wounded for our transgressions, He was bruised for our iniquities, the chastisement of our peace was upon Him'?"

"I have never preached on that either."

"What *do* you preach, then?" I asked.

He hesitated for a little, and then said, "I preach moral essays."

"You leave out atonement?"

"Yes."

"Well," I said, "it would all be a sham to me if I did that; I could not understand it. I would be away home tomorrow, I would not know what to preach. Moral essays on Christ without His death!"

The young man said, "Well, it does seem a sham sometimes."

He was honest enough to confess that. Why, the whole thing is a myth without the atonement. The crucifixion of Christ is the foundation of the whole matter. If a man is unsound on the blood, he is unsound on everything. "Without shedding of blood there is no remission."

Turn now to Hebrews 10:11. Hebrews is full of the blood. "And every priest standeth daily ministering and offering oftentimes the same sacrifices, which can never take away sins. But this man"— what Man? The Man Christ Jesus—"after he had offered one sacrifice for sins for ever, sat down on the right hand of God." One sacrifice for sins forever! He has offered as a sacrifice *Himself*. You need no lambs now, no bullocks now. The High Priest has offered Himself. The high priest of old could not take his seat; his work was never done. But our great High Priest went up on high, and took His seat on the right hand of the Father's throne; the work is done. "It is finished," He said. All the types and shadows are fulfilled in Him, and now they have vanished away.

I believe if a man could get to heaven without the blood of Christ, he would not be happy there. He could not join in the great song that is sung around the throne; he could not sing the song of Moses and the Lamb; he could not say he was redeemed by the blood of the Lamb. You would see him away in some corner, out of tune with the rest; he would not be in harmony with them, and would not wish to stay there. But he could not get there. The only way is by the new and living way that Christ opened.

Turn back again to Hebrews 10:19: "Having, therefore, brethren, boldness to enter into the holiest by the blood of Jesus, by a new and living way, which he hath consecrated for us, through the veil, that is to say, his flesh." Those Jews, before Christ died, had to have the high priest intercede for them. He used to go in once a year into the holy of holies with blood to make intercession; but since Christ, our great High Priest, came, we do not need any Aaron to intercede for us. When Christ died, He opened a new and living way. He made us all kings and priests. It is said that the veil that was rent was His flesh. When He cried on the cross, "It is finished," the veil of the temple was rent in twain. God seized it with His right hand and tore it away. No veil between God and man now! We need no one to intercede for us now. Christ has died, yea, is risen again. Yes, we are all kings and priests now; we can go straight to the holy of holies ourselves. We need no man to intercede for our souls. The moment a man is saved by the blood he becomes a king and a priest. God calls him "My son." He is an heir of heaven and of glory. He is redeemed by the blood; he is made nigh by the blood. He gets victory over the world, the flesh, and the devil, by the blood.

There are very solemn verses found in Hebrews 10:28–29. "He that despised Moses' law died without mercy under two or three witnesses: of how much sorer punishment, suppose ye, shall he be thought worthy, who hath trodden under foot the Son of God, and hath counted the blood of the covenant, wherewith he was sanctified, an unholy thing, and hath done despite unto the Spirit of grace?" If a man despised Moses' law, they led him out and stoned him to death. Sinner, let me ask you, What are you going to do with the blood of God's only Son? I tell you it is a terrible thing to make light of the blood, to laugh and ridicule the doctrine of the blood. I would rather fall dead on this platform than do such a thing. It makes my heart shudder when I hear men speak lightly of it.

Some time ago a very solemn thought came stealing over me, and made a deep impression on my mind. The only thing that Christ left of His body on the earth was His blood. His flesh and bones He took away, but when He went up on high, He left His blood down here. What are you going to do with the blood? Are you going to make light of it and trample on it? May God give us all a glimpse of Christ crucified!

Revelation is full of the doctrine of the blood. "They overcame him by the blood of the Lamb, and by the word of their testimony." That is the only way to overcome the devil, the lion of hell—by the blood of the Lamb. He knows that the moment a poor sinner flees to the blood he is beyond his reach.

As I have traveled up and down Christendom I have found out

that a minister who gives a clear sound upon this doctrine is successful. A man who covers up the cross, though he may be an intellectual man, and draw large crowds, will have no life there, and his church will be but a gilded sepulcher. Those who preach the doctrine of the Cross, and hold up Christ as the sinner's only hope of heaven, and as the sinner's only substitute, who make much of the blood, God honors. Souls are always saved in the church where the blood of Christ is preached.

May God help us to make much of the blood of His Son. It cost God so much to give us His Son, and shall we try to keep Him from the world which is perishing from the want of Him? The world can get along without us, but not without Christ. Let us preach Christ in season and out of season. Let us go to the sick and dying, and hold up the Savior who came to seek and save them—who died to redeem them. "They overcame him by the blood of the Lamb, and by the word of their testimony."

Once more, in Revelation 7:14. "These are they which came out of great tribulation, and have washed their robes, and made them white in the blood of the Lamb." Sinner, how are you going to get your robes clean if you do not get them washed in the blood of the Lamb? How are you going to wash them? Can you make them clean?

I pray that at last we may all get back to the paradise above. There they are singing the sweet song of redemption. May it be the happy lot of each of us to join them. It will be a few years at the longest before we shall be there to sing the sweet song of Moses and the Lamb. But if you die without Christ, without hope, and without God, where will you be? O sinner, be wise; do not make light of the blood. An aged minister of the Gospel, on his dying bed, said:

"Bring me the Bible."

Putting his finger upon the verse, "The blood of Jesus Christ His Son cleanseth us from all sin," he said. "I die in the hope of this verse."

It was not his fifty years' preaching, but the blood of Christ. May God grant that when we come at last to stand before the great white throne, our robes may be washed in the cleansing blood of Christ!

23

THE SECOND COMING OF CHRIST

In Second Timothy, third chapter, verse sixteen, Paul declares: "All scripture is given by inspiration of God, and is profitable for doctrine, for reproof, for correction, for instruction in righteousness." But there are some people who tell us, when we take up prophecy, that it is all very well to be believed, but that there is no use in one trying to understand it; that future events are things that the Church does not agree about, and it is better to let them alone, and deal only with those prophecies which have already been fulfilled.

But Paul doesn't talk that way; he says: "ALL scripture is . . . profitable for doctrine." If these people are right, he ought to have said: "Some scripture is profitable; but you can't understand the prophecies, so you had better let them alone." If God did not mean to have us study the prophecies, He would not have put them into the Bible. Some of them are fulfilled, and He is fulfilling the rest, so that if we do not see them all completed in this life, we shall in the world to come. Prophecy, as has been said, is the mold in which history is cast. About one-third of the Bible is prophetical, and a large portion of the remainder is typical of things that were to come.

Three great comings are foretold in the Word of God. First, that Christ should come; that has been fulfilled. Secondly, that the Holy Ghost should come; that was fulfilled at Pentecost, and the Church is able to testify to it by its experience of His saving grace. Third, the return of our Lord from heaven—for this we are told to watch and wait "till He come."

I do not want to teach anything dogmatically, on my own authority; but to my mind this precious doctrine—for such I must call it—of the return of the Lord to this earth is taught in the New Testament as clearly as any other doctrine in it. If you read the twenty-sixth chapter of Matthew, the sixty-fourth verse, you will find that it was just this very thing that caused His death. When the high priests asked Him who He was, and if He was the true Messiah, what does He reply:

"I say unto you, Hereafter shall ye see the Son of man sitting on the right hand of power, and coming in the clouds of heaven."

That was enough. The moment they heard that, they accused Him of blasphemy, and condemned Him to death, just because He said He was coming again.

Whoever neglects this has only a mutilated Gospel, for the Bible teaches us not only of the death and sufferings of Christ, but also of His return to reign in honor and glory. His second coming is mentioned and referred to over three hundred times, yet I was in the Church fifteen or sixteen years before I ever heard a sermon on it. There is hardly any church that does not make a great deal of baptism, but in all of Paul's epistles I believe baptism is spoken of only thirteen times, while he speaks about the return of our Lord fifty times; and yet the Church has had very little to say about it. Now, I can see a reason for this:

The Devil Does Not Want Us To See This Truth,

for nothing would wake up the Church so much. The moment a man realizes that Jesus Christ is coming back again to receive His followers to Himself, this world loses its hold upon him. Gas stocks and water stocks and stocks in banks and railroads are of very much less consequence to him then. His heart is free, and he looks for the blessed appearing of His Lord, who, at His coming, will take him into His blessed kingdom.

Some people say, "The prophecies are all well enough for the priests and clergy, but not for the rank and file of the Church."

But Peter says, "The prophecy came not in old time by the will of man: but holy men of God spake as they were moved by the Holy Ghost," and those men are the very ones who tell us of the return of our Lord. Look at Daniel, where he tells the meaning of that stone which King Nebuchadnezzar saw in his dream, that was cut out of the mountain without hands, and that broke in pieces the iron, the brass, the clay, the silver, and the gold. "The dream is certain, and the interpretation thereof sure," says Daniel. Now, we have seen the fulfillment of that prophecy, all but the closing part of it. The kingdoms of Babylon and Medo-Persia and Greece and Rome have all been broken in pieces, and now it only remains to smite the image and break it in pieces till it becomes like the dust of the summer threshing-floor, and for this stone to become a great mountain and fill the whole earth.

BUT HOW WILL HE COME?

We are told how He is going to come. When the disciples stood looking up into heaven at the time of His ascension, there appeared two angels, who said unto them (Acts first chapter, verse eleven): "Ye men of Galilee, why stand ye gazing up into heaven? this same Jesus, which is taken up from you into heaven, shall so come in like manner as ye have seen him go into heaven."

How did He go up? He took His flesh and bones up with Him. "Look at me; handle me; a spirit has not flesh and bones as ye see me have. I am the identical one whom they crucified and laid in the grave. Now I am risen from the dead and am going up to heaven."

"He is gone," say the angels, "but He will come again just as He went."

An angel was sent to announce His birth to the Virgin. Angels sang of His advent in Bethlehem. An angel told the women of His resurrection. Two angels told the disciples of His coming again. It is the same testimony in all these cases.

I do not know why people should not like to study the Bible, and find out all about this precious doctrine of our Lord's return. Some have gone beyond prophecy, and tried to tell the very day He would come. Perhaps that is one reason why people don't believe this doctrine. He is coming—we know that; but just when He is coming we don't know. Matthew settles that: "But of that day and hour knoweth no man, no, not the angels of heaven, but my Father only." The angels don't know. It is something the Father keeps to Himself.

In Luke we read: "The Son of man cometh at an hour when ye think not."

McCheyne, the Scottish preacher, once said to some friends, "Do you think Christ will come tonight?"

One after another they said, "I think not."

When all had given this answer, he solemnly repeated this text: "The Son of man cometh at an hour *when ye think not*."

Commenting on the text: "It is not for you to know the times or the seasons, which the Father hath put in his own power," Spurgeon says: "If I were introduced into a room where a large number of parcels were stored up, and I was told that there was something good for me, I should begin to look for that which had my name

upon it, and when I came upon a parcel and I saw in pretty big letters, 'It is not for you,' I should leave it alone. Here, then, is a casket
of knowledge marked, 'It is not for you to know the times or the seasons, which the Father hath put in his own power.' Cease to meddle
with matters which are concealed, and be satisfied to know the
things which are clearly revealed."

If Christ had said, "I will not come back for 2,000 years," none
of His disciples would have begun to watch for Him until the time
was near, but it is

The Proper Attitude Of A Christian

to be always looking for his Lord's return. So God does not tell
us when Christ is to come, but He tells us to watch. Just as Simeon
and Anna watched and waited for His first coming, so should true
believers watch and wait for His return. It is not enough to say you
are a Christian, and that you are all right. You are not all right unless you obey the command to watch.

We find also that He is to come unexpectedly and suddenly.
"For as the lightening cometh out of the east, and shineth even unto
the west; so shall also the coming of the Son of man be." And again,
"Therefore be ye also ready: for in such an hour as ye think not the
Son of man cometh."

Some people say that means death; but the Word of God does
not say it means death. Death is our enemy, but our Lord has the
keys of death. He has conquered death, hell, and the grave, and at
any moment He may come to set us free from death, and destroy
our last enemy for us.

In the last chapter of John there is a text that seems to settle this
matter. Peter asks the question about John, "Lord, and what shall
this man do? Jesus saith unto him, If I will that he tarry *till I come,*
what is that to thee? Follow thou me. Then went this saying abroad
among the brethren that that disciple *should not die*." They did not
think that the coming of the Lord meant death; there was a great difference between these two things in their minds. Christ is the Prince
of Life. There is no death where He is. Death flees at His coming.
Dead bodies sprang to life when He touched them or spoke to them.
His coming is not death; He is the resurrection and the life. When He
sets up His kingdom, there is to be no death, but life forevermore.

Look at the account of the last hours of Christ with His disciples. What does He say to them? "If I go away, I will send death after
you to bring you to Me" or "I will send an angel after you?" Not at

all. He says: "I will come again, and receive you unto myself."

It is this that makes the fourteenth chapter of John so sweet.

There is another mistake, as you will find if you read your Bibles carefully. Some think that at the second coming of Christ everything is to be brought about in a few minutes, but I do not so understand it.

The First Thing He Is To Do

is to take His Church out of the world. He calls the Church His bride, and He says He is going to prepare a place for her. We may judge, says one, what a glorious place it will be from the length of time He is in preparing it, and when the place is ready He will come and take the Church to Himself.

In the closing verses of the fourth chapter of 1 Thessalonians, Paul says: "If we believe that Jesus died and rose again, even so them also which sleep in Jesus will God bring with him . . . We which are alive and remain unto the coming of the Lord shall not prevent them which are asleep. For the Lord himself shall descend from heaven with a shout, with the voice of the archangel, and with the trump of God: and the dead in Christ shall rise first: Then we which are alive and remain shall be caught up together with them in the clouds, to meet the Lord in the air: and so shall we ever be with the Lord. Wherefore comfort one another with these words." That is the comfort of the Church.

If my wife were in a foreign country, and I had a beautiful mansion all ready for her, she would a good deal rather I should come and bring her to it than to have me send some one else to bring her. He has prepared a mansion for His bride, the Church, and He promises for our joy and comfort that

He Will Come Himself

and bring us to the place He has been all this while preparing.

There was a time when I used to mourn that I should not be alive in the millennium; but now

I Expect To Be In The Millennium.

Dean Alford says—and almost everybody bows to him in the matter of interpretation—that he must insist that this coming of Christ to take His Church to Himself in the clouds, is not the same event as His coming to judge the world at the last day. The deliverance of the Church is one thing, judgement is another. Christ will save His Church, but He will save them finally by taking them out of the world.

Some may shake your heads and say: "Oh, well, that is too deep for the most of us. Such things ought not to be said before young converts. Only the very wisest characters, such as the ministers and the professors in the theological seminaries, can understand them."

But, my friends, Paul wrote about these things to the young converts among the Thessalonians, and he told them to comfort one another with these words. Here in the first chapter of 1 Thessalonians Paul says: "Ye turned to God from idols to serve the living and true God; and to wait for his Son from heaven, whom he raised from the dead, even Jesus, which delivered us from the wrath to come." To wait for His Son—that is the true attitude of every child of God. If he is doing that, he is ready for the duties of life, ready for God's work; yes, that makes him feel that he is just ready to begin to work for God.

Then over in the next chapter he says: "For what is our hope, or joy, or crown of rejoicing? Are not even ye, in the presence of our Lord Jesus Christ at His coming?" And again, in the third chapter, thirteenth verse: "To the end that he may stablish your hearts unblamable in holiness before God, even our Father, at the coming of our Lord Jesus Christ with all his saints." Still again, in the fifth chapter and twenty-third verse: "I pray God your whole spirit and soul and body be preserved blameless unto the coming of our Lord Jesus Christ." He has something to say about this same thing in every chapter; indeed, I have thought this Epistle to the Thessalonians might be called the Gospel of Christ's Coming Again.

Take the account of the words of Christ at the communion table. It seems to me the devil has covered up the most precious thing about it. "For as often as ye eat this bread, and drink this cup, ye do shew the Lord's death *till he come*." But most people seem to think that the Lord's table is the place for self-examination, and repentance, and making good resolutions. Not at all; they spoil it that way. It is to show forth the Lord's death, and we are to observe it till He comes.

Some people say, "I believe Christ will come on the other side of the millennium."

Where do they get it? I can't find it. The Word of God nowhere tells me to watch and wait for signs of the coming of the millennium (such as the return of the Jews), but for the coming of the Lord; to be ready at midnight to meet Him, like those five wise virgins.

At one time I thought the world would grow better and better until Christ could stay away no longer; but in studying the Bible I don't find any place where God says so, or that Christ is to have a spiritual reign on earth of a thousand years. I find that

The World Is To Grow Worse And Worse

and that at length there is going to be a separation. The Church is to be translated out of the world, and of this we have two examples already, two representatives (as we might say) in Christ's kingdom, of what is to be done for all His true believers. Enoch is the representative of the first dispensation, Elijah of the second, and, as a representative of the third dispensation, we have the Savior Himself, who entered into the heavens for us, and became the firstfruits of them that slept. We are not to wait for the great white throne judgement, but the glorified Church is set on the throne with Christ, and to help to judge the world.

Now, some think this is a new and strange doctrine, and that they who preach it are speckled birds. But let me say that many spiritual men in the pulpits of Great Britain, as well as in this country, are firm in this faith. Spurgeon preached it. I have heard Newman Hall say that he knew no reason why Christ might not come before he got through with his sermon. But in certain churches, where they have the form of godliness, but deny the power thereof—just the state of things which Paul declares shall be in the last days—this doctrine is not preached or believed. They do not want sinners to cry out in their meetings, "What must I do to be saved?" They want intellectual preachers who will cultivate their taste, brilliant preachers who will rouse their imagination, but they don't want the preaching that has in it the power of the Holy Ghost. We live in the day of

Shams In Religion.

The Church is cold and formal; may God wake us up! And I know of no better way to do it than to get the Church to look for the return of our Lord.

Some people say, "Oh, you will discourage the young converts if you preach that doctrine!"

Well, my friends, that hasn't been my experience. I have felt like working three times as hard ever since I came to understand that my Lord was coming back again.

I look on this world as a wrecked vessel. God has given me a lifeboat, and said to me, "Moody, save all you can." God will come in judgment to this world, but the children of God don't belong to this world; they are in it, but not of it, like a ship in the water; and their greatest danger is not the opposition of the world, but their own conformity to the world. This world is getting darker and darker; its ruin is coming nearer and nearer; if you have any friends on this wreck unsaved, you had better lose no time in getting them off.

But someone will say, "Do you then make the grace of God a failure?"

No; grace is not a failure, but *man is*. The antediluvian world was a failure. The Jewish world was a failure. Man has been a failure everywhere when he has had his own way and been left to himself. When the Son of God left heaven, and came to this sin-cursed earth to open up a new and living way whereby we might return to God, the earth would give Him no better quarters than a manger for His birthplace, no place to lay His head during the years of His ministry, and only the cruel cross in His death.

Nowhere in the Scriptures is it claimed that the whole world shall be brought to the feet of Christ in this dispensation. In the fifteenth chapter of Acts, James says: "Simeon hath declared how God at the first did visit the Gentiles, to take out of them a people for his name." That is one reason for our Lord's delay. He is waiting until the elect are all gathered out, until His Gentile bride is complete.

Now, don't take my word for it. Look this doctrine up in your Bibles, and, if you find it there, bow down to it, and receive it as the Word of God. Take Matthew, twenty-fourth chapter, verses fifty and fifty-one: "The lord of that servant shall come in a day when he looketh not for him, and in an hour that he is not aware of, and shall cut him asunder, and appoint him his portion with the hypocrites: there shall be weeping and gnashing of teeth." Take Second Peter, third chapter, fourth and fifth verses: "There shall come in the last days scoffers, walking after their own lusts, and saying, Where is the promise of his coming? for since the fathers fell asleep, all things continue as they were from the beginning of the creation." Go out on the streets, and ask men about the return of our Lord, and that is just what they would say:

"Ah, yes; the Lord delayeth His coming! I don't propose to trouble myself about it. It will not be in my day."

But Peter goes on to say, verse ten: "But the day of the Lord will come as a thief in the night; in the which the heavens shall pass away with a great noise, and the elements shall melt with fervent heat, the earth also and the works that are therein shall be burned up." We have no right then to say when it will *not* come, any more than we have a right to say when it will come. As some one has said, Christ's second coming does not occur so quickly as impatience, nor yet so late as carelessness, supposes.

There is another thought I want to bring to your attention, and that is: Christ will bring our friends with Him when He comes. All who have died in the Lord are to be with Him when He descends from His Father's throne into the air. An interval of time ensues between this meeting of all His saints in the air and His coming with all His saints to execute judgement upon the ungodly, to chain Satan in the bottomless pit for the thousand years, and to establish the millennial reign in the great power and glory. "Blessed and holy is he that hath part in the first resurrection: on such the second death hath no power, but they shall be priests of God and of Christ, and shall reign with him a thousand years." "But the rest of the dead lived not again until the thousand years were finished. This is the first resurrection." That looks as if the Church was to reign a thousand years with Christ before the final judgement of the great White Throne, when Satan shall be cast into the Lake of Fire, and there shall be new heavens and a new earth.

When Christ returns, He will not be treated as He was before. There will be room for Him at Bethlehem. He will be welcome in Jerusalem. He will reveal Himself as Joseph revealed himself to his brethren. He will say to the Jews, "I am Jesus," and they will reply: "Blessed is He that cometh in the name of the Lord." And the Jews will then be that nation that shall be born in a day.

"Behold, I come quickly," said Christ to John. Three times it is repeated in the last chapter of the Bible. And almost the closing words of the Bible are the prayer: "Even so, come, Lord Jesus." Were the early Christians disappointed then? No; no man is disappointed who obeys the voice of God. The world waited for the first coming of the Lord, waited for 4,000 years, and then He came. He was here only thirty-three years, and then He went away. But He left us a promise that He would come again; and, as the world watched and waited for His first coming and did not watch in vain, so now, to them who wait for His appearing, shall He appear a second time unto salvation.

Now, let the question go round. "Am I ready to meet the Lord if He comes tonight?"

"Be ye also ready, for in such an hour as ye think not the Son of man cometh."

24

THE PRODIGAL

The Prodigal Son

This young man, the prodigal son, started wrong—that was the trouble with him. He was like hundreds and thousands of young men in our cities today who have a false idea of life; and when a man has a false idea of life, it is very hard for his father or mother or any of his friends to do anything with him.

I do not know where his mother was. Perhaps he had sent her to the grave with a broken heart. The Lord did not speak of his mother; if she had been living, He would have probably referred to her.

The father is to be censured; we cannot help but blame the father. When the son said, "Father, divide, and give me my portion," the father should have said:

"You show a bad spirit. I will let you go without your portion."

A great many fathers make that mistake now. I do not think this father could have done a greater unkindness to the boy than to give him his goods and money and let him go. It showed a contemptible spirit in the boy when he came to his father and said:

"Divide: give me my portion and let me go."

He wanted to go away from his father's prayers and influence and get into a foreign land where he could go on as he pleased, where he could run riot and plunge into all kinds of sin, and where there was no restraint. And that indulgent father gratified his wish and divided his goods with him. I have two sons, and if either should ask me for a portion I'd say:

"Go and earn it by the sweat of your brow."

Of all classes I most pity rich men's sons with nothing to do. It's a good deal better for your sons to earn wealth for themselves than for you to earn it for them. I have more respect for a rich man's son who makes anything of himself than for a poor man's son. Self-

made men are the only men good for anything. The rich men's sons
are spoiled. Their fathers do everything, even their thinking, for
them. They are subject to all kinds of temptations, which poor
men's sons never know.

Perhaps this young man did not get on well with his elder
brother. Or perhaps he grew restive under home restraints. We are
not told the reason why he left home, but not many days after he
had received his portion, he went around to his old companions
and bade them all good-bye and went off to a foreign country, perhaps to Egypt. He started out with a false idea of life; nine-tenths of
the young men do. He thought he'd find better friends and have a
better time in that far off country.

How Satan blinds men! With some it is money, with others
pleasure; with all of us, it is selfishness under one form or another.

He started off, holding his head very high that morning. He
was full of pride and conceit, and he had very lofty ideas. If anyone
had told him what he was coming to, he would have laughed in
scorn. But mind you, once a man starts on the downward trace, he
will sink lower and lower, unless by the grace of God he turns from
sin to righteousness.

A CRISIS IN A MAN'S LIFE

The first lie, the first drink, the first petty theft, is often a crisis
in a man's life. I suppose, like young men of today, he went to Memphis or some other large city. He put up at the best hotel, he smoked
the best cigars, he drank none but the best wines, and drove none but
the fastest horses. He did not mix with the common men. He gathered a number of choice friends around him and thought he was
having a high time. The very first thing we hear of him is that he was
in bad company. He began to waste his substance in riotous living. I
never knew a young man who treated his father unkindly who would
not go off into bad company. We hear of his going on in all kinds of
vice. He devoured his living with harlots. He was guilty of adultery—
the shortest, quickest, surest road to ruin. If they had theaters in
those days (and I do not doubt but they had), he would be in the theater every night of the week. We should find him in the billiard hall
and the drinking saloon. We should find him in the ways of those
whose feet take hold on hell. He was a popular young man; he had
plenty of money, and his money was popular. He was a grand com-
panion for the young men in that far country; they liked his society.
If you had asked him to come to a religious meeting, he would

have been indignant. What need had he of a Savior? What did he care for his father's Bible or his mother's prayers?

That first year he was very independent. He had a great many admirers fluttering around him. His friends were the leading young men—the upper ten. He moved in very high circles. The aristocratic mothers were foolish enough to introduce him to their daughters, who were very glad to make his acquaintance.

That was the first year, but he cleared it all out in five years or less. Perhaps his portion was $100,000. It does not take long for a young man to go to ruin when he gets among harlots and wild young fellows. It takes one generation to accumulate; the next spends it.

Where are his friends now? He had plenty to gamble with him at first. They liked to take a helping hand in spending his money, but gradually he hasn't money enough to pay the tailor. He is getting a little shabby in appearance. His clothes are not so good as they were. He once had a good wardrobe, but now he goes to the pawnshop, and he pawns his overcoat for a strong drink; and one thing after another soon goes. He might have had some gift which his mother gave him when she was dying, and at last that goes; and yet he does not come to himself. When he first came to Memphis he used to get drunk at least once a week. Now you see him hanging around the pawnbroker's. He asks one of his former friends to lend him a dollar. They were ready enough to strip him of his money; now they point him out as the biggest fool in all Memphis.

"He came here five years ago," one of them says, "with $100,000 and he's gone through the whole of it. He actually asked me to lend him a dollar. I wouldn't lend him a cent." His friends were the friends of his circumstance. Give me the friend who is my friend for what I am, not for what I've got. I want a friend who will stand by me in the time of calamity.

He pawns his ring, the sign of sonship, and his clothes. And then a mighty famine strikes the land. There is always a famine in the devil's territory. A mighty famine struck the land, and this young man began to feel the want of food.

The fact is, it doesn't take long to drain the cup of pleasure dry. There may be pleasure in sin, but it does not last. It ends in want and misery every time. Satan never gives enduring satisfaction. When this young man got home they "began to be merry," but now in the far country he begins to be in want. And "no man gave unto him." Generosity is a virtue which does not flourish in that kind of soil.

ONE REDEEMING POINT

He had one redeeming point—he would not beg or steal. God have mercy on a young man in perfect health who will beg! He is not far from being a thief.

The prodigal looked round for a job. Would any bank president have him for cashier? "I couldn't trust him," they would say. Would any leading merchant take him? "I couldn't," they would answer; "he has lost his character."

"Look at his hands," one said; "he can't earn anything at manual labor."

He went round for a number of days and at last was hired to look after swine. He was so hungry that he would have eaten husks if he could have got them. No man gave him even husks. This wealthy man's son, who was brought up amid good influences and surroundings, is now living in that foreign country like a man who had never seen a decent home.

Now, just for a moment think what that man lost in all these years.

He lost his *home;* he had no home. His friends, when he had money, might have invited him around to their homes; but it was not home for him. There is not a prodigal upon the face of the earth but has lost his home. You may live in a gilded palace, but if God is not there, it is not home. If your conscience is lashing you, it is not home.

He lost his *food*. His father's table did not go to that country. He would have fed on the husks that the swine did eat. This world cannot satisfy the soul.

Then he lost his *testimony*. I can imagine that some of the young men of that country saw him among the swine, feeding them, and they said:

"Look at that poor wretched young man, with no shoes on his feet and with such shabby garments."

They looked at him and called him a beggar and pointed the finger of scorn at him.

He said, "You need not call me a beggar. My father is a wealthy man."

"Your father a wealthy man?"

"Yes."

"You look like a wealthy man's son!" Not a man believed him when he said he was a wealthy man's son. His testimony was gone.

So when a man goes into the service of the devil he sinks lower and lower; it is not long before everyone loses confidence in him. One sin leads on to another. His testimony is gone.

He lost his *health,* his *good name*, his *time*.

And he did not gain much to compensate him for these losses. He got a good many things; however. He got the jeers of his former companions. He got rags and filth. He got a gnawing hunger and a depraved appetite. He got a sad experience of the unsatisfying nature of worldly pleasures.

ONE THING HE DID NOT LOSE

But there is one thing he did not lose, and if there is a poor backslider reading this, there is one thing you have not lost. That young man never lost *his father's love*.

I can imagine one of his father's neighbors met him in that place and said to him:

"My boy, I have just come from your home. Your father wants you to return."

I can imagine the young man said, "Did my father speak of me? I thought he had forgotten me."

"Why," says the man, "he thinks of nothing else. He thinks of you day and night. Do you think he has forgotten you? No, never. He cannot forget you. He loves you too well for that."

One morning he got his work done sooner than usual and got to thinking. I wish I could get men to think about what they are and where they are going. His mind went back over his past conduct, and he saw nothing but sin. In the future he saw nothing but death and judgement. In his childhood days he remembers how he used to play with his brother, and how the old birch tree in front of the house looked. He remembers his mother used to bend over him at night and teach him some little prayer, such as, "Now I lay me down to sleep." He remembered the morning when he left home.

"Father tried to pray for me," he meditated, "but he couldn't finish his prayer. His grip was like a vice as he said, 'It's just breaking my heart to have you go. Remember, I shall always be glad to see you back. Hope you won't be away long.'

"If I stay here much longer, I'll starve to death, and they will bury me like a pauper. Here I am, perishing with hunger, while my father's hired servants have bread enough and to spare. I will arise and go to my father and say to him, 'Father, I have sinned against heaven and before thee.'"

ONE OF THE GREATEST BATTLES EVER FOUGHT

One of the greatest battles ever fought was being waged then. Everything holy and heavenly was beckoning him home. The powers of darkness were trying to keep him from returning.

"You go back and they'll all laugh at you. What'll they say?" said the devil.

No doubt there was an angel hovering over him, watching for the decision, and when he arose and said, "I will arise," the angel bore it on high.   .

"Make another crown. Get another robe ready. There's another sinner coming!"

That "I will" echoed and re-echoed, and there was joy in the presence of the angels. He is saved already. His heart has got home already. The battle with pride and sin is over.

As the Scripture puts it, "He came to himself." It is a grand thing to see a man coming to himself. When he began to come to himself, then there was hope for him. It teaches us clearly that all these years he had been out of his mind. Very likely he thought Christians were out of their minds. There is not a drunkard, harlot, thief, or gambler, but thinks Christians are mad; and they call us fanatics. But Solomon says, "Madness is in their heart while they live, and after that they go to the dead."

When he came to himself, he said, "I will perish here. I will arise and go to my father." That was the turning point in that young man's life. There is always hope for a man when he begins to think. I wish you would bear in mind that if you are willing to own your sin and own that you have wandered from God, God is willing to receive you. The very moment you are willing to come, that moment God is willing and ready to receive you. He delights in forgiveness. I do not care how vile you have been; if you are willing to come back, God is willing and ready to receive you.

It did not take long, after his mind was made up, to go. He had no friends to visit and bid good-bye to. There was no one to love and pity him. He asked his employer to settle up—he didn't get much. He came just as he was—poor, ragged, dirty; he did not wait to get fixed up.

I see him as he starts home. He has a hard journey. He is almost starved. Day after day he travels on. He has no fear of thieves, for he has squandered all he had.

If a man had seen him going along the road when he started for home, he'd have said:

"There goes a tramp."

A tramp? He is an heir of glory, going to sit on the throne with Christ. He is already in the kingdom. If a man is not saved, it is not because he *can't,* but because he *won't.* The only obstacle in the way of receiving pardon for sins are those you make yourself.

One day he gets to the top of the hill—and then he's across the line. There is a strange feeling about getting back into your own country, under the old flag; there's an excitement about it. He gazed at the blue hill in the distance and said to himself:

"When I get on that hill I can see how the old house looks."

When he arrives on that hill-top, how his eyes feast on the homestead!

Now let us take a look into the home. It is the hour of family worship. The old father reads a psalm, one of the psalms of David, the ninety-first or the forty-sixth, perhaps. After reading, they sing, and the old man prays. He prays for the servants, the elder brother, the neighbors, then his voice begins to falter a little, and he prays: "God bring home my wandering boy!"

That cry had gone up from that altar every evening for five years.

"Who's that your master was praying for?" you ask the servants.

"His youngest son."

"Why, I've lived here for three years and never knew he had one. What kind of a young man is he?"

"A good-for-nothing, miserable wretch," they answer.

Then you inquire of the elder son.

"Yes, sir, I've a younger brother. He's off down at Memphis."

"Is he in business down there?"

"No, sir, my father gave him his fortune, and he spent it all with harlots and riotous living."

You notice that it's the elder brother that says this. Not a bit will the father tell. Go and sit down by that gray-haired father and ask him:

"Would you forgive him?"

"Forgive him? Why, there's been nothing in my heart but love for him all along. Let him come home, and you'll see how gladly I'll restore him."

The father in the parable represents your God and mine. His heart is full of love for us, no matter how we turn our backs on Him and disobey. He so loved us that He sent His only begotten Son to die for us.

One day the old father is on the flat roof on the top of the house. It is about three o'clock in the afternoon. The old man is praying with his face turned towards Jerusalem. He takes his usual look along the highway and sees a stranger in the distance. He holds up his hands to keep the sun out of his eyes, and looks. Love makes the eyesight very keen. He cannot recognize his boy by his rags, but he knows his son's very gait.

"That's my boy! That's my son! He's coming back!" he exclaims.

Downstairs he rushes, his gray hair flying in the wind; he has never been seen to go so fast for years. He leaps into the highway. The servants wonder to see him rushing to meet a stranger. God never allows us to get ahead of Him.

"Father, I've sinned," begins the prodigal. But the old man won't hear a word.

"Run quickly and get the best robe. You run and bring a new ring. You fetch the best pair of shoes. You go and kill the fatted calf. Send for the musicians. We are going to have music and rejoice."

The whole house is in excitement.

What a picture that is of the love of God and His joy over the return of a sinner! Come, reader, are you not ashamed to stay away from such a Father? Will you not say, "I will," this moment, and turn your face homewards? God is waiting to welcome you.

I see the old man weeping tears of joy. In that home there is gladness. The boy is eating that sumptuous meal; he has not had as good a meal for many a year. It seems almost too good to be true. Picture the scene. While he is there he begins to weep; and his old father, who is weeping for joy, looks over to him and says:

"What are you weeping for?"

The boy says, "Well, Father, I was thinking it would be an awful thing if I should leave you again and go into a foreign country."

But if you sit down at God's feast, you will not want to go back into the devil's country again. He go back? He will never go back to the swine and the husks.

Oh, my friends, come home! God wants you. His heart is aching for you. I do not care what your past life has been. Upon the authority of God's Word I proclaim salvation to every sinner. "This man receiveth sinners, and eateth with them." Every sinner has a false idea of God; he thinks God is not ready and willing to forgive him. He says it is not justice. But God wants to deal in mercy. If the old father had dealt in justice, he would have barred the door and said to his son:

"You cannot come into my house."

That is not what fathers are doing. Their doors are not barred against their own children. Their doors are wide open, and they bid you come home. There is no father on earth who has as much love in his heart as God has for you. You may be black as hell; yet God stands ready and willing to receive you to His bosom and to forgive you freely.

When I was preaching once in Philadelphia, a poor, fallen woman came into the meeting. The sermon did not touch her until I got to that part where I said: "There is no sinner so vile but Jesus will receive that one"; and it went like an arrow to her soul. She came to the inquiry-room and made up her mind never to go back. In the course of forty-eight hours she found her way to the feet of Jesus. Two Christian ladies went to see her mother; and when they came to her house, she was not going to let them in. She was sick, and did not want to receive any callers; but the thought came to her that perhaps they were bringing good news from her husband. When these two angels of light came in, they said they came to talk about her daughter, Mary. The woman said:

"My daughter? Have you brought news of my child? Where is she? Oh, how my heart has ached for fifteen long years. Why did you not bring her with you?"

They said: "We did not know that you would receive her."

She said: "Oh, how my heart has been aching! Won't you bring her back tomorrow morning?"

If the mother received that child, do you tell me God would not receive her? There is not a sinner on earth whom God will not receive if he repents.

William Dawson, the celebrated Yorkshire farmer, once said that there was no man so far gone in London that Christ would not receive him. A young lady called on him and said:

"I heard you say that there was no man so far gone in London that Christ would not receive him. Did you mean it?"

"Yes," he said.

"Well," she said, "I have found a man who says he is so bad that the Lord will not have anything to do with him. Will you go and see him?"

He said, "I will be glad to go." She took him to a brick building in a narrow street, and he was in the fifth story. She said:

"You had better go in alone."

He went in and found a young man lying in the garret, on an

old straw bed. He was very sick. Mr. Dawson whispered in his ear some kind words and wanted to call his friends.

The dying man said, "You are mistaken in the person."

"Why so?" said Mr. Dawson.

"I have no friends on earth," said the dying man.

It is hard indeed, for a man to serve the devil and come down to no friends.

"Well," said he, "you have a friend in Christ"; and he told him how Jesus loved and pitied him and would save him. He read different portions of Scripture and prayed with the man. After praying with him a long time, the light of the Gospel began to break into his dark soul, and his heart went out towards those whom he had injured. He said:

"If my father would only forgive me, I could die happy."

"Who is your father?"

He told him, and Mr. Dawson said, "I will go and see him."

"No," the sick man said, "he has cast me off."

But William Dawson knew he would receive him, so he got his father's address and said:

"I will go."

He came to the west end of London and rang the bell of the house where the father lived. A servant in the livery came to the door, and Mr. Dawson asked if his master was in. The servant showed him in and told him to wait a few minutes. Presently the merchant came in. Mr. Dawson said to him:

"You have a son by the name of Joseph."

The merchant said, "No, sir; if you came to talk to me about that worthless vagabond, you shall leave the house. I have disinherited him."

Mr. Dawson said, "He will not be your boy by night, but he will be as long as he lives."

The man said, "Is my boy sick?"

"Yes, he is dying. I do not ask you to help bury him, I will attend to that; but he wants you to forgive him, and then he will die in peace."

The tears trickled down the father's cheeks. Said he, "Does Joseph want me to forgive him? I would have forgiven him long ago if I had known that."

In a few minutes he was in a carriage, and they went to the house where the boy was; and as they ascended the filthy stairs, he said:

"Did you find my boy here? I would have taken him to my heart if I had known this."

The boy cried, when his father came in, "Can you forgive me all my past sins?"

The father bent over him and kissed him and said, "I would have forgiven you long ago." And he added, "Let my servant put you in my carriage."

The dying man said, "I am too sick—I can die happy now. I think God, for Christ's sake, has forgiven me."

The prodigal told the father of the Savior's love; and then, his head lying upon his father's bosom, he breathed his last and rose to heaven.

If your father or mother forsake you, the Lord Jesus Christ will not. Oh, press into the kingdom of heaven now. Come home!

Mr. Spurgeon once summed up the things his audience had gotten over. Some, he said, had gotten over the prayers of faithful Sabbath-school teachers who used to weep over them and come to the house and talk to them. They resisted all their entreaties and got over their influence. And some had gotten over their mothers' tears and prayers, and she, perhaps, sleeps in the grave today. Some had gotten over the tears and prayers of their father and of their minister, who had prayed with them and wept with them, a godly, faithful minister. There was a time when his sermons got right hold of them, but they have gotten over them now, and his sermons make no impression. Some had been through special meetings, and they have made no impression; they have not touched them. Still they say they are getting on. Well, so they are, but, bear in mind, they are getting on as fast as they can to hell, and there is not one man in ten thousand who can hope to be saved after he has grown so hard-hearted.

Oh, reader, if you are not already a child of God, safe bound for the Father's home, or if you are a wandering child, off in the far country, say, "I will arise" now! Let there be joy in heaven today over your return.

25

WHAT IS FAITH?

Trust

We have for our subject at present one word—trust. It means really the same as *belief on,* or *faith in,* the Lord Jesus Christ. Many people have been brought up to believe intellectually, and when we talk to them about faith they do not exactly understand what we mean. Perhaps, however, the use of this word—*Trust*—will help to make it plainer. The word "Believe" in the New Testament is the same as "Trust" in the Old Testament. Where it is "Believe, believe" in the New, it is "Trust, trust, trust" in the Old. Some people get hold of that word "Trust" when they don't understand what is meant by believing on the Lord Jesus Christ. It seems a simpler word.

Once when I was preaching, I noticed a lady looking very steadily at me, and she seemed to fetch home to her heart every word that fell from my lips. After the sermon I went down and asked her if she was a Christian. She said:

"No, but I wish I was. I have been seeking Christ for three years, and can not find Him. What am I to do?"

Said I, "There must be some mistake. He has been seeking you for twenty years; and if you have been seeking Him, you would have met long before now."

She asked, "What am I to do?"

"Do nothing; just believe on the Lord Jesus Christ and be saved."

"I have heard that until my head aches. Everybody says believe, believe, believe; and I am none the wiser."

I said, "I will drop that word. *Trust* the Lord Jesus Christ, as you stand here."

"If I say I will trust the Lord, will He save me?"

"No, you might *say* that a thousand times, and not *do* it. Will you do it?"

"I do trust in the Lord Jesus Christ with all my soul," she said, "and I don't feel any difference."

I said: "You have been seeking after feeling; you have been seeking for feeling in your heart. Now, there is no promise in the Word of God that you will get feeling. There is no verse, from Genesis to Revelation, where feeling is attached to salvation."

I quoted the verse: "He is able to keep that which I have committed unto Him."

"Now," I said, "will you not put your trust in Him? Trust Him and let your feelings take care of themselves."

She looked at me about five minutes it seemed, but I don't suppose it was more than one; and then she reached out her hand, and said:

"I trust the Lord Jesus Christ this night to save my soul."

There was no tear, no prayer, but there was a decision.

"I trust."

She turned to the pastor of the church, and calling him by name, said: "I trust the Lord Jesus Christ to save my soul." Turning to one of the elders she said: "I trust the Lord Jesus Christ to save my soul." She started and went down the aisle, and just as she was going out the door she met another officer of the church, and she said: "I am trusting Jesus to save me."

The next night she was in front of me. I did not have to go down that night and ask her if she loved Jesus. At the close of the meeting she was the first to go into the inquiry-room, and when I got there she had her arm around a young lady's neck, and she was saying:

"It is only to *trust* Him."

She led more people to Christ in two weeks in that church than anyone else.

My first point is

Whom Are You To Trust?

You know the 8th verse of the 118th Psalm is the middle verse in the whole Bible. A convict in one of our prisons is said to have counted the verses in the Bible, and he found that was the middle verse. I think that is a good place to begin, and run both ways, and we will then have the whole Bible. At least we will take up a few passages that will help us to get hold of this truth, beginning with that verse:

"It is better to trust in the Lord than to put confidence in man."
You will say "Amen" to that. You that have put confidence in
man and have been disappointed, can say that is true. Every infidel
will admit that. It is better to trust God than yourself. I would rather
trust God than my own deceitful heart. It is better to make yourself
a liar and make God true. It is better to trust in the Lord than to put
confidence even in princes. That is what the Lord said.

The Psalmist says, "I will not be afraid what man can do unto
me, because my trust is in God." Why? Because his heart is fixed—
trusting.

If God has hid me in the secret pavilion, let men slander me
and abuse me if they like! If I can say that God is my Father, Jesus
is my Savior, and heaven is my home; let the world rail—let the
flesh do what it pleases—I will not be afraid of evil tidings, for my
trust is in God! Is not that a good footing for eternity? "Heaven and
earth shall pass away, but my word shall not pass away." If you get
your feet fair and square on the rock, let the waves beat if they will.
A Christian once said that he trembled sometimes, but the foundation never did: he had his foot upon the rock. We want good footing
for eternity, and there is no better footing than the Word of God.

One of the greatest enemies of the human family is the *self-
righteousness* and *self-confidence* that people have. In the Gospel by
Luke, Christ spoke a parable "to certain of those who trusted in
themselves." Every one is either trusting in Christ as his risen Savior, or in himself, or in the church, or in other people's opinions.

You must guard against trusting in *churches*. A good many
men are converted to a church. They say: "I like that church. It is a
beautiful church, and there is beautiful singing. I like the quartet
and the grand organ; and there is a good minister." And so they are
converted to the church, and to the singing, and to the organ, and
to the minister. Or perhaps they are converted to the people who go
there; they get into good society. But that is not being born of God,
or being converted to God.

Churches are good in their place; but when we put them in the
place of salvation, they become a snare. All the churches in the
world cannot save you. If the bitten Israelite had looked to Moses,
or only to the pole, he could not have been saved. He had to raise
his eye above the pole, and above Moses, and to fix it on the serpent.
Then God's word was fulfilled. We must guard against trusting in
anything but the Word of God, and the Lord Himself. If you pass by
all obstacles, and come right to Him, and put your trust in Him, you

will have rest, and peace of mind; and you need not doubt your salvation from this day until you go to your grave.

Again, God has warned us not to put trust in *man*. Jeremiah 17:5–9: "Thus saith the Lord: Cursed be the man that trusteth in man, and maketh flesh his arm, and whose heart departeth from the Lord. For he shall be like the heath in the desert, and shall not see when good cometh; but shall inhabit the parched places in the wilderness, in a salt land and not inhabited.

"Blessed is the man that trusteth in the Lord, and whose hope the Lord is. For he shall be as a tree planted by the waters, and that spreadeth out her roots by the river, and shall not see when heat cometh, but her leaf shall be green; and shall not be careful in the year of drought, neither shall cease from yielding fruit.

"The heart is deceitful above all things, and desperately wicked: who can know it?"

The same thought is brought out in Isaiah 30: "Woe to the rebellious children, saith the Lord, that take counsel, but not of me; and that cover with a covering, but not of my spirit, that they may add sin to sin: that walk to go down into Egypt, and have not asked at my mouth; to strengthen themselves in the strength of Pharaoh, and to trust in the shadow of Egypt! Therefore shall the strength of Pharaoh be your shame, and the trust in the shadow of Egypt your confusion."

In one place He says, "Woe," and in another place He says, "Cursed be the man." It is a terrible thing for a man to put faith in man.

Then Psalm 146:3–5: "Put not your trust in princes, nor in the son of man, in whom there is no help. His breath goeth forth, he returneth to his earth; in that very day his thoughts perish. Happy is he that hath the God of Jacob for his help, whose hope is in the Lord his God."

Here we are told very plainly by God that we are not to put our trust in this man or that man—not to lean upon an arm of flesh.

How often we hear a man say: "There is a member of the church who cheated me out of five dollars, and I am not going to have anything more to do with people who call themselves Christians." But if the man had had faith in Jesus Christ, you do not suppose he would have had his faith shattered because some one cheated him out of five dollars, do you? What we want is—to have faith in the Lord Jesus Christ. If a man has that, he has something he can anchor to, and the anchor will hold; and when the hour of temptation comes to him, and the hour of trial, the man will stand firm. If we are only converted to man, and our faith is in man, we will certainly be disappointed.

In the eleventh chapter of Hebrews, the writer tells us of the faith of Abel, and Enoch, and Abraham, and Moses, and the others; but in the next chapter he takes the eye away from the contemplation of them, and says:

"Look at Jesus. Do not look at these now, but look unto Jesus, the author and finisher of our faith. Look to Him alone."

Let us learn a lesson, that we are not to pin our faith even to good men; we are not to have supreme faith in them. They can not save us. We may have confidence in them, but when it comes to the great question of salvation, we are to have

Faith In God Alone.

If you are trusting friends, they may turn against you, or death may take them from you. If you trust in riches, they may take to themselves wings and fly away; and if you keep them to the last, you must ultimately leave them.

Creeds can not save you. Creeds are very good in their place, but if you stop there and live upon your creed, you get no strength. A creed is like a street to take me to my house; but if I don't go into my house, I don't get my dinner. We must go beyond our creed to the person, the Lord Jesus Christ.

Let us look at the ninth Psalm and tenth verse: "And they that know thy name will put their trust in Thee: for thou, Lord, hast not forsaken them that seek thee."

A man that knows God can not help but trust Him. That is a good proof we have that these things are true. Men who know most about God trust Him the most. It is men who don't know God who don't trust Him. Did you ever see a man who was well acquainted with the Bible and with the teachings of the Spirit, who didn't have full confidence in God? I never did.

Suppose a man made me a hundred promises, and had ten years to fulfill them, and that next month the ten years will expire. He has fulfilled ninety-nine of the promises, and is able to fulfill the other. Would not I have good reason to trust him that he would fulfill it?

Has not God fulfilled all His promises? And shall we doubt Him, and say we can not trust Him? They that know Him trust Him.

A party of gentlemen in Scotland wanted to get some eggs

from a nest on the side of a precipice, and they tried to persuade a poor boy that lived near to go over and get them, saying they would hold him by a rope. They offered him a good deal of money; but they were strangers to him, and he would not go. They told him they would see that no accident happened to him—they would fasten him securely.

At last he said, "I will go if my father will hold the rope."

He trusted his father.

A man will not trust strangers. I want to get acquainted with a man before I put my confidence in him. I have known God for forty years, and I have more confidence in Him now than I ever had before; it increases every year. In the Bible, some things that were dark ten years ago are plain today; and some things that are dark now will be plain ten years hence. We must take things by faith. You take the existence of cities on the testimony of men that have been in those cities; and we ask you to take our testimony, who have found joy in believing. We ask you to trust in God.

How many are kept back from Christ because

They Think They Have Not The Right Kind Of Feeling.

Let feelings take care of themselves. Satan can change your feelings, and make you feel almost any way; but he can not change the Word of God. If our feelings change, we know the Word of God is true; and it is a great deal better to build upon God's Word than it is to build upon the best of feelings. Tell the world, tell your feelings, tell your friends—that you are going to trust God, be you sick or well; and whether you live or die, whatever happens to you, you can and will trust Him. Behold, God is my Savior and my Redeemer; not prayers, or feelings, or works, or tears, or anything in or of myself. "God is my salvation; I will trust, and not be afraid: for the Lord Jehovah is my strength and my song: he also is become my salvation." There is salvation in front of you, and salvation behind you, salvation to begin with, and salvation to end with. So now, just pray to the Lord to help you to trust Him from this hour—from this minute—trust Him with your body, and with your soul.

There is a verse in Proverbs teaching us

How To Trust:

"Trust in the Lord with all thine heart; and lean not unto thine own understanding. In all thy ways acknowledge him, and he shall direct thy paths."

I never knew a man who was willing to trust the Lord with all his heart, but the Lord saved him, and delivered him from all his doubts. The great trouble is that we do not trust Him *with all our heart*. God says, "Ye shall find me when you search for me with all your heart." God says, "Trust me with all your heart." Is there anything to hinder you from putting your whole trust in Him?

If Satan comes to you and wants to hear you explain some mysterious sayings in the Bible, do not lean on your own understanding; tell him you are going to trust the Lord, and not yourself. If God cannot be trusted, who can? Trust Him without any doubts. There cannot be true faith where there is doubt; the very fact that you doubt should show you that you do not trust with all your heart.

It is said that Alexander the Great had a favorite physician who followed him through all his battles. This favorite doctor had an enemy who wanted to get him out of the way. The latter wrote a letter to Alexander, stating that the favorite physician intended to give him a poison cup on the following morning. The man thought the Emperor would order the physician to be put to death. Next morning, however, the Emperor took the message, and read it out loud; and before the physician had time to reply, he drank what was in the cup before his eyes, to show his friend that he did not believe one word that his enemy had said.

That is believing with all the heart; and when Satan comes with some insinuation about God not being love, tell him that you believe God with all your heart.

People get many of these doubts from reading infidel books. They say, "You should read both sides of the question." If a man writes me scandalous letters about my wife, must I read them? I made up my mind forty years ago about Jesus Christ, and when an infidel book is put into my hand, I tear it up. I would take poison into my system as soon as read an infidel book. If you doubt Christ being the Savior, ask yourself—Has He not done more to elevate mankind than any other man who ever lived? There is but one side to truth after all; and is not Christ the truth?

Do not entertain these doubts for a moment. If Satan darts an evil thought into your mind about Christ, that is not sin if you do not entertain it. Meet it with the shield of faith, "wherewith ye shall be able to quench all the fiery darts of the wicked." Drive it off and let your mind be filled with good thoughts that will crowd out the evil ones. A great many people are troubled with evil thoughts and doubts and fears; but my experience is that if they would go and work, they would not have any time to doubt.

People say, "If I could only get rid of these doubts and fears, I think I would be ready to work."

Go to work, and these doubts will disappear. There is work to be done. Life is short at the longest, so let us be about our Master's business; and while you are engaged in His work, these doubts will not assail you so much. I believe any Christian would have doubts in less than six months if he did nothing.

We should trust God with all our hearts, and not with our heads. The trust must be down in the heart; and that will carry our hands and feet, and whole life, right into the current of God's work.

Not "Try" But "Trust."

I can imagine some one says: "I have tried to trust Him over and over again."

The very word "try" implies that you don't do it. If a man said to me—"I will try to believe you," it would imply that I had deceived him some time, and he had hard work to believe me now. Drop the word "try," and say "trust."

When shall we trust?

A great many say: "I would like to become a Christian, but you don't pretend to say I can trust now and be saved?"

There is not anything to hinder a man from trusting at once if he will. You say:

"Have I not to feel a little, and repent more, and weep more, and have a deeper conviction of sin?"

A deep conviction of sin is all you want. I don't object to seeing men weep over their sins. Some people think it is not manly. I don't know why it is not manly for a man to weep over his sins. It is more manly than to trifle with salvation, and make light of serious things. A great many men seem to be ashamed to shed tears over their sins.

In the eighth verse of the sixty-second Psalm we read: "Trust in him at all times, ye people."

There are a good many who trust God when we see all is light and clear before us, but not in the dark. We will trust when everything is fair and bright—no opposition, no persecution, or bitterness, but all smooth sailing. Well, that is walking by sight, and not by faith. We are to trust in the Lord at all times, and the Lord will not have one who can not be tried. If you are starting out in the Lord's work, you are going to be tempted. St. Augustine said that

God had one Son without sin, but He had no Son without trial.

You must expect trial and temptation, but you must trust God

At All Times.

My experience has been this: that Christians who are all the time trying to walk by sight instead of faith, are the most faulty Christians we have. All the time Jacob was walking by sight, he was in trouble; and when he got into Egypt, and the King of Egypt wanted to know what kind of a journey he had had through life, all he could say was that it had been stormy. Few and evil had been his days! He had had an awful time of it. Look at Joseph! He walked by faith; and in God's good time He took him out of slavery and prison, and put him on the throne, and made him ruler over all Egypt. One walked by sight, and the other by faith.

You may be put into some dark place; but in the darkness KEEP TRUSTING! It takes no faith at all to trust when we can see the whole thing. People may say it is a leap in the dark; but we are constantly making such leaps.

Suppose I have a sick boy. I know nothing about medicine; but I call in the doctor, and put that boy's life and everything into his hands. I do not fail to believe in him; and I do not interfere at all. Do you call that trusting in the dark? Not at all! I need my best judgement, and I put that boy's life into the hands of a good physician.

You have a soul diseased. Put it into the hands of the Great Physician! Trust Him, and He will take care of it. He has had some of the most hopeless cases. He was able to heal all that came to Him while on earth. He is the same today.

Take another illustration. Suppose you have one thousand dollars, and there are forty thieves who want to rob you of it. I tell you that there is a bank here, and that I will introduce you to the president so that you can deposit the money. You do not know anything of the bank, save by repute: you know nothing about how the books are kept; but you take my word, and you believe my testimony, that if you deposit the money, it will be safe; and you go in and place the thousand dollars there.

We must trust God in time of trouble, in time of bereavement. You can trust Him with your soul until your dying day, if you will. Will you not do it?

Several years ago, a minister in a town much resorted to by invalids was requested to see a gentleman reported to be very ill. He went accordingly. The patient was a man between fifty and sixty, and had been a successful merchant in the metropolis. He had been ordered to this health resort; but, as it proved, only to die there. The minister soon saw that it was no earnest desire for spiritual benefit that had prompted the request. On the contrary, he felt there was little or no sense of the gravity of the case, and no sympathy with his own concern for the sufferer. He felt as if, on the part of the relatives at least, there was almost suppressed ridicule of his efforts to guide the dying man to the truth.

Altogether the case was about as hopeless a one as my friend had ever dealt with. Still he persevered . . . I cannot remember whether it was during the first visit, or upon a second call, that it occurred to him, seeing the sufferer was a Scotchman, to take advantage of a line in the metrical version of the psalms used in Scotland, to convey the saving truth he was trying to state.

"There is a line in one of your Scotch psalms," said my friend, "that contains in five words all I would tell you. I do not know the psalm, or the rest of the verse; but here are the words, and the whole Gospel is in them:

"'None perish that Him trust.'"

The invalid looked up from his pillow, and slowly repeated:

"'I'll shall the wicked slay; laid waste

Shall be who hate the just;

The Lord redeems His servants' souls:

None perish that Him trust.'"

"That is it," said my friend; "believe on the Lord Jesus Christ. None perish that *Him* trust. Where did you learn that psalm?"

"My mother taught me it when I was a boy. She used to go to Dr. Alexander's church at Edinburgh."

Old recollections seemed awakened. Attentively he listened to what more it was thought proper to add. He requested a repetition of the visit. How often after the minister saw him I do not recollect, but from that hour there was a marked change, and an evident growing interest as the way of salvation was explained.

The last time my friend was sent for, he went without delay, but it was too late, or seemed to be too late, for the dying man to receive aught from human lips. He was already far down the valley—alone—and friends could only look after him as he descended. As they gazed in silence, they saw his lips moving. My friend bent down to catch the faint whispers that followed each other in slow succession; they were:

"None—perish—that—Him—trust."

He heard no more; but left, indulging a cheerful confidence that the seed cast into the heart of her boy by a mother long, long years before, had borne fruit to eternal life.

If we are to die trusting in Christ, let us live trusting in Him.

SECTION 4
DAILY DEVOTIONS

January 1st

Peace I leave with you, my peace I give unto you: not as the world giveth, give I unto you. Let not your heart be troubled, neither let it be afraid—John 14:27.

Did you ever think that when Christ was dying on the cross, He made a will? Perhaps you have thought that no one ever remembered you in a will. If you are in the kingdom, Christ remembered you in His. He willed His body to Joseph of Arimathea, He willed His mother to John, the son of Zebedee, and He willed His spirit back to His Father. But to His disciples He said,

"My peace, I leave that with you; that is My legacy. My joy, I give that to you."

"My joy," think of it! "My peace"—not *our* peace, but *His* peace!

They say a man can't make a will now that lawyers can't break, and drive a four-in-hand right straight through it. I will challenge them to break Christ's will; let them try it. No judge or jury can set that aside. Christ rose to execute His own will. If He had left us a lot of gold, thieves would have stolen it in the first century; but He left His peace and His joy for every true believer, and no power on earth can take it from him who trusts.

March 7th

Thine own wickedness shall correct thee, and thy backsliding shall reprove thee: know therefore and see that it is an evil thing and bitter, that thou hast forsaken the Lord thy God, and that my fear is not in thee, saith the Lord God of hosts—Jeremiah 2:19.

I do not exaggerate when I say that I have seen hundreds of backsliders come back, and I have asked them if they have not found it an evil and a bitter thing to leave the Lord. You cannot find a real backslider, who has known the Lord, but will admit that it is an evil and a bitter thing to turn away from Him; and I do not know of any one verse more used to bring back wanderers than this very one.

Look at Lot. Did not he find it an evil and a bitter thing? He was twenty years in Sodom and never made a convert. Men would have told you that he was one of the most influential and worthy men in all Sodom. But alas! Alas! He ruined his family. And it is a pitiful sight to see that old backslider going through the streets of Sodom at midnight, after he has warned his children, and they have turned a deaf ear to him.

March 11th

Moreover thou shalt provide out of all the people able men, such as fear God, men of truth, hating covetousness; and place such over them, to be rulers of thousands, and rulers of hundreds, rulers of fifties, and rulers of tens—Exodus 18:21.

Isn't it extraordinary that Jethro, the man of the desert, should have given this advice to Moses? How did he learn to beware of covetousness? We honor men today if they are wealthy and covetous. We elect them to offices in church and state. We often say that they will make better treasurers because we know them to be covetous. But in God's sight a covetous man is as vile and black as any thief or drunkard. David said: "The wicked boasteth of his heart's desire, and blesseth the covetous, whom the Lord abhorreth." I am afraid that many who profess to have put away wickedness also speak well of the covetous.

June 15th

To every man his work—Mark 13:34.

If you notice that verse carefully, it does not read "to every man some work," or "to every man a work," but "to every man *his* work." And I believe that every man and woman living has a work laid out for them to do; that every man's life is a plan of the Almighty, and that away back in the councils of eternity God laid out a work for every one of us. There is no man living who can do the work that God has for me to do, no one but myself. And if any man's work is not done, he will have to answer for it when he stands before the bar of God.

August 16th

Ye shall receive power, after that the Holy Ghost is come upon you: and ye shall be witnesses unto me both in Jerusalem, and in all Judea, and in Samaria, and unto the uttermost part of the earth—Acts 1:8.

If these early Christians had gone out and commenced preaching then and there without the promised power, do you think that scene would have taken place on the day of Pentecost? Peter would have stood up and beat against the air, while the Jews would have gnashed their teeth and mocked at him. But they tarried in Jerusalem; they waited ten days.

"What!" you say, "with the world perishing and men dying! Shall I wait?"

Do what God tells you. There is no use in running before you are sent; there is no use in attempting to do God's work without God's power. A man working without this unction, a man working without this anointing, a man working without the Holy Ghost upon him, is losing time after all. We shall not lose anything if we tarry till we get this power.

September 24th

Though I speak with the tongues of men and of angels, and have not charity, I am become as sounding brass, or a tinkling cymbal—1 Corinthians 13:1.

If we want to be wise in winning souls and to be vessels fit for the Master's use, we must get rid of the accursed spirit of self-seeking. That is the meaning of this chapter in Paul's letter. He told the Corinthians that a man might be full of faith and zeal, he might be very benevolent, but if he had not love, he was like sounding brass and a tinkling cymbal. I believe many men might as well go into the pulpit and blow a tin horn Sabbath after Sabbath as go on preaching without love. A man may preach the truth; he may be perfectly sound in doctrine; but if there is no love in his heart going out to those whom he addresses, and if he is doing it professionally, the apostle says he is only a sounding brass.

October 15th

Peter said, Ananias, why hath Satan filled thine heart to lie . . . ?—
Acts 5:3.

"Mr. Moody," you say, "how can I check myself? How can I overcome the habit of lying and gossip?" A lady once said to me that she had got so into the habit of exaggerating that her friends said they could never understand her.

The cure is simple, but not very pleasant. Treat it as a *sin*, and confess it to God and the person whom you have wronged. As soon as you catch yourself lying, go straight to that person and confess you have lied. Let your confession be as wide as your transgression. If you have slandered or lied about anyone in public, let your confession be public. Many a person says some mean, false thing about another in the presence of others, and then tries to patch it up by going to that person alone. This is not making adequate confession. I need not go to God with confession until I have made it right with that person, if it is in my power to do so; He will not hear me.

December 16th

*Now when Daniel knew that the writing was signed, he went into his house; and his windows being open in his chamber toward Jerusalem, he kneeled upon his knees three times a day, and prayed, and gave thanks before his God, as he did aforetime—*Daniel 6:10.

There is many a business man today who will tell you he has no time to pray: his business is so pressing that he cannot call his family around him, and ask God to bless them. He is so busy that he can not ask God to keep him and them from the temptation of the present life—the temptations of every day. "Business is so pressing." I am reminded of the words of an old Methodist minister: "If you have so much business to attend to that you have no time to pray, depend upon it that you have more business on hand than God ever intended you should have."

But look at this man. He had the whole, or nearly the whole, of the king's business to attend to. He was Prime Minister, Secretary of State, and Secretary of the Treasury, all in one. He had to attend to all his own work, and to give an eye to the work of lots of other men. And yet he found time to pray: not just now and then, nor once in a way, not just when he happened to have a few moments to spare, but "three times a day."

27

THEY WALKED WITH GOD

Love for Your Neighbor

Do you want to know how you can reach the masses? Go to their homes and enter into sympathy with them. Tell them you have come to do them good, and let them see that you have a heart to feel for them. When they find out that you really love them, all those things that are in their hearts against God and against Christianity will be swept out of the way. Atheists may tell them that you only want to get their money and that you do not really care for their happiness. We have to contradict that lie by our lives and send it back to the pit where it came from.

We are not going to do it unless we go personally to them and prove that we really love them. There are thousands of families that could easily be reached if we had thousands of Christians going to them and entering into sympathy with their sorrows. That is what they want. This poor world is groaning and sighing for sympathy—human sympathy. I am quite sure it was that in Christ's life that touched the hearts of the common people. He made Himself one with them. He who was rich for our sakes became poor. He was born in the manger so that He might put Himself on a level with the lowest of the low.

I think that in this manner He teaches His disciples a lesson. He wants us to convince the world that He is their friend. They do not believe it. If once the world were to grasp this thought, that Jesus Christ is the friend of the sinner, they would soon flock to Him.

—*To The Work*

She Has Done What She Could

Thank God, every one of us can love Christ, and we can all do something for Him. It may be a small thing; but whatever it is shall be lasting; it will outlive all the monuments on earth. The iron and the granite will rust and crumble and fade away, but anything done for Christ will never fade. It will be more lasting than time itself. Christ says: "Heaven and earth shall pass away, but My word shall not pass away."

Look again and see that woman in the temple. Christ stood there as the people passed by and cast their offerings into the treasury. The widow had but two mites, and she cast it all in. The Lord saw that her heart was in it, and so He commended her. If some nobleman had cast in a thousand dollars, Christ probably would not have noticed it, unless his heart had gone with it. Gold is of little value in heaven. It is so plentiful there that they use it to pave the streets with; and it is transparent gold, much better gold than we have in this world. It is when the heart goes with the offering that it is accepted of Christ. So He said of this woman: "She hath cast in more than they all." She had done all she could.

I think this is the lesson we are to learn from these Scripture incidents. The Lord expects us to do what we can. We can all do something. In one of our Southern cities a few Christian people gathered together at the beginning of the war to see what could be done about building a church in a part of the city where the poor were very much neglected. After they had discussed the matter they wanted to see how much could be raised out of the congregation.

One said he would give so much; others said they would give so much. They only got about half the amount that was needed, and it was thought they would have to abandon the project. Away back in the meeting there sat a washerwoman. She rose and said her little boy had died a week before. All he had was a gold dollar. She said: "It is all I have, but I will give the dollar to the cause." Her words touched the hearts of many of those who heard them. Rich men were ashamed at what they had given. The whole sum was raised within a very short time.

—*To The Work*

The Prize

The world scoffed at Paul, but he did not heed its scoffing. He had something the world had not; burning within him he had a love and zeal the world knew nothing about. And the love that Paul had for Jesus Christ! But, oh, the greater love the Lord Jesus had for Paul!

The hour had come. The way they used to behead them in those days was for the prisoner to bend his head, then a Roman soldier took a sword and cut it off. The hour had come, and I seem to see Paul, with a joyful countenance, bending his blessed head, as the soldier's sword comes down and sets his spirit free.

If our eyes could look as Elisha's looked, we might have seen him leap into a chariot of light like Elijah; we would have seen him go sweeping through limitless space.

Look at him yonder!

See! He is entering now the Eternal City of the glorified saints, the blissful abode of the Savior's redeemed. The prize he so long has sought is at hand. See the gates yonder; how they fly wide open. And he goes sweeping through the pearly gates, along the shining way, to the very throne of God, and Christ stands there and says, "Well done, thou good and faithful servant; enter thou into the joy of the Lord."

Just think of hearing the Master say it! Will that not be enough for everything?

Oh, friends, your turn and mine will come by and by, if we are but faithful. Let us see that we do not lose the crown. Let us awake and put on the whole armor of God; let us press into the conflict; it is a glorious privilege, and to us too, as to the glorified of old, will come that blessed welcome from our glorified Lord: "Well done, thou good and faithful servant."

—*Heaven*

His Yoke Is Easy

Do you mean to say that God is a hard master? Do you say it is a hard thing to serve God, and do you say that Satan is an easy master, and that it is easier to serve him than God? Is it honest—is it true? God a hard master! If I read my Bible right, I read that the way of the transgressor is hard. Let me tell you, it is the devil who is the hard master. Yes, "the way of the transgressor is hard." The Word of God cannot be changed.

If you doubt it, young man, look at the convict in prison, right in the bloom of manhood, right in the prime of life. He has been there for ten years and must remain for ten years more—twenty years taken out of his life, and when he comes out of that miserable cell, he becomes a branded felon! Do you think that man will tell you, "The way of the transgressor has been easy"? Go ask the poor drunkard, this man who is bound hand and foot, the slave of the infernal cup, who is hastening onward to a drunkard's hell. Ask him if he has found the way of the transgressor easy. "Easy?" he will cry—"Easy? The way of the transgressor is hard and gets harder and harder every day!" Go ask the libertine and the worldling, go ask the gambler and the blasphemer—with one voice they will tell you that the service has been very hard. Take the most faithful follower of the devil and put questions to him.

The best way to settle this matter is to find out by the testimony of those that have served both masters. I do not think a man has any right to judge until he has served both. If I heard a man condemn a master, I should be very apt to ask if he had served him; and if he had not, he could not very well testify. Now, if you have served two masters, then you are very good judges.

I want to stand as a witness for Christ. I have been in this school for forty years, and I want to testify that I have found Him an easy master. I used to say, as you do, "It is a hard thing to be a Christian," and I thought it was; but now I tell you that the yoke is easy and the burden light.

—*Select Sermons*

Heartfelt Repentance

Heaven is a prepared place for a prepared people. If your boy has done wrong and will not repent, you cannot forgive him. You would be doing him an injustice. Suppose he goes to your desk and steals ten dollars and squanders it. When you come home, your servant tells you what your boy has done. You ask if it is true, and he denies it. But at last you have certain proof. Even when he finds he cannot deny it any longer, he will not confess the sin but says he will do it again the first chance he gets. Would you say to him, "Well, I forgive you," and leave the matter there? No! Yet people say that God is going to save all men, whether they repent or not—drunkards, thieves, harlots, whoremongers, it makes no difference. "God is so merciful," they say. Dear friend, do not be deceived by the god of this world. Where there is true repentance and a turning from sin unto God, He will meet and bless you; but He never blesses until there is sincere repentance.

David made a woeful mistake in this respect with his rebellious son, Absalom. He could not have done his son a greater injustice than to forgive him when his heart was unchanged. There could be no true reconciliation between them when there was no repentance. But God does not make these mistakes. David got into trouble on account of his error of judgement. His son soon drove his father from the throne.

Speaking of repentance, Dr. Brookes, of St. Louis, well remarks: "Repentance, strictly speaking, means 'a change of mind or purpose'; consequently it is the judgement which the sinner pronounces upon himself, in view of the love of God displayed in the death of Christ, connected with the abandonment of all confidence in himself and with trust in the only Savior of sinners. Saving repentance and saving faith always go together; and you need not be worried about repentance if you will believe.

"Some people are not sure that they have 'repented enough.' If you mean by this, that you must repent in order to incline God to be merciful to you, the sooner you give over such repentance the better. God is already merciful, as He has shown fully at the cross of Calvary; and it is a grievous dishonor to His heart of love if you think that your tears and anguish will move Him, 'not knowing that the goodness of God leadeth thee to repentance.' It is not your badness, therefore, but His goodness that leads to repentance; hence the true way to repent is to believe on the Lord Jesus Christ, 'who was delivered for our offences, and was raised again for our justification.'"

—*The Way To God*

His Promises

God is always true to what He promises to do. He made promises to Abraham, Jacob, Moses, Joshua, and the others, and did He not fulfill them? He will fulfill every word of what He has promised; yet how few take Him at His word.

When I was a young man I was clerk in the establishment of a man in Chicago, whom I observed frequently sorting and marking bills. He explained to me what he had been doing; on some notes he had marked B, on some D, and on others G. Those marked B, he told me, were bad, those marked D meant they were doubtful, and those with G on them meant they were good; and, said he, you must treat all of them accordingly. And thus people endorse God's promises by marking some as bad and others as doubtful; whereas we ought to take all of them as good, for He has never once broken His word, and all that He says, He will do in the fullness of time.

I heard of a woman once who thought there was no promise in the Bible for her; she thought the promises were for someone else, not for her. There are a good many of these people in the world. They think it is too good to be true that they can be saved for nothing. This woman one day got a letter, and when she opened it she found it was not for her at all; it was meant for another woman who had the same name; and she had her eyes opened to the fact that if she should find some promises in the Bible directed to her name, she would not know whether it meant her or someone else that bore her name. But you know the word "whosoever" includes everyone in the wide world.

—*Moody's Stories*

A Warning

No matter how painful it may be, break with sin at once. Severe operations are often necessary, for the skillful surgeon knows that the disease cannot be cured by surface applications. The farmer takes his hoe and his spade and his axe, and he cuts away the obnoxious growth and burns the roots out of the ground with fire.

If your right eye offend you, pluck it out, as Christ says, and cast it away, for it is better for you that one of your members should perish, rather than your whole body should be cast into hell. And if your right hand offend thee, cut it off and cast it from you rather than that your whole body should be cast into hell.

Remember that the tares and the wheat will be separated at the judgement day, if not before. Sowing to the flesh and sowing to the Spirit inevitably lead in diverging paths. The axe will be laid at the root of the trees, and every tree that brings not forth good fruit will be hewn down and cast into the fire. The threshing floor will be thoroughly purged, and the wheat will be gathered into the garner, while the chaff will be burned with unquenchable fire.

Beware of your habits. A recent writer has said: "Could the

young but realize how soon they will become mere walking bundles of habits, they would give more heed to their conduct while in the plastic state. We are spinning our own fates, good or evil, and never to be undone. Every smallest stroke of virtue or of vice leaves its ever-so-little scar. The drunken Rip Van Winkle, in Jefferson's play, excuses himself for every fresh dereliction by saying, "I won't count it this time." Well, he may not count it, and a kind heaven may not count it, but it is being counted nevertheless. Down among his nerve cells and fibers the molecules are counting it, registering and storing it up, to be used against him when the next temptation comes.

—*Sowing And Reaping*

28

DAILY GEMS

February 5th

(*Mr. D. L. Moody's birthday.*)

He asked life of thee, and thou gavest it him, even length of days for ever and ever—Psalm 21:4.

I was down in Texas some time ago, and happened to pick up a newspaper, and there they called me "Old Moody." Honestly, I never got such a shock from any paper in my life before! I had never been called old before. I went to my hotel, and looked in the looking glass. I cannot conceive of getting old. I have a life that is never going to end. Death may change my position but not my condition, not my standing with Jesus Christ. Death is not going to separate us.

Old! I wish you all felt as young as I do here tonight. Why, I am only sixty-two years old! If you meet me ten million years hence, then I will be young. Read Psalm 91, "With long life will I satisfy him." That doesn't mean seventy years. Would that satisfy you? Did you ever see a man or woman of seventy satisfied? Don't they want to live longer? You know that seventy wouldn't satisfy you. Would eighty? Would ninety? Would one hundred? If Adam had lived to be a million years old, and then had to die, he wouldn't be satisfied. "With long life will I satisfy him"—life without end! Don't tell me old. I am only sixty-two. I have only begun to live.

February 8th

If I speak with the tongues of men and of angels, but have not love, I am become sounding brass, or a clanging cymbal. And if I have the gift of prophecy, and know all mysteries, and all knowledge; and if I have all faith, so as to remove mountains, but have not love, I am nothing—1 Corinthians 13:1, 2 (A.S.V.).

A man may have wonderful knowledge, may be able to unravel the mysteries of the Bible, and yet be as cold as an icicle. He may glisten like the snow in the sun. Sometimes you have wondered why it was that certain ministers who have had such wonderful magnetism, and who preach with such mental strength, haven't had more conversions. I believe, if the truth were known, you would find no divine love back of their words, no pure love in their sermons.

April 26th

For the zeal of thine house hath eaten me up—Psalm 69:9.

I heard of someone who was speaking the other day of something that was to be done, and who said he hoped zeal would be tempered with moderation. Another friend very wisely replied that he hoped moderation would be tempered with zeal. If that were always the case, Christianity would be like a red hot ball rolling over the face of the earth. There is no power on earth that can stand before the onward march of God's people when they are in dead earnest.

May 2nd

It is high time to awake out of sleep—Romans 13:11.

As I have said, there are a great many in the church who make one profession, and that is about all you hear of them; and when they come to die you have to go and hunt up some musty old church records to know whether they were Christians or not. God won't do that. What we want is men with a little courage to stand up for Christ. When Christianity wakes up, and every child that belongs to the Lord is willing to speak for Him, is willing to work for Him, and, if need be, willing to die for Him, then Christianity will advance, and we shall see the work of the Lord prosper.

June 4th

Arise ye, and depart; for this is not your rest—Micah 2:10.

This world that some *think* is heaven is the home of sin, a hospital of sorrow, a place that has nothing in it to satisfy the soul. Men go all over it and then want to get out of it. The more men see of the world the less they think of it. People soon grow tired of the best pleasures it has to offer. Someone has said that the world is a stormy sea, whose every wave is strewed with the wrecks of mortals that perish in it. Every time we breathe someone is dying. We all know that we are going to stay here but a very little while. Only the other life is enduring.

June 30th

But the fruit of the Spirit is love, joy, peace, longsuffering, gentleness, goodness, faith, meekness, temperance: against such there is no law—Galatians 5:22, 23.

The fruit of the Spirit begins with love. There are nine graces spoken of, and of these nine Paul puts love at the head of the list; love is the first thing, the first in that precious cluster of fruit. Someone has said that all the other eight can be put in terms of love. Joy is love exulting; peace is love in repose; long-suffering is love on trial; gentleness is love in society; goodness is love in action; faith is love on the battlefield; meekness is love at school; and temperance is love in training. So it is love all the way; love at the top, love at the bottom, and all the way along down this list of graces. If we only just brought forth the fruit of the Spirit, what a world we should have! Men would have no desire to do evil.

July 24th

After these things the word of the Lord came unto Abram in a vision, saying, Fear not, Abram: I am thy shield, and thy exceeding great reward—Genesis 15:1.

Abram might have thought that the kings that he had defeated might get other kings and other armies to come, and he might have thought of himself as a solitary man, with only 318 men, so that he might have feared lest he be swept from the face of the earth. But the Lord came and said:

"Abram, fear not."

That is the first time those oft-repeated words *fear not* occur in the Bible.

"Fear not, for I will be your shield and your reward."

I would rather have that promise than all the armies and all the navies of the world to protect me—to have the God of heaven for my Protector! God was teaching Abram that He was to be his Friend and his Shield, if he would surrender himself wholly to His keeping, and trust in His goodness. That is what we need—to surrender ourselves up to God, fully and wholly.

September 7th

*Work out your salvation with fear and trembling. For it is God which worketh in you both to will and to do of his good pleasure—*Philippians 2:12–13.

I have very little sympathy with any man who has been redeemed by the precious blood of the Son of God, and who has not got the spirit of work. If we are children of God, we ought not to have a lazy drop of blood in our veins. If a man tells me that he has been saved, and does not desire to work for the honor of God, I doubt his salvation.

Laziness belongs to the old creation, not to the new. In all my experiences I never knew a lazy man to be converted—never. I have more hope for the salvation of drunkards, and thieves, and harlots than of a lazy man.

November 11th

*Ye are the light of the world. A city that is set on an hill cannot be hid—*Matthew 5:14.

God has left us down here to shine. We are not here to buy and sell and get gain, to accumulate wealth, to acquire worldly position. This earth, if we are Christians, is not our home; it is yonder. God has sent us into the world to shine for Him—to light up this dark world. Christ came to be the Light of the world, but men put out that light. They took it to Calvary, and blew it out. Before Christ went up on high, He said to His disciples: "Ye are the light of the world. Ye are My witnesses. Go forth and carry the Gospel to the perishing nations of the earth."

November 14th

*Verily, verily, I say unto you, He that heareth my word, and believeth on him that sent me, hath everlasting life, and shall not come into condemnation; but is passed from death unto life—*John 5:24.

The cross of Christ divides all mankind. There are only two sides, those for Christ, and those against Him. Think of the two thieves; from the side of Christ one went down to death cursing God, and the other went to glory.

What a contrast! In the morning he is led out, a condemned criminal; in the evening he is saved from his sins. In the morning he is cursing—Matthew and Mark both tell us that those two thieves came out cursing; in the evening he is singing hallelujahs with a choir of angels. In the morning he is condemned by men as not fit to live on earth; in the evening he is reckoned good enough for heaven. In the morning nailed to the cross; in the evening in the paradise of God, crowned with a crown he should wear through all the ages. In the morning not an eye to pity; in the evening washed and made clean in the blood of the Lamb. In the morning in the society of thieves and outcasts; in the evening Christ is not ashamed to walk arm-in-arm with him down the golden pavements of the eternal city.

December 7th

And I was afraid, and went and hid thy talent in the earth: lo, there thou hast that is thine—Matthew 25:25.

I read of a man who had a thousand dollars. He hid it away, thinking he would in that way take care of it, and that when he was an old man he would have something to fall back upon. After keeping the deposit receipt for twenty years he took it to a bank and got just one thousand dollars for it. If he had put the money at interest in the usual way, he might have had about three times the amount.

He made the mistake that a great many people are making today throughout Christendom, of not trading with his talents. My experience has been as I have gone about in the world and mingled with professing Christians, that those who find most fault with others are those who themselves do nothing. If a person is busy improving the talents that God has given him, he will have too much to do to find fault and complain about others.

SECTION 5
SERMONS

29

TALKS TO CHRISTIANS

Affliction

You will find in Psalm 119:67 these words: "Before I was afflicted I went astray; but now have I kept thy word"; and again, in
verse 71: "It is good for me that I have been afflicted; that I might
learn thy statutes." We can stand affliction better than we can prosperity, for in prosperity we forget God. When our work is light, our
prospects good, and everything looks smooth and easy, we are more
apt to give ourselves over to pleasure. Somebody said: "It is the dead
level of affairs that makes us go to ruin." A great many have a wrong
idea of God, and think He sends afflictions because He doesn't love
them; they think that, because they don't know Him. He sends afflictions to humble our hearts and make us look to Him, and because
He loves us so, He cannot let us leave Him and forget Him. Mr.
Moody read a letter from a young lady in London, who would not go
to the meetings when he was there for fear she might be converted,
but who, since then, had been brought to God through suffering.

PERSONAL EFFORT

Let me say one thing now about personal effort. I think if we
will first begin to talk with our friends, those that we come in contact with personally, quietly and gently about the Savior, although
they may not previously be interested, I think that we will be greatly rewarded.

I went out to Cambridge to spend Saturday, and the father and
mother wanted to have me speak to their oldest son, a young man
who is preparing for Harvard College. I asked him if he had any interest in the subject of religion; he said he hadn't. I talked with him
on other subjects that he was interested in; and then I brought up
again the subject of religion. Finally we took a ride out to Mount

Auburn, and I talked to him a little more about it, and said: "I wish you would come down to the meeting next Monday night, and hear the young converts speak." And he was there; and when I asked the inquirers to go upstairs, he started and went up. Yesterday that father came to me and said his dear boy went home Monday night and told his father and mother that the question of eternity was settled—that he had found a Savior; and I don't think you can find a happier mother and father perhaps in all Cambridge today than that father and mother. And yet there is a man that said he was not at all interested.

And a great many think and tell you that they are not interested; but when the Spirit of God is working, you will find that those who are careless will soon become interested. Now let us pray that God will do His work and that each one of us may be watching for souls, and that He may revive His work in all these churches.

SEVEN "COMES"

I would like to speak to you of seven instances where we are invited to come to the Lord. In Isaiah 55:1 we read: "Ho, every one that thirsteth, come ye to the waters," and again in verse 3: "Incline your ear, and come unto me: hear, and your soul shall live." I have great hopes that a man may be saved when he will stop and listen. People are so engrossed with the affairs of this world that but few find time to stop. It is all rush and hurry, and they don't think about their souls.

I was out to dinner the other day, and they were trying there to teach a little child to walk. They would say to her, "Come," and she would try to go a few steps. So Christ is calling the world to come, but the trouble is they do not heed and won't go. After the Chicago fire, when such quantities of money, clothes, and provisions were sent there, the only question asked those who applied for assistance was, "Were you burned out?" If they could prove it, they got help. All you have to do is to show that you want help from God, and He will give it.

In Isaiah 1:18 we find: "Come now, and let us reason together, saith the Lord: though your sins be as scarlet, they shall be as white as snow." Sin can keep us out of heaven, but not out of Christ. If you are out of Christ, decide now to come to Him. As the old Negro woman said, "When I made up my mind, then I was there."

Will you turn to Mark 6:31? Christ said to His disciples: "Come ye yourselves apart into a desert place, and rest awhile." It is a good thing to be alone with God. We lead two lives—one in the world and one apart with God. In Matthew 11 is the invitation, "Come unto me, all ye that labor." If any man or woman among you is carrying a burden, take it to Christ. In Hebrews 4:16 we are told to come boldly to the throne of grace. Those who are afraid to become Christians lest they can't hold out should remember that at the Throne we can find grace in time of need.

The next "come" is in Matthew 22:4: "Come unto the marriage"—the parable of the marriage of the king's son.

The seventh and last invitation I want to call your attention to is, "Come and inherit eternal life." "Come up hither." These are blessed words, which will last forever.

Christ the Good Samaritan

And, behold a certain lawyer stood up, and tempted him, saying, Master, what shall I do to inherit eternal life?—Luke 10:25.

In this picture we get the whole Gospel. Jerusalem was the city of peace. Jericho was a city condemned, and from one to the other was all the way down hill—an easy road to go, as the unfortunate man thought when he started on his journey. But he fell among thieves, who stripped him and left him half dead, and the priest and the Levite passed him by. These two men represent a large class of people. We can imagine the priest asking himself, "Am I my brother's keeper?" and complaining, "What did he want to go down there for anyway? Why didn't he stay at home? He was a great deal better off in Jerusalem—he might have known something would happen to him." Some people think they have done their duty when they blame the poor for their poverty, and the unfortunate for the accidents which happen to them.

There is another class who always begin to philosophize the minute they see suffering. "Why does God have these things? Why does He have sin and poverty in the world, I would like to know? He needn't have it; He could just as well have made a world without it." But here comes the good Samaritan; he does more than pity and philosophize; he helps, gives oil, and lifts the poor fellow on his beast. He is not afraid to touch him. He doesn't stop to ask whether he is Jew or Gentile, or just what he is going to do with the man if he takes him away from there. Now a great many people ask us,

"What are you going to do with these young converts when you get them? Where will you put them—into what church—Methodist, Baptist, Episcopal?" "Well, we don't know; we have not thought of that; we are trying to get them out of the ditch first." "Oh, well then, we don't want to have anything to do with it; we want it to be done decently and in order if we are going to have a hand in it."

These people are no Samaritans; they won't have anything to do with the poor fellows by the wayside if they cannot dispose of them ever afterward to suit themselves. Let us not condemn those who have fallen into the ditch. Christ is our Good Samaritan; He has done for us, and tells us to do for others.

CHRIST OUR MODEL

When a house is to be built, before the masons and the carpenters commence work, the architect is called in to make a drawing of the building. As the workmen conform to his plans, they realize the ideal that was in his mind.

The trouble with most people is that their lives are not formed according to any plan. They are not striving to resemble any model. They have no definite aim or purpose.

This is the cause of sorrow and suffering and disappointment. We owe it to ourselves to set an ideal before us, and then press toward the attainment of it with all our being. The ideal should be the highest possible, and we cannot aim higher than Christ.

He is a perfect Model in every way. The Bible tells us how perfectly He conformed to His Father's will, leaving us an example in service, in love, in prayer, in self-sacrifice, in dependence upon God. And all this because He is divine.

And yet if He had been only divine and not human too, He could never have served as our Model. It is because He took upon Himself our form and likeness, passing through human experiences, realizing human needs, and undergoing human temptations and trials, that He is possible as our Model.

His atoning death opened the door for us into the Christian life. But that is only the entrance. There is a path to be trod, and here Christ in His life on earth is the Model for every believer to follow.

How thankful I am that we have a record of His life! Gladstone once said that precept freezes while example warms; precept is a marble statue, while example is a thing of flesh and blood. The great defect of other religions and philosophies is that, while they may contain beautiful maxims and exhortations, they do not give the power to follow these out. But Christ embodied what He taught. He practiced what He preached. He was a living example that we may imitate.

There is a story of a Bohemian king, St. Wenceslaus, going to devotions to a distant church one snowy winter night. His servant followed trying to imitate his zeal; but the way was rough, and he began to faint. The king told him to step in the marks he made, and he was able to follow. Christ commanded us to follow in His steps. The path is smoother because He trod it.

Is it possible really to be like Christ? Doubt and unbelief say, No. Faith says, Yes. God commands it, and therefore it must be possible. But how? Because we can have the same life, the same mind in us as was in Christ. If we are "partakers of the divine nature," if we are branches of the true Vine, the same fruit will show in our life as in His. He will dwell in our hearts by faith, and our lives may thus become the expression of His own.

I do not say that here we shall ever be like our Model in measure or degree. But light is light, whether it be candlelight, gaslight, electric light, or sunlight. It is the same in kind or nature, if not in degree. So we may really resemble Christ, although we do not realize the full measure of His divine perfection. A good definition of sanctification of holiness would be conformity to His example. He is the Light of the world; we are to shine as lights in the world. He is the Word; we are epistles.

HOW CAN WE GET POWER TO COPY OUR MODEL?

1. Learn of Christ. Do not look to men. In Hebrews 11 Paul tells of Old Testament worthies, but lest we should try to imitate them he immediately turns away our eyes and fixes them on Jesus—"looking unto Jesus."

2. Claim by faith the promises of the indwelling Christ. Until we are born again, and He lives in us by the Spirit, all our efforts will be vain.

3. Keep in touch with Him. Get better acquainted with Him. Talk to Him in prayer. Let Him talk to you through the Bible. It is a recognized fact that two persons thrown together a good deal are apt to become alike in habits of thought and conduct, and even in looks. It is said of the early disciples that the rulers "took knowledge of them that they had been with Jesus." Moses had a shining face after he had been with God.

30

SELECT SERMONS

What Think Ye of Christ?

Matthew 22:42.

I suppose no one is reading this who has not thought more or less about Christ. You have heard about Him, and heard men preach about Him. For nearly nineteen hundred years men have been talking about Him, and thinking about Him. Some have their minds made up about Him, who He is, and doubtless some have not. And although all these years have rolled away, this question comes up, addressed to each of us, today:

"What think ye of Christ?"

I do not know why it should not be thought a proper question for one man to put to another. If I were to ask you what you think of any prominent public man, you would already have your mind made up about him. If I were to ask you what you think of the President, you would speak right out and tell me your opinion in a minute. If I were to ask about the secretary of state, you would tell me freely what you had for or against him. And why should not people make up their minds about the Lord Jesus Christ, and take their stand for or against Him? If you think well of Him, why not speak well of Him, and range yourselves on His side? And if you think ill of Him, and believe Him to be an impostor, and that He did not die to save the world, why not lift up your voice, and say you are against Him? It would be a happy day for Christianity if men would just take sides—if we could know positively who was really for Him, and who was against Him.

It is of very little importance what the world thinks of anyone else. Kings and princes, presidents and generals must soon be gone. Yes, it matters little comparatively, what we think of them. Their lives can only interest a few; but every living soul on the face of the earth is concerned with this Man. The question for the world is, "What think ye of Christ?" I do not ask you what you think of the Episcopal Church, or of the Presbyterians, or the Baptists, or the Roman Catholics; I do not ask you what you think of this minister or that, of this doctrine or that; but I want to ask you what you think of the living person, Jesus Christ?

I should like to ask, was He really the Son of God—the great God-man? Did He leave heaven and come down to this world for a purpose? Was it really to seek and to save? I should like to begin with the manger, and follow Him up through the thirty-three years He was here upon earth. I should like to ask you what you think of His coming into this world, and being born in a manger when it might have been a palace; why He left the grandeur and glory of heaven, and the royal retinue of angels; why He passed by palaces and crowns and dominion, and came down here alone?

I should like to ask what you think of Him as *a teacher*. He spake as never man spake. I should like to take Him up as *a preacher*. I should like to bring you to that mountain side that we might listen to the words as they fall from His gentle lips. Talk about the preachers of the present day! I would rather a thousand times be five minutes at the feet of Christ than listen a lifetime to all the wise men in the world!

I should like to ask you what you think of Him as a *physician*. A man would soon have a reputation as a doctor if he could cure as Christ did. No case was ever brought to Him but He was a match for it. He had but to speak the word and disease fled before Him. Here comes a man covered with leprosy. "Lord, if Thou wilt Thou canst make me clean," he cries. "I will," says the great Physician, and in an instant the leprosy is gone. The world has hospitals for incurable diseases, but there were no incurable diseases with Him.

Now see Him in the little home at Bethany, binding up the wounded hearts of Martha and Mary, and tell me what you think of Him as a *comforter*. He is a husband to the widow, and a father to the fatherless. The weary may find a resting-place upon His breast, and the friendless may reckon Him their friend. He never varies, He never fails, He never dies. His sympathy is ever fresh, His love is ever free. O widow and orphans, O sorrowing and mourning, will you not thank God for Christ the comforter?

But these are not the points I wish to take up now. Let us go to those who knew Christ, and ask what they thought of Him. If you want to find out what a man is nowadays, inquire about him from those who knew him best. I do not wish to be partial; we will go to Christ's enemies and friends. We will ask His friends and His enemies, What think ye of Christ? If we only went to those who liked Him, you would say, "Oh, he is so blind; he thinks so much of the man that he can't see His faults. You can't get anything out of him, unless it be in His favor; it is a one-sided affair altogether." So we shall go in the first place to His enemies, to those who hated Him, persecuted Him, cursed and slew Him. I shall put you in the jury-box, and call upon them to tell us what they think of Him.

I.

First, among the witnesses, let us call upon *the Pharisees*. We know how they hated Him. Let us put a few questions to them.

Come, Pharisees, tell us what you have against the Son of God! What do *you* think of Christ?

Hear what they say! *"This man receiveth sinners."*

What an argument to bring against Him! Why, it is the very thing that makes us love Him! It is the glory of the Gospel. He receives sinners. If He had not, what would have become of *us?* Have you nothing more to bring against Him than *this?* Why, it is one of the greatest compliments that was ever paid Him!

Once more: when He was hanging on the tree, you had this to say of Him, "He saved others, Himself He cannot save." And so He died to save others, but He could not save Himself and save us too? He laid down His own life for yours and mine. Yes, Pharisees, you have told the truth for once in your lives! *He saved others.* He died for others. He was a ransom for many; so it is quite true what you think of Him—*"He saved others, Himself He cannot save."*

Now, let us call upon *Caiaphas*. Let him stand up here in his flowing robes; let us ask him for his evidence.

Caiaphas, you were chief priest when Christ was tried. You were president of the Sanhedrin. You were in the council-chamber when they found Him guilty. You yourself condemned Him. Tell us; what did the witnesses say? On what grounds did you judge Him? What testimony was brought against Him?

"He hath spoken blasphemy," says Caiaphas. "He said, 'Hereafter shall ye see the Son of Man sitting on the right hand of power, and coming in the clouds of heaven.' When I heard that, I found Him guilty of blasphemy, I rent my mantle, and condemned Him to death."

Yes, all that they had against Him was that He was the Son of God; and they slew Him for the promise of His coming for His bride.

Now, let us summon *Pilate*. Let him enter the witness-box.

Pilate, this man was brought before you. You examined Him. You talked with Him face to face. What think *you* of Christ?

"I find no fault in Him," says Pilate. "He said he was the King of the Jews" (just as he wrote it over the cross), "but I find no fault in Him."

Such is the testimony of the man who examined Him! And as he stands there, the center of a Jewish mob, there comes along a man, elbowing his way, in haste. He rushes up to Pilate, and thrusting out his hand, gives him a message. He tears it open; his face turns pale as he reads—"Have nothing to do with *this just man,* for I have suffered many things this day in a dream because of Him." It is from *Pilate's wife*—her testimony to Christ. You want to know what His enemies thought of Him? You want to know what a heathen thought? Well, here it is, "no fault in Him"; and the wife of a heathen, "this just man"!

And now, look—in comes *Judas*. He ought to make a good witness. Let us address him.

Come tell us, Judas, what think *you* of Christ? You knew the Master well. You sold Him for thirty pieces of silver. You betrayed Him with a kiss. You saw Him perform those miracles. You were with Him in Jerusalem. In Bethany, when He summoned Lazarus from the dead, you were there. What think you of Him?

I can see him as he comes into the presence of the chief priests; I can hear the money ring as he dashes it upon the table—*"I have betrayed innocent blood!"* Here is the man who betrayed Him, and this is what he thinks of Him!

Yes my friend, God has made every man who had anything to do with the death of His Son put their testimony on record that He was an innocent Man.

Let us take *the Centurion*, who was present at the execution. He had charge of the Roman soldiers. He had told them to make Him carry His cross. He had given orders for the nails to be driven into His feet and hands, for the spear to be thrust in His side. Let the Centurion come forward.

"Centurion, you had charge of the executioners. You saw that the order for His death was carried out. You saw Him die. You heard Him speak upon the cross. Tell us, *what think you of Christ?*"

Hark! Look at him! He is smiting his breast as he cries, *"Truly, this was the Son of God!"*

I might go to *the thief on the cross,* and ask what he thought of

Him. At first he railed upon Him and reviled Him. But then he thought better of it. "This man hath done nothing amiss," he said. I might go further, I might summon the very *devils* themselves and ask them for their testimony. Have *they* anything to say of Him? Why, the very devils called Him the Son of God! In Mark we have the unclean spirit crying, "Jesus, Thou Son of the most High God." Men say, "Oh, I believe Christ to be the Son of God, and because I believe it intellectually, I shall be saved." I tell you the devils did that. And they did more than that; *they trembled*.

II.

Let us now bring in His friends. We want you to hear their evidence.

Let us first call that prince of preachers. Let us hear the forerunner, the wilderness preacher, *John*. Save the Master Himself, none ever preached like this man—this man who drew all Jerusalem and all Judea into the wilderness to hear him; this man who burst upon the nations like the flash of a meteor. Let John the Baptist come with his leathern girdle and his hairy coat, and let him tell us what he thinks of Christ.

His words, though they were echoed in the wilderness of Palestine, are written in the Book forever, "Behold the Lamb of God which taketh away the sin of the world." This is what John the Baptist thought of Him. "I bare record that He is the Son of God." No wonder he drew all Jerusalem and Judea to him, because he preached Christ. And whenever men preach Christ, they are sure to have plenty of followers.

Let us bring in *Peter*, who was with Him on the Mount of Transfiguration, who was with Him the night He was betrayed.

"Come, Peter, tell us what you think of Christ. Stand in the witness-box and testify of Him. You denied Him once. You said, with a curse, you did not know Him. Was it true, Peter? Don't you know Him?"

"Know Him!" I can imagine Peter saying; "it was a lie I told them. I *did* know Him." Afterward I can hear him charging home their guilt upon these Jerusalem sinners. He calls Him "both Lord and Christ." Such was his testimony on the day of Pentecost. "God hath made that same Jesus both Lord and Christ." And tradition tells us that when they came to execute Peter, he felt he was not worthy to die in the way his Master died, and he requested to be crucified with his head downwards. So much did Peter think of Him!

Now let us hear from the beloved disciple, *John*. He knew more about Christ than any other man. He had laid his head on his Savior's bosom. He had heard the throbbing of that loving heart. Look into his gospel if you wish to know what he thought of Him.

Matthew writes of Him as the Royal King come from His throne, Mark as the servant, and Luke as the Son of Man. John takes up his pen, and with one stroke, forever settles the question of His divinity. He goes right back before the time of Adam. "In the beginning was the Word, and the Word was with God, and the Word was God." Look into Revelation. He calls Him "the bright and the Morning Star." So John thought well of Him because he knew Him well.

We might bring in *Thomas*, the doubting disciple.

"You doubted Him, Thomas. You would not believe He had risen, and you put your fingers into the wound in His side. What do you think of Him?"

"My Lord and my God!" says Thomas.

Then go over to Decapolis and you will find Christ has been there casting out devils. Let us call the men of that country and ask what they think of Him. *"He hath done all things well,"* they say.

But we have other witnesses to bring in. Take the persecuting *Saul*, once one of the worst of His enemies. Breathing out threatenings, he meets Him. "Saul, Saul, why persecutest thou me?" says Christ; and He might have added, "What have I done to you? Have I injured you in any way? Did I not come to bless you? Why do you treat me thus, Saul?" And then Saul asks, "Who art Thou, Lord?" "I am Jesus of Nazareth, whom thou persecutest." You see, He was not ashamed of His name; although He had been in heaven, "I am *Jesus of Nazareth.*" What a change did that one interview make in Saul! A few years after we hear him say, "I have suffered the loss of all things, and do count them but dung, that I may win Christ." Such a testimony to the Savior!

But I shall go still further. I shall go away from earth into the other world. I shall summon the *angels* and ask what they think of Christ. They saw Him in the bosom of the Father before the world was. Before the dawn of creation, before the morning stars sang together, He was there. They saw Him leave the throne and come down to the manger. What a scene for them to witness! Ask these heavenly beings what they thought of Him then. For once they are permitted to speak; for once the silence of heaven is broken. Listen to their songs on the plains of Bethlehem, "Behold, I bring you good tidings of great joy, which shall be to all people, for unto you is born this day, in the city of David, a Savior, which is Christ the Lord." He leaves the throne to save the world. Is it a wonder the angels thought well of Him?

Then there are *the redeemed saints*—they that see Him face to face. Here on earth He was never known, no one seemed really to be acquainted with Him; but He was known in that world where He had been from the foundation. What do they think of Him there?

If we could hear from heaven, we should hear a shout which would glorify and magnify His name. We are told that when John was in the Spirit on the Lord's day, and being caught up, he heard a shout around him, ten thousand times ten thousand, and thousands and thousands of voices, "Worthy is the Lamb that was slain to receive power, and riches, and wisdom, and strength, and honour, and glory, and blessing!"

Yes, He is worthy of all this. Heaven cannot speak too well of Him. Oh, that earth would take up the echo, and join with heaven in singing, "WORTHY to receive power, and riches, and wisdom, and strength, and honor, and glory, and blessing!"

But there is yet another witness, a higher still. Some think that the Jehovah of the Old Testament is the Christ of the New. But when Jesus came out of Jordan, baptized by John, there came a voice from heaven. God the Father spoke. It was His testimony to Christ: "This is my beloved Son, in whom I am well pleased."

Ah, yes! God the Father thinks well of the Son. And if God is well pleased with Him, so ought we to be. If the sinner and God are well pleased with Christ, then the sinner and God can meet. The moment you say as the Father said, "I am well pleased with Him," and accept Him, you are wedded to God. Will you not believe this witness, this last of all, the Lord of hosts, the King of kings, Himself? Once more He repeats it, so that all may know it. To Peter and James and John, on the Mount of Transfiguration, He says again, "This is my beloved Son; hear Him." And that voice went echoing and re-echoing through Palestine, through all the earth from sea to sea; yes, that voice is echoing still, *"Hear Him! Hear Him!"*

My friend, will you hear Him now? Hark! What is He saying to you? "Come unto me, all ye that labour and are heavy laden, and I will give you rest. Take my yoke upon you, and learn of me: for I am meek and lowly in heart: and ye shall find rest unto your souls. For my yoke is easy, and my burden is light." Will you not think well of such a Savior? Will you not believe in Him? Will you not trust in

Him with all your heart and mind? Will you not live for Him? If He laid down His life for us, is it not the least we can do to lay down ours for Him? If He bore the cross and died on it for me, ought I not be willing to take it up for Him? Oh, have we not reason to think well of Him? Do you think it is right and noble to lift up your voice against such a Savior? Do you think it is just to cry, "Crucify Him! Crucify Him!"?

Oh, may God help all of us to glorify the Father by thinking well of His only-begotten Son.

31

MOODY'S GREAT SERMONS

Be Not Deceived

You will find my text this evening in the sixth chapter of Galatians, the seventh and eighth verses: "Be not deceived; God is not mocked: for whatsoever a man soweth, that shall he also reap. For he that soweth to his flesh shall of the flesh reap corruption; but he that soweth to the Spirit shall of the Spirit reap life everlasting."

When Mr. Sankey was singing that hymn tonight about sowing the seed, I thought of a meeting we had in Chicago three years ago this month. There was a poor man came into that meeting discouraged, disheartened. He had run away from his friends in the hope that he might come to Chicago and die in the gutter. He had given up all hope of becoming a sober man. He was the son of a good man; he was the husband of a lovely wife; he was the father of two beautiful daughters. But he had become such a slave to strong drink that he had given up all hope. That night he came into the Tabernacle because it was cold and he wanted to get into a warm place. He went up into the gallery and got behind a post, and he said, as the people came in well dressed and looking so happy, he looked down upon them and gnashed his teeth, and cursed the day that he was born. At last Mr. Sankey struck up that hymn, "Sowing the Seed." The man said he did not take any interest in the singing until he came to the third verse, and that was the verse that reached him. And when Mr. Sankey was singing tonight I was in hopes it would reach someone else. Let me read you the verse that God used to rouse that man.

"Sowing the seed of a lingering pain,
Sowing the seed of a maddened brain,
Sowing the seed of a tarnished name,
Sowing the seed of eternal shame!

O, what shall the harvest be?"

Three years have rolled away. One of the most efficient workers today in Chicago is that man. I have seen him move an audience as I think I never saw an audience moved. God reached very low when He picked him up. His wife and children are with him now— a happy home. I hope God will arouse some one here tonight. I hope there will be some one aroused tonight by the Spirit of God. And I want to say to you Christians that if you pray and are looking right up to God for power tonight there may be some one convicted. The sermon is not going to convict anyone. It is the Spirit of God that convicts men of sin. Man has not the power to rouse men. He can speak to the outward ear, but God has got to speak to the ear of the soul. God has got to make these dead souls live. What we want is the Holy Ghost power here tonight.

I remember the first time I ever preached from that text was in the city of Boston. I commenced, "Be not deceived," and I pointed down in the audience and said, "Young man, 'be not deceived!'" and a man had been coming there for two weeks—he had just come, he said, out of curiosity. He had lost all hope. He was a poor prodigal turned out of his own home, and a wanderer in the city of Boston. But God had just used these words, "Be not deceived," and he waked up to the fact that he had been deceived. From his childhood all along up he had been deceived, and that young man became a Christian, and when I was at Cooper Institute two weeks ago tonight, I found him clothed and in his right mind. He has been working for Jesus Christ all these months, and now he is a very efficient worker.

My friends, let us pray tonight that the text may do its work. The sermon is of very little account after all. It is the text we want. The sermon is just to drive the nail. And now, never mind the sermon, but pray God to carry the text down into the hearts of the people. Infidels and skeptics tell us the Word is not true; but who can deny that text, "Be not deceived; God is not mocked: for whatsoever a man soweth, that shall he also reap." We can see that all about us. A man is doubly blind that can not see that fulfilled every day. These gray-haired men know that; they have lived long enough to see men reaping today what they have sown. "Be not deceived!" It is a decree of high heaven that a man must reap what he sows. These farmers, when they sow, expect to reap. A man learns a trade. He is learning that trade because he expects to reap, by and by, a harvest. A man that is toiling hard to get a profession—you take some of these lawyers that have toiled for ten or fifteen years; they expect to reap by and by a harvest. They expect it. That is what they are sowing for. You take some of these medical men; they commence practice, and they have hard work for years to get a-going; and some people say, "Why don't you give it up?" "Why," they say, "I expect to reap by and by." They are looking forward to the reaping time. They are just laying the foundation—sowing the seed, but they say, "I expect to reap by and by."

Then there is another thing. A man expects to reap the same kind of seed that he sows. "Whatsoever a man soweth that shall he also reap." If a man sows wheat, he does not look for watermelons. If a man plants potatoes, he does not look for grapes; he expects to dig potatoes. If he sows wheat, he looks for wheat; he does not look for oats; he does not look for anything else but wheat. He expects to reap the same kind of seed that he sows.

Well, now, that is true in the natural world, and, my friends, it is true in the spiritual world. A young man says in a flippant, fluent way, that he is just sowing his wild oats; he is a young man. He forgets that it is a decree of high heaven that he has got to reap those wild oats. It is no laughing matter. It is astonishing just to see men hold their heads up with a scorning look and say, "Oh, well, we are young men now, and you know we must have our time sowing our wild oats. We must have a little of the world and see a little of its pleasures"; but they seem to forget that if they sow to the wind, they must reap the whirlwind.

And you will find that this runs all through life. You let me be a deceitful man and let me deceive others, and I will be paid back in my own coin—others will deceive me. You let me teach my children to disobey God, and they will turn around and disobey me. Many a man has got a broken heart because he taught his children to be disloyal to God, and they have turned around and been disloyal to him. God knows that, and He tells us to train our children to honor Him so they may honor us in our old age. I have a case in my mind now where a man reaped just the same kind of seed that he sowed. He was a wealthy man. He was what the world would call a prosperous man. He had a good bar, and right near him lived a widow with an only son, and that son was enticed into that place night after night, and at last he came home drunk. When the widow waked up to the fact that her only son was becoming a drunkard she went to that rum seller and begged him not to sell her boy any more liquor; and he told her to mind her own business, and he would mind his; that he would sell to whom he pleased; he had a license, and he would go on selling. And he did continue selling to that boy until at last he went down to a drunkard's grave; and that gray-haired mother is now tottering upon the brink of the grave with a broken heart. But it was not five years before that rum sellers's only son, in a drunken spree, put a revolver to his head and blew out his own brains; and that father went down to his grave with a broken heart. He had to reap just what he sowed. If I sell another man's son rum and ruin him, someone will ruin my boy. That is a decree of heaven. You cannot get around it. It is madness for a man to shut his eyes to these facts. You can close up the Bible and see this constantly carried out.

I remember reading in history that in the days of Louis XI, he had a cruel, wicked bishop that was persecuting some of the saints of the Most High God; and the king wanted to know how he could make their punishment more cruel and bitter. "Well," said the bishop, "make them a cage, and have it so short and narrow they cannot lie down, and so low they cannot stand straight, and they will have to be in a bent position all the while." The king ordered the cage made, and the very first one that went into that cage was the bishop himself. He had offended the king before he got the cage finished; and for fourteen long years the king kept him in that cage. He had to reap what he sowed.

Another thing: When a man sows he expects to reap more than he sows. You sow a handful of grain, and you will reap a bushel. Some men think that it is pretty hard to have to reap more than they sow. But, then, you ought to think of that when you are sowing. That is a law of nature. You must reap more than you sow. Why, many a man has brought ruin upon himself and his whole family by one act—for just one night's pleasure; and he has blasted his reputation, his character, and the hopes of his friends—all gone. Sometimes a man has to reap when he sows; it comes quick; judgement follows right on after the act, as in the case of Judas, and of Cain. Sometimes, as I said last night, sentence is delayed, but it is surely coming. There is one thing a man can always count on, and that is that his sin will overtake him.

The Bible says, "Be sure your sin will find you out." A man may laugh at that and say, "I will cover up my tracks so they cannot find me out. I will bury the deed so deep that it shall never have a resurrection." Young man, "Be not deceived; God is not mocked; for whatsoever a man soweth, that shall he also reap." You may sow it in darkness, and you may say that no eye has seen you; but God has seen you. His eyes go to and fro through the earth. He knows what the sons of men are doing, and you cannot deceive Him. I will venture to say there is not a man or woman in this audience tonight but has been deceived. You know what it is to be deceived. You have been deceived by some of your neighbors. You have been deceived and "taken in," as you call it, by some stranger that has come along. You know what it is to be deceived. There is not a man or woman in this audience but what has been deceived. You have been deceived by some bosom friend—by some brother or first cousin, perhaps. But more than that, you have been deceived by your own heart. I will venture to say we have been deceived more by our own treacherous hearts than anything else. "The heart is deceitful above all things, and desperately wicked." Therefore, if a man is guided by his own dark mind and dark heart, he will be led astray. What we want is not to be deceived by our own heart. God does not deceive us, and He does not want us to attempt to deceive Him. "Be not deceived; God is not mocked." When man sins it is known. God knows it. It is blindness and folly for him to think it will never come to light. It may be twenty years afterwards, but sin will overtake him as it did Jacob. Look at those sons of Jacob, when Joseph was taken and thrown into prison. "We do remember our fault this day, how our loved brother Joseph pleaded." Twenty long years had rolled away and their sin had overtaken them in a strange land. Be sure that your sin, young man, will find you out. It may be this very day you took out of your employer's till twenty-five cents. Perhaps last week you took fifty cents and went to the theater with it. But you say, "I will put it back some time." That is the way these defaulters begin. Men don't go to a precipice and jump down. They come down step by step. It is these little things—twenty-five cents or a dollar. You say, "I can replace that any time; that don't amount to anything." Ah, my friends, "Be not deceived." A man that steals twenty-five cents is just as much a thief as one that steals $5,000. He has made his conscience guilty. He is not the man he was before he took it. He is laying a bad foundation, and if he attempts to build on that foundation the structure will fall.

When we were in New York City a man came up from the boat to the Hippodrome. He was out of money, had no friends, and was a perfect stranger. He was a fine looking young man, and I said to him, "How is this? How is it you come over here, a perfect stranger; without money and without friends?" The poor fellow took me off

to one side and told me the story. He said he had held a high position in England, but one night he was out gambling with his employer's money; he was the confidential man and carried the money
that belonged to his employers; these men that were gambling with
him got him drunk, and he gambled away all his employer's money,
and the only thing for him to do was to go to prison or escape—flee
to this country. I talked with him and found he had left a beautiful
wife and a beautiful family of children. I said, "How is it, do they
know where you are?" "No," says he, "they don't." I said, "Was not
that pretty hard?" The poor man wrung his hands and says, "I am
broken-hearted; not only my own character gone, but I brought
ruin upon my wife and children." Ah, just one night's pleasure, one
night in that gambling den, and he was stripped of all. There was a
stain and he could not wipe it out. God in mercy may forgive him,
but at the same time a man has got to reap what he sows. I can
imagine I hear some one say, "I would like to hear you explain
that—if Jesus Christ forgives, how is it a man has got to reap what
he sows?"

You know the Bible tells us the penalty of sin is death—the
soul that sinneth, it shall die. Now Christ will meet that penalty because He will save my soul; but, at the same time, if God forgives
me, I have to reap what I sow; for instance, I send a man out to sow
wheat and he gets mad at me and sows thistles. When the reaping
time comes I ask him, "Do you know anything about these thistles?"
and he says, "Mr. Moody, I got mad at you that day when you sent
me out to sow wheat and I sowed thistles; I am very sorry, will you
forgive me?" I will forgive you, but I tell you when you reap that
wheat you will have to reap thistles too. God may forgive a man, but
at the same time he has got to reap what he sows. One act may make
me reap all the rest of my days with sorrow, with shame. God may
forgive me, yet I have to reap. I think I can make that still plainer.

When we were preaching in the Tabernacle in Chicago one
night, a young man came into the inquiry-room, a fine looking
young man. The minister tried to talk to him, but he did not seem
to open up. The minister said to me, "I wish you would come and
see this young man." I went down and sat down by his side. The
poor fellow trembled. He was greatly agitated. I could not talk with
him as much as I would like to, so I said, "I wish you would come
tomorrow at 1 o'clock at the close of the noon meeting." At 1 o'clock
that young man was there. He was from Ohio, not far from Cleveland. He went on and told me his history. He told me he was a

telegraph operator. The boys in the express office where they officed and himself used to meet nights and play cards. One night they suggested they would break into the express office out of fun. He said at last they broke into the express office. He was arrested, tried, and acquitted. When they found him innocent they took him right up in their arms and carried him out in the street and just cheered and cheered. He said it went like a hot iron into his soul. He said he was guilty, and for seven months he had not known what peace was. Now, says he, "I would like to know if I can become a Christian without giving myself up to the law and confessing my guilt." I said, "I never like to advise a man to do what I would not do myself, and I don't know what I would do if I was in the situation. But it is always safe to ask God. Let us get down and pray about this matter." We got down and I prayed, and the minister that was with us prayed, and then we asked this young man to pray. He said, "No, sir." Said I, "Why not?" "I know what that means; if I pray, I have to give myself up to the law." Said I, "My friend, it is always safe to do what God wants you to do. You had better ask Him for guidance." At last the young man opened his lips in prayer. After prayer he said, "Well, gentlemen, I thank you for the interest you have taken in me. My duty is very plain. I will submit to the law. I am going down to Ohio to give myself up."

He took the train that afternoon. When he got about fifty miles out of the city he sent me back a dispatch that he had set his face to do right, and God revealed Himself to him and the Lord blessed him on the train. And he came down home. I wish I had the letter he wrote me. I think I never wept so much over a letter as I did over that. He had a Christian mother down here, not far from Cleveland, and father, and there were eight brothers and sisters. When he got home they were all glad to see him. They had not seen him for seven months. He said that evening, after they had all got in the house and quiet, he just told them how God had met him, and how he was then coming home to confess his guilt.

His father and mother and family thought him innocent up to that night; but he said: "I stole that money, and I am a perjured man; I am on my way now to give myself up to the law." He says to his father: "I know I have brought disgrace upon you. I have done wrong. I want you to forgive me." The old man says, "Yes, I will forgive you." He says to his mother: "Can you forgive me, can you forgive your boy?" The mother says: "Yes, I will forgive my son," and the brothers and sisters all said they would forgive him.

Then he got down and prayed—the first prayer he had made, except the one he had made there in Chicago. The next morning he left that home of weeping and gave himself up to the law. He was tried at Akron and sent to the penitentiary. His mother was taken down some time afterward with typhoid fever and the boy could not go to see the mother. Tell me that he did not have to reap what he sowed. Tell me that the reaping was not fearful! That godly, praying mother dying in his own state and he could not go and see her. Though God in His infinite mercy had forgiven him yet the boy had to reap what he sowed. He had sowed the wind and he was reaping the whirlwind. Don't make light of sin. Sin is a fearful thing. It makes life so dark.

At last the father was taken down with typhoid fever and it was thought he was dying, and some Cleveland men went to the Governor of the State and the first pardon your present Governor granted was for that young man. When he got out he telegraphed me that he had got his release and went home to nurse his father, and, as he supposed, to see him die. But the father recovered. Then a brother was taken down. He watched over that brother and the brother died. At last this young man was taken down and when he was given up to die, he asked that the Christians of that town should come to his bedside to pray with him; and he lifted up his voice in prayer, and in a little while he passed away and he is in the world of light tonight. The poor boy has had to reap. Do you think he ever forgave himself? God forgave him, but he did not forgive himself.

It is a fearful thing to sow wild oats. You may laugh at it now, but the reaping time is coming by and by, and there will be no laughing when the reaping time comes. Cain would like to have changed places with Abel when the reaping time came. Do you think Ahab would not like to take Elijah's place? If a man goes on sowing, he has got to reap. If he don't reap here, he has got to reap hereafter, because it is a decree of high heaven, "Whatsoever a man soweth, that shall he also reap."

O, friends, I beg of you tonight, be wise and turn from sin; hate it with a perfect hatred; ask God this night to forgive you and help you to do right, because He wants you to do right.

32

THE GREAT REDEMPTION

Their Rock Is Not Our Rock

For their rock is not as our Rock, even our enemies themselves being judges—Deuteronomy 32:31.

This was Moses' farewell address. He was about to leave the children of Israel in the wilderness. He had led them up to the borders of the Promised Land. For forty long years he had been leading them in that wilderness, and now, as they were about to go over, Moses takes his farewell; and among the good things he said, for he said a great many very wise and very good things on that memorable occasion, this is one: "For their rock is not as our Rock, even our enemies themselves being judges." There was not a man on the face of the earth at that time that knew as much about the world, and as much about God, as Moses. Therefore he was a good judge. He had tasted of the pleasures of the world. In the forty years that he was in Egypt he probably sampled everything of that day. He tasted of the world, of its pleasures. He knew all about it. He was brought up in the palaces of a king, a prince. Egypt then ruled the world, as it were. He had been forty years in Horeb, where he had heard the voice of God; where he had been taught by God; and for forty years he had been serving God. You might say he was God's right hand man, leading those bond men up out of the land of Egypt, and out of the house of bondage, into the land of liberty; and this is his dying address—you might say, his farewell address. This is the dying testimony of one that could speak with authority, and one that could speak intelligently. He knew what he was saying, "Their rock is not as our Rock, even our enemies themselves being judges."

Now, tonight I want to take up the atheist, the deist, the pantheist, and the infidel; and I want to show, if I can, and I think it is not a very difficult thing to show, that their way is not as our way.

I know there is a good deal of dispute now about the definition of these words. So, to avoid any trouble, instead of going to the Bible I went to Webster's dictionary, and I have got the meaning. I suppose you will give in, most of you, that Webster is wiser than yourselves. There are a few men that are a little wiser than Webster, for infidelity is generally very conceited. One of the worst things about infidelity is the conceit. You seldom meet an infidel that is not wiser in his own estimation than the God who created him, and he wants to teach God instead of letting God teach him. But for those that are willing to bow to Webster we will refer to his definition of these words.

An atheist is "one who disbelieves or denies the existence of God." I am thankful to say that they are very scarce. You meet them now and then. I am sorry to say that you will occasionally meet a young man that will tell you that he is an atheist. He believes there is no God; he believes that there is no hereafter; that when he dies, that is the end—that ends all.

I don't know of anything that is darker; I don't know of anything that is colder, bleaker, than that doctrine; for, of course, an atheist has feelings like the rest of us. If he is a father, he has love for his children. Here is a boy that has gone astray; he has been taken captive by Satan; he has become a victim to strong drink, we will say, and strong drink has got the mastery; and you can see that boy as he is going down to a drunkard's grave. He says to that father that believes there is no God, and no hereafter, "Father, is there no deliverance for me? Is there no way that I can become a sober man? Is there no way that I can become a free man?" "Yes," says the atheist, "assert your manhood. Resolve that you will never drink any more." "Ah, but, Father, I have done that a thousand times, and I can't keep those resolutions. The tempter is too strong for me. My appetite is stronger than my will power, Father. Is there no God that created me that can help me?" "No, my son, no hope; nothing outside of yourself." "And if I die in this condition, what is going to become of me?" "Oh, that will be the last of you." "And shall we never meet again in the universe of God?" "No, never." Pretty dark, isn't it? And that atheist sees that boy go down to a drunkard's grave. There is no arm to deliver, no eye to pity. There is no help.

Look again. He has got a beautiful little child. It had lived long enough to twine itself around that father's heart, and the cold, icy hand of death is feeling for the chords of life, and that little flower is going to be plucked. You can see that little child wasting away upon a bed of pain and sickness. The child calls the father to its bedside and says, "Father, is there no hereafter?" "No, my child." "Shall we never meet again?" "No, my child." "When I die, is that the last of me?" "Yes, my child." Pretty dark, isn't it? That atheist goes and lays away that child without one ray of hope—without one star to relieve the midnight darkness and gloom.

A prominent infidel of this country stood at the grave of a member of his family. He is an orator—an eloquent man; and he said he committed him back to the winds and the waves and the elements; it was the last they would ever see of him. Pretty dark, isn't it?

And yet there are some men that want to go over to atheism. They want to believe that there is no God. I can not for the life of me see where you get any comfort in it. I turn away from it, and I say from the very depths of my heart, "Their rock is not as our Rock." I thank God I have got a better foundation than that; I thank God I have got a better hope than that. If my boy is led astray, I can preach to him Jesus Christ, and I can tell him that God Almighty has got power to deliver him from sin, and from its mighty power; and if God should take my child from me, I can say to that dear child, "I will meet you on the glorious morning of the resurrection. It won't be long. We may be separated for a little while, but the night will soon pass, and the great morning of the world will dawn upon us." Yes, "their rock is not as our Rock, even our enemies themselves being judges."

But I must pass on. That is the definition of an atheist—one that believes there is no God. I want to say if there were many atheists in this country, we would have a great many more suicides than we have. These men that have got tired of life, if they thought that death ended all, they would quickly put themselves out of the way, and you could not blame them for it. But I think there is something down in man's heart that tells him there is a hereafter; that there is not only a God, but there is a judgement to come.

Now a deist. A deist is one that believes in one God only. He denies Christ and revelation. Deism is not much better, I think, than atheism, for I never yet knew a deist that knew anything about his God. He believes there is a God, and that is all you can get out of him.

Deists live on their doubts. They live on what they do not believe—on negatives. You meet a deist and he would tell you, "I don't believe this, and "I don't believe that," and he is all the time telling you what he doesn't believe. You seldom, if ever, find a deist who will tell you what he does believe, because he knows nothing about his God. If a man denies revelation, how is he to know anything about God? How are we to know our God if we are only deists, and just close that Book, and not believe in the Book? Is he a God of mercy? We know nothing about it. Is he a God of truth, and equity, and justice? We know nothing about it. How are we to know anything about God, if we cast away the Bible, and say we don't believe in revelation; that we don't believe that Jesus Christ came down here to declare His Father, and believe that that Book is not written by inspiration, and doubt that blessed Word of God? I would like to have a deist come forward and declare to us his God—and tell us who and what he is.

The pantheist. Let us see what Webster's definition of a pantheist is. He believes that the universe is God. He believes that God is in the wind, God is in the water, God is in the trees, and all the God we know anything about is the god we see about us. A pantheist will say, "Why, yes I believe in God. You are God and I am God. We are all Gods." That is their idea—that God is in everything. I strike that board and I strike the pantheist's god, because that is as much a god as the god he knows. I stamp upon the floor, and I stamp the pantheist's god. That is all he knows. God is in everything; God is everywhere; God is nowhere; that is the summing up of pantheism. Now, you will find a great many of these pantheists that will tell you they believe more in God than we do, because they believe God is in every thing all around. But when you ask a deist or a pantheist if his God answers prayer, he will tell you no. "Does he hear the cry of distress?" "No." "Does he hear the cry of the humble?" He will tell you that the Lord of the universe and the God of the universe has just made this world, and has wound it up as a clock, and it is going to run; that His laws are fixed; that He never answers prayer. If your child has gone astray, you can't pray to Him, because He has no mercy. There is no mercy but in the wind, and you may as well go out and pray to the thunder, to a storm, or a shower, to the moon, the sun, the stars, because God is every thing and everywhere, and yet is nowhere. They don't believe in the personality of God. You may just take pantheism, deism, and atheism, put them all together, and there is not much difference. I would as soon be the one as the other, because they are in midnight darkness and gloom. They know nothing about the God of love and the God of the Bible.

But now we come, perhaps to the most difficult class, because I think that there are a great many infidels, and don't like that name. I suppose that saying they were infidels had offended quite a number of Cleveland people. They stand up and deny it. But when you come to put the question right to them according to Webster's definition of infidelity, they are nothing but infidels. Now, an infidel is one that does not believe in the inspiration of the Scriptures.

I am sorry to say that we have got today a good many infidels. The first step towards atheism is infidelity. The first step towards pantheism is infidelity. The first step towards deism is infidelity. The moment you can break down that Word in one place and make out that it is not true, then, of course, the whole Word goes. Now, you ask an infidel if he really believes in the Bible, and he says, "Well, I believe part of it. I believe all that corresponds with my reason, but I don't believe anything supernatural. I don't believe anything I can't reason out."

Now, if a man takes that ground he might as well throw away the whole Bible and go over to atheism at one leap. He need not be weeks and months going, because that is where it is going to bring him. If you take out of that Book all that is supernatural, you might as well take out the whole of it. From beginning to end it is a supernatural Book. Look into Genesis. You ask an infidel if he believes in the Flood. No sir; not he. Then throw out Genesis; because, if the man who wrote Genesis put in one lie, why is not the whole of it a lie? If he did, he must have known it was a fraud when he wrote it, so that condemns Genesis. You ask a man if he believes the story of the Red Sea—about bringing the children of Israel through the Red Sea. Not he. That is contrary to reason, contrary to man's intellect. Out goes Exodus. That throws out the decalogue—throws out the commandments. It all goes together. If the man who wrote Exodus told a lie in the beginning of Exodus and that the children never went through the Red Sea, then away goes the whole book.

Then take up Leviticus. It is said in Leviticus if we will do so and so, He will come down and walk with us, would be among His people, and the shout of the king is heard in the camp. "Do you believe that?" "No, sir," the infidel says, "I don't believe anything of that kind." Out goes Leviticus. Throw it all out.

Do you believe God told Moses to make a brazen serpent, and that all the bitten Israelites that looked upon it shall live? The skeptic turns up his nose and says with a good deal of contempt, "No, you don't think I am fool enough to believe that?" Out goes the whole book of Numbers; throw it out, because if the man that wrote that book, put that lie in, the whole of it is a lie. You just prove that I tell a willful lie here tonight and my whole sermon is gone. You go into court and testify to a lie and let it be proven that you have told a willful lie (and untrue in one thing, untrue in all), out goes your testimony. The jury won't take it. Now, if the man that wrote the book of Numbers put down that lie—if he never did make a brazen serpent for the children of Israel, then the whole book of Numbers is gone. Throw it out.

Then we come to Deuteronomy. Do you believe Moses went up into the mountain and his natural force was not abated, his eye had not grown dim, and he died there and God buried him; God kissed away his soul, as some one has said? The infidel says, "I don't believe one word of it; that is supernatural; that is against reason." Then throw out the whole of Deuteronomy. There goes the first five books of Moses.

Then go into Joshua. "Do you believe Joshua took Jericho by going around Jericho blowing rams' horns?" "Don't believe a word of it." Tear it to pieces. Throw it away. Out it goes. If the writer of that book would tell a lie like that at the beginning of the book, he lied all through it—why not? That is what an infidel is—one who does not believe in supernatural things.

"Do you believe that Samson took the jaw-bone of an ass and slew a thousand men?" "No, I don't believe it." Out goes the book. Because from the beginning of Judges to the end it is all supernatural.

"Do you believe God called Samuel when he was a little boy— that God called him?" "Why, no," says the infidel, "I don't believe anything that is contrary to my reason. I don't believe anything supernatural." Out goes the two books of Samuel.

"Do you believe that David went out and met Goliath and slew him?" "No, I don't believe it." Out goes the two books of Kings. And so I can go on through the whole Bible. Take out the supernatural in it and you have to throw away the whole Bible. You can't touch Jesus Christ from His birth until He went up into glory, but what He was supernatural. The work that is going on now is supernatural. Things are happening every day that are supernatural. Every man that is born of the Holy Ghost, born of God—it is supernatural. Yet an infidel will stand right up and tell you today that he will not believe a thing in that Book that doesn't correspond to his reason; therefore the infidels are just tearing the Bible all to pieces. That is where we are drifting to. "Their rock is not as our Rock, even our enemies themselves being judges."

Now, I would like to ask the infidels what earthly motive could the early Christians have had in writing that Book? What motive could Jesus Christ have had in coming down here and living such a life as He led? Some of you accuse us of working for gain. You say that we are after your money and that we don't care anything about your soul. You cannot accuse our Master of that, can you? He didn't carry off much money, did He? His cradle was a borrowed one. The only time that He rode into Jerusalem that we have recorded He rode in on a colt, the foal of an ass. It would be a strange sight to see Him coming into Cleveland in that way. You would not own Him. And He did not own this beast. It was a borrowed beast. It was a borrowed guest chamber in which He instituted His Supper. It was a borrowed grave in which they laid Him. He that was rich become poor for our sakes. What motive could He have had in coming down here if He had not been true and real—if He had been an impostor, a hypocrite, coming down here and teaching us a falsehood? If Jesus Christ was not God manifest in the flesh, He was the greatest impostor that ever came into this world, and every Christian throughout Christendom today is guilty of idolatry, of breaking the first commandment, "Thou shalt have no other god before me." He comes and says unto the world, "Come unto me and I will give you rest." Elijah never said that; Moses never said that; no man that ever trod this earth dared to have said it; and if Jesus Christ had not been divine as well as human, it would have been blasphemy, and the Jews ought to have put Him to death. They had a right by the Jewish law to put Him to death. He was an impostor! He was a deceiver! He a fraud! Away with such doctrine! And yet people will stand right up here in this community and tell you it is all a fiction about His conception by the Holy Ghost, and at the same time they will stand right up and say they are Christians. They don't like that word infidel. They say they are not infidels. But, ah, my friends, if we break down the testimony of Jesus Christ, and make Him out a fraud and deceiver, it all goes.

Now, when people tell me that that Book is not to be relied upon, I tell them that I will throw it away when they will bring me a better one. I am ready to throw it away tonight if you will bring me a better one. But where is there any book to be compared with it? Bring it on will you! When you bring on a better man than Jesus Christ I will follow him. But don't ask me to follow these skeptics and infidels down here who are trying to tear down the works of Jesus Christ when they have no better to leave in their place.

Now Jesus Christ was without spot or blemish. You can find no fault with Him or in Him. We don't want to follow anyone else until we can find a better man. If these men that are scoffing and sneering at Christ will bring on a better man, we will follow him. If they will bring on a better book, we will take it. But until they do, let us cling to the Bible, and defend it and stand by it, and let us stand by Jesus Christ and let us defend Him.

Infidelity takes everything away from us and gives us nothing in return. When Lord Chesterfield went to Paris he was invited out to dine with Voltaire, the leading infidel of that day. Lord Chesterfield was a Christian man. A lady at the table when they were at dinner, said: "Lord Chesterfield, I am told that you have in your English Parliament five or six hundred of the leading men of thought in the nation." Well, he said he believed that was so. She said, "Then why is it that those wise men tolerate Christianity?" Well, he said he supposed because they could not get anything better to take its place.

Do you ever stop to think what you would put in the place of Christianity? It is easy enough to tear down, or at least try to tear down. There are some people that spend all their lives in trying to tear down things that are good, but they give us nothing in the place of them. Now, the trouble with infidelity is it gives us nothing in the place of what we have got. The Bible holds out a hope to man. It holds out something that is beyond this life, and gives him hope. Infidelity gives him no hope. It tears down all the hope he has got. He has got nothing to build on. If this Book fails, what have we got? Now, just think a moment. Take the Bible away from us, and what have we got? I would like to say to the people here tonight, if you step into a church—for I am sorry to say some of these infidels have got into the pulpit—if you step into a church and hear a man talking about Jesus Christ not being Divine, if you take my advice, you will get out of that church as quick as you can get out. But you say, "My father and mother belong to that church." Suppose they do. You get out, as Lot got out of Sodom. Make haste. You think a man who would sell you poison and kill your children is a horrid man; but I tell you a man who would plant infidelity in the mind of my child is worse than a man who gives it poison—to have their young minds poisoned and infidelity taught them under the garb of Christ and Christianity; and yet there are some men who profess to be friends of that Book who are all the time trying to tear it to pieces, and make out that it is not written by inspiration—that it is not from God, and that it cannot speak with authority.

Now, to show that their rock is not as our Rock, our enemies themselves being judges, I want to tell you a thing that happened some time ago. I was in the room with a man, and he said he wanted to have a talk with me. "But," he says, "I wish you would let that man go out." "Oh!" I said, "he is here to take care of the things." We had some of our things in the cloak-room back of the platform, and he was there so that no thief should come in and steal what we had. And this man said, "I would like to have him go out." "Well," I said, "he belongs here. I will ask him to go out if you insist upon it, but," says I, "I will talk at this end of the room." "Well," he said, "I would like to have him out." I spoke to the man and asked him to leave the room, and he hadn't more than got out before he opened his lips, and such a tirade against Christianity! I said to him, "My friend, why did you want that man to go out?" "Well," he said, "I thought it might hurt him." I said, "If it is good for you, why is it not good for him?" Well, he said he did not like to have his children know his views. He said his wife was a Christian and he wanted his children brought up differently. "Their rock is not as our Rock, even our enemies themselves being judges." I want my children to believe as I believe. I want them to be taught to love and fear and honor God. If these infidels think infidelity is good for them, why is it they don't want it taught to their children, why is it, that so many infidels want their children to be taught the Lord's prayer?

Very often when I have been in an infidel's house he has wanted his wife and children to leave the room, and then he has gone on and talked his infidelity. "Their rock is not as our Rock, even our enemies themselves being judges." That proves it.

A man ordered his servant out of his dining room, and after his servant went out he began to talk his atheism to a Christian man that was there. The Christian man said to him, "Why did you order out your servant?" "Well," said he, "I'm afraid if he held my views, he might cut my throat some time, for my money."

You laugh at it, but if there is no God, why not? If there is no hereafter, why not? If this country is as bad as it is with all the religion we have got, what would it be without it? Let this country go over to infidelity; what would become of the nation? It was not a great many years ago that, in a convention at Lyons, in France, they voted that the Bible was a fiction, that it was not true, and that there was no God; that there was no hereafter; that death was an eternal sleep; and it was not very long before blood flowed very freely in France. And you let atheism, and pantheism, and deism, and infidelity go stalking through this land, and life and property won't be safe. You know it very well.

Lord Lyttleton and Gilbert West were going to expose the fraud of Christianity. One was going to take up the resurrection and expose that. The other was going to take up Saul's conversion and expose that. And they went about it—went to studying up those two facts. The result was they were both converted. The testimony was perfectly overwhelming. If a man will look at the testimony, I can't see for the life of me how he can doubt these are facts. What did Paul have to gain by his conversion? Would you call such a man as Paul a fraud? What did he give up for the Gospel's sake? Reputation, position, standing—every thing he had. What did he get in return? Hunger, persecution, prison, stocks, stripes, and death. He died the death of a common criminal. He died at Rome as a poor and miserable outcast in the sight of the world. What earthly motive could he have had, if these things are not true? Why, we have all the proof that any man could ask for, that Jesus Christ rose from the dead. He was seen ten different times, and was here among us forty days, and then He was seen, by the holiest and best men on earth at that time, ascending into heaven. They went and looked into the sepulcher and found it was empty.

There was no doubt about His body coming out of the grave. Some men say they believe in Christianity, but they don't believe Christ's body came up. Do you think they could have stolen that body and palmed that fraud off on the world for these eighteen hundred years? Do you think those keen Jews of Jerusalem would never have found out the fraud and deception? Away with such a delusion. Christ rose; He burst asunder the bands of death. He has come out of the sepulcher and passed into the heavens and taken His seat at the right hand of God.

We don't worship a dead Savior. Our Christ lives. He is on the throne tonight. Let us look up; for the time of our redemption is nigh. Let us gird up our loins afresh. Let us buckle on the whole armor and fight for Christ. Let us hold to the faith. Let us not be influenced by the infidelity around us, but let it drive us to the Bible. Let us cling to this good old Book. It will be darker than midnight ere long if we let our confidence go in that Book.

I saw an account some time ago of an infidel who was dying. So many infidels recant when they die. Did you ever hear of a Christian recanting? I never did. Did you ever hear of a Christian dying that was sorry that he had served the Lord Jesus Christ? I never did. I have heard of good men that regretted that they had not served Him a good deal better than they had; that they had not lived more like Him. The infidel friends of this infidel gathered around him. They were afraid he was going to recant, and if he did, the Christians would make capital out of it. They gathered around him and said, "Hold on, hold on to your principles; don't give it up now." The poor dying man said, "What have I got to hold on to?" You answer the question, will you? What has an infidel got to hold on to?

Some time ago I was drawing a contrast between the end of that talented man, Lord Byron, and Paul. Byron died at the early age of thirty-six. The time allotted to man is three score years and ten.

A fast life—a life of dissipation carried him off early. These are about the last lines he penned:

"My days are in the yellow leaf
The flower and the fruit of life are gone;
The worm, the canker and the grave
Are mine alone."

That is all he had at the close of life. But look at Paul's farewell. He writes to Timothy: "I have fought the good fight. I have kept the faith; henceforth there is laid up for me a crown of righteousness." There is a good deal of difference between the death of a skeptic and an infidel, and the death of the righteous. "Their rock is not as our Rock, even our enemies themselves being judges." How often you have heard men say, "I wish I could believe as you do." What do they want to believe as we do for, if they are satisfied with their rock? "I wish I had your hope." What do you want our hope for if you are satisfied with your rock? "Oh, I wish I had the assurance you have." What do you want our assurance for if you are satisfied with your rock? The fact is, "Their rock is not as our Rock, even our enemies themselves being judges." We will bring them in as witnesses and let them testify. Let us, my friends, hold on to the Word of God. When these skeptics and infidels talk about the Book, let us love it all the more. Let it drive us to the Word. Let us say we will give up life rather than that Book. We will hold on to that, let it cost us what it will. The world may call us fanatics and fools, and all that, but they can not give us any worse name than they gave the Master. They called Him Beelzebub, the Prince of Devils, and we can afford to be called fools for Christ's sake for a little while, and by and by we will be called home, and, if we will hold right on, the end will be glorious.

A soldier, during the war, got in one of our meetings in Chicago. He had just come from the battle of Perryville. He said his brother came home one day and said he had enlisted. He went down to the recruiting officer and put his name next to his brother's; there was no name between them; he said they had never been separated one day in their lives, and he said he did not mean to have his brother go into the army without him. He said they went into the army, and they went into a good many battles together. The terrible battle of Perryville came on. About 10 o'clock in the morning his brother was mortally wounded. A minié ball passed through his lungs. He fell by his side, put his knapsack under the head of his dying brother, pillowed his head, and made him as comfortable as he could, bent over and kissed him, and started away. The dying man says, "Charlie, come back here. Let me kiss you upon your lips." He came back, and his brother kissed him on the lips and said, "There, take that home to my dear mother, and tell her that I died praying for her." And he said as he turned away, and his brother was wallowing in his blood, and the battle was raging all around him, he heard him say, "This is glorious." He turned around and went back, and said, "My brother, what is glorious?" "Oh," he said, "it is glorious to die looking up. I see Christ in heaven."

It is glorious to die looking up. But if we die looking up, we have got to live looking up. O, in this dark day of infidelity, when it is coming up all around, let us hold on to the glorious old Bible, and to the blessed teachings of the Lord Jesus Christ.

33

THE BEST OF D. L. MOODY

On the Death of Mr. P. P. Bliss

Therefore be ye also ready—Matthew 24:44.

I expected to enjoy this afternoon coming around here and hearing our friend Mr. Bliss sing the Gospel, and our friend Mr. Whittle preach. I was telling my wife, when I got home Friday night, that I was really glad I didn't have to work so hard on this Sabbath. I have looked forward to those two men of God coming to this city. I had arranged and made my plans to stay over a few days, in order to hear and enjoy their services. Ever since I heard that I would have to take their place this afternoon, there has been just one text running in my mind. I can not keep it out: "Therefore be ye also ready." You who have heard me preach the past three months, I think will bear witness to this, that I haven't said much about death. Perhaps I haven't been faithful in this regard. I'd always rather tell about life; perhaps there's not been warning enough in my preaching. But I feel that, if I should hold my peace this afternoon, and not lift up my voice and warn you to make ready for death, God might lay me aside and put some one else in my place; I must speak and forewarn you.

Today has been one of the most solemn days in my life. The closing hours of every year, for the past ten or twelve years, have been very solemn to me. I think I never spent such a day as I have today. This world never seemed so empty, and men never looked so blind away from God, as they do today. It seems, as never before, that I can not understand how life can go on in madness, how a man can keep away from Christ, when in just a stroke he is gone to eternity, and there is no hope. Those men I mean that really believe, intellectually, that the Bible is true; that if they die without regeneration, without being born again, they can not see God's kingdom. How it is they can believe, and yet they can still stay away from Christ when such judgments are brought near to them, is a mystery to me. I hope the words of the Lord Jesus will find their way to your hearts, as they have to mine; I hope you will hear Him this afternoon, saying: "Therefore be ye also ready." He had been warning them; for in a verse preceding this text He said, "As in the days of Noah, they were eating and drinking, marrying and giving in marriage, until the flood came and took them all away." It came suddenly. How often the judgements of God come suddenly upon us. I want to call your attention to a few words we find in the Old Testament, in the 6th chapter of Jeremiah, at the 10th verse: "To whom shall I speak, and give warning, that they may hear? Behold their ear is uncircumcised, and they cannot hearken: behold, the word of the Lord is unto them a reproach; they have no delight in it." Also in the 33rd chapter of Ezekiel, 4th, 5th, and 6th verses: "Then whosoever heareth the sound of the trumpet, and taketh not warning; if the sword come, and take him away, his book shall be upon his own head. He heard the sound of the trumpet, and took not warning; his blood shall be upon him. But he that taketh warning shall deliver his soul. But if the watchman see the sword come, and blow not the trumpet, and the people be not warned; if the sword come, and take any person from among them, he is taken away in his iniquity; but his blood will I require at the watchman's hand." Do you ask me, now, why I am so anxious to warn you? Because, if I don't, the blood of your soul will be required at my hand.

I want to warn you today; I want to plead with you today. And it is because I love you that I come to plead with you. I am sure there is nothing else that could induce me to speak this afternoon. I felt rather like going into my room and locking the door, and trying to learn what this providence means. I don't expect to find out yet; I'm not sure I'll ever know. But—(the speaker paused in deep emotion), I just felt I'd got to come down here this afternoon and cry out: "Therefore be ye also ready!" Make ready before the close of this sermon! Just ask yourselves this question, "Am I ready to meet God this moment?" If not, when will you be? God would not tell us to be ready, if He did not give us the power, unless it was something within our reach.

The thought is put into some of your minds that I am trying to take advantage of the death of this good man to frighten you and scare you; and I haven't any doubt Satan is doing this work at this moment. Right here let me notice that some say I'm preaching for effect. That's what I am doing. I want to affect you; I want to rouse you out of your death-sleep, when I warn you to prepare to meet your God; for "in such an hour as you think not the Son of man cometh." It is just from pure love, pure friendship to you, that I warn you; the thought that I am trying to frighten you from selfish motives is from the pit of hell. You take a true mother; if she does not warn her child when playing with fire, you say she's not what she professes to be, not a true mother. If a father sees his boy going to ruin and doesn't warn him, is he a true father? I say, it is the single power of love that makes me warn you. Suppose I walk by a house on fire, with a man and woman in it, and their seven children. If I don't call out, hammer on the door, smash in the windows if necessary, and cry out, "Escape if you can," what would you say? You would say, I ought not to live. If souls are going down to death and hell all around me—I verily believe such live today, and some are in this building—how can I hold my peace, and not cry out at the top of my voice: "Therefore be ye also ready; for in such an hour as ye think not the Son of man cometh."

There is a legend, that I read some time ago, of a man who made a covenant with death; and the covenant was this: that death should not come on him unawares—that death was to give warning of his approach. Well, years rolled on, and at last death stood before his victim. The old man blanched and faltered out; "Why, Death, you have not been true to your promise; you have not kept your covenant. You promised not to come unannounced. You never gave me any warning." "How, how!" came the answer. "Every one of those gray hairs is a warning; every one of your teeth is a warning; your eyes growing dim are a warning; your natural power and vigor abated—that is a warning. Aha! I've warned you—I've warned you continually." And death would not delay, but swept his victim into eternity.

That is a legend; but how many the past year have heard these warning voices. Death has come very near to many of us. What warnings have come to us all. The preacher's calls to repentance, how again and again they have rung in our ears. We may have but one or two more calls yet, this year, in the next few hours; but I doubt it. Then how many of us in the last twelve months have gone to the bedside of some loved friend, and kneeling in silent anguish unable to help, have whispered a promise to meet that dying one in heaven. Oh, why delay any longer! Before these few lingering hours have gone, and the year rolls away into eternity, I beg of you, see to it that you prepare to make that promise good. Some of you have kissed the marble brow of a dead parent this year, and the farewell look of those eyes has been, "Make ready to meet thy God." In a few years you will follow, and there may be a reunion in heaven. Are you ready, dear friends?

When visiting the body of my brother, just before he was put in the grave, I picked up his Bible, of the size of this in my hand; and there was just one passage of Scripture marked. I looked it up, and I found it read: "Whatsoever thy hand findeth to do, do it with thy might." As I read it that night, the hand that wrote it was silent in death. It was written in '76. Little did he think, when he wrote it, that in that same year he would be silent in the grave. Little did he think that the autumn wind and the winter snow would go roaring over his grave. Thank God, it was a year of jubilee to him! That year he found salvation; it was a precious year to his soul. That year he met his God. How often have I thanked God for that brother's triumphant death! It seems as though I could not live to think he had gone down to the grave unprepared to meet his God—gone without God and hope. Dear friends—dear unsaved friends—I appeal to you that you will now accept Christ. Seize the closing hours of this year; let not this year die till the great question is decided. I plead with you once more to come to the Lord Jesus. Oh, hear these blessed words of Christ, as I shout them again in your hearing: "Therefore be ye also ready."

Now death may take us by surprise. That's the way it has taken our dear friends, Mr. and Mrs. Bliss. Little did they know, as they rode toward Cleveland last Friday night, what was to be the real end of the journey. About the time I was giving out notice, last Friday night, of their being here this afternoon, they were then struggling with death. That was about the time they passed into glory-land. It was a frightful death, by surprise. But, beautiful salvation! Star of hope! In that time of gloom, darkness, and death: they both were ready. They were just ripening for the kingdom of God. I do not think I ever saw two persons who have grown more in Christ than these dear friends have in the past four or five years. I do not think a man walks the streets of Chicago today who has so few enemies as P. P. Bliss. He was a man we will love in another world. When the summons came, it must have been terrible; it must have brought cruel pain for a few minutes. But it lasted only a few minutes, and— they were in glory. Only a few minutes—and they were all together in that world of light, perhaps raising the shout of praise, "Alleluajah, what a Savior!" I think the heavenly choir has had a great accession today. I doubt whether many around the throne of God sing sweeter than P. P. Bliss. I doubt whether many have loved the Son of God more than he. With that golden harp of the glorified, how sweetly shall he sing!

But, my friends, while we are mourning here, are we ready? We can not call them back. We may mourn for them; we may mourn for the sad misfortune that has befallen ourselves. But what is our loss is their gain. It is better for them there than here; it is better to be "absent from the body, and present with the Lord." Shall you join him in that blessed land? Say, are you ready?

Now there are three things which every man should be ready for in this world: ready for life, ready for death, and ready for judgement. Judgement after death is as sure as life; judgement is as sure as death. There are three sure things. "It is appointed unto man once to die, but after this the judgment." It is of very little account how we die, or where we die, if we are only prepared, if we are only ready. We don't know what may happen any day. It seems to me, we ought to be ready any hour, any moment; we know not what may happen any moment. Oh, let us get ready! It seems the sheerest folly to delay this matter a single moment. Look at that train, where great numbers were ushered into eternity unexpectedly. Little did they think that their time was so near at hand. Little did our friends, Mr. Bliss and wife, think that they were going to be ushered into eternity, as they stepped light-hearted on that railway train. It would seem that people ought to resolve never to step aboard a railway train again, until they're ready to meet their God. It would seem as though no one would lie down and go to sleep tonight, until he knows he is ready to meet the Bridegroom.

Dear friends, are you ready? This question this afternoon, it seems to me, ought to go down into all our hearts. And then, if we are ready, we can shout over death and the grave; that death is overcome, the sting of death is gone, and the grave opens terrorless. Suppose we do go on and live thirty or forty years; it is all only a little moment. Suppose we die in some lone mountain, like Moses on Pisgah; or like Jacob, in the midst of our family; or like Joshua, with the leaders of Israel around us; or suppose God lets us die surrounded with the comforts and luxuries of home; or suppose death comes on unexpectedly and suddenly, as it did on Stephen; it may be we shall be called to die the death of the martyr, and be put to death unexpectedly; but if we are only ready, what care we just how our summons comes. If I am ready, I would as soon die like Stephen, or Moses on Pisgah. I would as soon die like our friend Mr. Bliss, as like Jacob with all his sons around him, if only I am ready for my glorious inheritance beyond the grave. That is the main question. It is not how we die. It is not where we die. At the worst, it may be but the sudden shock of a few minutes, and all will be over; and we enter upon eternal joy, joy for evermore. Millions and millions and millions of years in this world will not yield the joy of one minute of heaven. O my friends, shall you have a place in that heavenly home? Oh! Will you not each one ask this question just now, "Am I ready, am I ready?"

I believe that every man in this Christian land has had some warning; some John the Baptist to warn him as Herod had, some Paul as Agrippa and Felix had, some friend like Nathan, sent to warn him, as David had; some friend to warn him such as Ahab had in Elijah. And, my friends, I think this is a day of warning to you. Are you not coming to God today? Will you not hear the Savior's loving voice today, "Come unto me"? God will forgive your sins and blot them out, and give you a new heart. Oh, let not the sun go down tonight without being reconciled to God.

Little did those people on that train, as it neared Cleveland Friday night, little did they think the sun was going down for them the last time, and that they should never see it rise again. It is going down tonight—as I am speaking, the last sun of the year; some of you in this assemblage may never see it rise again. Dear friends, are you ready for the call, if it comes to you between now and tomorrow morning? This very night you may be called away; your soul may be required by God your Maker. Are you ready to meet the King and Judge of all the earth? Let me put, urgently but kindly, these questions to every soul here tonight. Can you say: "I have Christ; I have eternal life through Jesus Christ my Savior"? If not, dear friends, let me ask you, what will you say when He shall come to judge you? If, this very night, He should summon you to stand before Him, what would you say?

Oh, how deceitful death is! Something may fall on us as we walk home tonight, or we may fall down and break some part of our body, and be ushered into eternity. We may be seized by some fit, and we're gone. We may have some disease around the heart, that is hidden from us and that we know nothing about, and this may be our last day on earth. "Boast not thyself of tomorrow"; we don't know what will happen, even before tomorrow. And then, another deception. A great many people, you know, because their parents have outlived the allotted years, because their parents were long-lived people, think that they're going to live long also. How many are deceived in that way. Then there is that lying deception: "Oh, it is time enough to be a Christian—time enough to cry to God—when He calls us." Look at that wreck! Look at those people being dashed down that frightful chasm to frightful deaths! That is no time to get ready; that is not the time! They have all they can do trying to get out of the wreck—bleeding, burning, drowning, frozen! How many in eternity in five minutes! How many instantly! No time for prayer in such chaos as that. I would not say God is not merciful; He may have heard even then, the penitent cry; but I would not dare to say, "Put it off till some calamity overtakes you." The word comes, now, at this moment, "Prepare to meet God," "Seek first the kingdom of God and his righteousness." Oh, that is the first duty and pleasure of life, not its last! It is more important than going home to look after the highest earthly affairs; more important than if you could win the wealth and honors of the universe! Let business be suspended and everything be laid aside, until this greatest question of life—this greatest question of time and eternity—is settled, "Prepare to meet thy God." Oh, prepare!

My friends, I call upon you to come to the Lord Jesus Christ. I call upon you to prepare this day and this hour to meet your God. I lift up my voice, in warning, to all of this assembly. Would you not rather be in the place of Mr. and Mrs. Bliss, and die as they did, in that terrible wreck, by that appalling accident—would you not rather choose that, than to live on twenty-five years, or a hundred years, and die without God, and go down in despair to dark rivers of eternal death! Oh, it was appalling! But I would rather, a thousand times, have been on that train that dark night, and taken that awful leap and met my God as I believe Mr. and Mrs. Bliss have met Him, than to have the wealth of worlds and die without God and hope! Oh, if you are not ready, make ready just now! I think a great many tears should be shed for the sins of the past year. If you take my advice, you will not go out of this Tabernacle this night until you have tasted repentance, and the joy of sins forgiven. Go into the inquiry-room and ask some of the Christian people to tell you the way of life, to tell you what to do to be saved. Say, "I want to be ready to meet my God tonight; for I don't know the day or the hour He may summon me."

I may be speaking to some this afternoon who are hearing me for the last time. In a few days, I will be gone. My friends, to you I want to lift up my warning voice once again. I want to speak as to brethren loved, hastening on to judgement: "Prepare to meet thy God." I beg of you, I beseech of you, this moment, don't let the closing hours, these closing moments of '76, pass, until you are born of God, born of the Spirit, born from death. This day, if you seek God, you shall find Him. This day, if you turn from sin and repent, God is ready to receive you. Let me say, He never will be more willing than today; and you'll never have more power than today. If you are ready, He is ready now to receive and bless you forever! Oh, may the God of our fathers have compassion upon every soul assembled here! May our eyes be opened; and all flee from the wrath to come! May the divine warnings take hold on every soul! May we profit by this sad calamity, and may many be raised up in eternity to thank God that this meeting was ever held.

34

THE LONDON DISCOURSES

Popular Present Day Excuses

I pray thee have me excused—Luke 14:18.

Those men that had been invited to this feast wanted to be excused. And bear in mind that it was to a feast that they were invited—not to a funeral—not to hear some dry, stupid sermon, nor to hear some dry lecture; they were not invited to go to prison, nor were they invited to go to a madhouse, but they were invited to go to a supper. And in all my travels I never met a man yet that really didn't like to go to a feast, especially if it was a royal feast. It is not very often that common people like us get an invitation to go to a royal feast; but I have got one here tonight. There isn't a man hardly in all London but would consider it a great honor if he should get an invitation from Her Majesty to go to Windsor Castle to her feast she was getting up in honor of her son that has returned from Russia with his young bride. Why, you know, if the honorable men in London get an invitation they would like it to get into the press and to have it noised abroad that they had been invited. They consider it a great honor; but there is something worth a great deal more than that tonight. Here is an invitation from the King of kings and the Lord of lords.

We read that down in the evening of this dispensation the marriage-supper of the Lamb is to take place, and now God is sending out the invitation to that grand feast. The messengers are crossing mountains, and rivers, and deserts, and going to the four corners of the earth to invite every creature to be present; and God doesn't want one to be absent; He wants us all there. Man gets up a feast, and what a rush there is to get the best seat; but God prepares His feast, and there are empty chairs. Men begin to send in excuses.

They fast rain in upon Him. Christ has not only to provide a feast, but to fill the chairs. "I pray thee have me excused."

A SOLEMN THOUGHT

Did you ever stop to think what would take place in a city like London if God should take every man and woman at their word, and just excuse them, and with one stroke clasp them all in the arms of death? I don't think there would be such a crowd here to-morrow night if that should take place within the next twenty-four hours. A good many of the congregation would be absent. All you people that are making excuses, you would be gone.

How many of you? If I should get down to the audience I should find that every one that is not already saved would have an excuse. You would have an excuse right on at the end of your tongue; and if you haven't one already, Satan would be ready to help you to make one. That has been his business for the last 6,000 years—making excuses. "With one consent they begin to make excuse." It would be a very strange thing that would take place, if every man and woman in this great city should be excused, and God should just take them right away. There would be no drunkards reeling along on your streets tomorrow, for I never heard of a drunkard yet that didn't want to be excused. If he accepts the invitation, he must give up the rum-bowl. No drunkards shall enter the kingdom of heaven; there will be none at the marriage-supper of the Lamb. A good many publicans would be gone, if not all of them. They would want to give up their businesses. But they say, "We didn't want to give up our businesses," and they go on in their hellish traffic, destroying the bodies and souls of men. A good many cabmen would be absent tomorrow; there wouldn't be so many cabs in the streets of London, because, if they accepted this invitation, they would have to give up their Sunday business. A good many merchants and shopkeepers would not be here tomorrow. They want to be excused. They say they are too busy, and haven't time to accept this invitation.

EXCUSED—FROM WHAT?

Well, the friends that are making excuses just stop now and think a little; and would you just ask yourselves what you are being excused from? From heaven; from the society of the pure; those that have "washed their robes and made them white in the blood of the Lamb"; those that have been gathering for the last 6,000 years, from the time that Abel went up, all along down to the present time, while the best of earth are not down here; they are in heaven. And when man says, "I pray thee, have me excused," it really means he doesn't want to be there. He wants to be excused from those mansions that Christ is preparing for those that love Him: they want to be excused from the society of angels and the society of God the Father, Christ the Son, and God the Holy Ghost; they want to be excused from the society of the redeemed ones that have already gone up on high.

Now, I can't speak for the rest of you, but if I know my own heart tonight, I would rather be torn from limb to limb on this platform, rather have my heart torn out of my body before I leave the platform, than to be absent from the marriage-supper of the Lamb. I would ten thousand times rather die tonight, and be sure of meeting with the blessed and the purified in yon world of light than to live a hundred years and have the wealth of the world rolled at my feet, and then die and miss that wonderful scene. I have missed a good many appointments, but by the grace of God I want to make that one; I want to be at the marriage-supper of the Lamb. Blessed is he that shall be at the marriage-supper of the Lamb.

What a glorious thing it would be if every man and woman in this audience would give up all their excuses tonight! It is said, "God's hail shall sweep away those refuges of lies." Some one has said, "Let some plague strike you, and half your excuse is gone." Let death give you one look, and the other half is gone. When we come down to the gate of death, how these excuses will blow away in the dim past!

THE ORIGIN OF EXCUSES

You know the origin, don't you, of excuses? Why, they are as old as man himself. No sooner had Adam fallen than God came down to find him with an excuse. Satan was there, and he helped Adam to make the excuse. Adam said, "It was this woman you gave me." He turned it back on God really, and Eve laid it on Satan; and so all Adam's children have been making excuses ever since; they are very good at it.

THE LANDOWNER'S CASTLE

Let us look at the excuses those other men make. One man "bought a piece of land," and he must go and see it. A strange time to go and see land at supper time! He ought to have gone in the morning, at breakfast time. As some one has said, if he had been a good business man, he would have gone and looked at it before he bought it. But now he had bought it, no one could steal the land and run off with it in his pocket. It was not that he had not got the title of it, or that some one had got another deed and that he lost the title of his land. Was it going to make his land any better by looking at it? Would it improve it by looking at it? There is not a person in this hall but says that on the face of it it was a lie. That is what it was. That little boy down there says that it was. The man says to the servant, "I will be happy to be at your feast, but I must go and look at my land, and you will excuse me." That is how people talk now. I want to go to heaven; there is no one wants to be saved more than I do, but I don't know the way. You should find the way, if you were in earnest, into the kingdom of God.

ANOTHER LIE

What is the next man's excuse? "I have bought five yoke of oxen, and I go to prove them." Why didn't he do so before he bought them? He could let his oxen stand in the stall until he accepted this invitation; but no; he must needs go and prove his oxen right at that very minute, just at supper time—a queer time to prove oxen—but he must needs go right off then to prove his oxen; and away he went. Another lie. You know it. There's not a man or woman here that's making excuse but will say it is a lie on the face of it. That wasn't the reason he didn't want to go. It is like people now. They don't believe the Gospel is good news; they don't believe that the Gospel is glad tidings; they don't believe that the Gospel is peace and joy.

THE MARRIED MAN'S EXCUSE

The next man's excuse, some one has said, was more absurd than the other two. He married a wife and couldn't come? Why didn't he take his wife with him? Who likes to go to a feast more than a young bride? But the invitation is to the whole family, not one left out. And then, if his wife didn't go with him, she would stay at home and let him accept the invitation. He might have left her at home to go to that feast; but the fact was he didn't want to go; it was a manufactured excuse. That is what Satan is doing, rocking people off to sleep in the cradle of excuses. May God wake you tonight that these excuses may flee away!

When you come before God not one of these excuses this man

gives would stand the light of eternity. Not one of them would man stand up and give to God. Eighteen hundred years have rolled away, and

Have Men Grown Wiser?

Have men got any better excuse today? Can you find any better excuse now right down in that hall tonight? If I ask that young lady what her excuse is, would she have a better one than that man had? Yon gray-haired man might be asked why he didn't accept the invitation—would he have any better reason? If I go to that young man in the gallery, and ask him what his excuse is, and why he didn't accept of this invitation, could he give a better one?

Now I have met with a great many people, and talked to them about their souls; and in all my travels I never found a man who had a better excuse than these three. When you analyze and look them over, you see they look absurd, don't they?

Come now, my friends, let us

Look At Your Excuses.

What are they? Let me take up some I find every night in the inquiry-room. Only last night I found one very anxious to be saved, but "it was such a hard thing to be a Christian." God, in other words, they meant, was a hard Master, and really they meant that Satan was an easy one. Now is that true? The best witness to testify in a court to the character of two masters would be he that had served those masters. If I had worked for two men, I could tell more about them than a man that hadn't worked for the two, couldn't I? Now, if you have worked for Satan and haven't worked for the Lord, if you have been a servant of Satan and haven't been a servant of the Lord Jesus, I contend you don't know anything about it, and you can't say He is a hard Master. No one can say God is a hard Master until they have been in His service. Now if I could summon up witnesses tonight that have been in the service of Satan and the service of the Lord Jesus, I contend there would not be a man that would rise in this audience and say, "I have found God a hard Master."

THE DEVIL A HARD MASTER

If I should ask the disciples of Jesus Christ tonight to speak out in this hall, would they say they found God a hard Master? Is it true, O disciples of the Lord Jesus, that He is a hard Master and the devil is an easy one? (Cries of "No.") What do you say? (Repeated cries of "No.") Hear the witnesses say it. They say "No." Let me ask you another question. "Is not the devil a hard master?" (Loud cries of "Yes.") "Who is the easiest master to serve?" (A number of voices, "Christ.") Not only that, my friends, but I will take the bitterest enemies Christianity has got here in London, and I might bring them up to this platform tonight and they would testify themselves that the devil is a hard master.

In New York City there is a little iron bridge running from the police-court, as we call it, where the men are tried; and on one side of the bridge is written,

"The Bridge Of Sighs,"

and on the other, written in iron letters, "The way of the transgressors is hard." I said to the officer of the prison, "What made you put that up there?" "Why," he says, "there is not a man that goes over that bridge that does not go weeping, and therefore we call it 'The Bridge of Sighs.'" Now, you go to the prison and ask the convict if he has not found the way of the transgressors hard. Ask the man who has been in prison ten years, and who has to be there ten years longer, if he hasn't found the service of Satan hard; if he hasn't found him to be a bad master. What did the Lord Jesus say to Saul? "Saul, Saul! It is hard for thee to kick against the pricks." "It is hard for *thee*"—not hard for the Lord Jesus—but it was hard for Saul. It is hard for a man to contend with his Maker. It is hard for a man to fight against God. But I will tell you why you found the way hard. It is because you have been trying to serve God in the flesh; it is because you have been trying to serve God with the old carnal heart, which is enmity against God and is not subject to the law of God. No man can serve God until he is born of the Spirit; and then the "yoke is easy," then the "burden is light," and then God is an easy Master.

I tried to serve God in the flesh. I tried and failed; and it was hard to be a Christian; but when God snapped the fetters and set free my captive soul, and when I was born of the Spirit, the "yoke was easy and the burden was light." I stand here tonight to testify of the Lord Jesus Christ that He is

An Easy Master.

He is not a hard Master; His yoke is easy and His burden is light. All His ways are ways of pleasantness. It is a delightful journey if you have Christ with you; but if you reject Him, and try to serve God without Christ, you will find it hard and dark and utterly impossible. So don't go out here tonight and say God is a hard Master and Satan is an easy one. If you believe it, go and ask that drunkard who has been a drunkard for the last ten years. Go down to his home. It is a little hell upon earth. Oh, how dark and gloomy that drunkard's home is! Ask that drunkard if he has found the devil an easy master, and he will tell you that it is hard and dark; not only that, it grows darker and darker, and harder and harder as he journeys on. And if you could go down to the lost world and summon up one that has been there for the last thousand years to come up from the infernal pit—the dark caverns of hell—to tell you of his woe and his agony, he would tell you it is not only hard in this life, but ten times harder in the life to come. But go and ask that humble disciple of the Lord Jesus that has been walking with Christ for the last twenty years. Let him come up to this platform. See his eye, and there is pure light from Calvary shining across his path, and the light of Calvary is flashing around his countenance. Let that man tell of the peace and the joy he has in the service of Christ—how the way is lighter and lighter as he journeys on, and his hopes brighter and brighter as he comes nearer his eternal home. Nay, if we could go up to glory and bring down one that has been there for the last thousand years, if he should come from that world of light and tell of the joy, and the peace, and the glory of the upper world, oh, my friends, then you would find that there is a difference between him who serves Satan and him who serves the Lord Jesus.

So, my friends, don't go away from here tonight and say God is a hard Master and Satan an easy one; for Satan is a liar, and he has deceived the whole human race. Now

Tonight Change Masters:

make up your mind you will accept of the invitation to be present at the marriage-supper of the Lamb. But a man over there says, "Mr. Moody, that is not my case at all—not my excuse. My excuse is, I don't know as I am elected. If I were, I would make sure of salvation; but I don't know I am one of the elect." Now, I won't give any uncertain sound on this point. I won't say that no unconverted man in London has nothing to do with the doctrine of election. Now, bear that in mind. You have no more to do with the doctrine of election than you have with the Government of China: not a bit more. Now, then, what else? Suppose I am walking down by the Agricultural Hall tonight, and I see the people going in; I step up to a

policeman and say, "Who is invited to that meeting?" and the policeman says, "No one is invited except those that have tickets." I
have no ticket, therefore I can't go in. I go down to another hall, and
see people crowding in, and I find there is a lecture, but no one is
admitted there but those that belong to the society. I don't belong to
the society, and can't get in. I find there is another meeting; but
none are admitted but women. I am not a woman, and can't go in.
I go on a little further, and find a public meeting. I make inquiries,
and find it is a club, and none but those belonging to the club can
go in. I can't go in there. I come to another building, and I find written up on its front, in great letters of fire,

"Whosoever Will, Come In";

and in I go—that's me. That's the way God puts His proclamation—"Whosoever will, let him come in from the highways and the
hedges, the blind, the lame, the halt, the deaf, the dumb, the sick—
rich and poor all alike, come to the feast, and come just as you are."

Well, then, you say, what am I to do with that observation
about election? Get into the Church, and we will talk to you about
that. I am talking now to those who are not in the Church. You must
deal with that word "whosoever" before you deal with election.
That must come first. When you begin to read you must begin with
the alphabet. You don't commence with the first reader: you must
commence at once with the ABC; and if you are to learn arithmetic,
you don't commence with geometry or algebra, you commence
clear on at the beginning; and if you want to go into God's kingdom,
you must go in God's way; and "whosoever will," let him go, and after you have got in we will talk to you about election. It will be time
enough to talk about it then.

I don't know if it is true, but I have thought that after the Lord
Jesus had gone to heaven, and Paul read that epistle he saw how
some people would go and tumble over it, and perhaps he would
look down to London here in the afternoon of the 19th century, and
he would see how some people would give an excuse for not going
to the feast. Whether He came down or caught up John, I don't
know which; but John and the Master came together again. He was
"in the spirit" on Patmos "on the Lord's day." Now John wrote these
things to the churches, and he took up a pen, and kept on and on
writing; and before he closed the book the Master said, "John, write
this: 'The Spirit and the Bride say, Come. And let him that heareth
say, Come'"; and I can imagine he would say, "There are some that

can't hear"; "Well, let him that is athirst come." Some will say, "I am not willing, and not authorized." But it is broader still, "Whosoever *will*, let him take of the water of life freely." Isn't that broad enough? If God says, "Let him take," all the devils in hell could not stop you. "I will take the cup of salvation, and call upon the name of the Lord." Who will take the cup tonight? Who will take salvation as the gift tonight? Who will accept of the invitation to be present at the marriage-supper of the Lamb tonight? Never mind about election, my friends. The invitation is to the broad, broad world. "Go ye into the world, and preach the Gospel to every creature." That means every one here. Will you believe the Gospel, and be saved? Will you accept of the invitation tonight? Oh, may God help you this night and this hour to accept of the invitation to be at the marriage-supper of the Lamb!

Ah! But I can imagine those young people send in their excuse. They are not troubled about election, not troubled at all with that excuse; but their excuse is this: if they become Christians, they will have to

Give Up All Pleasure

and all joy; they will have to put on a long face, and walk right straight through the world, and have no more joy, no more pleasure until they get to heaven. That kept me away from Christ for years. I used to think I should like to die a lingering disease, to know when death was coming, and before I died I would become a Christian, and get to heaven, making the most of both worlds, enjoying this world, and enjoying the world to come. I thought if I became a Christian, I should have to give up all true pleasure and all true joy until I got to heaven. There was never a greater lie told in hell or on earth than that. Does it make a man gloomy to become an heir of heaven? Does it make a man gloomy to become a child of the Lord, and to have the great God look down from His throne in heaven, and say, "That is My son; I have set My love upon him. That is My daughter!"

THE ONLY SOURCE OF JOY

Why, there is a man on his way to the execution. In a few minutes his soul is to be launched into eternity! See him tremble from head to foot when he is being led out to execution! Flash across the wires comes a message from the Queen. She sends a reprieve, and I run in haste and take it to the condemned man, and say, "Good

news! You haven't to die. Here is a reprieve from the Queen." Is that
to make him gloomy? Is that to give a man a long face? Here is a
man dying for want of water, and I go and give him a tumbler of
clear crystal water. Is that to make him gloomy? Christ is the Water
of Life. Here is a man dying for want of bread, and I give him bread.
Is that to make him gloomy? That is what Christ is; He is the Bread
of Life. Why should it make me gloomy to get an invitation to a
feast? When my little children get an invitation to go to a party, I am
not long in the house before I hear of it. My little boy claps his
hands with glee, and jumps for joy. That little girl down there likes
to go to a party—to a feast. My little child, I have got an invitation
for you; God wants you to go to the marriage-supper of the Lamb.
You are invited, little child—mother too; come along; all are invited. All ye young people, come to Christ tonight. Make haste and
accept of this invitation. Don't believe Satan's lies any longer that it
makes a man gloomy to be a follower of the Lord Jesus Christ. Men
are gloomy for the want of Christ. All the trouble in this world is because men have rejected Christ and salvation.

Then there is another excuse I heard from a man in the inquiry-
room the other night. "I should like to go to Christ, but God will not
receive me." "Why not?" "Because I am such a sinner." "You don't
know God. If you did, you wouldn't talk in that way."

HE RECEIVETH SINNERS

"This man receiveth sinners and eateth with them." O sinner!
Come along tonight. I don't care who you are or what your past life
has been. It may be as black as hell itself, but "the blood of Jesus
Christ cleanseth from all sin." He will clothe you with His own garment, and bring you into His banqueting-house, and the banner
over you will be Love. It may be I have been speaking to some poor
prodigal who has been strolling along the streets for the last few
weeks, who saw the crowd going into the Agricultural Hall, and was
drifted along into this hall. Perhaps his mother is dead and in her
grave; perhaps the father has cast him off because he is a prodigal,
wanderer, and a drunkard, and he says to himself, "Nobody cares
for my soul. There's no eye on earth to pity me, no hand reached
out to help me."

O prodigal! If you are here tonight, I bring you good news. I
have an invitation to you from the King of kings—the Lord of Glory. He wants you to go to the marriage-supper of His own Son. You
are invited tonight as much as any king or prince that has ever lived,

and you are as precious in the sight of God as any soul in London. Come now, just as you are. Don't wait another minute. Say now, "By the grace of God I will accept the offer of the invitation; I will be at the marriage-supper of the Lamb. If the Lord Jesus will receive me, He will have me." My dear friends, I tell you He *will* receive you. I challenge any man that ever was upon the face of the earth to say that when he came to Christ, Christ didn't receive him. Did you ever hear of such a case? Did you ever read of such a case? That never happened yet. "Him that cometh unto me I will in no wise cast out," says the Son of God. Those are the words of Christ, and He *will* receive you.

I wish I could tell you how willing He is; I wish I could tell you how He is longing to receive every soul here, and that He will never "see of the travail of His soul and be satisfied" until sinners come flocking to Him. What He wants is to give life. What He wants is to bless. What He wants is to receive. Why! There is joy in heaven over one sinner that repenteth. If there should be thousands here who repent tonight, what joy there would be in heaven! What a shout around the throne! How they would lift their high hallelujahs, and sing tonight sweeter than they have sung for many a night, if there is a great rush into the kingdom of God. Oh, may God lead you to accept the invitation; and if you go, He will receive you.

A CHAPTER OF AUTOBIOGRAPHY

Let me tell you a little incident that happened in our own family to illustrate God's willingness to receive sinners. The first thing I remember in my life was the death of my father. He died before I was four years old. One beautiful day in June he fell suddenly dead on the floor, and his sudden death gave me such a shock that I have never forgotten it. It made an impression on my young mind that followed me through life. I can't remember the funeral. The only thing I remember of my father was his sudden death. The next thing I remember was that my mother was laid away upon a sick bed; and the third thing—for afflictions don't come generally singly—was that my oldest brother became a prodigal and ran away. I well remember how that Mother mourned for that boy. I well remember away back in my early childhood how that mother thought of that boy, and I used to think Mother loved him more than all the rest of us put together—and I think she did; it was the love of pity. I remember the cold winter nights, as we used to sit round the old family fireside, and we talked to our mother about our father—how he acted and what he used to do, and we would sit for hours and hear Mother talk of him; but if we mentioned that elder brother all would be silent. Mother never heard his name mentioned without tears coming; and some nights when there would be gales of wind, Mother didn't sleep at all. She thought, "He may be on the sea, and in that gale. He may be in trouble"; and these nights she was ever praying for him.

THE MOTHER'S CRY

I remember some nights waking past midnight and hearing a voice in my mother's chamber; and I heard that mother weeping and saying, "O God, send back my boy. O God, shelter him and protect him, and take care of him." That was her cry. And when there came a day when the nation returned thanks for the harvest, a day when all the family comes together, Mother used to say to us and raise our hopes, "Perhaps he will come back today," and his chair was kept vacant, and the place at the table. And yet he never returned. We wrote to different parts of the country as we grew up. If we found any paper that had a man named with the name of our brother, we would write to see if it was our brother. I remember once finding a notice in a Californian paper of a man bearing that name, and I thought it was him. I wrote out there, and was very disappointed at receiving a letter telling me he wasn't the man. Yet Mother prayed on and hoped on, seemingly against hope, until the hair once black turned gray, and the step once firm began to tremble, and I could see grief carrying that dear mother into an untimely grave. How my heart used to bleed for her!

THE PRODIGAL'S RETURN

One day, as she was sitting in her little cottage, her two youngest children, that were infants when brother left home, and were now grown up almost to manhood and womanhood, sitting at the table with her, a stranger appeared at the gate, and he came up to the east piazza and stood with his arms folded, looking on that mother he hadn't seen for years. Mother didn't recognize her boy; but when she saw those tears rolling down over the long black beard, through those tears she saw it was her long-lost boy; and when she saw it was her lost boy she said, "Oh, my son, come in." And he says with his arms folded, "No, Mother; I will not come across your threshold until you forgive me." Sinner, do you believe she was ready to forgive him? She didn't wait for him to come in, but ran to the door, threw her arms around his neck and wept for joy. The dead was alive, the lost was found, the wanderer was come home, and the joy it gave that mother—I cannot tell it to you. None but the mother that had the prodigal boy can realize that mother's joy. I cannot tell you what joy it gave us as family; but it was nothing compared to the joy in heaven tonight, if you will only come home. Your Father wants you; and so come home this very night. He will receive every one of you if you will only come. May God help you to come now! May the Lord incline you to come, and you will find a warm welcome. He will give you a hearty response! Oh, may God incline you now to believe on the Lord Jesus Christ and to be saved!

A Sermon About Hell

Son, remember—Luke 16:25.

In another place in the Scriptures we read of the "worm that dieth not" and the "fires that are not quenched." I believe the "worm" spoken of is memory. I believe that is what is going to make hell so terrible to those that have lived in a Gospel land—to think what they might have been, to think how they might have spent eternity in that world of light. Now we read in this portion of the Scripture that this rich man is in another world. His soul has left the body, he has gone beyond time, and he is now in another world. Some people say that when we preach about hell it is only to terrify people, only to alarm them. Now, I am no alarmist, and if I could terrify any one, and try to scare them into the kingdom of God, I would not. But, at the same time, if I am to be a messenger for God, I must tell the whole message—I must not keep back any part of the Word of God. The same Christ that tells us of heaven with all its glories tells us of hell with all its horrors; and I am sure there is no one here will accuse Christ of drawing this picture to terrify people, or to alarm them, if it is not true. This picture is one that He has drawn Himself. Now, I have read some sermons about hell, but I never read one more terrible than this one. I never have seen a picture drawn more fearful than this one that is drawn here, of a rich man "clothed in purple and fine linen," and who "fared sumptuously every day" while he was in this world; but now we catch a glimpse of him in another world, and we find him there lifting up his voice in hell, and crying in torment.

NO HELL, NO HEAVEN

Some tell us there is no hell and some there is no heaven, and, if I had to give up one, I would have to give up the other. The same Bible that tells us of heaven tells us of hell. The same Savior that came down from heaven to tell us about heaven, told us about hell. He speaks about our escaping the damnation of hell, and I am sure there is no one that has lived since that could tell us as much about it as Himself. If there is no hell, let us burn our Bibles. Why spend so much time studying the Bible, why spend so much time and so much money in building our churches? Let us turn our churches into places of commerce or of amusement; let us eat and drink and be merry, for we will soon be gone if there is no hereafter. Let us build a monument for Paine and Voltaire; let us build a tomb over Christianity and shout over it: "There is no hell to receive us, there is no God to condemn sin, there is no heaven, there is no hereafter!" Let us be real too. If there is a heaven and a hell, then let us act as God would have us act. God was in earnest when He gave Christ to die for us. Christ was in earnest when He went to Calvary and suffered that terrible death—it was to save us from that terrible hell. If I believed there was no hell, I am sure I would be

Off Tomorrow For America.

You would not find me here going from town to town, spending day and night preaching and proclaiming the Gospel, and urging men to escape the damnation of hell. I would go back to my own country, and take things easy. Oh, my friends, I can not but believe it! And now, if there is anyone here in doubt about it, why not be honest? If you believe you have a Creator, why not ask Him to give you light about the future? There was a time when I did not believe it; but God revealed it to me. It is a matter of revelation. It is Satan that is telling us that there is no hereafter or there is no hell, because the Word of God teaches it so plain. And if there is a hell, we had better find it out before we get there; it is a good deal better for us to find it out here than it is to be laughing and joking about it. It makes me feel terrible to hear men speaking so flippantly about hell, and making jokes about it. God is not to be trifled with. Think of this man in that lost world crying for one drop of water, and then crying that Abraham might send one to comfort him, but there was a gulf fixed that no man could cross. God has fixed that gulf.

THE TIME OF SEPARATION

The time is coming when there will be separation; the time is coming when that praying wife and that godless, Christless husband shall be separated; the time is coming when that godly, sainted mother will be lifted up to heaven, and that scorning, infidel son will be cast down to hell unless he is wise and accepts salvation. Now the thought I want to bring out is just this—that is, memory in hell. What did Abraham say to this man? "Son, remember." Oh, may this text be fired down into many a heart tonight.

"Son, remember." God wants you to wake up and remember before it is too late. It is a good deal better for a man to be wiser and stop and think while he has the privilege of changing his mind, if he is wrong, than it is to go on like a madman and be cast into the prison house of hell. Then he will have to think; yes, memory will be keen then to act, but it will be too late to make any change. I have been twice

At The Point Of Death.

I was drowning once, and just as I was going down the third time I was rescued. In the twinkling of an eye my whole life came flashing across my mind. I can not tell you how it was. I can not tell you how a whole life can be crowded into a second of time; but everything I had done from my earliest childhood, it all came flashing across my mind. And I believe that when God touches the secret spring of memory every one of our sins will come back, and if they have not been blotted out by the blood of the Lord Jesus Christ, they will haunt us as eternal ages roll on. We talk about forgetting, but we cannot forget if God says, "Remember." We talk about the recording angel keeping the record of our life. I have an idea when we get to heaven or into eternity we will find that recording angel has been ourselves. God will make every one of us keep our own record; these

Memories Will Keep The Record,

and when God shall say, "Son, remember," it will all flash across our mind. It won't be God that will condemn us, it will be ourselves; we will condemn ourselves, and we will stand before God speechless. By and by God shall change our countenance, and He will send us away to read our own biography, to read our own record, and that will be what will condemn us.

There is a man in prison. He has been there five years. Ask that young man what makes the prison so terrible to him. Ask him if it is the walls and the iron gates—ask him if it is his hard work, and he will tell you no; he will tell you what makes the prison so terrible to him is memory; and I have an idea if we got down into the lost world we would find that is what makes hell so terrible—memory that they once heard the Gospel, that they once had Christ offered them, that they once had the privilege of being saved, but they made light of the Gospel, they neglected salvation, they rejected the offer of mercy, and now if they would they could not.

A MISSIONARY SPIRIT IN HELL

We find this rich man had a desire to get out of that place of torment. He had a missionary spirit when he got there, for he said, "Send some one to my father's house and warn my five brethren. Oh, send some one to tell them not to come to this place of torment." Yes, it would have been better if he had had a missionary spirit before he had got there; it would be better for you that you should wake up and come to the Lord Jesus Christ, and go to work to save your friends while you are on praying ground, and in this world. Your missionary spirit won't help you when you are in hell; it won't help you when you are in the lost world. Yes, memory, memory—"Son, remember."

CAIN'S MEMORY

If Cain is in that lost world tonight, no doubt he can remember the pleading of his brother Abel. He can remember how he looked when he smote him; he can hear that piercing cry tonight, he has not forgotten it. All these long years Cain can remember what he might have been, how he despised the God of grace, and how he lost his soul. Thousands of years have rolled away, but still Cain has to think; he can not help but think. I have not any doubt but Judas remembers how Christ preached that sermon he heard on the mountain, how Christ looked when He wept over Jerusalem; he can see those tears tonight, he can hear that voice as He cried over Jerusalem, "O Jerusalem, Jerusalem, that thou killest the prophets and stonest them that are sent unto thee, how often would I have gathered thy children together, even as a hen gathereth her chickens under her wings, and ye would not." He hears that cry; he can see that kind, mild, gentle look of the Son of God. He can hear that voice as Christ said to him in Gethsemane, "Betrayest thou the master with a kiss?" Yes, memory is at work. His memory woke up before he died, when he went out and destroyed himself, taking his remorse and despair with him into the lost world.

NOAH'S COUNTENANCE

Do you think those antediluvians have forgotten how Noah pleaded with them? They laughed at the ark. I have not any doubt if you had gone and preached to them a week before the flood, and told them that there was a hell, not one would have believed it. If you had told them that there was to be a deluge, they would not have believed it. But did it change the fact? Did not the flood come and take them all away? You might have gone to Sodom and told the Sodomites that God was going to destroy Sodom, and they would have laughed at you, just as men make light of and laugh at hell. But did it change the fact? Did not God destroy the cities of the plain? So with Jerusalem. Christ told them how destruction would come upon it, and they mocked at Him and crucified Him. But look down the stream of time. In forty short years Titus came up against that city and besieged it, and there were 110,000 that perished within it. Yes, those Jerusalem sinners can remember in the lost world tonight how Christ wept over Jerusalem, how He walked their streets, how He went into the temple and preached, and how He pleaded with them to escape for their life, and to flee the damnation of hell; but they mocked on, and laughed on, they made light until it was too late, and they are gone now. Oh, may God wake up this audience, and may every man and woman here before it is too late escape for their lives! "How shall you escape," says the apostle, "if ye neglect so great salvation?"

NO BIBLE IN THE LOST WORLD

But now, my friends, "remember!" and we want tonight to have you think—"remember." There will be no Bible in the lost world to be a lamp to your feet and a light to your path, to guide you to eternal mansions. You make light of the Bible now, you laugh at its teachings; but bear in mind, there will be no Bible in the lost world. You have a Bible here; had not you better take it now, had not you better read it, had not you better believe it? I have not any doubt if a man had gone to that rich man a week before he was taken away he would have told you he did not believe in the Bible, he did not believe in a place of torment, he did not believe in a word of it. But did that change the fact? He found it out when it was too late; and there was no Bible there to help him out, there was no minister to go there and preach to him; and bear in mind if you get into that lost world, there will be no minister to pray for you, no earnest sermons preached there—it will be too late then.

There will be no Sabbath-school teacher there. I am speaking now to some young people that are in the Sabbath-school, and who have a praying teacher. Bear in mind you will have no teacher there to weep over you, to pray for you, to plead with you to come to Christ. I may be speaking to some young man, and he has had some friend come and put his hand upon his shoulder, and ask him to come to Christ. You made light of that, young man; you laughed at him, and you caviled at him. Bear in mind there will be no friend to come and put his hand upon your shoulder, and speak loving words to you there. "Son, remember." If you have friends that are anxious for your soul's salvation here, and they are pleading for you, treat them kindly; you will not have them in that lost world. Do not laugh at them; it is God that sent the loving message to you. You laugh now at the church. There will be no church for you to attend in that world, no church-bells to warn you of the Sabbath, no tolling of the bell for the death of some friend. It will be

Too Late Then.

You may have a praying wife now that weeps over you, pleads with you to come to Christ; but there will be no wife there to weep over you and pray for you—you will be separate then. Oh, my friend, treat that wife kindly, make her heart glad tonight by telling her that her heaven shall be your heaven, and that you will start tonight on pilgrimage with her. I may be speaking to some young man that has a godly praying mother. You are hastening to ruin, and breaking a mother's heart. Oh, young man, make that mother's heart glad tonight by telling her you have accepted her God as your God, her Savior as your Savior, that you are not going down to death and ruin, but that you will meet her in glory! Oh, may God meet every soul in this assembly, and may every eye and heart be opened to receive the truth. You come here tonight to hear Mr. Sankey sing, "Jesus of Nazareth Passeth By"; but bear in mind you will not hear that song in the lost world; or if you do, it will not be true—He does not pass that way. Tonight He is passing by. There have been many praying for this meeting.

THE LIVERPOOL CONVERTS PRAYING FOR LONDON

Last night at Liverpool the young converts gathered round me,

and how they made my heart glad as they told me they were praying for London. Many silent prayers are going up for you. I beg of
you do not make light of the Lord Jesus and His offer of mercy. He
comes to save you from a terrible hell; He wants to redeem every
soul here tonight, and now while I am speaking hundreds and thousands of Christians are lifting up their hearts silently to God for
your salvation, and may God answer their prayers, and may there
be many tonight that shall be saved. Now you have a golden opportunity. Jesus is truly passing this way. Why do you doubt that He has
been in our midst tonight? There has not been a night that a great
many have not gone into the inquiry-room and have taken us by the
hand and said, "I have accepted Christ and have found Him tonight,"
showing that the Lord Jesus Christ is in our midst. He is saving
some, why should He not save you? And while He is passing, and so
many are believing on Him, why won't you receive Him? My
friends, God does not want you to perish, but he wants you to be
saved. God does not want a soul in His vast assembly to be lost, but
He wants every one to be in glory; and if you will accept of His Son
as a gift from Him, if you will accept of the Lord Jesus, you can be
saved.

AN UNBELIEVING MOTHER

I was standing by the inquiry-room door in another place a few
months ago, and I saw a lady weeping. I spoke to her, but a woman
seized her by the hand and shoved her away from me. I said, "What
is the trouble?" "Why," she said, "this is my daughter, and I don't
want her to be associated with Christians; I hate Christians." Well,
I tried to reason with that mother, but she pulled her daughter away
weeping, the daughter pleading with her mother to stay. Is there
such a mother here tonight? May God have mercy upon you! It is a
thousand times better for your daughter and your children to be associated with Christians than it is to have them go down to death
and be associated with fiends as eternal ages go on.

TERRIBLE APPEAL TO YOUNG LADIES

If a young lady going home tonight should be spoken to by
some drunken man, how alarmed she would be; but did you ever
think in that lost world libertines and drunkards and murderers shall
be your companions? You are terrified now at the sight of one; but
they shall be your boon companions in that lost world. All workers
of iniquity shall be cast into the lake of fire, but those whose names

are written in the Book of Life shall have a right to the Tree of Life, and shall walk the crystal pavement of heaven. Oh, may God help you to be wise tonight, and to flee from your old companions and associates, and lay hold of eternal life! Do not trifle with this great subject. Be wise, and accept salvation as it comes from God.

STORY OF AN UNFILIAL SON

I was told some time ago of a father that had a son who had broken his mother's heart. After her death he went on from bad to worse. One night he was going out to spend it in vice, and the old man went to the door as the young one was going out, and said, "My son, I want to ask a favor of you tonight. You have not spent one night with me since your mother was buried, and I have been so lonesome without her and without you, and now I want to have you spend tonight with me; I want to have a talk with you about the future." The young man said, "No, Father. I do not want to stay; it is gloomy here at home." He said, "Won't you stay for my sake?" and the son said he would not. At last the old man said, "If I cannot persuade you to stay, if you are determined to go down to ruin, and to break my heart, as you have your mother's—for these gray hairs can not stand it much longer—you shall not go without my making one more effort to save you"; and the old man threw open the door, and laid himself upon the threshold, and said, "If you go out tonight you must go over this old body of mine"; and what did he do? Why that young man leaped over the father, and on to ruin he went.

Now, there is not a man or woman here who would not say that young man was an ungrateful wretch. Did you ever think that God has given His Son? Yes, He has laid Him, as it were, right across your path that you might not go down to hell; and if there is a soul in this assembly that goes to hell, you must go over

The Murdered Body Of God's Son,

you must trample the blood of Christ under your feet. No sooner did the news reach heaven that Adam had fallen than God came down and made a way of escape. God so loved the world that He gave Christ to die that you and I might live. Do not make light of that blessed Savior. Do not sit here and have that scornful look upon your brow; but lift up your heart to God, and say, "God be merciful to me, a sinner." Receive the gift of God.

If the Spirit of God is striving with any of you here, let me plead with you. Treat the Spirit kindly. Bear in mind that God has said His Spirit shall not always strive. There have been many, I believe, that have been awakened, and the Spirit of God has been striving with you; and now let me plead with you as a friend—just give yourself up to the leading of the Spirit of God. The Spirit of God will lead us aright; He never makes any mistake. God has sent Him from heaven into this world to lead us out of darkness into light, and the Spirit is drawing you. Do not resist Him; do not reject Him. I do not ask you to think or to believe what I say; all I ask is, believe what God tells you; believe what the Spirit of God will reveal to you; and if the Spirit of God is striving with you, do not quench or resist Him, do not resist the Holy Ghost, but tonight just open the door of your heart and let the Spirit come in, and it will be a thousand times better for you in this life and in the life to come.

A MAN WHO LACKED MORAL COURAGE

A few years ago I went to close a meeting, and said, "Is there anyone here that would like to have me remember them in prayer? I would like to have them rise!" and there was a man rose, and when I saw him stand up, my heart leaped in me for joy. I had been anxious for him a long time. I went to him as soon as the meeting was over, and took him by the hand, and said, "You are coming out for God, are not you?" He says, "I want to, and I have made up my mind to be a Christian, only there is one thing that stands in my way." "What is that?" I said. "Well," he says, "I lack moral courage." Naming a friend of his, he said, "If he had been here tonight, I should not have risen, and I am afraid when he hears I have risen for prayer he will begin to laugh at me, and I won't have the moral courage to stand up for Christ." I said, "If Christ is what He is represented in the Bible, He is worth our going out for, and if heaven is what we are told it is in the Bible, it is worth our living for." He said, "I lack moral courage," and the man was trembling from head to foot.

I thought he was just at the very threshold of heaven, and that one step more was going to take him in, and that he would take the step that night. I talked and prayed with him, and the Spirit seemed to be striving mightily with him, but he did not get light. Night after night he came, and the Spirit still strove with him, but just that one thing kept him: he lacked moral courage. At last the Spirit of God that had striven with him so mightily seemed to leave him, and there was no more striving. He left off coming to church, was off among his old companions, and would not meet me in the street; he was ashamed to do so.

About six months afterwards, I got a message from him, and found him on what he thought his dying bed. He wanted to know if there was any hope for him at the eleventh hour. I tried to tell him there was hope for any man that would accept Christ. I prayed with him, and day after day I visited him.

TEMPTING GOD

Contrary to all expectations, he began to recover, and when he was convalescent, finding him one day sitting in front of his house, I sat by his side, and said, "You will soon be well enough to come up to the church, and when you are, you will come up, and you are just going to confess Christ boldly, are not you?" "Well," says he, "I promised God when I was on what we thought my dying bed I would serve Him, and I made up my mind to be a Christian; but I am not going to be one just now. Next spring I am going over to Lake Michigan, and I am going to buy a farm, and settle down, and then I am going to be a Christian." I said, "How dare you talk in that way! How do you know you are going to live till next spring? Have you a lease of your life?" He says, "I never was better than I am now; I am a little weak, but I will soon have my strength. I have a fresh lease of my life, and will be well for a good many years yet." I said, "It seems to me you are tempting God," and I pleaded with him to come right out boldly. "No," he says; "the fact is, I have not the courage to face my old companions, and I can not serve God in Chicago." I said, "If God has not grace enough to keep you in Chicago, He has not in Michigan." I urged him then and there to surrender soul and body to the Lord Jesus, but the more I urged him the more irritated he got, till at last he said, "Well, you need not trouble yourself any more about my soul; I will attend to that. If I am lost, it will be my own fault. I will take the risk."

A FEARFUL DEATHBED

I left him, and within a week I got a message from his wife. Going to the house, I met her at the door weeping. I said, "What is the trouble?" "Oh, sir, I have just had a council of physicians here, and they have all given my husband up to die; they say he cannot live." I said, "Does he want to see me?" She replied, "No." "Why did you send?" "Why," she said, "I cannot bear to see him die in this terrible state of mind." "What is his state of mind?" "Why, he says that his damnation is sealed, and he will be in hell in a little while."

I went into the room, but he turned his head away. I said, "How is it with you?" Not a word; he was as silent as death. I spoke the second time, but he made no response. I looked him in the face, and called him by name, and said, "Will you not tell me how it is with you?" He turned and fixed that awful deathly look upon me, and, pointing to the stove, he said, "My heart is as hard as the iron in that stove; it is too late, my damnation is sealed, and I shall be in hell in a little while." I said, "Don't talk so, you can be saved now if you will."

He replied, "Don't you mock me; I know better." I talked with him, and quoted promise after promise; but he said not one was for him; "Christ has come knocking at the door of my heart many a time, and the last time He came I promised to let Him in, and when I got well I turned away from Him again, and now I have to perish without Him." I talked, but saw that I was doing no good, and so I threw myself on my knees. He said, "You can pray for my wife and my children; you need not pray for me, it is a waste of your time, it is too late." I tried to pray, but it seemed as if what he said was true—it seemed as if the heavens were as brass over me.

I rose and took his hand, and it seemed to me as if I was bidding farewell to a friend that I never was to see again in time or in eternity. He lingered till the sun went down. His wife told me his end was terrible. All that he was heard to say were these fearful words, "The harvest is past, and the summer is ended, and I am not saved." There he lay, and every little while he would take up the awful lamentation, "The harvest is passed, the summer is ended, and I am not saved." And just as the sun was sinking behind those western prairies he was going into the arms of death. As he was expiring, his wife noticed that his lips were quivering; he was trying to say something, and she reached over her ear, and all she could hear was, "The harvest is past, the summer is ended, and I am not saved," and the angels bore him to judgement. He lived a Christless life, he died a Christless death; we wrapped him in a Christless shroud, nailed him in a Christless coffin, and bore him to a Christless grave. Oh, how dark! Oh, how sad! I may be speaking to some one tonight, and the harvest may be passing with you, the summer may be ending—oh, be wise tonight, and accept of the Lord Jesus Christ! May God's blessing rest upon us all, and may we meet in glory, is the prayer of my heart!

BIBLIOGRAPHY

Bell, James S., comp. *They Walked with God*. Chicago: Moody, 1993.

Fitt, Arthur P. *The Shorter Life of D. L. Moody*. Chicago: Moody, n.d.

Fitt, Emma Moody. *The D. L. Moody Year Book*. Chicago: Revell, 1900.

Moody, D. L.. *Bible Characters*. Chicago: Revell, 1888.

_____. *Calvary's Cross*. Chicago: Revell, 1900.

_____. *Daily Gems*. Chicago: BICA, n.d.

_____. *Heaven*. Chicago: Revell, 1884.

_____. *The Faith Which Overcomes*. London: Morgan and Scott, n.d.

_____. *Finding God*. Chicago: Moody 1958.

_____. *The Fullness of the Gospel*. London: Robert Scott, 1907.

_____. *The Great Redemption*. Chicago: J. Fairbanks, 1880.

_____. *The London Discourses of Mr. D. L. Moody*. London: James Clarke, 1875.

_____. *Men of the Bible*. Chicago: Revell, 1898.

_____. *Moody's Great Sermon's*. Chicago: Laird & Lee, 1900.

_____. *The Overcoming Life*. Chicago: BICA, 1896.

_____. *The Peril of Unbelief and the Danger of Doubt*. Chicago: BICA, 1910

_____. *Pleasure and Profit in Bible Study*. Chicago: Revell, 1895.

_____. *Prevailing Prayer*. Chicago: BICA, n.d.

_____. *Moody's Select Sermons*. Chicago: BICA, n.d.

_____. *Secret Power*. Chicago: Revell, 1881

_____. *Sovereign Grace*. Chicago: Revell, 1891

_____. *Sowing and Reaping*. Chicago: Revell, 1896.

_____. *Talks to Christians*. Chicago: BICA, n.d.

_____, ed. *Thoughts for the Quiet Hour*. Chicago: Moody, n.d.

_____. *To the Work*. Chicago: BICA, n.d.

_____. *The Way to God*. Chicago: Revell, 1884.

_____. *The Way Home*. Chicago: BICA, 1904.

_____. *The Way of Life*. Chicago: BICA, 1895.

_____. *Weighed and Wanting*. Chicago: Revell, 1898.

Moody, D. L., Charles Spurgeon, George Mueller, and J. C. Ryle. *The Second Coming of Christ.* Chicago: Moody, n. d.

_____. *The Story of the Prodigal.* Chicago: BICA, 1896.

_____. *What Is Faith?* Chicago: BICA, 1924.

Smith, Wilbur M. *The Best of D. L. Moody.* Chicago: Moody, 1971.

Spurgeon, Charles H., and D. L. Moody. *The Empty Tomb.* Chicago: BICA, 1896

Torrey, R. A. *Why God Used D. L. Moody.* Chicago: BICA, 1923.

A SELF-EVALUATION GUIDE

After reading the preceding thirty-five entries from the various works of D. L. Moody and two of his biographers, you may be moved to ask, "What can I learn from his life?" That may seem an overwhelming question to answer, yet this guide should help you find many answers and applications to your own life. Here, chapter by chapter, are sets of questions that will help you reflect on the ministry and impact of Moody as well as apply some of his principles to your own life.

1. SHORTER LIFE OF D. L. MOODY

1. What one event in the life of D. L. Moody most inspires you and why?

2. What aspect of his Christian life would you most want to imitate?

3. What teaching does he emphasize that you feel you need the most help with and how might you obtain it?

2. WHY GOD USED D. L. MOODY

1. Of all the reasons God used Moody, what do you think are the three most important? And why?

2. When God uses you effectively, what three reasons correspond to those of Moody, and how can you improve on those areas?

3. What area of service that Moody excelled in do you most struggle with, and what can you learn from your struggle?

3. THE WAY TO GOD

1. Are you certain that you are born again of the Spirit of God, and can you give a scriptural reason why you are going to heaven?

2. Do you look to Jesus on a regular basis for forgiveness and righteousness in your life?

3. What evidence in the events and blessings of your own life prove Christ to be your Shepherd?

4. MEN OF THE BIBLE

1. Have you ever been made to wait like Moses, not able for a time to be productive? What effect did this have on you?

2. Have you, like Moses, given up the acclaim of the world to stand up for truth and had to pay a price because of that stand?

3. Have you been reluctant to obey God in some area of service? Did you later move ahead like Moses, or did you shrink back?

5. THE FAITH WHICH OVERCOMES

1. If humility must precede all other virtues, how would this affect the other virtues that you possess?

2. Have you ever purposely "counterfeited" humility by false pretense or affectations? What is true humility?

3. What Bible character best exemplifies humility in a way you would like to imitate?

6. SOWING AND REAPING

1. Where in your life have you both (to some degree) reaped the consequences of your behavior and yet been forgiven and spared serious loss?

2. In what ways, upon repentance, has God turned around lost opportunities and given you something better?

3. How might the idea of future reward spur you on to seek forgiveness as well as renew your efforts to please God in new ways?

7. THE PERIL OF UNBELIEF AND THE DANGER OF DOUBT

1. What obstacles in your life or in yourself block or soften your assurance of either salvation or God's daily care?

2. Find three Scripture verses that clearly demonstrate the absolute certainty of your salvation in Christ.

3. How might acts of love toward others strengthen your own assurance of salvation and knowledge that God loves you?

8. FINDING GOD

1. What do you seek most in your life, that is, what do you spend most time with and is closest to your heart?

2. How much do you value the price paid for your salvation and thus seek God to enjoy it and grow in it?

3. As Spurgeon says, we need a new heart before a new head. Do you seek God with all your heart so that head knowledge will follow?

9. THE OVERCOMING LIFE

1. Where have you tried to find rest and peace in the world as opposed to finding it in God? Describe how these sources are very different.

2. How can Christ carry our burdens when we still have to live through our difficulties without necessarily seeing circumstances change?

3. How well do you follow the command, "Come!"? Do you spend time giving Christ your burdens?

10. THE FULLNESS OF THE GOSPEL

1. Faith is the foundation of life; list ways you exercise faith outside the spiritual realm and then apply these to God.

2. How often and in what ways do you study and claim the promises of God? Do you have evidence when they are applied to your circumstances?

3. When you face difficulties of many kinds, what particular teachings of the Christian faith give you hope? Are you growing in this area?

11. HEAVEN

1. How can we become more like Christ in order to be better prepared for heaven, where Christlikeness will be a necessity?

2. What stories of family, friends, or saints in various books have inspired you related to a deathbed hope in Christ?

3. Do you ever think of heaven as your home because you are familiar with it because of study and meditation?

12. THE WAY HOME

1. How has Christ exerted compassion and long-suffering in your life, seeking to save, spare, and bless you over and over?

2. Name two or three incidents from the Gospels where Christ exhibited His great pity and compassion. What could He have done instead?

3. When have you demonstrated a compassion or mercy to others that goes beyond your capabilities? How do you seek Christ for more of this?

13. SECRET POWER

1. What is the true content of your witness? How can you better express the truth of the Gospel so it is clear to others?

2. Do you tend to use your own techniques and reasoning rather than witnessing in the power of the Spirit?

3. If unbelief is one of the greatest sins, ask God to forgive you as it applies in various ways to your reluctance to witness for Him.

14. TO THE WORK

1. If the word enthusiasm means "in God," do you regularly abide in Christ in order to serve Him with your whole heart?

2. What keeps the fire burning in your service of God? Try to improve even more in your faithfulness in that spiritual exercise.

3. In what specific area do you lack an earnest desire to glorify God in your life? Ask God to increase His grace and strength here.

15. PREVAILING PRAYER

1. If your prayers aren't answered, what obstacles to getting those answers may be in your way? Check your motives, Scriptures, sins, will of God, and so on.

2. Search the Scriptures for verses about stories related to God answering every prayer. Know that He longs to answer "yes" to prayers according to His will.

3. Recall some personal answers to specific prayers. With renewed faith, choose two requests and ask God again to meet your needs.

16. SOVEREIGN GRACE

1. Explain in fifty words or less the difference between being under law and under grace.

2. In what ways has grace softened your behavior, attitudes, and words? What areas of your life need more softening?

3. Look at your past life and identify the ways in which the law has led you to grace, especially through failure and fear.

17. THE EMPTY TOMB

1. Would you say that all of our best efforts are in vain if Christ hasn't risen? Why does that make a difference, even in seeming failure?

2. What does it mean to walk in resurrection life? How do we participate in this type of life on a moment-by-moment basis?

3. The author says that, "If Christ is not risen, it is impossible to admire His words and character." How so?

18. WEIGHED AND WANTING

1. Coveting what others have is a subtle sin, yet a deadly one. Name three things you would say are wrong and harmful concerning desiring what others have.

2. What are some of the illusions or falsehoods attached to the idea that someone is better off than we are because they own more or better things?

3. What are the values that our American culture espouses that make coveting acceptable? How can you overcome these values?

19. PLEASURE AND PROFIT IN BIBLE STUDY

1. How well do you know the Bible and how regularly do you study it? Do you do the digging in the Word yourself or does some Bible help do it for you?

2. Do you have all the necessary tools for in-depth study? How about a book that will teach you a method, such as inductive study?

3. Does your study include meditation, memorization, and application of Scripture to various life situations?

20. BIBLE CHARACTERS

1. How can you be like John the Baptist by decreasing before Christ so that He might increase in your life and in the world?

2. How may you be unselfish like John, who, though he had much recognition and authority, gave it up for a higher cause?

3. Jealousy is sin, which, striking unexpectedly, as seen with John's disciples, can do great damage. Has jealousy struck you, even in the spiritual realm?

21. WAY OF LIFE

1. Does too much emphasis on obedience make you uncomfortable? Check your heart to see if you're willing to obey in every area of your life.

2. Often we "sacrifice" by giving God what we choose rather than following Him wherever He leads. Has any sacrifice of yours really been a cover-up?

3. Do you submit completely to those God has placed in authority over you?

22. CALVARY'S CROSS

1. The author mentions in one sentence five things that the blood of Jesus does for us. What are they and what does this mean for your life?

2. Many hymns speak eloquently of the power of the blood. Choose one and memorize part or all of it.

3. When do you invoke or pray about the power of the blood in your life? How might it help especially in spiritual warfare?

23. THE SECOND COMING OF CHRIST

1. If Jesus Christ were to come back tomorrow, how would you change your life today? How would He evaluate your faithfulness?

2. Do you spend each day waiting for His return, or living as if it may be your own last day on earth? How might you do so?

3. How might the near return of Christ affect how you relate to others, especially the unsaved?

24. THE PRODIGAL

1. What false ideas about the "good life" have led you from time to time down the wrong path? What caused you to see your error?

2. In what ways has God demonstrated His compassion and patience toward you when you took a wrong path?

3. In what small area do you need to "return" to the Lord? Where has the full inheritance for your life been withheld?

25. WHAT IS FAITH?

1. Besides your salvation, what have you truly trusted God for? What needs or desires have you held back?

2. In what areas in your Christian life do you most struggle with doubt and unbelief? Why?

3. What crises or major challenges in your past life have caused you to either trust God more or less?

26. THE D. L. MOODY YEAR BOOK

1. (March 11) Being covetous, greedy, or envious of anyone or anything is a serious sin, yet often undetected. Search your heart and seek forgiveness.

2. (September 24) When have you had the correct doctrines or Christian behavior but lacked true Christian love? Ask God for more.

3. (October 15) Gossip can be subtle as well as addictive. How have you secretly spread information about others that might be inappropriate?

27. THEY WALKED WITH GOD

1. ("The Prize") How well do you know the atmosphere of heaven? Study Scripture verses as well as the book of Revelation.

2. ("His Yoke Is Easy") Why do the pleasures of sin actually prove to be a hard master? Has His yoke been easy in difficulties?

3. ("His Promises") Take five promises from the Bible and address them to yourself as your very own. Repeat them throughout the day.

28. DAILY GEMS

1. (September 7) Are you doing whatever you can to cooperate with God's grace, or has laziness obstructed spiritual growth?

2. (May 2) Where in your life are you spiritually asleep, that is, not fully active and alert, and working hard for Him?

3. (November 11) What gifts, skills, talents, knowledge, etc., do you possess that can shine in the darkness? How can you shine brighter?

29. TALKS TO CHRISTIANS

1. ("Affliction") Though afflictions seem counterproductive or wasteful, describe how at times they draw you closer to God and make you stronger.

2. ("Personal Effort") When, through much determination and prayer, have you seen someone come to Christ? Is it always easy?

3. ("The Good Samaritan") Whom do you see in a "ditch" today—
   be it sin, infirmity, or ignorance—that you, as a good Samaritan,
   can help pull out?

30. SELECT SERMONS

1. When judging who Christ is, in what ways might we be like the
   Pharisees, preferring our systems to His demands?

2. Similarly, how might we be like Pilate, afraid of the crowd, and
   pressured at times to judge incorrectly?

3. In what ways may we be similar to Peter, strong and outspoken
   in our desire to serve Him and yet timid when challenged?

31. MOODY'S GREAT SERMONS

1. Look back to a point in your life when the Spirit of God enlightened you as to some deception. Ask Him now for fresh
   light.

2. You reap more than you sow. Examine your life and see where
   this is true both in good and bad deeds.

3. Think of a time in your life when you were forgiven a sin, yet
   suffered later consequences. How can this help you avoid sin in
   the future?

32. THE GREAT REDEMPTION

1. What are some of the tactics of those who wish to undermine
   the authority of Scripture? How can they be overcome?

2. Many people profess Christianity but have a different "rock"
   they really trust in. Name some of these false foundations.

3. Why is it that many non-Christians want Christian values and
   even beliefs in the society or even within their families?

33. THE BEST OF D. L. MOODY

1. Like it did in Mr. Bliss's life, much seeming tragedy can happen in a believer's life, yet it is better than not knowing God. Do you have a similar tale?

2. Are you ready to meet your Lord today unexpectedly as did Mr. Bliss? How can you better prepare?

3. How does this sermon move you to reach out to friends who may still not have found Christ? What if today is their last?

34. THE LONDON DISCOURSES

1. What are some of the typical excuses made in the present day when a strong Christian commitment is called for?

2. Though you may be committed to Christ in terms of the big picture, what small excuses do you make with the difficult demands?

3. Name some of the great benefits of not making excuses but entering into all God has for you. Why are excuses so pitiful?